Inside Lincoln's
White House

John Hay

Inside Lincoln's
White House

THE COMPLETE CIVIL
WAR DIARY OF
JOHN HAY

Edited by

MICHAEL BURLINGAME

and

JOHN R. TURNER ETTLINGER

SOUTHERN ILLINOIS UNIVERSITY PRESS

Carbondale and Edwardsville

Frontispiece: Photograph of John Hay, 1861, by Albert Bierstadt,
signed by Hay, courtesy of Brown University Library.

Library of Congress Cataloging-in-Publication Data
Hay, John, 1838–1905.
Inside Lincoln's White House : the complete Civil War
diary of John Hay / edited by Michael Burlingame and
John R. Turner Ettlinger.
p.   cm.
Includes bibliographical references and index.
1. Hay, John, 1838–1905—Diaries. 2. Statesmen—
United States—Diaries. 3. Lincoln, Abraham, 1809–1865.
4. Lincoln, Abraham, 1809–1865—Personal narratives.
I. Burlingame, Michael, 1941– . II. Ettlinger, John R. T.
III. Title.
E664.H41A3 1997
973.7'092—dc21   96–47791
ISBN 0-8093-2099-1 (alk. paper)   CIP

To John Y. Simon,
scholar and friend extraordinary,
with respect, affection, and gratitude

M.A.B.

In Memoriam.
David Jonah. Bess Jonah.

J.R.T.E.

CONTENTS

ACKNOWLEDGMENTS

THE BROWN UNIVERSITY LIBRARY STAFF HAS PROVIDED INDIS-
pensable help in the preparation of this book. John Ettlinger is most
thankful to Martha Mitchell of the library's Department of Archives. Jennifer Lee of the John Hay Library at Brown kindly called Michael Burlingame's attention to the manuscript prepared by Ettlinger. She and her
colleagues, including Samuel Streit and Jean Rainwater, have been unfail-
ingly helpful throughout the completion of this project. To them is owed
a great deal.

John Y. Simon, the dean of documentary editors in the field of American history, has been an inspiration, a goad, and a friend to Burlingame,
encouraging him throughout the years he worked on this book and other
Lincoln studies. Burlingame counts himself supremely lucky to have
Simon's counsel and friendship.

Wayne C. Temple, the chief deputy director of the Illinois State Archives
in Springfield, and Thomas F. Schwartz, the Illinois state historian, have
examined the manuscript and generously shared their extensive knowledge of Lincoln and his times. Lois Erickson McDonald (Brown '59), who
has a special affinity for John Hay and the John Hay Library, has helped
more than she knows to make this book possible.

Other librarians across the country have also provided invaluable assistance, especially at the Library of Congress, the National Archives, the
Huntington Library, the New York Public Library, the New-York Historical Society, Allegheny College, the Illinois State Historical Library in
Springfield, and particularly at Connecticut College in New London,
where Burlingame has taught since 1968. The college's R. Francis Johnson
Faculty Development Fund has helped defray some of the expenses involved in the research and writing of this book.

Lloyd Burlingame of Manhattan and Sue Burlingame Coover of Chevy
Chase, Maryland, have been emotional rocks of Gibraltar as well as generous hosts who make Burlingame's research visits to New York and Washington, D.C., not only enjoyable but affordable. Cynthia Love McCollom
and Kathy Nolan were very helpful in checking the accuracy of the annotations.

EDITORS' INTRODUCTION

THE DIARY OF ASSISTANT PRESIDENTIAL SECRETARY JOHN HAY has been aptly described as "the most intimate record we have or ever can have of Abraham Lincoln in the White House." It is one the richest deposits of high-grade ore for the smelters of Lincoln biographers and Civil War historians, especially for the years 1863 and 1864, when Hay was a more conscientious diarist than he had been earlier. The diaries of cabinet members and other political associates of the president—like Treasury Secretary Salmon P. Chase, Attorney General Edward Bates, Navy Secretary Gideon Welles, and Senator Orville Hickman Browning—also shed much light on Lincoln's presidency, but none of those has the literary flair of Hay's journal, which is, as Lincoln's friend Horace White noted, as "breezy and sparkling as champagne." An aspiring poet, Hay recorded events in a scintillating style that the lawyer-politician diarists conspicuously lacked.[1]

Living in the White House, Hay enjoyed easy access to Lincoln, who, according to one observer, "loved him as a son." Galusha Grow, the Speaker of the House during the first half of the Civil War, recalled that "Lincoln was very much attached" to Hay "and often spoke to me in high terms of his ability and trustworthiness." Grow knew "of no person in whom the great President reposed more confidence and to whom he confided secrets of State as well as his own personal affairs with such great freedom." Hay and the chief presidential secretary, John G. Nicolay, were (as they later put it) "daily and nightly witnesses of the incidents, the anxieties, the fears, and the hopes, which pervaded the Executive Mansion and the National Capital." Lincoln, they claimed, "gave them his unlimited confidence."[2]

Born in Salem, Indiana, in 1838, Hay was raised in Warsaw, Illinois, where his father practiced medicine. A precocious boy, Hay had mastered much Latin by the age of twelve, when he was shipped off to live with his uncle, Milton Hay, in Pittsfield, where the schools were superior to those in Warsaw. There the youngster befriended an older lad, John G. Nicolay. Hay attended Brown University, from which he graduated in 1858. Leaving Providence, he returned to Illinois and once again stayed with his uncle, who was then practicing law in Springfield, which he called "a city combining the meanness of the North with the barbarism of the South." Shakespeare's Dogberry, he quipped, "ought to have been an Illinoisan."[3]

After Lincoln's nomination in May 1860, the candidate needed help answering mail. He knew Nicolay, who had been serving as an assistant to the Illinois secretary of state, Ozias M. Hatch, since 1857. Lincoln spent much time in Hatch's office, which was "practically the Republican campaign headquarters for both city and State," and thus got to know Nicolay well and decided to hire him.[4]

To cover the expense, several friends contributed to a special fund. At the suggestion of Milton Hay, his nephew John, who was then desultorily studying law with him in Springfield, was chosen to assist Nicolay. Following his electoral victory in November, Lincoln wished to retain both Nicolay and Hay as secretaries, but federal law provided money enough for only one. Milton Hay, who said that his nephew "had much enjoyed working with Mr. Lincoln," volunteered to pay John's expenses in Washington for half a year. The president-elect asked young Hay to assist Nicolay in the White House. There Lincoln insisted on paying Hay out of his own pocket, but that proved unnecessary when the young man was named clerk in the Interior Department, then detailed to duty in the White House. In 1864 he was appointed a major in the army.[5]

The relationship between Lincoln and Hay resembled that between earlier wartime father-and-son surrogates George Washington and Alexander Hamilton. As the journalist John Russell Young noted, Hay "knew the social graces and amenities, and did much to make the atmosphere of the war environed White House grateful, tempering unreasonable aspirations, giving to disappointed ambitions the soft answer which turneth away wrath, showing, as Hamilton did in similar offices, the tact and common sense which were to serve him as they served Hamilton in wider spheres of public duty."[6]

Young, who regularly visited the White House during the war, described Hay as "exceedingly handsome—a slight, graceful, boyish figure—'girl in boy's clothes,' as I heard in a sniff from some angry politician." Young observed that Hay was "brilliant" and "chivalrous," quite "independent, with opinions on most questions," which he was not shy about expressing. Gifted with "a poetic nature," Hay was "proud of army associations"; though sociable, Hay could be "reserved" and aloof, "with just a shade of pride that did not make acquaintanceship spontaneous." Young concluded that Hay, "honest as sunshine, as strong and brave as the seas," managed to combine "the genius for romance and politics as no one . . . since Disraeli," and that he was well "suited for his place in the President's family."[7]

Hay's appearance was striking. Young described him as "a comely young man with peach-blossom face." This "young, almost beardless, and almost boyish countenance did not seem to match with official responsibilities and the tumult of action in time of pressure, but he did what he had to do, was always graceful, composed, polite, and equal to the complexities of any situation which might arise." Hay's "old-fashioned speech" was "smooth, low-toned, quick in comprehension, sententious, reserved." People were "not quite sure whether it was the reserve of diffidence or aristocracy," Young recalled. Hay was "high-bred, courteous," and "not one with whom the breezy overflowing politician would be apt to take liberties." Young detected "a touch of sadness in his temperament"; he thought Hay "had the personal attractiveness as well as the youth of Byron" and "was what Byron might have been if grounded on good principles and with the wholesome discipline of home."[8]

Others added touches to Young's portrait. His college roommate, William Leete Stone, described Hay as "of a singularly modest and retiring disposition," yet with "so winning a manner that no one could be in his presence, even for a few moments, without falling under the spell which his conversation and companionship invariably cast upon all who came within his influence." A cousin, Logan Hay, deemed John "a different type from the rest of the Hay family. He had a magnetic personality—more culture." A journalist who enjoyed a nodding acquaintance with Hay in 1861 recalled that he was "a young, good-looking fellow, well, almost foppishly dressed, with by no means a low down opinion of himself, either physically or mentally, with plenty of self-confidence for anybody's use, a brain active and intellectual, with a full budget of small talk for the ladies or anybody else, and both eyes keeping a steady lookout for the interests of 'number one.'" Hay's casual insouciance impressed F. A. Mitchel early in 1861 when he found the young secretary lounging at Willard's Hotel, leaning against a cigar stand with his arms stretched out to either side. When Mitchel and his father congratulated the young man on his appointment, Hay responded: "Yes. I'm Keeper of the President's Conscience."[9]

Apparently, he was attractive to the opposite sex. Stone recalled that at college, Hay "was always a great favorite with the ladies." In 1860 Anna Ridgely of Springfield described him as "a very pleasant young fellow & very intelligent." Later she recalled that at twenty-one, Hay was "a bright, handsome fellow of medium height and slight build, with good features, especially the eyes, which were dark, lustrous brown; red cheeks and clear dark complexion; small, well-shaped hands which he had a habit of locking together interlacing the fingers, and carrying at arm's length, which the girls thought particularly fetching." His sartorial taste also appealed to young women, Miss Ridgely noted: "He wore a long, loose overcoat, flying open, his hands thrust into the pockets, which was also thought very graceful and attractive as he swung himself along the street, for he had a rocking walk in those days."[10]

A young woman visiting Washington in 1862 reported that the "nicest looking man I have seen since I have been here is Mr Hay the President's Secretary. I do not know him personally but he came into the Senate the other day to deliver a message from the President. He is very nice looking with the loveliest voice." His eyes also attracted women. "Hay's marked feature was his eyes," recalled Helen Nicolay; they were "always kindly" and "sometimes depressed." His "wonderful hazel eyes" were remembered fondly by his college sweetheart, Hannah Angell: "you could look into them a mile, & he looked a mile into yours." She also thought him "very attractive as a talker"; in conversation he was "given to abrupt, swift phrases." Not every young woman concurred in this assessment. In 1864 a Springfield maiden "was disgusted with him" in part because "he talked in a most affected manner."[11]

T. C. Evans, a journalist who saw Hay almost daily during the Civil War, recalled that he "was born to moderation and calmness in mien as in action, and they walked with him on either hand throughout his length of days, tokens of the equity of a balanced character, working with Nature as one who had discovered that her central note is calm and that she is commanded only by those who obey her." He appeared "to possess in a high degree a silent power of work, doing a great deal and saying little about it," while "his spirit was ever of unruffled serenity, his manner of invariable sweetness and charm, and that his talk was apt, varied, refined, and of a markedly literary quality."[12]

A gentleman who saw a great deal of Hay from 1862 to 1865 and who boarded at the same club and dined with him frequently, recollected that he was "smooth-faced, ruddy-cheeked, vivacious, witty, polished, urbane and withal as full of intellectual activity as an egg of meat." Although "he constantly pursued his *belles lettres* studies and went much into society," Hay was "a hard practical worker" who spent "twelve or fourteen hours a day of hard work at the White House." A "trusted and intimate friend of Lincoln's," Hay "probably lived nearer to that good man's heart during the years of the civil war, than any other man." Whenever he saw Hay "he was always the same witty, genial, agreeable, effervescent and fascinating fellow." Hay obviously "had decided genius and unusual literary culture."[13]

William O. Stoddard, a clerk who assisted the two principal White House secretaries during the Civil War, described Hay as "quite young, and looks younger than he is; of a fresh and almost boyish complexion; quite a favorite among the ladies, and with a gift for epigram and repartee." He could also tell a good joke, as Stoddard recalled. One Sunday when the Executive Mansion was "silent as the graveyard," Hay burst into Stoddard's office, "all one bubble," and regaled him with a hilarious joke. Hearing uproarious laughter, Nicolay hastened over, pen in hand, and Hay repeated his story. Suddenly Lincoln appeared at the door: "Now John, just tell that thing again." As Stoddard remembered the scene, "His feet had made no sound in coming from his room, or our own racket had drowned any footfall, but here was the President, and he sank into Andrew Jackson's chair, facing the table, with Nicolay seated by him and Hay still standing by the mantel. The story was as fresh and was even better told that third time up to its first explosive place. Down came the President's foot from across his knee with a heavy stamp on the floor, and out through the hall went the uproarious peal of laughter."[14]

Another young man who worked in the Executive Mansion during the Civil War, Charles H. Philbrick, reported at the end of 1864 that "Hay does the ornamental . . . and the main labor is divided between three others of us who manage to get along tolerably well with it." In 1863 Thomas Wentworth Higginson deemed Hay "a nice young fellow, who unfortunately looks about seventeen and is oppressed with the necessity of behaving like seventy." Captain Henry King believed that Hay physically "most resembles Edgar A. Poe" and considered him "a thorough gentlemen, and one of the best fellows in the world." Thurlow Weed called Hay "a bright, gifted young man, with agreeable manners and refined tastes."[15]

Not everyone thought so highly of the assistant secretary. Henry Smith patronizingly called him "a nice beardless boy" and lamented that "Mr. Lincoln has no private secretary that fills the bill and the loss is a national one." A journalist described Hay as "a proper ladies' man" who "might with due change of garb have passed creditably as a lady's maid," while another critic declared of Hay's "vanity" that it "was inordinate almost to the point of being disgusting." The journalist and historian David Rankin Barbee expressed the same sentiment more bluntly: "Hay was such a damned intellectual snob, . . . so superior to everybody, including Jehovah, that you want to puke as you read him." Hay, in fact, made no pretentions to modesty, which he called "the most fatal and most unsympathetic of vices."[16]

Hay quit the White House in part because of sharp conflicts with Mary Lincoln, whom he called the "Hellcat," and partly because he could not abide the grasping petitioners who besieged his office. In 1881, when president-elect James A. Garfield asked him to become his secretary, Hay declined, saying, "The contact with the greed and selfishness of office-seekers and the bull-dozing Congressmen is unspeakably repulsive. The constant contact with envy, meanness, ignorance and the swinish selfishness which ignorance breeds needs a stronger heart and a more obedient nervous system than I can boast."[17]

Hay kept his White House diary in three medium-sized notebooks. The first volume, 177 pages, opens with 4 pages of miscellaneous jottings, probably made at different times in the summer of 1863. It then switches to an entry for 30 June 1864 and continues for 22 pages through 7 July 1864, then abruptly switches again, to 18 April 1861, and continues through 17 October 1863. The second notebook, consisting of 190 pages, starts with 18 October 1863 and ends on 25 June 1864. The third begins on 23 September 1864 and runs for 41 pages through 18 December 1864. The remaining pages—headlined with the names of various states, below which appear the names of generals from those states—are in Lincoln's hand.

Hay also kept three small pocket diaries to record his jottings while traveling. One contains entries from 4 April to 1 June 1863, when he visited South Carolina, as well as miscellaneous notes and some poetry. A similar pocket diary chronicles his journey to Niagara Falls in 1864. Another covers his trip to South Carolina and Florida, 14 January–23 March

1864. All the diaries were donated to the Brown University Library by Hay's daughter, Mrs. James W. Wadsworth, of Geneseo, New York, in 1954.

Hay's diary and letters were first printed in 1908 in a private edition, compiled by Henry Adams and Clara Louise Stone Hay, John Hay's widow, in which only the initials of proper names were given. Thirty-one years later, Tyler Dennett published a more scholarly and useful version.[18] Like Adams and Hay (but unlike the editors of the present volume), Dennett included letters by Hay.

Though it represented a great improvement over the Adams and Hay edition, Dennett's version was "rather casually edited," in the words of Allan Nevins, the dean of Civil War historians.[19] Dennett omitted several Civil War entries, annotated the text skimpily (and sometimes inaccurately), and transcribed passages erroneously. Approximately 10 percent of Hay's entries between 1861 and 1864 were excluded from Dennett's version, often with no ellipses or any other indication of the omission. (It should be noted that the only ellipses in the present edition replace the occasional string of periods used in the original diary.)

Most of the omitted entries were written when Hay was out of Washington on troubleshooting missions for Lincoln, but a few of the excised passages deal directly with the president. Inexplicably, Dennett left out one of the wisest and most eloquent of Lincoln's writings, the letter to Captain James M. Cutts, dated 16 October 1863:

> Although what I am now to say is to be in form a reprimand, it is not intended to add a pang to what you have already suffered upon the subject to which it relates. You have too much of life yet before you, and have shown too much of promise as an officer, for your future to be lightly surrendered. You were convicted of two offences. One of them, not of great enormity, and yet greatly to be avoided, I feel sure you are in no danger of repeating. The other you are not so well assured against. The advice of a father to his son, "Beware of entrance to a quarrel, but being in, bear it that the opposed may beware of thee," is good & yet not the best. Quarrell not at all. No man resolved to make the most of himself can spare time for personal contention. Still less can he afford to take all the consequences including the vitiating of his temper & the loss of self-control. Yield

larger things to which you can show no more than equal right; and yield lesser ones though clearly y[ou]r own. Better give y[ou]r path to a dog than be bitten by him in contesting for the right. Even killing the dog would not cure the bite.

In the mood indicated deal henceforth with your fellow men, and especially with your brother officers; and even the unpleasant events you are passing from will not have been profitless to you.

A copy of this remarkable document, which was unknown until the Robert Todd Lincoln Collection of Abraham Lincoln Papers was opened to the public in 1947, was pasted into the diary. An unidentified portion of it had appeared in Nicolay and Hay's biography of Lincoln.[20]

Dennett also left out the president's hilariously sarcastic response to a presumptuous Kentucky state senator, though he had published it in his 1934 biography of Hay.[21] Dated 6 May 1861 and signed by Hay, this letter to John M. Johnson of Paducah masterfully put that gentleman in his place: "The President has the honor to acknowledge the receipt of your communication of the 26th ult. protesting against the stationing of U. S. Troops at Cairo [Illinois]. The President directs me to say that the views so ably stated by you shall have due consideration: and to assure you that he would certainly never have ordered the movement of troops, complained of, had he known that Cairo was in your Senatorial district."

One of Lincoln's more ingenious puns also did not appear in Dennett's version of the diary: "A man caught in a disgraceful affair said he could bring a man to prove an alibi. 'I have no doubt,' said the President, 'you can bring a man to prove a lie by.'"[22]

Also omitted, without ellipses, was Hay's description of Lincoln's desire to move an army corps from South Carolina to Virginia in the spring of 1864: "The President looks favorably on General Gillmore's plan of coming north with the 10th Corps, but no decision will be made until Grant returns. He advised me to go down to the Army of the Potomac and talk things over with the General." Hay's description of another shift in military forces was likewise omitted: "in the evening [26 September 1863] came Slocum [of the] 12th Corps. He said he would call in the morning. He did so Sunday morning accompanied by Governor Seward. The result of the visit, a request by the President to Genl. Rosecrans urging him to take

Slocum from Hooker's force and give Hooker some corresponding force."[23]

In general, Dennett transcribed the diary accurately, but errors do crop up now and then. He rendered "Beast" as "Prest."; "gemmen" (black dialect for "gentlemen") as "gunmen"; "Frenchman" as "punchman"; "Hogeboom" as "Hopboon"; "drabs" as "Arabs"; "Sec'y Watson" as "Sec'y Nation"; "Mayor" as "Major"; "Gen. Augur" as "Gen. Agnew"; "granting of passes" as "guaranty of the voters"; "Mrs. Young" as "Mrs. Long"; "D'Arcy" as "Davey"; "sleep" as "ship"; "Fox" as "Fry"; "Green Clay Smith" as "Gen. Clay Smith"; "McMaster" as "McMastin"; "Hammacks" (a restaurant) as "hammocks"; "Eames" as "Ann's"; "Tuesday" as "Thursday"; "ruts" as "nets"; "lost" as "last"; "Durrell" as "Dowell"; "Erith" as "Guth"; "Col. Serrell" as "Col. Sewell"; "Stono River" as "Stone River"; "black" as "[a] block [of]"; "The occup[ation] perm[anent] as "We occupy present"; "ordnance" as "ordinance"; and "boats' crews" as "boatscrews."

Dennett provided few annotations (approximately one-seventh of the number included in this edition), and some of them are inaccurate. He rendered "Pet Halsted" as "Pit Halsted," and then, instead of identifying him as an influential lobbyist and notorious Washington character, guessed that he was "Possibly Murat Hasted." (He meant Murat Halstead, a Cincinnati journalist.)[24]

More than three decades ago, John Ettlinger, then in charge of Special Collections at the Brown University Library, made a careful and literal transcript of the text of the diary, which involved deciphering Hay's difficult and occasionally confused writing. In particular, passages were restored that had been canceled, sometimes heavily, by the first editors, for reasons of confidentiality and propriety.[25] Unfortunately, Ettlinger's plans to publish the diary fell through. In 1992 Michael Burlingame began to explore the Hay manuscripts at Brown University and realized that a new edition of the dairy was needed. From Jennifer Lee of the John Hay Library, Burlingame learned about the work of Ettlinger, by then a professor emeritus at Dalhousie University in Halifax, Nova Scotia. Ettlinger gave Burlingame permission to use his typescript as the basis for the new edition. Burlingame then took Ettlinger's text, compared it with the original diary, added material to his annotations, and supplemented them with annotations of his own. Ettlinger's text thus forms the basis of the present edition, which also incorporates, with many additions and much updating, a body of notes providing a critical apparatus to the diary identifying historical events and persons.

All diary entries in this edition are preceded by the date in the order day-month-year, followed by the day of the week (which Hay himself occasionally included). Brackets enclose all editorial insertions in the text. A word followed by a question mark and enclosed in brackets represents one that could not be deciphered with complete confidence; empty brackets are left in place of illegible words. All decipherable words of any significance that were crossed out in the diary (whether by Hay, his widow, or someone else) are reproduced as canceled text ~~like this~~. When a word was inadvertently repeated, the second occurrence of the word is silently omitted. When a period was used where a comma is called for, the comma is put in its place. Otherwise, Hay's sometimes eccentric punctuation is unchanged and his misspellings are retained. Familiar foreign terms are untranslated; less well-known expressions in foreign languages are translated in notes. Where Hay used shorthand such as an inverted caret for *of the*, a slash for *that* or *which*, or a dot for *the*, those words are silently substituted. Words that had been added above the line are simply inserted into the text. Contractions are retained. Raised letters are reproduced as if they were not raised. Persons mentioned by Hay are identified in notes when their name first appears, if information on them has been found. No annotation is made for those about whom nothing could be discovered.

Inside Lincoln's
White House

1

1861

THE WHITE HOUSE IS TURNED INTO BARRACKS. JIM LANE MAR-
shalled his Kansas Warriors today at Willard's and placed them at the
disposal of Maj. Hunter, who turned them tonight into the East Room. It
is a splendid company—worthy such an armory. Besides the western Jayhawkers it comprises some of the best *materiel* of the East. Senator Pomeroy
and old Anthony Bleecker stood shoulder to shoulder in the ranks. Jim
Lane walked proudly up and down the ranks with a new sword that the
Major had given him. The Major has made me his aid, and I labored under
some uncertainty as to whether I should speak to privates or not.[1]

The President today received this despatch.

"We entreat you to take immediate measures to protect American Commerce in the Southern waters and we respectfully suggest the charter or
purchase of Steamers of which a number can be fitted from here without
delay." Signed by Grinnell Minturn, & many others of the leading business
men of the place. The President immediately sent for the Cabinet. The[y]
came together and Seward answered the despatch in these words.[2]

Despatch to the President received and letters under consideration.
W H Seward.[3]

All day the notes of preparation have been heard at the public buildings and the Armories. Every body seems to be expecting a Son or brother
or "young man" in the coming regiments.

Tonight, Edward brought me a card from Mrs Ann S. Stephens expressing a wish to see the President on matters concerning his personal
safety. As the Ancient was in bed, I volunteered to receive the harrowing
communication. Edward took me to his little room adjoining the Hall and
I waited. Mrs. Stephens, who is neither young nor yet fair to any miraculous extent came in leading a lady who was a little of both whom she introduced as Mrs. Col. Lander. I was ~~infinitely~~ delighted at this chance
interview with the Medea, the Julia the Mona Lisa of my stage struck ~~salad~~
days. After many hesitating and bashful trials, Mrs. Lander told the im-

pulse that brought them. Some young Virginian long haired swaggering chivalrous of course and indiscreet friend had come into town in great anxiety for a new saddle, and meeting her had said that he and half a dozen others including a daredevil guerilla from Richmond named Ficklin would do a thing within forty eight hours that would ring through the world. Connecting this central fact with a multiplicity of attendant details she concluded that the President was either to be assassinated or captured. She ended by renewing her protestations of earnest solicitude mingled with fears of the impropriety of the step. Lander has made her very womanly since he married her. Imagine Jean M. Davenport a blushing hesitating wife.[4]

They went away and I went to the bedside of the Chief *couché*. I told him the yarn; he quietly grinned.

Going to my room, I met the Captain. He was a little boozy and very eloquent. He dilated on the troubles of the time and bewailed the existence of a garrison in the White House "to give éclat to Jim Lane."[5]

Hill Lamon came in about midnight saying that Cash. Clay was drilling a splendid company at Willard's Hall and that the town was in a general tempest of enthusiastic excitement. which not being very new, I went to sleep.[6]

19 APRIL 1861, FRIDAY

Early this morning I consulted with Maj. Hunter as to measures proper to be taken in the matter of guarding the house. He told me that he would fulfill any demand I should make. The forenoon brought us news of the destruction of Govt. property at Harper's Ferry. It delighted the Major, regarding it as a deadly blow at the prosperity of the recusant Virginia.[7]

I called to see Joe Jefferson & found him more of a gentleman than I had expected. A very intellectual face, thin and eager with large intense blue eyes, the lines firm, and the hair darker than I had thought. I then went to see Mrs. Lander and made her tell the story all over again "just by way of a slant." Miss Lander the sculptor was there. I like Jean M. more and more. Coming up, I found the streets full of the bruit of the Baltimore mob & at the White House was a nervous gentleman who insisted on seeing the President to say that a mortar battery has been planted on the Virginia heights commanding the town. He separated himself from the information and instantly retired. I had to do some very dexterous lying to calm the awakened fears of Mrs. Lincoln in regard to the assassination suspicion.[8]

After tea came Partridge and Petherbridge from Baltimore. They came to announce that they had taken possession of the Pikesville Arsenal in the name of the Government—to represent the feeling of the Baltimore conservatives in regard to the present imbroglio there and to assure the President of the entire fidelity of the Governor and the State authorities. The President showed them Hicks and Browns despatch which [said] "Send No troops here. The authorities here are loyal to the Constitution. Our police force and local militia will be sufficient." meaning as they all seemed to think, that they wanted no Washington troops to preserve order, but, as Seward insists, that no more troops must be sent through the city. Scott seemed to agree with Seward. His answer to a despatch of inquiry was, "Gov. Hicks has no authority to prevent troops from passing through Baltimore." Seward interpolated, "no right." Partridge and Petherbridge seemed both loyal and helpful. They spoke of the danger of the North being roused to fury by the bloodshed of today and pouring in an avalanche over the border. The President most solemnly assured them that there was no danger. "Our people are easily influenced by reason. They have determined to prosecute this matter with energy but with the most temperate spirit. You are entirely safe from lawless invasion."[9]

Wood came up to say that young Henry saw a steamer landing troops off Fort Washington. I told the President. Seward immediately drove to Scott's.[10]

About midnight we made a tour of the house. Hunter and the Italian exile Vivaldi were quietly asleep on the floor of the East Room and a young and careless guard loafed around the furnace fires in the basement. Goodlooking and energetic young fellow, too good to be food for gunpowder,—if any thing is.

Miss Dix called today, to offer her services in the Hospital branch. She makes the most munificent and generous offers.[11]

20 April 1861, Saturday

Col. Washington called this morning but could not see the President. It would seem like a happy omen to have a General Washington living and fighting among us at this time.[12]

The streets were full of the talk of Baltimore. It seems to be generally thought that a mere handful of men has raised this storm that now threatens the loyalty of a state.

I went up with Nicolay Pangborn and Whitely to see the Massachusetts troops quartered in the Capitol. The scene was very novel. The contrast was very painful between the grey haired dignity that filled the Senate Chamber when I saw it last and the present throng of bright-looking Yankee boys, the most of them bearing the ~~inevitable~~ signs of New England rusticity in voice and manner, scattered over the desks chairs and galleries some loafing, many writing letters, slowly and with plough hardened hands, or with rapid [glancing?] clerkly fingers, while Grow stood patient by the desk and franked for every body. The Hall of Representatives is as yet empty. Lying on a sofa and looking upward the magnificence of the barracks made me envy the soldiers who should be quartered there. The wide-spreading skylights over arching the vast hall like heaven blushed and blazed with gold and the heraldic devices of the married States, while all around it the eye was ~~relieved~~ rested by the massive simple splendor of the stalagmitic bronze reliefs. The Spirit of our institutions seemed visibly present to inspire and nerve the acolyte, sleeping in her temple beside his unfleshed sword.[13]

This evening Speed Butler came from Illinois, bearing despatches in relation to the garrisoning of St. Louis and Cairo, and the state of the Sub Treasury at St. Louis. Scott listened with great satisfaction to the plans proposed by the State Government & with his own hand wrote an order which Cameron signed, commanding the Commander at the Arsenal to provide accommodations for the Illinois troops, at the Arsenal or Jefferson Barracks and to furnish to the order of the Govr. of Ills. ten thousand stand of arms. Speed will instantly return with these.[14]

The town is full tonight of feverish rumours about the meditated assault upon this town, and one, which seems to me more probable, on Fort McHenry. The garrison there is weak and inadequate and in spite of the acknowledged bravery of Robinson and Hazzard it must fall if attacked. ~~Let us hope that the widows of Baltimore may bewail the night.~~[15]

Ellsworth telegraphs that his regiment has been raised, accepted and that he wants them sent to Ft Hamilton for preliminary drill. Cameron authorized the answer that the Commander there should have orders to that effect. Much is hoped from the gallant Colonel's Bloodtubs. They would be worth their weight in Virginia currency, at Ft McHenry tonight.[16]

The Massachusetts men drilled tonight on the Avenue. They afford a happy contrast to the unlicked patriotism that has poured ragged and unarmed out of Pennsylvania. They step together well and look as if they meant business.[17]

Jim Lane wrote a note to the President today offering to bring any assignable number of Northern fighting men over the border at the shortest possible notice.[18] This the Tycoon quietly shelved. Gen. Scott seems to think that four or five thousand men will be a sufficient garrison to hold this town against any force that may be brought from the Maryland or Virginia woods.

21 APRIL 1861, SUNDAY

This morning came a penitent and suppliant crowd of conditional secessionists from Baltimore, who having sowed the wind seem to have no particular desire to reap the whirlwind. They begged that no more federal troops should be sent through Baltimore at present; that their mob was thoroughly unmanageable and that they would give the government all possible assistance in transporting its troops safely across the State by any other route. The President, always inclined to give all men credit for fairness and sincerity consented to this arrangement contrary to the advice of some of his most prominent counselors. And afterwards said, that this was the last time he was going to interfere in matters of strictly military concernment. That he would leave them hereafter wholly to military men.[19]

I spoke of the intended resignation of Col. Magruder. The Tycoon was astonished. Three days ago, Magruder had been in his room making the loudest protestations of undying devotion to the Union. This canker of secession has wonderfully demoralized the army. Capt. Fry is the firmest and soundest man I meet. He seems to combine great honesty of purpose with accurate and industrious business habits and a lively and patriotic [soldier?] spirit that is better than any thing else, today.[20]

This morning we mounted the battlements of the Executive mansion and the Ancient took a long look down the bay. It was a "water-haul".[21]

Any amount of feverish rumours filled the evening. The despatch from Mead Addison in regard to 1500 Mass. troops being seen off Annapolis seemed to please the Prest very much.[22] Then there was a Fort Monroe Rumour and a 7th Regt. Rumour and R I rumour, all of which tomorrow will sift.

We passed the evening pleasantly at Eames where were the English Legation and returned to find Vivaldi and his borderers guarding the imperial palace pacing in belted and revolvered dignity up and down the wide portico, to give style and tone to the defensive guard, looking as he said like gentlemen in feature and dress. We went up and found a despatch stating that no troops had arrived at the Navy Yard.[23] *Tant pis* we said and slept.

22 APRIL 1861, MONDAY

The President this morning recommended the appointment of Peck of Chicago to a Lieutenancy and of Capt. Todd to the vacant Quartermaster-generalship. Chase and the Chief were talking together Chase said, "all these failures are for want of a strong young head. Everything goes in confused disorder. Gen Scott gives an order, Mr. Cameron gives another. Half of both are executed neutralizing each other."[24]

The whining traitors from Baltimore were here again this morning. The President I think has done with them. In conversation with Major Hunter last night, in reply to the Major's blunt assertion that the troops should have been brought through Baltimore if the town had to be leveled to the earth, he said, that that order commanding their return to Pa. was given at the earnest solicitation of the Maryland conservatives who avowed their powerlessness in Baltimore but their intention to protect the federal troops elsewhere; granted them, as a special extension, as an exhaustion of the means of conciliation & kindness. Hereafter however, he would interfere with no war measures of the army.[25]

A young lady called today from Baltimore, sent by her father H Pollock Esq. to convey to the Govt. information as to the state of affairs in the plug-ugly city. She was very pretty and Southern in features and voice and wonderfully plucky and earnest in the enunciation of her devotion to the Stars and Stripes. She stated that the mails had been stopped at the Balto. P. O—Arms expected from Va—Ft. McHenry to be attacked tonight—The scared comrs here thoroughly traitorous & other things. I met her again this afternoon and talked three hours. Her quiet courage and dauntless patriotism brought back to me the [flush?] times of De Montfort and Queen Eleanor and the girl of Dom Remy.[26] I gained a new idea of the possibilities of true brave hearts being nourished in Republics. Just as she stepped into her carriage, her friend called her "Lilie" and I knew her name. She seemed so heart-whole in her calm devotion to the Union, that flirtation died in her presence and better thoughts than politicians often know, stole through the mind of one who listened to the novelty of an American woman, earnest, intelligent patriotic and pretty.

This afternoon the Pocahontas and the Anacostia came peacefully back from their cruise and folded their wings in the Harbor. The Pocahontas has done her duty at Norfolk and is welcome to our bay, with its traitor haunted shores. She reports no batteries at the White House Point and makes no record of any hostile demonstrations from the banks of Alexandria. The very fact of the Pocahontas coming so quietly in, is a good one.[27]

A telegram intercepted on its way to Baltimore states that our Yankees and New-Yorkers have landed at Annapolis. Weary and foot-sore but very welcome, they will probably greet us tomorrow.[28]

This little incident reminds me irresistibly of Capt. Hazard.

[pasted into the diary is a newspaper clipping:]

FORT McHENRY—On Saturday night a rumor that this fort was to be attacked kept a great many people on the streets until morning. Shortly before midnight the Maryland Guards were ordered out with a strong police force, and proceeded to the vicinity of the Fort for its protection. They were ordered away from the fort by the officer in command, who threatened to turn the guns on them if they did not retire. The officer evidently mistook their mission. All day yesterday crowds remained in the neighborhood but out of range of the guns. They were prompted more by curiosity than anything else.—*Balt. Sun.*

I can imagine the cool air of determination with which he gave that warning to the protecting force that came too near for comfort. I will be glad if circumstances favor him enough to make him heroic. He is brave.

It is amusing to drop in some evening at Clay's Armory. The raw patriots lounge elegantly on the benches—drink coffee in the Ante-room—change the boots of unconscious sleepers in the hall—scribble busily in editorial note books, while the sentries snore at the doors and the grizzled Captain talks politics on the raised platform and dreams of border battle and the hot noons of Monterey.

It was melo-dramatic to see Cassius Clay come into the Presidents reception room today. He wore, with a sublimely unconscious air, three pistols and an Arkansas toothpick and looked like an admirable vignette to 25-cents-worth of yellow-covered romance.

Housekeepers here are beginning to dread famine. Flour has made a sudden spring to $18.00 a bl and corn meal rejoices in the respectable atmosphere of $2.50 a bushel. Willard is preparing for war, furling all sails for the storm.[29] The dinner-table is lorn of *cartes* and the tea table reduced to the severe simplicity of pound-cake.

23 APRIL 1861, TUESDAY

This morning Doug. Wallack came rushing into the office looking for Seward with what he called important news. He said that the two ships at the Navy Yard were the Pawnee and the Keystone. They brought Marines and naval stores from Norfolk. Which place they left after carrying out to the letter their instructions, to destroy what Government property they could not remove. The premier cursed quietly because the Baltic had not come, told Wallach not to contradict the report that the Baltic had come—said the treason of Hicks would not surprise him—that the Seventh could cut their way through three thousand rioters—that Baltimore delenda est—and other things, and strolled back into the audience Chamber.[30]

At dinner we sat opposite old Gen. Spinner who was fierce and jubilant. No frenzied poet ever predicted the ruin of a hostile house with more energy and fervor than he, issuing the rescript of destiny against Baltimore "We've got em," he said. "It is *our* turn now. We keep steadily one week ahead of them, as Scott says. We have burned their hospital and poorhouse, Harper's Ferry and the Norfolk Navy Yard. Now let them fight or starve." He was peculiarly disgusted with the impertinence of Delaware. "The contemptible little neighborhood, without population enough for a decent country village, gets upon her hind legs and talks about armed neutrality. The only good use for traitors is to hang them. They are worth more, dead than alive." Thus the old liberty-loving Teuton raged.[31]

A gaunt, tattered, uncombed and unshorn figure appeared at the door and marched solemnly up to the table. He wore a rough [rusty?] overcoat, a torn shirt and suspenderless breeches. His neck was innocent of collar, guileless of necktie. His thin hair stood fretful-porcupine-quill-wise upon his crown. He sat down and gloomily charged upon his dinner. A couple of young exquisites were eating and chatting ~~beside~~ opposite him. They were guessing when the road would be open through Baltimore. "Thursday" growled the grim apparition, "or Baltimore will be laid in ashes." ~~It was the ally of Montgomery, the King of the Jayhawkers, and the friend of John Brown of Ossawatomie.~~[32]

It was Jim Lane.

Tonight there seem to be reliable news at the State Department that the Seventh Regiment and the Mass. troops would start from Annapolis tonight and through the favoring moonlight march to the Junction, where the Government has possession of the Road. The hostile peasantry can harass them fearfully on the way from fence corners and hillsides, if they are ready and brave.[33]

Cameron today informed Lord Lyons that he could not give a friend of his Lordship a safe passage to Baltimore as the Government only holds this end of the Road.[34]

We got some three-days-old New York Papers and it seemed like a glimpse of a better world to contrast the warm open enthusiasm of the Empire City with the cold distrust and grim earnestness that mark the countenance of the dwellers in Washington.

A large and disappointed throng gathered at the Depot this morning hoping to get deliverance. But the hope was futile. They seem doomed to see the rising of the curtain.

24 APRIL 1861, WEDNESDAY

On account of the stoppage of trains on the Northern Rail Roads, we have nothing this morning but a Southern mail. I have been reading it with new surprise & astonishment at the depth of degradation of which the human mind, in unfavorable conditions of existence, is capable. Nothing but the vilest folly & feculence, that might have simmered glimmeringly in the narrow brain of a chimpanzee, flow from the pens of our epistolary southern brethren. I have seen rough company in the west and north, but never in the kennels of great cities or the wild licence of flat boating on the Mississippi, did I ever hear words that were not purity, compared with the disgusting filtrations of the Chivalric Southern mind. Then the style! the noble disregard of grammar or orthography evinced by these colonels and generals. It is bad enough to be called hard names, anyway. But it is harrowing to have a Georgia Major sit calmly down, and cold-bloodedly write you in black and whitey-brown, "a godam ole foole." There is style in cursing as in other things, and elegant oaths as the Scotch baroness said are "a great sett-off to conversation." But only a gentleman can swear with grace, and blasphemy rolls as awkward and malformed from a seceding pen, as patriotism or piety from the lips of James Gordon Bennett.[35]

One Southern letter in a dozen, differs from the rest in being comparatively decently written and expressed. But we have the same lamentable hebetude of conscience, the same lack of vividness of moral perception, the logic that assumes as its major premise "All Southerners are honest generous and brave" and for its minor, "All northerners are faithless, tyrannical and cowardly," & deduces from these all needful conclusions. The defence of the capital is coercion. The succor of starving soldiers is trampling on the dearest rights of the South. The stoning to death of inoffensive strangers is a calm and earnest protest against lawless invasion. Slavery is the persecuted princess of faery. The long haired whiskey ruiners of the piney woods are her gentle and brave Knights-errant. The vile deformed and malevolent North is wooed in the tenderest terms to forego his wicked spite and lay down his oppressive arms, vacate the throne he has usurped to dishonor, and kneel in penitent allegiance at the feet of the adored and restored goddess of the chain and thong.

Abe Lincoln is adjured in the name of God to resign in favor of Jeff. Davis. The Northern Congress is requested with Arctic coolness, to recommend the Constitution of the C S A to the people of the North, at the same time distinctly avowing that it is by no means probable that Northern States will be admitted into this holy congregation, on any terms.

~~The history of the world is leprous with thick-scattered instances of national folly and crime, but it was reserved for the Southern States to exhibit an infamy to which other crimes show white as mother's milk, and a madness to which an actor's phrensy is sane.~~

The wounded soldiers from Massachusetts came up to the Presidents House today. He received them kindly and cordially. They came in confused and flushed, they went out easy proud and happy. A few kind words are very powerful if they go down. Coming up, they have less weight.[36]

This has been a day of gloom and doubt. Every body seems filled with a vague distrust and recklessness. The idea seemed to be reached by Lincoln, when chatting with the volunteers this morning he said, "I dont believe there is any North. The Seventh Regiment is a myth. R. Island is not known in our geography any longer. *You* are the only Northern realities." Seward's messengers sent out by the dozen do not return. The Seventh & Butlers are probably still at Annapolis.[37] A rumour this evening says the RR. is in the hands of the Govt. and the 7th's sappers & miners are at work repairing it.

The Pocahontas went puffing down the River at sundown to meet the New York Companies in the transport fleet that left there Sunday night. She looked busy and resolute.[38]

25 April 1861, Thursday

At the request of the Tycoon who imagined he had seen something significant steaming up the River, I went down to the Navy Yard. Saw Dahlgren who at once impressed me as a man of great coolness & power. The boat was the Mt. Vernon who reported everything right in the River.[39]

About noon the 7th Regiment came. I went to the Depot and saw Lefferts who communicated the intelligence of their peaceful passage with which I straightway gladdened the heart of the Ancient. Cale Smith was with him as I returned. He was just reading a letter from Hamlin advising the immediate manufacture of rifled cannon from the Chicopee Works. Lincoln seemed to be in a pleasant hopeful mood, and in the course of conversation partially foreshadowed his present plan. He said, "I intend at present, always leaving an opportunity for change of mind, to fill Fortress Monroe with men and stores: blockade the ports effectually: provide for the entire safety of the Capitol: keep them quietly employed in this way, and then go down to Charleston and pay her the little debt we are owing her." I felt like letting off an Illinois yell. I never heard words that so utterly pleased me. I begged the privilege of scattering an intimation of the coming glory through the host, but he quickly said "Not yet."[40]

This morning a jolly whole-hearted old Shaker from N H came in & filled the room with the freshness of his presence. He said they were late getting here, as their driver who was a constable had to stop to whip a nigger! It was a rich and novel idea to the broadbrimmed Northerner.

Gen Butler has sent an imploring request to the President to be allowed to bag the whole nest of traitorous Maryland Legislators and bring them in triumph here. This the Tycoon wishing to observe every comity even with a recusant State, forbade.[41]

Today we got a few letters and papers & felt not quite so forlorn.

Ash my exquisite acquaintance from Phila. came in, looking ghastly & worn, belted and profusely armed.[42]

26 APRIL 1861, FRIDAY

Massachusetts & Rhode Island troops in large numbers arrived today from Annapolis. Helme tells me that all through Maryland the slaves followed begging to be allowed to come with them as servants. One fellow who had bought himself said, If I had known you gemmen was a coming Id a saved my money.[43]

I called on Sprague the Governor of R. I. with Nicolay—A small, insignificant youth, who bought his place. But who is certainly all right now. He is very proud of his Company of its wealth and social standing.[44]

Carl Schurz was here today. He spoke with ~~wild~~ enthusiasm of his desire to mingle in this war. He has great confidence in his military powers, and his capability of arousing the enthusiasm of the young. He contemplates the career of a great guerilla chief with ardent longing. He objects to the taking of Charleston & advises forays on the Interior States.[45]

27 APRIL 1861, SATURDAY

Jackson Grimshaw has come here from Illinois to urge upon the Government the absolute necessity in a military point of view for the Government to seize the Hannibal & St Joe R.R. His views are very sound. He objects to the President conferring any important military trusts upon those who have been fighting in the interests of the slave power all their lives.[46]

The President recd a letter from Wm F. Channing advising abolition of

Slavery by martial law as the surest way to conquer rebellious states & preserve the border ones.[47]

The Seventh Regiment Band played gloriously on the shaven lawn at the South front of the Executive Mansion. The scene was very beautiful. Through the luxuriant grounds the gaily dressed crowd idly strolled, soldiers loafed in the promenades, the martial music filled the sweet air with vague suggestions of heroism, and Carl Schurz and the President talked war.[48]

28 April 1861, Sunday

All this blessed Sunday, free from war's alarms we have lounged sans souci. Sprague & his staff called on the President, and the Cabinet dropped in and gave a last word as to the new proclamation, blockading Va.[49]

Yesterday the President sent an order to Genl. Scott authorizing and directing him to suspend the writ of habeas corpus on all necessary occasions along the lines of military occupation leading to this city from Philadelphia &c.[50]

29 April 1861, Monday

Going into Nicolays room this morning, Carl Schurz and Jim Lane were sitting. Jim was at the window filling his soul with gall by steady telescopic contemplation of a Secession flag impudently flaunting over a roof in Alexandria. "Let me tell you" said he to the eloquent Teuton, "We have got to whip these scoundrels like hell Cairl Schurz. They did a good thing stoning our men at Baltimore & shooting away the flag at Sumpter. It has set the great North a howling for blood and theyll have it."[51]

"I heard" said Schurz "you preached a sermon to yr. men yesterday."

"No sir, this is no time for preaching. When I went to Mexico, there were four preachers in my regiment. In less than a week, I issued orders for them all to stop preaching and go to playing cards. In a month or so they was the biggest devils & best fighters I had."

An hour afterward Carl Schurz told me he was going home to arm his clansmen for the wars. He has obtained three months leave of absence from his diplomatic duties & permission to raise a cavalry regiment. I doubt the propriety of the movement. He will make a wonderful land pirate, bold, quick brilliant and reckless. He will be hard to control and difficult to direct. Still, we shall see. He is a wonderful man.[52]

The R. I. troops passed in review today. They look wonderfully well in their simple coarse uniforms relieved only by the fierce coloring in blankets.

30 APRIL 1861, TUESDAY

I went up to the Interior Department to see the Rhodian heroes. I saw Goddard Hoppin DeWolf, Sackett, Pearce and others of the whilom loungers of Westminster, all dressed in the coarse blue flannel and all doing duty the severest duty without a murmur, and without any apparent consciousness that there was anything at all remarkable about it. Scattered through the rubbish and camp litter of Company C's quarters there was enough of breeding and honor to retone the society of the Gulf, and wealth enough to purchase the entire State of Florida, and take the poor beggarly Montgomery loan. When men like these leave their horses, their women and their wine, harden their hands, eat crackers for dinner, wear a shirt for a week and never black their shoes,—all for a principle, it is hard to set any bounds to the possibilities of such an army. The good blood of the North must now be mingled with that of the South in battle, and the first fight will determine which is the redder.[53]

Horatio J Perry was this morning appointed Secretary of Legation at Madrid, *ad interim* to give Carl Schurz the benefit of his three months' leave. Perry is living at the Capital city of Spain at present, is married to the Poet Carolina Coronado & is certainly the best man for the place. I wish his appointment were permanent instead of temporary.[54]

Three Indians of the Pottowatomies called today upon their Great Father. The spokesman's English was very exceptional, the other two were mute. One was a magnificent broadchested bare armed giant with a barbaric regal adornment of bears claws. The second a quiet Uncas looking fellow. The Spokesman was dressed in a wonderful style of shabby genteel. The ~~Tycoon~~ President amused them ~~immensely~~ greatly by airing the two or three Indian words he knew. I was amused by his awkward efforts to make himself understood by speaking bad English, e. g. Where live now? When go back Iowa?

Frederick Hassaurek & I dined together. He seems stung by the inaction which his lameness besides his foreign duties imposes upon him. He evidently chafes with generous emulation of the coming glories of Schurz in the field. He is a delicate souled and thoughtful genius, but has not the ~~raw~~ vigor and animal arrogance that help Schurz to bully his way through life. Hassaurek will probably indulge his bent for literature in the high solitude of Quito. He intimated a course of articles in the Atlantic and an ultimate book.[55]

Coming home from the theatre I met Blair, Schurz and Fox coming out of the audience chamber.[56] Going in, I saw the great Map of Virginia, newly hung and fronted by conscious-looking chairs. The air is full of ghastly promises for Maryland & Virginia. ~~Destiny is even now casting over them the gloom of her shadowing wings.~~

Meanwhile the North is growing impatient. Correspondents talk impertinently, and ~~the "little villain" of~~ the N. Y. Times, advises the immediate resignation of the Cabinet, & warns the President that he will be superseded.[57]

Van Wyck is here occasionally. I never saw him so jolly as when he came up Sunday morning with Capt Viele.[58] He had manned a gun all the way up river & was flushed with the honor. He had artistically inked his shot pouch to the following effect.

"We will go through to Washington
Or sleep in the Potomac."
On the reverse.
"What our fathers died to establish
We will maintain."

1 May 1861, Wednesday

Yesterday I read a letter from prominent Unionists of Western Virginia, asking help from the Government in resisting the coercion of the Eastern & rebellious portion of the State. Their plan is to endeavor to remove the State Government from Richmond west of the mountains, or failing in that to cut themselves off from the Eastern District, or rather by remaining in the Union let the Eastern portion cut itself off. The letter was signed by G. W. Caldwell. Nicolay answered it cautiously today, leaving the door open for future negotiations. This morning some of the same men called upon the President. Loyalty will be safer in Western Virginia than rebellion will be on the Eastern slopes of the Blue Ridge.[59]

There were a half-dozen goodlooking members of the Seventh Regiment called upon the Commander-in-chief of the Armies & Navies this afternoon. He was very frank & cordial with them. He spoke amusedly of the Times' proposition of deposing him and said that the Government had three things to do: defend Washington: Blockade the Ports: and retake Government property. All possible despatch was to be used in these matters & it wd be well if the people would cordially assist in ~~these matters~~ this work, before clamoring for ~~additional work~~ more. The proclamation calling out the troops is only two weeks old. No people on earth could have done what we have in that time.

Montgomery Blair came in with the Intelligence that our office holders had been quietly installed at Baltimore under the floating of the constellated banner and that the Police Board had removed the restrictions on the sale of flour. He thought the outbreak at the Massachusetts passage was the work of secession officials who were unwilling to lose their lease of plunder. He thoroughly believed in the loyalty of Maryland. The President seemed to think that if quiet was kept in Baltimore a little longer Maryland might be considered the first of the redeemed.

The little Jew who has so singularly attached himself to Seward's ~~for-tunes~~ who is named in the Directory Herrman but whom the Premier has rechristened Flibbertygibbet came in with advices that Ellsworths regiment was at Annapolis in good order and well conditioned. Also that the R. I. Artillery was now on its way hither by water.[60]

Ellsworth's whereabouts pleased the Tycoon as it enabled him to correct a funk of Scotts that the Firemen were cutting their way through Baltimore. They will find the subterraneans of Wilson's command a thousand times worse than Ellsworths in insubordination & rowdyism. I think the best use for them will be to detail them at once to the retaking of Sumter. They will probably all perish, & provide themselves with a numerous escort of Palmetto rebels to the warm regions down below.[61]

2 MAY 1861, THURSDAY

Tonight Ellsworth & his stalwart troup arrived. He was dressed like his men, red cap, red shirt, grey breeches grey jacket. In his belt, a sword, a very heavy revolver, and what was still more significant of the measures necessary with the turbulent spirits under his command, an enormously large and bloodthirsty looking bowie knife, more than a foot long in the blade, and with body enough to go through a man's head from crown to chin as you would split an apple. His hair was cut short. His face thin from Constant labor and excitement. His voice had assumed that tone of hoarse strength that I recognized at the end of the triumphant trip last year. He seemed contented and at ease about his regiment. He indulged in a little mild blasphemy when he found that no suitable quarters had been provided but was mollified by the proffer of the 69th's rooms & the Capitol.[62]

I went up. It was a jolly gay set of blackguards. They had reduced their hair to a war footing. There was not a pound of capillary integument in the house. Their noses were concave, their mouths vulgar but goodhumoured, the eyes small crafty and furtive.

They were in a pretty complete state of dont care a damn, modified by an affectionate and respectful deference to the Colonel. He thought only of his men. We went, after making all possible provisions for their suppers, to Hammacks.[63] The Zouave could not enjoy his tea, as he thought it unbecoming an officer to eat before his men.

He spoke with honest exaltation of the fruitless attempt made to stop him the morning of embarkation.[64]

3 MAY 1861, FRIDAY

This morning in the Presidents mail I came across some warlike documents. One from Fernandy Wood offering his services in a military capacity, which was very cool but not so arctic as the cheekiness of Govr. Harris of Tenn, who demanded an immediate explanation of the seizing of the Hillman at Cairo (which the ~~Tycoon~~ President glanced at & quietly observed, "He be d——d.") A New Jersey General White offers his division for an unlimited time.[65]

4 MAY 1861, SATURDAY

The Maryland Disunionists, that branch of them represented by Bob McLane called today upon the President. ~~Their roaring was exquisitely modulated. It had lost the ferocious timbre of the April days.~~ They roared as gently as twere any nightingale. The only point they particularly desired to press was that there was no ~~particular~~ special necessity at present existing for the armed occupation of Maryland. That it would irritate and inflame. Still they admitted that the right of the Government to occupy the City and State was undeniable: That the people were on the side of the Union: a majority unconditionally and a majority of the minority favorably inclined, while nearly all were for avoiding any conflict with the federal authorities. They also implored the President not to act in any spirit of revenge for the murdered ~~soldiery~~ soldiers. The President coolly replied that he never acted from any such impulse & as to their other views he should take them into consideration and should decline giving them any answer at present.[66]

Genl. Scott gave orders to Genl. Butler to occupy the Relay House as soon as practicable and Butler instantly replied that he should hold divine service with his command there tomorrow (Sunday)[67]

5 MAY 1861, SUNDAY

Which he did.

6 MAY 1861, MONDAY

Maj. Sparks of Baltimore, who seems alarmingly tricky, came noisily in with a yarn that the Secessionists, who are hovering 10,000 strong around Harper's Ferry, are removing gun barrells, gun stocks, and machinery away from there—that there are batteries scattered among the rocks which thoroughly command the situation—that they can only be fought successfully from the Maryland side—that Ben McCullough is there & had recently sent a budget of information to the Legislature at Frederick—that Butler was snug at the Relay, unconscious until Sparks told him that the enemy were rigging up a battery on the opposite heights which would rake his camp, and other items to the like sensational purpose. I gave them to Howard who straightway sent them Tribune-wards.[68]

The President came into Nicolays room this afternoon. He had just written a letter to Hamlin, requesting him to write him a daily letter in regard to the number of troops arriving departing or expected each day. He said that it seemed there was no certain knowledge on these subjects at the War Department, that even Genl. Scott was usually in the dark in respect to them.[69]

I told him of a truculent letter written by a State Senator of Kentucky protesting against the occupation of Cairo by Federal troops. He directed an answer & I wrote as follows "Executive Mansion, May 6, 1861. Hon John M. Johnson. My Dear Sir, The President has the honor to acknowledge the receipt of your communication of the 26th ult. protesting against the stationing of U. S. Troops at Cairo.

The President directs me to say that the views so ably stated by you shall have due consideration: and to assure you that he would certainly never have ordered the movement of troops, complained of, had he known that Cairo was in your Senatorial district.

Allow me sir to subscribe myself with sentiments of high regard, Your humble Servant John M. Hay Assistant Sec to the President.

To Hon John M. Johnson State Senator, &c. Paducah Ky.

I wanted to add that the President respectfully requested that in all future occasions he would spell "solemly" with an "n." But this hypercritical orthography the Chief disapproved. So the missive went. It will take the quiet satire of the note about a half an hour to get through the thick skull of this Kentucky Senator, and then he will think it a damned poor joke.[70]

7 May 1861, Tuesday

~~Ellsworth came in this mo~~ I went in to give the President some little items of Illinois news, saying among other things that Singleton was behaving very badly. He replied with emphasis that Singleton was a miracle of meanness, calmly looking out of the window at the smoke of the two Navy steamers puffing up the way, resting the end of the telescope on his toes sublime.[71]

I spoke of the proposition of Browning to subjugate the South, establish a black republic in lieu of the exterminated whites, and ~~establish~~ extend a protectorate over them, while they raised our cotton.[72] He said, Some of our northerners seem bewildered and dazzled by the excitement of the hour. Doolittle seems inclined to think that this war is to result in the entire abolition of Slavery. Old Col. Hamilton a venerable and most respectable gentleman, impresses upon me most earnestly the propriety of enlisting the slaves in our army."

I told him his daily correspondence was thickly interspersed by such suggestions.

"For my own part," he said, "I consider the central idea pervading this struggle is the necessity that is upon us, of proving that popular government is not an absurdity. We must settle this question now, whether in a free government the minority have the right to break up the government whenever they choose. If we fail it will go far to prove the incapability of the people to govern themselves. There may be one consideration used in stay of such final judgement, but that is not for us to use in advance. That is, that there exists in our case, an instance of a vast and far reaching disturbing element, which the history of no other free nation will probably ever present. That however is not for us to say at present. Taking the government as we found it we will see if the majority can preserve it."[73]

He is engaged in constant thought upon his Message: It will be an exhaustive review of the questions of the hour & of the future.[74]

In the Afternoon we went up to see Ellsworth's Zouave Firemen. They are the largest sturdiest and physically the most magnificent men I ever saw collected together. They played over the sward like kittens, lithe and agile in their strength.

Ellsworth has been intensely disgusted at the wild yarns afloat about them which are for the most part, utterly untrue. A few graceless rascals have been caught in various lapses. These are in irons. One horrible story which has been terrifying all the maiden antiques of the city for several days, has the element of horror pretty well eliminated today, by the injured fair, who proves a most yielding seducee, offering to settle the matter for 25 dollars. Other yarns are due to the restless brains of the press-gang.[75]

The youthful Colonel formed his men in a hollow square, and made a great speech at them. There was more commonsense, dramatic power, tact, energy, & that eloquence that naturally flowers into deeds in le petit Colonels fifteen minute harangue, than in all the speeches that stripped the plumes from our unfortunate ensign in the spread eagle days of the Congress that has flitted. He spoke to them as men, made them proud in their good name, spoke bitterly & witheringly of the disgrace of the recreant, contrasted with cutting emphasis which his men delighted in, the enlistment of the dandy regiment[76] for thirty days, with *theirs* for the war—spoke solemnly & impressively of the disgrace of expulsion—roused them to wild enthusiasm by announcing that he had heard of one officer who treated his men with less consideration than himself and that, if on inquiry the rumor proved true, he would strip him & send him home in irons. The men yelled with delight clapped their hands & shouted "Bully for you." He closed with wonderful tact and dramatic spirit, by saying "Now laddies, if any one of you wants to go home, he had better sneak around the back alleys, crawl over fences, and get out of sight before we see him." which got them again. He must have run with this crowd some time in his varied career. He knows them and handles them so perfectly.

8 May 1861, Wednesday

Eames called this morning & brought to my notice a singular omission in Jeff. Davis' manifesto, His ignoring all mention of the right of revolution and confining his defense of his position to the reserved constitutional right of a state to secede. By this means he estops his claim upon the recognition of the world. For even those ~~governments~~ cabinets that acknowledge the necessity of recognizing all governments, which by virtue of revolution have a defacto existence, would most naturally say to a new government basing its claim to nationality on the constitution of the government vs. which it rebels, "We can entertain no such question of legal construction. The contest as stated by you between you and your government is a municipal one. We have no right to interfere or prejudge the issue of such a case of conflicting interpretation." Jeff. Davis seems to have been so anxious to satisfy the restless consciences of the Borderers, that he utterly overlooks the importance of conciliating the good opinion of the outside world. "There is a hole in your best coat Master Davis.[77]

9 May 1861, Thursday

~~Saw at breakfast this morning a quiet, shrewd looking man with unobtrusive spectacles, doing his devoir to an egg. I was informed that it was Anderson. The North has been strangely generous with that man. The red tape of military duty was all that bound his heart from its traitorous impulses. His Kentucky brigade will be like himself fighting weakly for a Union they scorn.~~[78]
There was a very fine matinee at the Navy Yard given by some musical members of the 12th New York. They sang well the Band played well and the President listened well. After the programme, the President begged for the Marseillaise. The prime gentleman gave the first verse and then gener-

ously repeated it, interpolating nonchalantly "Liberty or Death" in place of "Abreuve nos sillons," which he had forgotten.

Then we went down to the Pensacola and observed the shooting of the great Dahlgren gun Plymouth. Two ricochette shots were sent through the target and one plumper. The splendid course of the 11 inch shell [hiving?] through 1300 yds of air, the lighting, the quick rebound & flight through the target with wild skips, throwing up a 30 ft column of spray at every jump, the decreasing leaps and the steady roll into the waves were scenes as novel and pleasant to me as to all the rest of the party. The Prest. was delighted. Capt. Gillis was bored at Dahlgren for laughing at the bad firing from the Pocahontas.[79]

This morning Ellsworths Zouaves covered themselves with glory as with a blanket in saving Willard's Hotel and quenching a most ugly looking fire.[80] They are utterly unapproachable in anything they attempt. Their respectful demeanor to their Chief and his anxious solicitude for their comfort & safety are absolutely touching to behold.

10 MAY 1861, FRIDAY

Carl Schurz loafed into my room this morning & we spoke of the slaves & their ominous discontent. He agreed with me that the Commandants at Pickens & Monroe were unnecessarily squeamish in imprisoning & returning to their masters the fugitives who came to their gates begging to be employed. Their owners are in a state of open rebellion against the government & nothing would bring them to their senses more readily than a gentle reminder that they are dependent upon the good will of the Government for the security of their lives and property. The action would be entirely just and eminently practicable. Schurz says that thousands of Democrats are declaring that now is the time to remove the cause of all our woes. What we could not have done in many lifetimes the madness and folly of the South has accomplished for us. Slavery offers itself more vulnerable to our attack than at any point in any century and the wild malignity of the South is excusing us, before God & the World.[81]

So we talked in the morning.

But tonight I saw a letter from Mrs. Whitman stating that Thomas Earl, T. W. Higginson the essayist of Boston and young John Brown, were "going to free the slaves." What we were dreaming of came over my mind with horrible distinctness and I shrunk from the apparition. This is not the time nor are these the men to do it. They should wait till the government gives some kind of sanction to the work. Otherwise the horrors of the brutal massacre will move the pity of the magnanimous North, and in the suppression of the insurrection the warring sections may fuse and compromise.[82]

11 MAY 1861, SATURDAY

I told Helme to come & see me, and I impressed as strongly as possible upon his mind the importance of the view just taken—that the Administration could do nothing but hang the insurrectionists, and that any such rash outbreak would terribly weaken the hands of the government. He said he would write Brown & Higginson.

This afternoon the Marine Band played on the South Lawn and Carl Schurz sat with Lincoln on the balcony. After the President had kissed some thousand children and retired, Carl went into the library and developed a new accomplishment. He played with great skill & feeling, sitting in the dusk twilight at the Piano, until the President came by & took him down to tea. Schurz is a wonderful man. An orator, a soldier, a philosopher, an exiled patriot, a skilled musician. He has every quality of romance and dramatic picturesqueness.

12 MAY 1861, SUNDAY

We spent this afternoon at Camp Lincoln the habitation of Ellsworth's "pet lambs." They seemed very comfortable and happy. Ellsworth was playing ball with them as we approached looking fine and blouzy in his red shirt. We went to his tent. Col. Pritchard (here from St Louis to gain indemnity for his losses on the C E Hillman) was jubilant over the capture of Frosts Brigade. They seemed to think it would prove the coup de grace to Secession in Missouri. Frank Blair writes today that St Louis is getting too quiet. He wants his regiment sent to Charleston.[83]

Wm P Thomasson was here today trying to gain authority for the Kentucky Unionists to raise troops in the State for service in the State. Col. Rousseau says that they can be more easily raised and controlled in this way than in any other.[84]

22 AUGUST 1861, THURSDAY

A long Hiatus. The nights have been too busy for jottings.

Today Dudley & Hunt the Ky Comrs called on the President begging for permission of neutrality. He told them professed Unionists gave him more trouble than rebels. They put their case strongly but gained no commitment from him. It is a deep scheme of Magoffin's to put the responsibility of the first blow upon the Govt. The President cannot consent to what they ask for neutrality *wont* continue long—we want to go through the state—and the North will not permit the disarming of the Unionists. On his refusal Davis of course will assent to all demands & place the Govt. wrong before the people.[85]

We went over to Seward's found him comfortably slippered & after talking about consular nuisances went over to McClellan's. Every thing seems going right. Discipline is perfecting. The Dry Tortugas have squelched mutiny. The drills & reviews keep the men alive. Hunter is soon to go to Illinois as they need a head. At first he wanted to take McDowell but Scott objected. Regiments are constantly coming in, and arms for them. McClellan is growing jolly. Seward is in a better humor than I have lately seen him.[86]

28 AUGUST [SEPTEMBER] 1861

I went west, and passed several days in St. Louis. Saw very much of Fremont and his wife. He was quiet earnest industrious, imperious. She very much like him, though talking more and louder.[87] ~~I wrote articles in the World and Journal for Fremont. Coming to New York I found Thurlow Weed had blabbed it to the President.~~[88]

10 OCTOBER 1861, THURSDAY

Tonight I went over to McClellans Quarters with the ~~Tycoon~~ President and Seward. Lander was with us, part of the way. Lander was gasconading a little. He said he would like a good place to die in with a corporal's guard, to set the nation right in the face of the world after the cowardly shame of Bull Run. The President as Lander walked off, said "If he really wanted a job like that I could give it to him—Let him take his squad and go down behind Manassas and break up their railroad." Seward said he disbelieved in personal courage as a civilized institution. He had always acted on the opposite principle, admitting you are scared and assuming that the enemy is. If this matter had been managed on his basis it would have been arranged satisfactorily and honorably before now.

We came to McClellan's quarters and met in the telegraph office a long and awkward youth who spoke in a high-pitched and rapid tone to Seward, "We are just in from a ride of all day." Seward introduced him to me as Captain Orleans. He went up stairs to call McClellan and the President said quietly "One doesnt like to make a messenger of the King of France, as that youth, the Count of Paris would be, if his family had kept the throne."[89]

McClellan came hurriedly in and began to talk with the President. They discussed the events of today and yesterday. McClellan was much pleased at the conduct of his men—no rowdyism or plundering today. He was merely today finishing yesterdays work. The rest of this week will be used in the same way. Says the ~~Tycoon~~ President, "We have gained a day on our Sea Expedition. The vessells will leave on the 14th it is thought instead of the 15th."[90]

As we left, McClellan said, "I think we shall have our arrangements made for a strong reconnaissance about Monday to feel the strength of the enemy. I intend to be careful, and do as well as possible. Dont let them hurry me, is all I ask." "You shall have your own way in the matter I assure you," said the ~~Tycoon~~ President, and went home.[91]

12 October 1861, Saturday

Tonight the President went to Seward's, I with him. At the door a telegram was handed him—from McClellan, Stating that the enemy was before him in force and would probably attack in the morning. "If they attack"—he added—"I shall beat them."[92] We went to Seward's and talked of many things. Seward spoke of Lander's restlessness & griefs at inaction, his offered resignation—and resolve to go West and begin again—that watching the Potomac was not congenial, and other such. Seward told him to be of good cheer. Genl. Scott was already fixing his orders for exactly the work he wanted to do.[93]

Col. Scott came in with despatches from McCl—one ordering Hooker's Bladensburgh Brigade in—one countermanding & one reaffirming. Scott then went out to order transportation for 6000.[94]

G V Fox came in and began to talk about the Great expedition that is fitting at Annapolis. He wants when they have sailed to have 14,000 more men detached from the Army of the Potomac to be held in readiness awaiting the result of the expedition. If it causes a retreat of the rebels, then this additional force can be easily spared. The fleet will probably sail on Tuesday and will have some work to do at Fernandina Pensacola, Mobile. Genl. Scott told Fox that 3500 men would be enough to take Mobile, assisted by their Ships. Fox himself seemed very confident that the expedition would succeed. His only nervousness was in relation to submarine batteries which modern science has rendered very destructive and entirely feasible.[95]

Seward spoke also of Motley's despatch which seems to contain a most cheering account of the real sentiment of honest sympathy existing in the best Class of English Society towards us. Motleys letter embraced free and cordial conversations with Earl Russell, Earl Grey, Cobden, Mr. Layard Prince Albert and the Queen.[96]

There was much talk of Daniel Webster in which the financial sanssouciism of the great man was strikingly prominent. Seward said he would not live nor Clay, a tithe as long as J. Q. Adams. The President disagreed with him and thought Webster will be read for ever.

17 OCTOBER 1861, THURSDAY

At Seward's tonight we met Capt. Shultz who showed very bad taste by alluding to the Chicago Convention and Seward.[97] The Prest. told a good yarn.

One day in Springfield shortly after some of the lower counties had held meetings and passed resolutions eulogistic of Trumbull, John Wentworth sitting near Lincoln at breakfast one morning said "Lincoln, have you seen them resolutions." "I have seen what I suppose you refer to."

"Them Trumbull fellers are going to trick you again."

"I dont see any trickery about it, and if there was, there is no way to help the matter"

"I tell you what, Lincoln," said John with a look of unutterable sagacity, "You must do like Seward does—get a feller to run you."[98]

It was vastly amusing to both the ~~Tycoon~~ President and Secretary.

The Sec. State talked about intercepted correspondence and the double-dealing and lying of our young English friends, Fergusson and Bourke.[99]

Going to McClellan's with Banks they talked about the Campaign. McC. thought the enemy were massing at Manassas. He said he was not such a fool as to buck against that place in the spot designated by the foe. While there, the President received a despatch from Sherman at Annapolis asking for the 79th N. Y. the Highlanders. The President was vexed at this and at Sherman's intimation that the fleet would not sail before Sunday. McC. was also bored by the request but Seward strongly seconded it. McC. said he would sleep on it.[100]

We came away the ~~Tycoon~~ President still vexed at Sherman. At Sewards door, he turned suddenly and said, "I think I will telegraph to Sherman that I will not break up McClellans command and that I havent much hope of his expedition anyway."

"No," said Seward, "you wont say discouraging things to a man going off with his life in his hand. Send them some hopeful and cheering dispatch."

[18 OCTOBER 1861, FRIDAY]

The ~~Tycoon~~ President came home and this morning telegraphed Sherman. "I will not break up McC's army without his consent. I do not think I will come to Annapolis." This was all. I think his petulance very unaccountable.[101]

22 OCTOBER 1861, TUESDAY

This has been a heavy day. Last night Col. Baker was killed at Leesburg at the head of his Brigade. McClellan & the Prest. talked sadly over it. McClellan said, There is many a good fellow that wears the shoulder-straps going under the sod before this thing is over. There is no loss too great to be repaired. If I should get knocked on the head Mr. President you will put another man immediately into my shoes." "I want you to take care of yourself" said the President.[102]

McClellan seemed very hopeful and confident—thought he had the enemy if in force or not—we left him making arrangements for the morrow. During this evening's conversation it became painfully evident that he had *no plan* nor the slightest idea of what Stone was about.[103]

Tonight we went over again. Mc was at Poolesville. Telegraphs that loss is heavy and the troops behaved well. All right in that quarter.

At Sewards tonight the President talked about Secession Compromise and other such. He spoke of a committee of Southern Pseudo Unionists coming to him before Inauguration for guarantees &c. He promised to evacuate Sumter if they would break up their Convention, without any row or nonsense. They demurred. Subsequently he renewed proposition to Summers but without any result. The President was most anxious to prevent bloodshed.[104]

I never heard secession made more absurd than by the conversation of tonight. Seward Chase Kennedy & Bp. McIlvaine.[105]

Today Dep. Marshal came today & asked what he should do with process to be served on Porter in contempt business. I took him over to Seward & Seward said,

"The President instructs you that the Habeas Corpus is suspended in this city at present and forbids you to serve any process upon any officer here." Turning to me, That is what the Prest. says, is it not Mr. Hay? "Precisely his words" I replied and the thing was done.[106]

26 OCTOBER 1861, SATURDAY

This evening the Jacobin club, represented by Trumbull Chandler and Wade, came up to ~~blackguard~~ worry the administration into a battle. The ~~wild howl~~ agitation of the summer is to be renewed. The President ~~stood up for~~ defended McClellan's deliberateness. We then went over to the General's Headquarters. We found Col Key there. He was talking also about the grand necessity of an immediate battle to clean out the enemy, at once. He seemed to think we were ruined if we did not fight. The President asked what McC. thot about it. Key answered, "The General is troubled in his mind. I think he is much embarrassed by the radical difference between his views and those of General Scott."[107]

Here McC. came in—Key went out—the President began to talk about his wonderful new repeating battery of rifled gun, shooting 50 balls a minute. The President is delighted with it and has ordered ten and asks

McC. to go down and see it, and if proper, detail a corps of men to work it. He further told the General that Reverdy Johnson wants the Maryland Vols in Maryld to vote in November. All right.[108]

They then talked about the Jacobins. McC said that Wade preferred an unsuccessful battle to delay. He said a defeat could be easily repaired, by the swarming recruits. McClellan answered "that he would rather have a few recruits before a victory—than a good many after a defeat."[109]

The President deprecated this new manifestation of ~~senseless~~ popular impatience but at the same time said it was a reality and should be taken into the account At the same time General you must not fight till you are ready."[110]

"I have everything at stake" said the General. "If I fail I will not see you again or anybody."

"I have a notion to go out with you and stand or fall with the battle."

The President has written a letter to St. Louis giving plan of campaign as suggestion the officer in Command, probably Hunter. It is to halt the pursuit of Price, go back in two columns to Rolla and Sedalia, and there *observe* taking the surplus for active operation in the South. The plan though entirely original with the ~~Tycoon~~ President seemed a good one both to Scott and McC. and will probably be followed.[111]

27 OCTOBER 1861, SUNDAY

We went over to Seward's tonight and found Chandler and Wade there. They had been talking to Seward to get up a battle saying that one must be fought, saying that defeat was no worse than delay & a great deal more trash. Morton & Speed then began to growl about their guns. Seward and the President soon dried that up. Wilson came in, a strong healthy hearty Senator soldier and man. He was bitter on the Jacobins saying the safety of the country demanded that the General should have his time. Going up to McClellan's we discussed the Leesburgh business. McC. saying that Stone's report would be in tomorrow, every one forebore comment.[112]

Yesterday the Prest. received two despatches from St. Louis—one from Lamon deprecating the removal of Fremont and one from Washburne who seems at last thoroughly frightened about the Missouri matter saying there is a promise of anarchy and revolution in case of Fremonts deposition. "Forewarned forearmed" he says.[113]

Today we got a despatch from Kelley announcing a victory at Romney and tonight one from Fremont announcing a brilliant charge of Zagonyi and the body Guard at Springfield, from which we learn that they have been rapidly advancing of late. The President was pleased therewith.[114]

[NOVEMBER 1861]

The night of the 1st November we went over to McClellans. The General was there and read us his general order in regard to Scotts resignation & his own assumption of command.[115] The President thanked him for it and said it greatly relieved him. He added "I should be perfectly satisfied if I thought that this vast increase of responsibility would not embarrass you."

"It is a great relief, sir. I feel as if several tons were taken from my shoulders today. I am now in contact with you, and the Secretary. I am not embarrassed by intervention.

"Well" says the ~~Tycoon~~ President, "~~Call~~ Draw on me for all the sense I have, and all the information. In addition to your present command, the supreme command of the army will entail a vast labor upon you."

"I can do it all," McC said quietly.

Going to Sewards he talked long and earnestly about the matter. He had been giving a grave and fatherly lecture to McC. which was taken in good part, advising him to enlarge the sphere of his thoughts and feel the weight of the occasion.[116]

Then we went up and talked a little while to the Orleans princes. De Joinville is deaf and says little. The boys talk very well and fluently.[117]

7 NOVEMBER 1861, THURSDAY

I talked tonight with the President about the opening of the cotton trade by our sea-side excursionists. I represented the interest felt by Northern spinners who want it still blockaded. He doubted their statement that they had a large supply on hand whose price would be reduced by opening the trade and seemed to think that we equally with France and England would gain by it. He said it was an object to show the world we were fair in this matter favoring outsiders as much as ourselves. That it was by no means sure that they would bring their cotton to the port after we opened it. But it would be well to show Europe that it was secession that distressed them and not we. That the chief difficulty was in discovering how far the planters who bring us their cotton can be trusted with the money they receive for it.[118]

I went in strong for the opening of the ports, I dont know why, using all the arguments I could think of, and rather gained the idea that he also slanted in that direction.

8 November 1861, Friday

Here is a cheeky letter just recd. ~~It displays a wild and absurd miracle of cheek.~~

My dear Sir

Genl Wool has resigned. General Fremont must. General Scott has retired.

I have an ambition and I trust a laudable one to be Major General of the United States Army.

Has any body done more to deserve it? No one will do more. May I rely upon you as you may have confidence in me, to take this matter into consideration?

I will not disgrace the position. I may fail in its duties.

Truly yours
Benj. F. Butler.

The President.

P. S. I have made the same suggestion to other of my friends.[119]

11 November 1861, Monday

Tonight Blenker's Germans had a torch-light procession in honor of McC promotion. I never saw such a scene of strange and wild magnificence as this nightmarch was. Afterwards we went over to McC.s and talked about the Southern flurry. The President thought this a good time to feel them. McC. said "I have not been unmindful of that. We will feel them tomorrow." The ~~Tycoon~~ President and the General were both very jolly over the news.[120]

13 NOVEMBER 1861, WEDNESDAY

I wish here to record what I consider a ~~dreadful~~ portent of evil to come. The President, Governor Seward and I went over to McClellan's house tonight. The Servant at the door said the General was at the wedding of Col. Wheaton at General Buell's, and would soon return. We went in, and after we had waited about an hour McC. came in and ~~learned~~ without paying any particular attention to the porter who told him the President was waiting to see him, went up stairs, passing the door of the room where the President and Secretary of State were seated. They waited about half-an-hour, and sent once more a servant to tell the General they were there, and the answer ~~coolly~~ came that the General had gone to bed.[121]

I merely record this unparrallelled insolence of epaulettes without comment. It is the first indication I have yet seen, of the threatened supremacy of the military authorities.[122]

Coming home I spoke to the President about the matter but he seemed not to have noticed it specially, saying it was better at this time not to be making points of etiquette & personal dignity.[123]

4 DECEMBER 1861, WEDNESDAY

Left New York [for] Philadelphia.[124]

5 DECEMBER 1861, THURSDAY

Called on St. G. Campbell and ———— touching the case of Smith the private. Left Philadelphia noon. Arrived in Washington 6:30 P.M. Hunted up Attorney General Bates.

6 DECEMBER 1861, FRIDAY

Sought Cox (his resolution). Counsel with Cox and Snow-white (O'-Gorman).[125]

7 December 1861, Saturday

War Office. Blair. Military Committee. Bates. President. McClellan's office. Colonel Hardy. Daly and Barney arrive. Co-operation of Crittenden and McDougal, Latham, etc.[126]

8 December 1861, Sunday

Expected message from Colonel Hardy for interview with General McClellan. Daly and Barney arrange for a meeting with Secretary Chase.

9 December 1861, Monday

Daly and Barney see Secretary Chase and President. O'Gorman and Savage have a lengthy interview with General McClellan. Letter to Secretary Cameron. Military Committee. Blair. Richardson Dunn. Joint resolution passed the House. Agreed that O'Gorman return to New York and J. Savage remain. Subsequently O'Gorman prevailed on to remain. Couldn't see Seward, he had to see President and General McClellan. Appointment made with Assistant Secretary F. A. Seward to see the Secretary Tuesday morning.[127]

10 December 1861, Tuesday

Daly, O'Gorman and Savage interview with Secretary Seward; position of the latter. O'Gorman alludes to the Massachusetts men. Judge puts ———— at Seward. To the War Department. Send in General McClellan's letter. Waiting in the lobby O'Gorman and Assistant Secretary Scott. Latter willing and desirous to aid. The Vice-President, his views favorable. "A few earnest men worth a dozen public meetings." Senator Simmons introduces Colonel Knight, Mayor of Providence, his brother a prisoner. Latham, etc. Colonel Knight rebuffed by Secretary Cameron. We unable to see latter. Press of Senators and Congressmen. Cabinet hour arrives. Our letter sent back. Cameron had to go to Cabinet. So had *we*. Joined Barney there. What took place there. O'Gorman returns to New York. We go across the Potomac. Butterfield, Wadsworth, McDowell, King, Blenker, etc.[128]

11 DECEMBER 1861, WEDNESDAY

Mulligan. We talk with Bates. Knight calls. Barney. Bancroft. Daly. S. Go to Blenker. Stahl, Steinwehr, Prince Salm-Salm, Count Valentini, Ingenheim, etc., etc. Seminoles, Creeks, Chickasaws, Commissioner of Indian Affairs. Ladies. Balcony. Review. Indian talk. "That my side," etc., etc.[129]

2

1862

[MARCH 1862]

ON THE 27TH DAY OF JANUARY, THE PRESIDENT ISSUED HIS GENeral War Order No. *One* to those whose direction it was to be. He wrote it without any consultation and read it to the Cabinet, not for their sanction but for their information. From that time he influenced actively the operations of the Campaign. He stopped going to McClellan's and sent for the General to come to him. Every thing grew busy and animated after this order. It was not fully carried out in its details. Some of the Corps anticipated others delayed action. Fort Henry and Ft Donelson showed that Halleck was doing his share. The Army of the Potomac still was sluggish. His next order was issued after a consultation with all the Generals of the Potomac Army in which as Stanton told me next morning, "we saw ten Generals afraid to fight." The fighting Generals were McDowell Sumner Heintzleman & Keyes, and Banks. These were placed next day at the head of the Army Corps.[1]

So things began to look vigorous. Sunday morning, the 9th of March the news of the Merrimac's frolic came here. Stanton was fearfully stampeded. He said they would capture our fleet, take Ft Monroe, be in Washington before night. The ~~Tycoon~~ President thought it was a great bore, but blew less than Stanton. As the day went on the news grew better. And at four oclock the telegraph was completed and we heard of the splendid performance of the Monitor. That evening also we heard of the evacuation of the Potomac batteries, the luckiest of all possible chances, as the most ~~appalling~~ worst thing about the Merrimac's damages was the fact that they would impede the enterprise of taking those batteries. This was McDowell's explanation to me when I told him of it.[2]

At Evening came the news of Manassas being evacuated; this came through contrabands. McClellan started instantly over the River. The next day the news were confirmed and the next night Manassas was occupied. People said a great deal about it and thought a great deal more.[3]

35

On the evening of the 11th of March the President requested me to call together the Heads of the Departments of War State & Treasury. Seward came first. The President read to him General Order no 3.[4] He approved it thoroughly. He agreed with the President when he the Prest said that though the duty of relieving Gen McClellan was a most painful one, he yet thought he was doing Gen McC. a very great kindness in permitting him to retain command of the Army of the Potomac, and giving him an opportunity to retrieve his errors. Seward spoke very bitterly of the imbecility which had characterized the generals operations on the upper Potomac. The Secretary of State urged that the War Order go out in the name of Stanton. He said it would strengthen the hands of the Secretary and he needed public confidence. While he was urging this Stanton came in and at once insisted that it go in the President's name. He said that a row had grown up between him and McCs friends and he feared it would be thought to spring from personal feeling. The President decided to take the responsibility.[5]

Blair was not consulted. The Prest. knew that he would object to the disposition of Fremont and preferred to have no words about it. Blair and the Prest. continued on very good terms in spite of the publication of Blairs letter to Fremont. Blair came to explain it to the Prest. but he told him that he was too busy to quarrell with him. If he, B, didnt show him the letter he would probably never see it. ~~Chase had previously forgiven him in a quietly careless sort of way & He retained his old status in Cabinet councils.~~[6]

Schuyler Colfax told me the other day that he had seen a letter from old F. P. Blair Sr. asking Fremonts influence to make Frank Blair a Major Genl of Missouri Militia: and the original manuscripts of the proposals for clothing contracts that Fremont had refused to Frank Blair on McKinstrys representation of their unfairness. So that is one point in that Fremont business settled.[7]

[five illegible lines]

[1 SEPTEMBER 1862, MONDAY]

Saturday morning, the 30th of August, I rode out into the country and turned in at the "Soldiers home." The President's horse was standing by the door and in a moment the President appeared and we rode into town together.[8]

We talked about the state of things by Bull Run and Pope's prospect. The President was very outspoken in regard to McClellan's present conduct. He said it really seemed to him that McC wanted Pope defeated. He mentioned to me a despatch of McC.s in which he proposed, as one plan of action, to "leave Pope to get out of his own scrape, and devote ourselves to securing Washington." He spoke also of Mcs dreadful ~~cowardice~~ panic in the matter of Chain Bridge, which he had ordered blown up the night before, but which order had been countermanded; and also of his incomprehensible interference with Franklin's corps which he recalled once, and then when they had been sent ahead by Halleck's order, begged permission to recall them again & only desisted after Hallecks sharp injunction to push them ahead till they whipped something or got whipped themselves. The President seemed to think him a little crazy. Envy jealousy and spite are probably a better explanation of his present conduct. He is constantly sending despatches to the President and Halleck asking what is his real position and command. He acts as chief alarmist and grand marplot of the Army.[9]

The President, on my asking if Halleck had any prejudices, rejoined "No! Halleck is wholly for the service. He does not care who succeeds or who fails so the service is benefited."

Later in the day we were in Hallecks room. H. was at dinner & Stanton came in while we were waiting for him and carried us off to dinner. A pleasant little dinner and a pretty wife as white and cold and motionless as marble, whose rare smiles seemed to pain her. Stanton was loud about the McC. business. He was unqualifiedly severe upon McClellan. He said that after these battles, there should be one Court Martial, if never any more. He said that nothing but foul play could lose us this battle & that it rested with McC. and his friends. Stanton seemed to believe very strongly in Pope. So did the President for that matter.[10]

We went back to the Headquarters and found General Halleck. He seemed quiet and somewhat confident. He said the greatest battle of the Century was now being fought. He said he had sent every man that could go, to the field. At the War Department we found that Mr. Stanton had sent a vast army of Volunteer Nurses out to the field, probably utterly useless, over which he gave Genl. Wadsworth command.[11]

Every thing seemed to be going well and hilarious on Saturday & we went to bed expecting glad tidings at sunrise. But about Eight oclock the President came to my room as I was dressing and calling me out said,

"Well John we are whipped again, I am afraid. The enemy reinforced on Pope and drove back his left wing and he has retired to Centerville where he says he will be able to hold his men. I dont like that expression. I dont like to hear him admit that his men need holding"

After a while however things began to look better and peoples spirits rose as the heavens cleared. The President was in a singularly defiant tone of mind. He often repeated, "We must hurt this enemy before it gets away." And this Morning, Monday, he said to me when I made a remark in regard to the bad look of things, "No, Mr Hay, we must whip these people now. Pope must fight them, if they are too strong for him he can gradually retire to these fortifications. If this be not so, if we are really whipped and to be whipped we may as well stop fighting."

It is due in great measure to his indomitable will, that ~~things~~ army movements have been characterized by such energy and celerity for the last few days. There is one man who seems thoroughly to reflect and satisfy him in everything he undertakes. This is Haupt the Rail Road man at Alexandria. He has as Chase says a Major General's head on his shoulders. The President is particularly struck with the businesslike character of his despatch, telling in the fewest words the information most sought for, which contrasted so strongly with the weak whining vague and incorrect despatches of the whilom General-in-chief. If heads or shoulder-straps could be exchanged, it would be a good thing, in either case, here. A good railroader would be spoiled but the General gained would compensate. The corps of Haupt starting from Alexandria have acted as Pioneers advance Guard, voltigeurs and every other light infantry arm of the service.[12]

5 SEPTEMBER 1862, FRIDAY

This morning I walked with the President over to the War Department to ascertain the truth of the report that Jackson has crossed the Potomac. We went to the telegraph office and found it true. On the way over the President said "McClellan is working like a beaver. He seems to be aroused to doing something, by the sort of snubbing he got last week. I am of opinion that this public feeling against him will make it expedient to take important command from him. The Cabinet yesterday were unanimous against him. They were all ready to denounce me for it, except Blair. He has acted badly in this matter, but we must use what tools we have. There is no man in the army who can man these fortifications and lick these troops of ours into shape half as well as he." I spoke of the general feeling against McClellan as evinced by the Prests mail. He rejoined, "Unquestionably he has acted badly toward Pope! He wanted him to fail. That is unpardonable. But he is too useful just now to sacrifice." At another time he said "If he cant fight himself, he excells in making others ready to fight."[13]

Going to breakfast, I sat down by Banks. He received the news I gave him of the enemy's crossing the river with a little elevation of the eyebrows—nothing more. Old Genl. Spinner sat down and began to gird at the Nat. Intl. for its alarm at the project of the New York Defense Committee for the raising of 50,000 fillibusters under Fremont and Mitchell. I condemned it. He defended it. I said he would soon have our country divided, as Italy is between V. E. & Garibaldi." He said "there is no question which is right? I said, "no! Victor Emmanuel is right." He replied that I was a worse conservative than he had thot me.[14]

Banks said that the war was steadily verging to one point and that no efforts of misguided friends or malignant enemies could prevent it. He said there was no real difference of opinion among loyal people. It was only their expressions that differed and caused quarrelling. Therefore he was opposed to proclamations & especially to Resolutions, that they would accomplish nothing.

Spinner said that neither the President the Congress nor the Military authorities would do this great and necessary thing of destroying the enemy, cause and effect, together, the people must do it. Banks thought the war would do it. He said he was in favor of the most rigorous measures, was ready to begin at noon today. But was for the Government, not the mob, doing it.

Banks went away and S. said "I hope to see him at the head of the army some day." I said I had little hope of it, as the right man was rarely seen in the right place in a Republic. He instanced Jackson as evidence to the contrary. I disagreed with him, thinking Jackson was a brawling and violent old loafer with no good quality but bravery.

Mayor Wightman has been here. He is a fussy little Democrat with strong anti-abolition prejudices. The African sits heavily on his mind. He thinks this is a Wight-man's war.[15]

~~Carl Schurz says his division is terribly thinned cut up but what is left of them is Iron and Steel. I proposed they should adopt as their motto "I run and Steal."~~

[MID-SEPTEMBER 1862?]

Today, going into the Executive Mansion, I met Governor Seward coming out. I turned back and walked home with him. He said our foreign affairs are very much confused. He acknowledged himself a little saddened. Walking on, he said, "Mr Hay what is the use of growing old? You learn something of men and things but never until too late to use it. I have only just now found out what military jealousy is. I have been wishing for some months to go home to my people but could not while our armies were scattered and in danger. The other day I went down to Alexandria and found General McClellans army landing. I considered our armies united virtually and thought them invincible. I went home and the first news I received was that each had been attacked and each in effect, beaten. It never had occurred to me that any jealousy could prevent these generals from acting for their common fame and the welfare of the country."[16]

I said it never should have seemed possible to me that one American general should write of another to the President, suggesting that "Pope be allowed to get out of his own scrape his own way."

He answered, "I dont see why you should have expected it. You are not old. I should have known it." ~~He said this gloomily and sadly.~~

[24 SEPTEMBER 1862, WEDNESDAY]

The President wrote the Proclamation on Sunday morning carefully. He called the Cabinet together on Monday made a little talk to them (see *a*) and read the momentous document. Mr. Blair and Mr. Bates made objections, otherwise the Cabinet was unanimous. The next day Mr. Blair who had promised to file his objections, sent a note stating that as his objections were only to the time of the act he would not file them, lest they should be subject to misconstruction.[17]

I told the President of the Serenade that was coming and asked if he would make any remarks. He said, no, but he did say half a dozen words,

& said them with great grace and dignity. I spoke to him about the editorials in the leading papers. He said he had studied the matter so long that he knew more about it than they did.[18]

At Governor Chase's there was some talking after the Serenade. Chase and Clay made speeches and the crowd was in a glorious humor. After the crowd went away, to force Mr. Bates to say something, a few old fogies staid at the Governors and drank wine. Chase spoke earnestly of the Proclamation. He said "this was a most wonderful history of an insanity of a class that the world had ever seen. If the Slaveholders had staid in the Union they might have kept the life in their institution for many years to come. That what no party and no public feeling in the North could ever have hoped to touch they had madly placed in the very path of destruction." They all seemed to feel a sort of new and exhilarated life; they breathed freer; the Prest. Procn. had freed them as well as the slaves. They gleefully and merrily called each other and themselves abolitionists, and seemed to enjoy the novel sensation of appropriating that horrible name.[19]

[26 September 1862, Friday]

Last night September 25 the President and I were riding to Soldiers Home; he said he had heard of an officer who had said they did not mean to gain any decisive victory but to keep things running on so that they the army might manage things to suit themselves. He said he should have the matter examined and if any such language had been used, his head should go off.[20]

I talked a great deal about the McClellan conspiracy but he would make no answer to any thing. He merely said that McC. was doing nothing to make himself either respected or feared.[21]

3

1863

4 April 1863, Saturday

L EFT NEW YORK AT NOON—GOT INTO ROUGH WEATHER IN THE
course of the afternoon—made an enormous dinner with a light and
defiant heart—cast it up with great heaviness of spirit—solitary agony—
weariness of living—disgust for the sea—enthusiastic promises of future
land residence—cold-blooded preparations made by the Steward—distant
echoes of troubled diaphragms—Sleep[1]

5 April 1863, Sunday

Feebleminded determination to get up—miserable failure, coldblooded
"bad sign" of Steward. Dr Green's Champagne—contemptuous scorn
of an irascible abdomen—Soup better success. Visit from Captain—
Comforting assurances—Details of sufferers around the table—heroic retreat and advance of Vogdes.[2] Van Wyck specially punished. No services—
Appearance of sufferers on deck. Vows for the future

6 April 1863, Monday

Fear and trembling. Try an apple. Breakfast. Large muster. Careful eating. Solid viands most popular. "Nobody much sick." On Deck. Discussions of the future. "The reign of rogues & demagogues over. The soldiers
begin to reorganize their men. A battle knocks the nonsense out of a man.
Charlie Train. Anecdotes of Camp-Discipline. The Alabama.[3] Dinner.

The porpoises—immense delight of the freshwater soldiers. Vandal
tricks.

Cocachilunk and the Greek initials.

Rage of the Vultures & love of the turtles. Dreams go by [contraries?]

The Fresh breeze in the evening Sunset & moonrise. "Don't like it. It fla-
vors of sea-sickness" Red & gibbous moon starting like a bloody portent
out of the tumbling waves.

7 April 1863, Tuesday

Too far to hear the sound of bombardment. The lost dinner.

Abreast of the Forts. Golden Gate comes alongside. Cunningham & Capt. Carbin. General on board—who? News from the North. The ball opens today in Charleston Harbor. The attack on Ft. Sumter begins at 3 oclock. Going ashore. Hilton Head. Search for transportation. Smith Skinner & Hawley.[4] Come aboard again. Vogdes asserts himself. The sunset scene. The wild tropical splendor of the dying day. The weirdlike mist that hangs over the woods. The gathering shadows of the water, & the lights glimering up one by one from the black bulks of the fleet.

A splendid harbor going to waste. A great country aroused & filling it with hostile power. Wabash.[5] Early night. A great city with its scattered lights. Moonrise. The liquid distances and sleeping ships make a city in the sea.

On board the propeller "Christian Commission"

8 April 1863, Wednesday

A rough morning. Lying at anchor in Edisto Harbor. Transports. V. W. leaves us. Picturesque scenery of the circling shores. White cottages nestling by the shores. Village to be burned

Out of Edisto. Smoke seen at Charleston Different surmises. Ch "Com" again. Banyan. At 2½ saw the Nahant going back disabled. Turn of the tide of surmise. Nearer approach. Flags of Moultrie & Sumpter. The Weed. Debarkation. Gen. Hunter & Col Halpine Recounting & prophesying—[6]

Supper on board the Canonicus.[7] Seymour. Duncan &c

Oysters.

Black Republican Congress. [   ]

9 April 1863, Thursday

Gen Terry's boat. Cruising up the Folly River. Bad news. The Admirals Despatches Col. Fess. & I take Navy Dep. to the Admiral. On the Lecor. The Ben De Ford. Up to the Bar. The wreck of the Keokuk & the watchers on the shore.—The Ironsides. Arriving on board the Ironsides I was met by an orderly and conducted to the Admiral in the after Cabin. Captain Rodgers presented me & I gave him the Adl my despatches which he at once sat down to read.[8] Rodgers said, "Mr Hay, you come to us at an unhappy time. Though unfortunate in view of the lively hopes that have been raised, as the issue is, we think that we may be grateful that what is an unsuccess, is not a disaster. The matter has been fairly tried. The Monitor fleet has been given into the hands of officers in whom the Dept. & the Country had confidence. Admiral Dupont has spared no possible effort and the only issue of it all is that we have reason to congratulate ourselves that with a loss of one vessel and the injury of many others we are still safely beyond the range of the enemy & the coast is still ours. The country must either follow its preconceived idea of the invincibility of the Ironclads and condemn us for too hasty a retreat, or take the deliberate and unanimous verdict of the Naval officers and justify us. We sailed into the harbor not sanguine of victory, we fought only about 40 minutes ~~in the midst of a concentrated fire never before seen~~ & the unanimous conclusion of the officers commanding was that another hour of that fire would have destroyed us. At the end of 40 minutes we had reached and touched the torpedoes and the obstructions. To have remained there long enough to remove them would have caused the destruction of some of the vessells. If the others had gone by the Fort they would still have been the target for the circling fire of the Forts, there were no sufficient land forces to take possession of the city, there was no means of supplying ammunition and provision for no wooden boat could live in that fire and the only issue of the matter would have been the capture of the surviving and the raising of the sunken vessells. This would have lost us the command of the coast, an irremediable disaster. So the Admiral took the responsibility of avoiding the greatest evil, by saving the fleet, and abandoning an enterprise which we think has been fairly proved impossible." The Admiral who had been listening and assenting to the latter portion of what Rodgers had been saying went on to add, "And as if we were to have a visible sign that an Almighty hand was over us protecting and guiding us, the orders you have given me show how vast was the importance of my preserving this fleet, whose power & prestige are still great and valuable for the work which the President considers the most momentous, the opening and the control of the Mississippi river. I made the attack in obedience to orders, under favorable circumstances; the vessels were managed, I presume to say with very great skill and spirit yet after a fight of only 40 minutes 7 guns of the Monitors were out of service, And two turrets had ceased to revolve. I might have pushed some of the vessells past Ft. Sumter but in that case we ran the enormous risk of giving them to the enemy & thus losing control of the coast. I cd. not answer for that to my conscience.[9]

Commodore Turner spoke with less earnestness but with more particular reference to the incidents of the fight.[10] He took me over the ship & showed the traces of the battle. When I left they were getting ready the torpedo raft to blow up the Keokuk.

Robert Small came back with us.[11]

10 APRIL 1863, FRIDAY

Wrote a letter to the President about Dupont.[12]
Cruised around shore. Gen Ferrys qrs.[13] Signal station. Legareville.
Wrote letter about Lawrence Williams.

11 APRIL 1863, SATURDAY

Came from Stono Inlet to Hilton Head on the Ben De Ford. Last of the fight & 1st of the feast. Came home to a crowded and noisy Wharf. Walked sulky to Headquarters. Evening Connecticut elections & Muggins.[14]

12 APRIL 1863, SUNDAY

Despatch from General Saxton announcing greater activity among the enemy than usual. After breakfast the General asked me break flag. Went up to Beaufort with the General on Wyoming. Robert Small on board. His ideas of the fight at Ft. Sumter. Plantations by the water side. Fullers. [   ] The old Huguenot forts. Broad River. Elliott. The Drumfish. Russell.[15]

Beaufort. General Saxton. Colonel Littlefield Captain Hooper. Heywards House. bathing arrangements. Rhetts. Bishop Bonwells. Orange Blossoms. Mimosa. School marms.[16]

Out to the ferry. The Picket. The forests. the Shell Road. Moss. the flowers Dogwood, Cherokee Rose, Honeysuckle, Jasmine. The 1st S. C.[17] Higginson. Secesh women.

The causeways. The batteries. The pickets.

Coming back. breakdown. Dinner Back to the Head.

Major Smith closed evening with hymns.

13 APRIL 1863, MONDAY

Went to ride with Wright & Smith. Stockton's Mare Fanny.[18] Stumble—through the woods to Gardners & Grahams. Back.

14 APRIL 1863, TUESDAY

Wrote letters. Charlie sick.[19] Great Storm. Waves up to the Breakwater. Couldnt dine on the Wabash.

15 APRIL 1863, WEDNESDAY

Took Dr. Craven to visit Charlie. Pneumonia. Rode in the afternoon with Wright Fessenden & Stockton. To Seabrooks, the coal depot.[20] Horses mired in the marsh. Fess stirrup To Stewarts plantation. Dress parade & home.

16 APRIL 1863, THURSDAY

Fighting orders. The delight of the general. Looking over map. Wrote to Nicolay.[21] Saw papers of 11th. Went to visit Col. Elwell. Spent the afternoon with Charlie.

The scene on the beach at night. Workmen caulking the barge loaded with Launches.

17 APRIL 1863, FRIDAY

Went with Major Smith and Fess. Wright & Kinzie to Fort Pulaski. Entering the Savannah River saw the Mortello Tower on Tybee Island and the line of the batteries. Coming nearer, saw the traces of the fight on the Fort. Landed. Walked up the boarded causeway built by the rebels. The appearance of the Fort. Speckled, slashed, & mottled, projectiles imbedded in the brick &c. Went in. Prim soldiers. The Col's quarters. The Colonel Chivalrous defenders through Mucilage bottles & ink on to walls. A walk around the parapet. Distant view of Savannah. Up the River. Elba Island. Rebel Steamers. Obstructions there. The barbette batteries. Incidents of the fight. The rebels surrendered because they feared for the magazine.[22]

The Theatre. John Bull & Rough Diamond. The workmanship. Chandeliers &c. The water battery beyond the Theatre. The dikes. drives. Base ball. Soldiers quarters. Pictures on wall. The goats. Shooting the loon.[23]

(James Bluffton & the Genl.s Story.) Dere is no better eatin. Coming back. Smiths Yankee friend. "I bloat." Col. ———. "There is channells." The darkies Weddings. March leaving to read.

The unanimity of the Navy *vs* another attack. The ideas of the Genl. The sandflies.

Sharked out of bed

18 APRIL 1863, SATURDAY

Mrs Gilman & her entomological researches

19 APRIL 1863, SUNDAY

Went with Genl to Beaufort cutting inspection & service on board Wabash. A fine cloudless day warm on the shore and cool on the sea. To Mr. French. To Church in the morning. The house & houseful. Black chancel-rails. Mrs Lander & Mrs Saxton The collection. After the paymasters. Dinner at French's. Spectacles & valetudinarianism. Major Strong & Lady & [Lister?]. The negro weddings discussed. Pecksniffianisms. What Capt Hooper said quoting Barney.[24]

The Hospital inspection. Means House Chisholm, Hamilton. To the Negro childrens Sunday School. Montgomery & the 3rd S. C. Vols.[25] Church filling up. The exercises of opening.

Singing Coronation as badly as poss. The children's singing. Tone shrill & mechanical at first. The speech of the Florida Private. Another. The earnestness of attention on the part of some of the soldiers & the flippant indifference & dandyism in the galleries.

Song by a Florida slavegirl. We will fight for liberty. The children join. Sergeant Proctor delighted. "Roll Jording Roll.

Genl. Saxton talks a little & we go home.

[several words crossed out]

Good things by Hooper. Talk about Linkum! No man see Linkum. Linkum walk as Jes. walk! no man see L.[26] 2 "I want a pass, sah, to git married again." (3) J. C. was no respectable person."

20 APRIL 1863, MONDAY

Took a ride Fessenden & Kinzie. Fess. lamed his horse jumping a log. Dress parade of young Africa. After some mutinous conduct the demoralized command dispersed to clam-hunting.

21 APRIL 1863, TUESDAY

Furious gale blowing all day.

22 APRIL 1863, WEDNESDAY

Arrival of Wrights & Halpines families. In the afternoon rode to Pope's plantation.[27] The rose garden & the human fauna. Tamar. Bucksheesh. Coming home. Halpine captured on the highway. Mail from Washington

23 APRIL 1863, THURSDAY

Wrote letters home. Nico & Marston & Kirk.[28] Preparations for starting to Florida Crowd on the wharf. The [Jacobin?] invasion. Order at last reigns.

Fort Pulaski. The Theatre, the plays were The Spectre bridegroom," pretty well done especially Aldwinkle & Nicodemus Diggory was also quite comic. The rest were sticky; the women parts were boys of hoarse utterance & unearthly ugliness. The plays following were The Jacobite & the New Footman, with a comic song.[29] It was very late when the performance closed, as it had been delayed for us till rather a late hour for beginning. We went back to the Fort whence the Colonel sent a Lieutenant to conduct us to the boat.

24 APRIL 1863, FRIDAY

We got away from Fort Pulaski at 5 oclock this morning. We skirted along within sight of land, among porpoises & Pelicans which were equally inaccessible till 3 P.M. when we entered the harbour of Fernandina. Dungeness house on the right going in. Showy white breakers. Took a walk around the town. White frame houses with verandahs & gardens. The Dr's folly. Shops. Sutlers & candy. Contrabands 1300 engaged here. Judge Latta, Commr. A secesh Lieutenant. Went with Latta to his quarters.[30]

Finegan's house. F. was a Q.M.-Segt & married a rich widow. A magnolia. Cider champagne. The land business. Evening on the boat. The female portion of the party resolve to start for St. Augustine in the morning.[31]

which they did

25 APRIL 1863, SATURDAY

Went to Fort Clinch with Captn. Sears in charge of the work.[32] When we got there the sea was too high to land. Beached the boat & we were carried to shore in the arms of negroes. The mazeppa-ride. The Fort. The Sand hills commanding it. The sea. The Alligators. The songs of the boatmen. "The bully boats a coming Oh ho, Oh ho Dont you hear the oars a humming Hang boys hang. Well all hang together, &c. We will hang one another &c &c. Perfect time harmonizing with the click of the oars by the falsetting of the voices. Coming back Capt. Janson gave some odd incidents of his experiences on the African coast & elsewhere.

Went to dine with Lt Col Gardner 7th Conn. Nice party & pleasant wife. "Realizing" Capt Gray's business & epistolary experiences.[33]

Tea with Col. Hawley & family. Best possible New England tea. A visit to the pet alligators. Bit in the thumb.

26 APRIL 1863, SUNDAY

The buzzards & the Kingfisher. The thieving darkey & the robbed contraband. Fishing on the pier.

With Col Gardiner to the Dungeness estate. The landing. Footprints & the trace of horses' hoofs on the moist sand, evidently made since the last tide proved the presence of strangers on the Island. Deployed the skirmishers who devoted themselves to blackberries on the way to the house. The house was ruinous. The upper rooms being somewhat finished while the lower ones never were. The garden a magnificent one. Bamboo, Banana, Fig & Pomegranate with commoner vegetation. Century plant &c.

Behind the house a road runs for 2 or 3 miles through a wonderful forest of moss-draped live oak.

The view from the top of the house was beautiful in the extreme. The most superb estate I ever saw. I was lost in wonder at the luxuriance of nature & the evident shiftlessness & idleness that had characterized the owners

Seth H. advocated tearing off the moss & selling it for the stuffing of mattresses. Seth beast.

Inscriptions on the walls by Yankee soldiers.

Came home having seen no rebels. Saw a turtle.

Some particulars about Stafford. Old man, neutral. 2 quadroon daughters to whom he has given a marriage portion of $50,000.

In the evening went to the Gowers with Latta. Gower an educated Englishman without income & his wife the daughter of Judge Burritt of Jacksonville.[34] Went afterward to Col. Hawley's

27 APRIL 1863, MONDAY

With Read the spectacled Comr. went to the colored Schools. Miss Harris & Miss Smith in charge of the Abcdarians. Their singing & exercises. Miss Foote & Miss Merrick in charge of the high school.[35] Light mulatto girls & white children. All together Singing

"Say my brother aint you ready
Get Ready to go home
For I hear de word of promise
At de breaking of the day
Ill take de wings of de morning
& fly away to Jesus
Ill take de wing of de morning
& Sound de Jubilee."
& Whittier's song of the boatmen. The contrast between Misses F & M.
Gen. Finegan's house tenanted by negroes. Talk at Latta's. The Gowers. Music.

Concert at the Baptist Church, Bones & Tambourine.

Good Byes & to bed.

28 APRIL 1863, TUESDAY

Waked up, the ship in motion. Arrived off the bar at 1. Shark in sight. After a few minutes saw the little skiff of Capo the pilot. Came on board.

A grave old fellow of some sixty years. His quiet ignoring the impertinent ribaldry of the purser. Crossing the bar. narrow & short. Hugging the Shore. The place for batteries. The wreck of the Jeff Davis. The lighthouse. The Fort of St Mark.[36] The English batteries. Anastasia Island. The city. The sea wall. Through the town. The houses. Narrow streets. [   ] Strong faces of the negroes. Buffington. The Domparado. Florida girls. Supper. Savory & abundant. Old Buff. Evening with the family. Spider. Back to the boat through the narrow little streets. Advantages to a tight man. Couldnt fall down & could dodge policemen. The roar of the breakers & bar. Night

29 APRIL 1863, WEDNESDAY

Fort St. Mark. The Demilune. The defaced arms of Spain. Through the sallyport. Ramp. The Parapets. The old Spanish guns. The caved-in hole. The bastions. The water batteries. The little look-outs. The coquina. The barbican. The city gates. Everything seeming of a past age. The donjon. The approaches thereto. The discovery. The Skeletons. The treasure chest. 3 keys. The King's retort. Expense of the erection of the fort.

Went to ride. Along the beach. fiddlers. Fairbanks. Through the woods. Over the flat. blackberries. The cactus. The banana. The palm. Spanish pinks. Roses. The [century?] plant. The pomegranate at Major Dormans.[37] The darkey girls delight at his return.

Porpoises catching fish. Herons. Hernandez' stories of Bear hunting & Indian fighting. St. Augustine in the old times. Living with visible means.

The Governor's palace. Plaza de la Constitution. The Cathedral.

Haldins fishing. The fiddler-man. The Mulatto fisherman. The drowning child. Walk with Charlie to the Soldiers' burying ground. In the evening went with Kinzie to visit Miss Mather & Miss Perrit.[38] Their reminiscences & statements. Finish evening at Buffs. Kinzie on rebel forts, &c. The rebel officer fattening at Hilton Head.

30 APRIL 1863, THURSDAY

Breakfast with Miss Mather & Miss Perritt. Their accounts of the administration of Col. Putnam.[39] Miss M's letter to the General. Grits, cakes & poached eggs on toast. Miss Hardin's boast & other rebel incidents.

Shooting at crows and porpoises. Small Africans catching crabs & [calemborin?]. Sisters of Charity going to the Orange groves on Fishers Island. Bitter Oranges. P. P. C.'s. Les Buffes. Mrs Anderson & Mrs Cobb Off. Goodbye to Capo. Music on the waters.

The Straw man of St. A. The difficulty of getting dry goods

1 MAY 1863, FRIDAY

Ran up to the lightship, turned & went to Fort Pulaski. Got away & met quite a stiff breeze. Got to Hilton Head about noon. Wrote letters &c.

Evening Muggins & music & the Savannah Republican.

Went to ride with the Genl. and Halpine. Halpineville. The 3rd S. C. Negro girls by the spring. The negro cabin and the indignant fisherman. Magnolia. Mimosa. Pride of India

2 MAY 1863, SATURDAY

Wrote letters. J. G. N: Stod: Mother: Gus: Clara Matteson: Phillips:

Saw young Merriam.[40] The radical man of John Brown's party: his purpose.

High tides. Ye [   ] Gambolier.[41]

3 MAY 1863, SUNDAY

Sick. in bed all day. New Orleans Era. Banks' successes.[42] General H's prescriptions. Toddies & sich.

4 MAY 1863, MONDAY

Drove on the beach with Genl & Mrs Wright[43] Rest of the day in the house. Merriam calls again.

5 MAY 1863, TUESDAY

The [liberliterarum?] The projected expedition to Savannah. My own impression of its feasibility. Strykens letter & talk with the General about it Reason why Seymour left the staff.

Went in afternoon to see Stockton draw his [   ]. Dark and lowering when K & I started. we walked over the quicksand to shore where S & his retainers were. A shower began to fall & K. went back. I trusting to my India Rubber Coat stayed. yellow western sky. falling curtain of rain nearing us. They pulled in slowly never minding rain. The fish were mostly tangled in the net. Sam finds a porpoise in the net. ~~Shrimp~~ Prawn. Angel fish. Trout. bass. Flounder. Horse-shoe crab. Stingray. Cuttlefish. Silver eel. Garpike. Louse. Catfish. Look out for your fingers. Started to draw again. I started home. rain falling fearfully. Creek too high to cross. Saw I was in for a wetting concluded to go back & see rest of the fun. Could scarcely see ten yards before me. Getting to the shore saw Sam & the men in water getting boat round the point. Got in as they passed. Sam & I went up the creek & getting out struck over the sand. Home. took a bath & brandy punch: no effect. Slept all evening & all night

6 MAY 1863, WEDNESDAY

Rode out on Clay-bank. Mrs Wright & Mrs Halpine. Wright & Genl. Com.[44] Went to Elliotts. The crowd surrounding the General. negro babies rolling each other over a barrel. Mimosa buds.

Melancholy. Kinzies black horse, Chivalry—discussion about his ears. Dicks raconte of the perfections of Geechee.

The cautious timidity of the Admiral. The General's proposition & the Ad's answer.

Col. Fessenden broke his collar bone while out riding alone this afternoon. Ships in distance. False hopes.

7 MAY 1863, THURSDAY

Charlie's new horse. The Genl. & staff go to Beaufort today to a review.

8 MAY 1863, FRIDAY

We rode to Stewart's plantation. Coming back met Preston.

The Arago arrives with accounts up to Sunday the 3rd of May of Hookers operations in Virginia—unsatisfactory.[45]

Skinner gives an account of the rebel pickets near Folly Island shouting Joe Hooker's licked. Hermit crabs.

9 MAY 1863, SATURDAY

Rode out with Charlie to Elliotts.

Did nothing else specially all day except read Charleston papers of 4 & 7 giving accounts of the fights on the Rappahannock.

10 MAY 1863, SUNDAY

Eugene, an intelligent contraband. His story. The condition of the rebels in Georgia. The secret understanding among the negroes. More wd come but they are afraid of being caught & sent back, and not until lately were they sure in reception. The Rebels more afraid of Rosecrans than anything else. Insurrection at Dahlonegah.[46]

Dined at 3 with the wardroom officers of the Wabash. After dinner talk. Longnecker &c. Nelson. Phillips. Smith on names.

The call to quarters. The men receiving their beds. The bear.

Came home & saw papers of the 6th

11 MAY 1863, MONDAY

Nothing in particular. Rode on the beach in evening with Charlie & Smith

Called with Smith on Arago

12 MAY 1863, TUESDAY

Arago sails. Write letters. Drive with General on the beach. buzzards & stingrees & shovelnose. was going to the Stono but postponed till tomorrow Hooper leaves for North—

13 MAY 1863, WEDNESDAY

Left Hilton Head at 9 A.M.. on the Mary Benton. Halpine & General play chess. I read No Name. A little perceptible motion. Dinner. Edisto Harbor. The five Ironclads. We go to Genl Stevenson's quarters. Ammen, Rodgers, Beaumont & others there. We go to ride. Captain Walker joins us. The enclosed camp. The Engineer Co. The Opossums. The forests. Palmetto. Cabbage. Lillandsia. Magnolia. Pines, spreading. Live oak. Water oak. Snakes. Seabrooks place: the cotton field. debatable ground. The clearings. Felled trees. The battery at the ford. Home through the camps. The Delaware comes in with General Ferry's flag at the fore.[47]

Dress parade by the shore in the warm light of sunset thin bayonets gleam like gold. The answering drumbeat from one island to the other

Night. black Steamer coming in. One of the Iron-clads moving in the quiet dusk by Botany Bay Island.

Long talk with H about New York Politics. The difference between a crusader and a reforming politician of our days. Things different at Paris and at N. Y.[48]

Getting to sleep Seymour & Dream. Shirttail caucus.

14 May 1863, Thursday

Early in the morning went to Botany Bay Island to see Col Guss.[49] Enormously good news from Hooker The encampment was on the site of a rebel fort. Saw a tame crow there and ate blackberries with the Col.

Went on board the Nantucket, Capt. Beaumont.[50] Saw her scars. Went into turret, saw it revolve. Big guns. Seaweeds on the bottom. Animalcules. The cabin &c. The slovenly appearance of the sailors compared to Wabash.

Patapsco, Ammen. Ammen on slavery &c. Nahant. Downes not on board Kaatskill, G Rodgers. Bouquet in his cabin from Seabrooks. Saw there Fairfax Comdg Montauk.[51]

After dinner took on board a half company of the 76th Pa Zouaves and went to the deserted plantation of Col Seabrook of the Rebel Army.[52] The finest place I have seen. A large roomy airy white house of wood. Splendid grounds well kept. The wharf with steps for boats. The boat house. the Sea entrance. The business office. The Aloe about to bloom. The conservatory. The summer houses. The Terrapin pond. The lakes & islands. waste-weir as fishes. The pic nic table. figs & artichokes. Quails & rabbits running at large. The negro quarters Tenants on St. Helena island now. The surrounding scenery marsh & river. The Gridiron over all dominant & haughty What this man wanted & what he got.

The pamphlets lying around. Controversial &c. David Copperfield left by Union soldier. Genl Wright in command a year ago. Our soldiers stole a cat. H carried off the weathervane.

Weird effect of the uninhabited village.

15 MAY 1863, FRIDAY

When I woke this morning the vessell had started for Stono. Weather very rough. Genl Orders boat back to Edisto. Rainy and cold day. Halpine pasquinades Mr. Welles. We visit the Nahant in the afternoon. Downes. The scars. Downes spoke slightingly of the Whitworth bolts. They strike with a clear sharp ring, doing no real harm having not sufficient weight of metal. The solid rifled shot do harm. The plating over the magazine objectionable in my opinion. The skylight ports never get struck. The scars on the turret. New plates & bolts. Inside the turret. The vast bulk of the 15 inch guns. The pilot house. 8 lookout holes The limited view from them The outside hammering. Downes' description. the inside jacket now on. The air-cushion above. The effects of concussion on the hair of the pilot, like Com Stockton on the Princeton. The sailing master killed by a bolt. Downes wounded in the leg & bruised all over. The impression while the fight was going on that the turret was coming to pieces like a pile of shingles. The sharp ringing sound of the hammering. Rifled guns to be used for penetrating & smoothbore for pounding and crushing. The torpedo excitement. People of any enterprise would have made it win.[53]

H says he cant speak without betraying his country

16 MAY 1863, SATURDAY

A rough morning. Judson & Merritt come on board. Play chess with Genl. Stalemate.

Leave Mary Benton & go on board Delaware at noon Halpine remains on Benton. At night I see for the first time the phosphorescent light on the waves. Ives & Greenleaf on board.[54] Captains.

17 MAY 1863, SUNDAY

Read Barren Honour. Met James Adger coming out.[55]

Got home to find papers of the 12, which took all the shine out of our former reports.

Ate pound cake with Mrs Halpine. Am shocked to find Charlie.

18 May 1863, Monday

Rode with Charlie around to the wood road to the beach. blackberries. darkeys.

Read Silver Cord all day.[56] Spent evening with Charlie.

19 May 1863, Tuesday

Went to Beaufort on the Gen Hunter at 10 A.M. Loafed with Saxton awhile. He says the Navy are frequently criminally slow and halfhearted in cooperating with the Army in this Department. He talked about early times in St. Louis & Sigel & Frost & Blair.[57] We dined with him, Smith & Charlie & I. We then drove out into the woods first visiting the house he has fitted up for Genl Hunter. Coming back heard the band play on the Green.

Tea and to Mrs Lander's.[58] Finished Silver Cord & went to bed. My first day in Blue & Gold—

20 May 1863, Wednesday

Went down to Hilton Head and stayed [ashore?] this morning, Genl S. Judge Smith & I.[59] Judge wanted to assess Edisto Id & get Genl H's consent. He opposes it at present.

21 May 1863, Thursday

Went with Genl Saxton to Helena and Lady's Island. The plantations neat and well tilled, people apparently contented and happy. Williams says they work better on their own grain crops than on Govt cotton crops. The women begging for their relations to be discharged from the army. The negro School taught by Miss Town, Miss Murray English and Miss Forten a bright mulatto of wealth & good position educated in Paris, who lives in Philada.[60] Little fellows afraid of the draft.

Bridge between Lady Id & Helena, rebels burnt & negroes extinguished. Sergeants out looking for deserters. Had talk with Col. Higginson.

Afternoon rode with Genl. and wife, heard music on the Green.

Mrs Lander sang Whall be king but Charlie

22 May 1863, Friday

Went this afternoon out to Barnwells place on the Broad River & had a blackberry picnic under charge of Mrs Lander. The house is old and tumbledown but the grounds are full of a rude beauty: the avenue of live oaks & pines is superb. We were in sight of the rebel pickets which added zest to the dancing. Col Higginson was there. Mrs Lander was the life & soul of the affair. Virginia reel. Vineclad doughnuts.[61]

Cotton furrows: long lasting. The 1st S. C. on guard for this occasion. Entrusted individ. who watched for rebels all afternoon with telescope.

Home through the magnificent avenue.

23 May 1863, Saturday

Started at noon with a party to Mrs Gage's plantation on Paris Island. Genl. & wife, Mrs Lander, Maj. Bannister, other ladies & gentlemen—went in the Flora—pulled ashore in boats.[62]

A vast number of bad jokes. Port & starboard. "*Port* is *left* to end of dinner." Mrs L = a *star-bored*—Mrs S said the Genl. was the *star* which guided her & wished it were two stars. I said it would make him a *biggerdear*—*Leaks*.

We went to the Plantation house & found the Gages—saw a chameleon. took lunch—went out to see darkies. Genl. Saxton made a little speech about their relatives in the Army. Revd. Moore followed & talked freedom & general politics & Littlefield was very characteristic in the same groove. I said ½ dozen words in behalf of the Tycoon.[63]

They then began to sing. They sang some strange & wild songs.

1. Death he is a little man
   He goes from do' to do' &c. &c.
Chorus
   Oh Lord remember me.
   Oh Lord remember me.
   Remember me when the year goes round
Oh L R me
2 Another
   Genl. Hunter sitting on the tree of life
   To hear the wind of the Jordan roll

Roll J. R. J. R J Roll
(Ch)
   March de Angel March
   March de Angel March
   My soul is rising heavenward
To hear the wind of the Jording roll.
I ax old Satan why follow me so?
Satan aint got nothing to do with me
Hold yr light (Bis) on Canaan's shore.
Oh Sister Ketchum dont you want to get religion
   Down in the lonesome valley, (my lord).
   And meet my Jesus there—

Prof Zachos history of these times—[64]

   We feed on milk & honey
   Johnny brought a letter
   Mary & Martha read it.

They swayed to & fro as they sang with great feeling. An old woman who came over fr. Africa. Says she was grown when she came. "was courted." tobacco. Littlefield taught them to cheer.

Their feast & we dispersed. Bannister having a convalescent appetite went off with me to eat plums & mulberries.

We came home filling Broad River with twilight music. The Arago is H. H. tonight.

24 MAY 1863, SUNDAY

A still fair day. I wore white trousers. Called on Gadsden. Talk with Halpine. Why Kinzie went north. Preston & McKenzie came in in the evening. we talked over the War. They pro McClellan & I contra—[65]

25 MAY 1863, MONDAY

Took long ride in morning on beach with Charlie and another in afternoon with Dick & Charlie.

26 MAY 1863, TUESDAY

A heavy North East Storm blowing all day. Rode out with Wright & Smith to Stoney's, a pretty place full of oleanders & magnolias in super-abundance. The old fort. The strange stillness & quiet in the interior of the island was strongly contrasted with the fury of the storm on the coast. A fine rapid gallop through the dust. Wind howled all night dismally—

27 MAY 1863, WEDNESDAY

The Noreaster continues all day Arago cant start

28 MAY 1863, THURSDAY

Halpine & I take a ride & are driven home by the storm. The storm too heavy for the Arago to sail. General, Halpine & I ride in the Afternoon. The barren fig tree, and fruitful one. The creek in the fields. We met the Provost Marshal who told us about the placard, "This man has been mean enough to steal from a negro." Home. Music in the Evening. Major Smith sang Scotch Irish ballads. John Brown—full chorus Genl joins in.

29 MAY 1863, FRIDAY

On my way to the Arago met my hero of the placard. Arago lying up the Beaufort now. we board her with the tug. Find a great crowd on board. Researches among passengers. Rapid disappearances & sinkings into oblivion. Paddlewheel views & reflections—

30 MAY 1863, SATURDAY

Still rather rough Cautious reappearances—feeble attempts at hilarity: an occasional song in the moonlight. Hatteras light Discussions about the Alabama. Im a British subject.

31 MAY 1863, SUNDAY

Today everybody appeared. The Genl looking still very peaked & rather shaky—The ship rolled more today than usual but every one seemed seasoned to it. The oscillating engine.

Moonlight again. Mess. Miss Clifton. Anderson son of the gambolier & looked like his father. "When this cruel War is over" Dissolute Legs. Im gittin' lame. "My venerable friend cannot be reached without profanity. Colloquy betw D. L. & Ives.

The frequent sails in the misty moonlight. The N. Y. Pilot.

1 June 1863, Monday

Early lunatics—Cold N Y morning breakfast & farewells—Hackman mildly remonstrative. Were all gentlemen. To the Hotel. Morning papers. Wall Street. Police Court. Joe D. Hotel. Beard. H W Buchan's pictures.

Start with Judge Dowling & detective Kelso on a tramp. Charlie & Gus along. First visit the Tombs.[66] Women washing the floors who are going to be released tomorrow. Conversation with the Judge. Youll be out tomorrow & be back the next day. Inside the Tombs. Bridge of sighs. The delirium patients. Forgers &c. The boys, packed like herrings or sardines—jolly & lively blackguards. What they were in for. Thieving—suspicion o' silk. Newspaper. Let us out & we'll never be caught again.

The station house. Drunk & disorderly. The sleeping rooms. The line of women. The telegraph. The Judge officiating. A woman locked up, 26 & born in America. Capt Jordan.

The streets. Crowds of children playing in the streets & [   ]. They breed like rats. The deference paid to Judge hotel policeman. Judge's explanation of it.

11 July 1863, Saturday

The President seemed in a specially good humor today, as he had pretty good evidence that the enemy were still on the North side of the Potomac and Meade had announced his intention of attacking them in the morning. The Prest. seemed very happy in the prospect of a brilliant success. He had been rather impatient with Gen Meade's slow movements since Gettysburg, but concluded today that Meade would yet show sufficient activity to inflict the Coup de grace upon the flying rebels.[67]

12 JULY 1863, SUNDAY

Rained all the afternoon, have not yet heard of Meade's expected attack.

13 JULY 1863, MONDAY

The President begins to grow anxious and impatient about Meade's silence. I thought and told him there was nothing to prevent the enemy from getting away by the Falling Waters, if they were not vigorously attacked. Eckert says Kelly is up on their rear.[68] Nothing can save them, if Meade does his duty. I doubt him. He is an engineer.

14 JULY 1863, TUESDAY

This morning the Prest. seemed depressed by Meade's despatches of last night. They were so cautiously & almost timidly worded—talking about reconnoitering to find the enemy's weak place and other such. He said he feared he would do nothing.

About noon came the despatch stating that our worst fears were true. The enemy had gotten away unhurt. The Prest was deeply grieved. We had them within our grasp" he said. "We had only to stretch forth our hands & they were ours. And nothing I could say or do could make the Army move."[69]

Several days ago he sent a despatch to Meade which must have cut like a scourge but Meade returned so reasonable and earnest a reply that the Prest concluded he knew best what he was doing & was reconciled to the apparent inaction which he hoped was merely apparent.[70]

Every day he has watched the progress of the Army with agonizing impatience, hopes struggling with fear. He has never been easy in his own mind about Gen Meade since Meades General Order in which he called on his troops to drive the invader from our soil. The Prest. says "This is a dreadful reminiscence of McClellan. The same spirit that moved McC. to claim a great victory because Pa & Md were safe. The hearts of 10 million people sank within them when McClellan raised that shout last fall. Will our Generals never get that idea out of their heads? The whole country is *our* soil."[71]

15 July 1863, Wednesday

~~Went with R. T. L. around town to concert saloons. Saw some very queer dancing and singing at one place and some very tolerable singing at a great hall where mann sauft and trinkt and raucht.~~[72]

R. T. L. says the ~~Tycoon~~ President is grieved silently but deeply about the escape of Lee. He said "If I had gone up there I could have whipped them myself." I know he had that idea.[73]

16 July 1863, Thursday

Nicolay leaves today for the Rocky Mountains.

Had a little talk with the ~~Tycoon~~ President about Milroy. Says Halleck thinks Schenck never had a military idea & never will learn one. Thinks Schenck is somewhat to blame for the Winchester business. ~~Tycoon~~ President says, however you may doubt or disagree from Halleck he is very apt to be right in the end.[74]

This evening at tea was talking with Lt. Col Alexander & Judge Whiting. We agreed in ascribing vast importance to the crushing of Lee at Wmsport. I thought that in the present aspect of affairs with Bragg deserting the lines of Corinth, Grant & Banks victorious & North Carolina mutinous, if Meade had destroyed Lee, the Rebellion would have been restricted to S. C. & Georgia.[75]

Genl Wadsworth came in. He said in Answer to Alexander's question "Why did Lee escape," "Because nobody stopped him" rather gruffly.

Wadsworth says that at a council of War of Corps Commanders held on Sunday the 12th, he was present, on account of the sickness of his Corps Commander, he Wadsworth being temporarily in command of the corps. On the question of fight or no fight the weight of authority was against fighting. French, Sedgwick, Slocum & ———[Sykes] strenuously opposed a fight. Meade was in favor of it, so was Warren, who did most of the talking on that side & Pleasonton was very eager for it as also was Wadsworth himself. The non-fighters ~~thought~~ or seemed to think that if we did not attack, the enemy would & even Meade, though he was in for action, had no idea that the enemy intended to get away at once. Howard had little to say on the subject.

Meade was in favor of attacking in three columns of 20,000 men each. Wadsworth was in favor of doing as Stonewall Jackson did at Chancellorsville, double up their left & drive them down on Williamsport. I do not question that either plan would have succeeded.[76]

Wadsworth said to Hunter who sat beside him, "General, there are a good many officers of the regular Army who have not yet entirely lost the West Point [notion] of Southern superiority. That sometimes accounts for an otherwise unaccountable slowness of attack."

In the course of the evening Hunter told me that he thought a failure of Gillmore was among probabilities by the enemy reinforcing by means of their causeway & gobbling him up.[77] The danger of a blow which would drive away the iron clads must also be considered.

18 JULY 1863, SATURDAY

Today we spent 6 hours deciding on Courtmartials, the President Judge Holt & I. I was amused at the eagerness with which the President caught at any fact which would justify him in saving the life of a condemned soldier. He was only merciless in cases where meanness or cruelty were shown.[78]

Cases of cowardice he was specially averse to punishing with death. He said it would frighten the poor devils too terribly, to shoot them. On the case of a soldier who had once deserted & reenlisted he endorsed, "Let him fight instead of shooting him."

One fellow who had deserted & escaped after conviction into Mexico, he sentenced, saying "We will condemn him as they used to sell hogs in Indiana, as they run."

~~He told one devilish good story about U. F. Linder, getting a fellow off who had stolen a hog, by advising him to go & get a drink & suggesting that the water was better in Tennessee. &c. &c.~~[79]

19 JULY 1863, SUNDAY

~~Spent this morning at St Aloysius. A dry priest declaimed against science & human reason & after demolishing both, glorified the dogma of Immaculate Conception.~~

The ~~Tycoon~~ President was in very good humour. Early in the morning he scribbled this doggerel & gave it to me.[80] In the afternoon, he & I were talking about the position at Williamsport the other day. He said "Our

Army held the war in the hollow of their hand & they would not close it." again he said, "We had gone through all the labor of tilling & planting an enormous crop & when it was ripe we did not harvest it. Still" he added, "I am very very grateful to Meade for the great service he did at Gettysburg."

~~They say now that McClernand has little show of probability of his claim that Vicksburg was taken by his plans. That at the time he moved on New Carthage Grant was preparing to go to digging again. Our state officers at Springfield are trying to keep out of the mess between McCler & Grant. Butler & Dubois are here.~~[81]

I was talking a few days ago with Mr Chase and he told me that he considered the subject of reconstruction one that should now be employing the best meditations of the statesmen of the country especially the Government. He thought that before any rebellious state were admitted to its former rights under the constitution, we should insist upon it as a necessary condition precedent that the people of the state should in convention remodel their existing laws on the basis of emancipation, taking as an accomplished fact the emancipation of the slaves by the Proclamation of the President. He thinks that a Union on other terms besides being a stultification of ourselves & our acts would be a delusion and a snare & would never enjoy a lasting or honorable peace.

Blair was talking the other day about his Concord Speech & Wendell Phillips' ~~blackguardly~~ outrageous reply. He began because I had ~~avowed myself no colonizationist~~ said I had no faith in colonization.[82]

He said that some time since in conversation with Henry Wilson he had referred to the dissensions rapidly rising & growing among loyal people, & had said that he thought Mr Lincoln the best name for the nomination, to unite the scattered elements, that Wilson agreed with him; and afterward went back on him. He says Seward & Chase are both scheming for the succession. Stanton would cut the President's throat if he could. &c.

Wilson was here the other day & says Phillips lied when he ~~said the~~ reported a conversation with the President in his 4th July speech at Framingham.[83] I knew that he did, but I was a little surprised to hear Wilson admit it. He would not do it at Framingham.

21 JULY 1863, TUESDAY

~~A fine day for the wedding of Carlota Wilhelmina Mariana von Gerolt and John Ward of the Bengal Civil Service. Everything was lovely and the~~

~~goose hung in a more elevated position than usual. Adjourned from the Church to the Legation. Rather dull for the first hour as people were fearful of coming too early, afterwards quite festive. I never saw three so pretty sisters together before. Madam was triste but the Baron walked in rose-colored clouds. Stanton was there which was strange rather. Seward of course was there officially. The diplomatic body, the deadest of all possible dead wood was there unmangled in plenary council.~~

~~I dined in the evening with Wise. I heard Dr Pyne say that Lee was within an ace of going with the North, that he said his whole life was bound up in the Union — that he cherished the profoundest contempt for this whole business of secession — that if he had a thousand negroes he would hold them all as nothing in comparison with the benefits conferred by the Union and that — (Oh! most lame & impotent conclusion!) he must go with his State. He hoped most earnestly that she would not secede, but in case she did &c. &c. That infernal heresy of State sovereignty was in the minds of many good men "the little speck within the garnered fruit, that rotting inward slowly ruined all."~~[84]

The Prest. recd. today a letter fr. Gen Howard in which he expressed his entire confidence in Gen Meade & said that fr. his standpoint Meade's whole action was justifiable.[85]

The Presdt. answered him stating his deep mortification at the escape of Lee rendered deeper by the high hopes excited by the brilliant conduct of our army at Gettysburg; referred to his own long cherished & often expressed conviction that if the enemy ever crossed the Potomac he might have been destroyed, said that Meade & his army had expended the skill & toil & blood up to the ripe harvest & then allowed it to go to waste. He then said that after the lapse of several days, he now felt profoundly grateful to Meade & his army for what they had done, without indulging in any criticisms for what they had not done & that Gen Meade had his full confidence as a brave & skillful officer & a true man.[86]

23 JULY 1863, THURSDAY

Today I gave the President a letter from Govr. Gamble in which he alternately whined and growled through many pages over the President's letter to Schofield. The ~~Tycoon~~ President told me to put it away. He wrote an answer to Gamble telling him he had not read the letter & would not as he wished to keep his temper and avoid irritants and that he meant no discourtesy by his Schofield letter.[87]

25 JULY 1863, SATURDAY

Halpine has been here. He tells me that Seymour is in a terrible state of nervous excitement. That there is absolute danger of the loss of his wits. He is tormented both by the terrible reminiscence of the riots & by the constant assertions of the Press that he is concerned in a conspiracy of which the outbreak was a mismanaged portion. He shudders even now at the dreadful picture which his imagination conjures up of the possible results of that miserable business. The mob he said aimed to destroy the great necessities of New York, light, water, & communication. They almost succeeded. The Harlem Bridge was at their mercy but a rain came up & wet them & somebody had neglected to supply the ~~conflagrating~~ incendiary party with kindling wood which alone prevented them. The Jersey City ferry boats hauled off & were saved. The Governors mind is tortured with visions of an isolated city without light or water, given over to a howling mob, whose accomplices in every kitchen in the city held the lives & property of the whole population at their mercy.[88]

~~Halpine was also talking about Gillmore. He says that his appointment is part of a programme arranged by the friends of Butler, to get as far as possible the "Soldiers influence for the Beast." Greeley was first fooled over and his influence got Gillmore a hearing at Washington. When he went south he took with him Turner and Strong, two special adherents of Butler.~~[89]

~~He says that Butler's party is growing enormously. All the fanatics—all the corruptionists—a vast stock-jobbing interest headed by Col Butler who has brought his stolen two millions to N.Y. & says he is willing to spend it all for this great object.~~[90]

~~Hunter wrote a letter to Greeley on hearing of his share in the appointment of Gillmore, congratulating him on his enlisting & receiving bounty in the "On to Charleston" movement, & hoping it would be as successful as the On to Richd in which he (G) howled shed some ink & other men some blood.~~[91]

~~I rode out to Soldiers Home with the Tycoon President tonight. Bob was down the river with Seward. I could not go as Chas. was here. Had a talk~~

~~on philology for which the T has a little indulged inclination. Rode home in the dark amid a party of drunken gamblers & harlots returning in the twilight from [——].~~

29 JULY 1863, WEDNESDAY

The President today wrote a letter to General Halleck, stating that as he inferred from one of Gen Meade's despatches that M. thought the Govt. were pressing him to an engagement with Lee, that the impression was erroneous, that He was opposed to it unless ~~that~~ such a course were in harmony with Hallecks & Meade's views; that if it were imprudent to attack them at Wmsport it was certainly more so now when Meade has no more than ⅔ of his then force; that he was in favor at Wmsport of Meade's crossing and harassing the enemy. This had been done and now he was rather in favor of delay than immediate attack & desired Gen Halleck to so communicate to Meade unless he saw good reasons to the contrary.[92]

31 JULY 1863, FRIDAY

Carl Schurz was in my room today: he spoke very highly of Meade. He says the rebels are deserting as much as they can in the face of their severe discipline.[93]

The President today received a letter from General Meade in answer to one he had written. Meade says that if Hooker is willing to serve under him he will be glad to have the benefit of his services. Hooker chafes in inaction. Fighting Joe has not finished his history yet by a great deal.[94]

The President today wrote a letter to Steve Hurlbut—who is talking about resigning,—urging him to reconsider his intention and remain in the service if he can without too serious detriment to his own private interests.[95]

He further urges him to see Sebastian, if he can, and ascertain if S. really intends to present himself next session for admission into the Senate. That he (The Presdt.) stands by the Proclamation—considers it valid in law—& to be sustained by the Courts—and that if Sebastian will come next winter prepared basing himself on that to try to bring in his state with a system of apprenticeship—not like the Missouri system which is faulty in *postponing* the benefits of freedom to the slave instead of giving him an immediate vested interest therein—he (L) will be glad to see him and Sebastian will be doing the greatest possible good that one man can do.[96]

I had considerable talk with the President this evening on this subject. It deeply interests him now. He considers it the greatest question ever presented to practical statesmanship. ~~While the rest are grinding their little private organs for their own glorification the old man is working with the strength of a giant and the purity of an angel to do this great work.~~

The President a day or two ago gave General Halleck directions to prepare an order for the protection of our black soldiers. Gen. Halleck brought him today a draft of it. He said he was troubled to know how to retaliate in kind for selling into slavery and concluded to make it imprisonment at hard labor.[97] ~~That will be rare. To see the swaggering lords of lash lazy & lousy longhaired & languid (a hell of an alliteration) in Zebra garb and Zouave scarcity of chevelure breaking stone or digging the first ditches instead of dying in the last.~~

1 AUGUST 1863, SATURDAY

Forney dedicated his new printing office today with a ~~blowout~~ spread at the Chronicle Buildings on 9th Street. The President went up. ~~with me.~~ Gen. Thomas was there. As the President shook hands with him & said Goodbye (Thomas being about to start for the West) he said "General! you are going about a most important work. There is a draft down there which can be enforced." "I will enforce it" Thomas replied. A few moments afterward at the lunch at Forney's quarters he used the ~~Tycoon's~~ President's expression as his own & was cheered for it. I regard his attitude as most significant. He is a man accustomed through a long lifetime to watch with eager interest the intentions of power and the course of events; till he has acquired an instinct of expediency which answers to him the place of sagacity & principle. He is a straw which shows whither the wind is blowing. The tendency of the country is to universal freedom, when men like Thomas make abolition speeches at public dinners.[98]

2 AUGUST 1863, SUNDAY

Spent the day on the River in the Steamer "Baltimore" with a navy party exclusively. The Secretary & family Fox Wise Faxon and Horwitz. We had a pleasant cool day. Enormous appetites fearfully disproportioned in fact to the lunch prepared. Went to Mathias Point and returned. Got to the

Navy Yard as it began to grow dark & kept yawing about trying to get in until later.[99]

3 AUGUST 1863, MONDAY

Dined with Wise. He and Aulick say the whole British Embassy here are actively secesh: Aided and abetted Lawrence to go South. And then assisted him out of jail when he was caught.[100]

6 AUGUST 1863, THURSDAY

This was the day of thanksgiving appointed by the President. We went to Dr Sunderland's but he was away so went to Gurley's. G. came out pretty strongly in prayer and sermon more decidedly than ever before. The President said after Church, that he supposed his faith in ultimate success must be decidedly strengthened or he would not have talked so.[101]

The ~~Tycoon~~ President says there is no foundation for the rumor of War with England.

~~Two good things on Hale. Got four votes out of a whole convention, against the Admn Found himself cut out of a job by a statute of Congress passed by himself. He then wanted the Secretary to construe it liberally.~~[102]

The President has recd. an enormous letter from Seymour about draft, and intends to enforce the draft with such arrangements as will take from the present enrollment its present look of unfairness. He says he is willing and anxious to have the matter before the Courts.[103]

Matters from Louisiana look very well. Banks in a letter to Boutwell says the state will do anything we want her to. In reference to that the President has written Banks this letter, a very careful & I think admirable one.[104]

~~Cuthbert Bullitt Collector at New Orleans is in hot water because he is not of the Chase dynasty devotees party.~~[105]

9 AUGUST 1863, SUNDAY

This being Sunday & a fine day I went down with the President to have his picture taken at Gardner's.[106] He was in very good spirits. He thinks that the rebel power is at last beginning to disintegrate that they will break to pieces if we only stand firm now. Referring to the controversy between two factions in Richmond one of whom believe still in foreign intervention, Northern Treason & other chimeras, and the other, the Administration party trust to nothing but the Army, he said "Davis is right. His Army is his only hope, not only against us but against his own people. If that were crushed the people would be ready to swing back to their old bearings."

He is very anxious that Texas should be occupied and firmly held in view of French possibilities. He thinks it just now more important than Mobile. He would prefer that Grant should not throw his army into the Mobile business before the Texas matter is safe. He wrote in that sense, I believe to Grant today.[107]

He wrote also to Rosecrans, in answer to Rosecrans letter to him, which is one of the worst specimens of epistolary literature I have ever come across. Rosecrans letter deprecated any dissatisfaction with his apparent slowness & gave his reasons for it: the extreme length of his lines: the scarcity of cavalry: the terrible mud of the roads: their narrowness which prevents trains from passing each other readily, &c.[108]

The President in his answer disclaimed all unkindness or any diminution of confidence and regard. He said that when Grant invested Vicksburg he was very anxious on account of Johnston and when he heard that Bragg had sent reinforcements to J. he thought that that was Rosecrans time to attack Bragg, & says with all kindness, he still thinks so. As time wore on he became convinced that Rosecrans should either attack the enemy, or stand on the defensive and send reinforcements to Grant. He gave that order to Halleck to send to R. H. said he had already done it in substance.

After Vicksburg fell his anxiety was relieved. He could not agree with Rosecrans in thinking that his best time for attacking Bragg would be after rather than before the fall of Vicksburg.

Now however he was relieved of anxiety & would trust to R. himself. He was very anxious that E. Tennessee should be relieved. But the question was, if we could take the country could we hold it? In conclusion he begged Rosey Rosecrans to believe that he was not blaming him, or watching him with an evil eye.[109]

10 AUGUST 1863, MONDAY

Today the answer of Presdt. to Seymour was printed: everybody seems to consider it a sock-dolager "settler" to the Govr.[110] Poor Seymour! A weak timid vacillating man, afraid to do either right or wrong. If he were under good influences, he would do yeoman's service for his country. Now, he is wearing himself into lunacy by trying to serve the plans of his owners and his own good impulses at once.

The President today wrote a letter to the East Tennesseans, who recently presented him a most touching petition, which, circulated by stealth among the mountains of that suffering but loyal district has obtained thousands of signatures. He answered that he had not seen them because he knew what they would say—the same true and painful story he had heard so often from Maynard & Johnson & Clements. That he was not indifferent to their sufferings, as they might know by the efforts he had made to build a railroad specially for their relief. That he could do no more than he had been doing if his own family & home were in Knoxville. That they were too much distressed to argue and he would not argue with them. The reasons of the long and agonizing delay could not be plainly seen by those who were mad and blinded by their sufferings. The impossibility so far, of supplying a great army in East Tennessee & the facility with which a small army could be concentrated upon and destroyed, were the main ones. He added that even now Stanton Halleck Rosecrans & Burnside were trying to do something which might result in their relief.[111]

~~Seymour writes a Coppery little letter in which he says the shameless frauds &c &c~~[112]

11 AUGUST 1863, TUESDAY

Seymour sends another ponderous document accusing the draft of partizanship.[113]

President read today Drake's letter and gave the substance of Gamble's each accusing him of outrageous partizanship with the other.[114]

Fred Douglass in company with Sen. Pomeroy visited the President yesterday. Frederick intends to go south and help the recruiting among his people.[115]

13 AUGUST 1863, THURSDAY

Rode today with the President and the Secretary of State to the Capitol. Saw the Statuary of the East Pediment. The Presdt. objected to Powers' statue of the Woodchopper, as he did not make a sufficiently clean cut.[116]

~~Attacks as usual by officious officials who were, however, easily snubbed~~.

Coming home the President told Seward of what Frank Blair said about an interview he had had with Poindexter in the West. Poindexter said "we are gone up, there is no further use of talking." "How about yr. institution?" Frank asked. "Gone to the Devil."

Seward said "Slavery is dead: the only trouble is that the fools who support it from the outside do not recognize this, and will not till the thing is over. In our Masonic warfare, we made a great fight. The Masons were beaten: they knew & felt it, and retired from the fight. But the Jack Masons as they were called kept up their dismal howls of sympathy for the Masons, long after *they* had given up the fight & forgotten all about it. So now, though slavery is dead, the Democratic party insists on devoting itself to guarding the corpse."[117]

Brady has recently written a letter in which he says he is sorry to say that Seymour is at present actuated by no higher ambition than to carry an election.[118]

Seward says "He is silly and short sighted. One fundamental principle of politics is to be always on the side of your country in a war. It kills any party to oppose a war. When Mr. Buchanan got up his Mormon War, our people Wade & Fessenden & the Tribune led off furiously against it.[119] I supported it to the immense disgust of enemies and friends. If you want to sicken your opponents with their own war go in for it till they give it up."

Presdt. says, "Butterfield of Illinois was asked at the beginning of the Mexican War if he were not opposed to it; he said 'no, I opposed one War. That was enough for me. I am now perpetually in favor of war, pestilence and famine.'"[120]

There is to be a diplomatic excursion to the North. Seward asked me to go. It will be a very ~~hefty~~ amusing affair.[121]

I saw Forney this morning. He says he thinks they will elect Curtin, though a bad choice for Govr. He would not have been nominated, had it not been for Cameron's foolish attack upon him.[122]

Conness has been here, the guest of Chase. James is made Collector at San Franco. in place of Low. I rather intimated to the Presdt. that this was Chases game and he replied good humoredly "I suppose C. thinks it is to his advantage. Let him have him."[123]

14 August 1863, Friday

Meade was in town today. In one thing he evinces want of candor or failure of memory. The President July 27, asked him if he would like to have Hooker with him. He replied by return mail that "he would be very glad to have the benefit of his services."[124] The President showed the letter to Hooker who was pleased with the prospect of fight and then wrote asking Meade if he would wish Hooker to come at once or could he as well wait till the 1st of September. In case there should be a battle Hooker would like to come at once. Meade answers that as to the probabilities of a battle, we at Washington can tell as well as he, as the army is now lying inactive, waiting reinforcements from the draft or orders to advance. What the enemy may please to do we dont know. As to Hooker, he says he never entertained or expressed any desire for him, that his part in the matter was simply one of acquiescence. This of course very much embarrasses the President. He must rely entirely on Hooker's generosity and magnanimity to get out of the snarl, As Meade evidently does not want him with the Army of the Potomac

The preparations for the draft still continue in New York. Dix is getting ready rather slowly. Fry goes to N. Y. tonight, armed with various powers. He carries a paper to be used in certain contingencies calling the militia of the State into the service of the General government, and calling upon rioters to disperse [K. T. A.?] Dix has already authority to declare Martial Law when it appears necessary. The devil of treason is pretty well muzzled there. We must tear out its fangs if it takes off the muzzle. Seymour is half lunatic half demagogue. He is a delicate soul without courage or honesty fallen on evil times. His reason, never the most robust is giving way under its overwork. If old Gen. Sandford is entirely sound, we may manage it without trouble.[125] The Govt. was never intended by the Constitution to be left helpless to the attacks of discontented State officers. I thank God for the riot if as one of its results we set a great authoritative precedent of the absolute supremacy of the National power, military and civil, over the State. Every nail that enters the coffin of that dead-and-gone humbug of State Rights is a promise of future & enduring peace & power.

19 AUGUST 1863, WEDNESDAY

This morning a letter came from Steve Hurlbut formally withdrawing his resignation and another a splendid letter full of the old arrogant and incisive energy of the man, saying that he thinks the rebellion is falling to pieces by disintegration in the West. He sends also a sketch of a letter he intends to write to the Mississippi planters, telling them to get themselves out of their miserable scrape by accepting the events of the war, including emancipation, as accomplished facts, and forming a plan of gradually lightening apprenticeship in accordance with them, and offering themselves back to the Union. He thinks the horrors of rebellion have so broken their spirits that they will do whatever seems best for peace and the old security.[126]

He says if East Tennessee were only redeemed, Tennessee would vote herself free and loyal in a few months, and send an earnestly loyal delegation to Congress from every district.

The whole letter is very like the old Hurlbut we used to know in Illinois the reliant arrogant brilliant leader in a political war.

This evening and yesterday evening an hour was spent by the President in shooting with Spencers new repeating rifle. A wonderful gun loading with absolutely contemptible simplicity and ease with seven balls & firing the whole readily & deliberately in less than half a minute. The President made some pretty good shots. Spencer the inventor a quiet little Yankee who sold himself in relentless slavery to his idea for six weary years before it was perfect did some splendid shooting. ~~My shooting was the most lamentably bad. My eyes are gradually failing. I can scarcely see the target two inches wide at thirty yards.~~[127]

An irrepressible patriot came up and talked about his son John who when lying on his belly on a hilltop at Gettysburg, feeling the shot fly over him like to lost his breath—felt himself puffing up like a toad—thought he would bust. Another seeing the gun recoil slightly said it wouldnt do; too much powder: a good piece of audience should not rekyle: if it did at all, it should rekyle a little forrid.[128]

22 AUGUST 1863, SATURDAY

The President today said John Logan was acting so splendidly now, that he absolved him in his own mind for all the wrong he ever did & all he will do hereafter.[129]

I said I thought Quantrell would murder Lane if he caught him. He replied that if he did Lane's friends wd hunt Quantrell to his death and[130]

23 AUGUST 1863, SUNDAY

Last night we went to the Observatory with Mrs Young. They were very kind and attentive. The Presdt. took a look at the moon & Arcturus. I went with him to the Soldiers' Home & he read Shakespeare to me, the end of Henry VI and the beginning of Richard III till my heavy eye-lids caught his considerate notice & he sent me to bed. This morning we ate an egg and came in very early. He went to the library to write a letter to Conkling & I went to pack my trunk for the North.[131]

[JULY–AUGUST 1863][132]

The Longnecker suggestion.

The forced loan.

Gen. Grant's supplementary despatch and the small boys explanation of his stained trousers.

The President said the Army dwindled on a march like a shovelfull of live fleas ~~being~~ pitched from one place to another.[133]

July 1863. Captain Cutts was in trouble about looking thro keyholes & over transoms at a lady undressing. The T said he should be elevated to the peerage for it with the title of Count Peeper.[134]

I am growing as thin as a shad—yea worse—as thin as a shadder.

The wren at my window & the wrencontre on the portfolio.

I. "The Richmond papers are trying to be jolly over Morgan's expedition which they call a success"[135]

Genl Spinner. "They remind me of a little fellow whom I saw once badly whipped by a bigger man, who was on top of him & jamming his head on the floor. The little cuss still full of conceit & pluck kept saying *Now*, damn you, will you behave yourself!"

The *Alabama* prisoner at Fort Lafayette, who didnt think matters were so dd bad & who wd be quite contented if he could have any security on occasions like this, for instance, that he was not cussing

Ben Wade says I prayed with earnestness for the life of Taney to be prolonged through Buchanan's Administration, and by God Im a little afraid I have overdone the matter.[136]

Wade says Chase is a good man, but his theology is unsound. He thinks there is a fourth Person in the Trinity, *S. P. C.*

A man caught in a disgraceful affair said he could bring a man to prove an alibi. I have no doubt said the Presdt. you can bring a man to prove a lie by.

Wise tells a good one of the Tycoon. I The fight of a ram with a bull suggested by the exploits of the Ram Arkansas.[137] II The starved but discriminating fox.

The Second Coming. If J. C. had ever been to Springfield once he would [never] come again.[138]

Who was to blame for the Winchester business. Lee.[139]

When Death called on [Deuceace?] no funk did he feel—
He shuffled this life off & cut for the De'il.

~~Lamon was passing the Canterbury. Cartter objected to this barelegged dancing. Cartter says, "A woman to be appreciated, must be covered."~~[140]

Cartter says "Millard Fillmore got a reputation for conservatism & Wisdom by never swearing in company, always wearing a clean shirt & never uttering a sentiment that the asses around him did not at once recognize as an old acquaintance."

Capt LeRoy told the other day an incident of the invasion of Pa. A meek looking soldier (McVeagh) was detailed as his clerk. He gave him some work—went to dinner—came back & found him a Major appointed in his absence & ranking him.[141]

Lamon says Gen. Mansfield is a good enough old man but he never had an idea till the next day.[142]

The Presidential aspirations of Mr Chase are said to have been compared by the President to a horsefly on the neck of a ploughhorse—which kept him lively about his work.[143]

Thos. Corwin's story about the meeting in Iowa "4 things past finding out" & the blue cotting Ambush. The original of Bob Blackwell's great thing.[144]

Corwin's story about the advertising pulpit—"fine powder at Bill Smithers"—& an indignant Auditor's reply Taint wuth a damn—grains big as rat tds—and I would walk through hell with a bag full of it.[145]

Corwins other story about the little boy on the wagon wheel.

[EARLY SEPTEMBER 1863]

Spent a day in New York. Dined with Andrews. He says Raymond came back from Washington full of admiration for the President, saying he had more clearly than anybody the issues of this matter in his mind. This explains those remarkably sensible articles which have appeared recently in the Times.[146]

Staid about a week at Long Branch. Fine air—disgusting bathing— pretty women and everything lovely. No politics, no war, nothing to remind me while there that there was such a thing as government, or a soul to save. Count Gurowski was an undertone of nuisance—That was all.[147]

~~Went to Providence to attend Commencement. I was charmed and surprised to find with what affectionate and hearty confidence Mr. Lincoln was there regarded. The refined and scholarly people of that ancient city seem utterly free from that lurking treason which so deforms some towns of more pretence. At the Commencement dinner especially I heard nothing but the most emphatic expressions of advanced and liberal Republicanism.~~[148]

9 SEPTEMBER 1863, WEDNESDAY

Dined with Wise. Met Hooker, Butterfield & Fox. Hooker was in a fine flow. Before dinner we talked about Halleck and his connection with

Hooker's resignation. He says he was forced to ask to be relieved by repeated acts which proved that he was not to be allowed to manage his army
as he thought best, but that it was to be maneuvered from Washington. He
instanced Maryland Heights whose garrison he was forbidden to touch,
yet which was ordered to be evacuated by the very mail which brought *his*
(H's) relief. And other such many.[149]

At Dinner he spoke of our Army. He says "it was the finest on the planet.
He would like to see it fighting with foreigners. It gave him an electric feeling to be with it. It was far superior to the Southern army in everything
but one. It had more valor more strength more endurance more spirit. The
rebels are only superior in vigor of attack. The reason of this is that in the
first place our army came down here capable of everything but ignorant
of everything. It fell into evil hands—the hands of a baby [McClellan] who
knew something of drill little of organization and nothing of the *morale*
of the army. It was fashioned by the congenial spirit of this man into a mass
of languid inertness destitute of either dash or cohesion. The Prince de
Joinville, by far the finest mind I have ever met with in the army, was struck
by this singular and as he said, inexplicable contrast between the character of American soldiers as integers and in mass. The one active independent alert, enterprising: the other indolent, easy, wasteful and slothful. It
is not in the least singular. You find a ready explanation in the character of
its original general. Stoneman is an instance of the cankerous influence of
that staff.[150] I sent him out to destroy the bridges behind Lee. He rode 150
miles and came back without seeing the bridges he should have destroyed.
He took with him 11000 men, he returned with 4500. His purposeless ride
had all the result of a defeat. He claimed to have brought in an enormous
train of negroes and other cattle. He brought 30 contrabands and not a
man or a mule. He is a brave good man but he is spoiled by McClellan and
the piles.

After the battle of Malvern and after the battle of Fair Oaks we could
have marched into Richmond without serious resistance. Yet the constitutional apathy of this man prevented."[151]

Says Butterfield On the night of the battle of Malvern I saw the red lights
of Meyer signal officer blazing near me and I went to him to gain information. He told me had just received a despatch from Gen McClellan asking where was General F. J. Porter, he wanted news. I volunteered a
despatch. "We have won a glorious victory and if we push on and seize our
advantage Richmond is ours." The day of Gaines' Mills I had taken my po-

sition, when Porter ordered me out of it into a hollow where I was compelled to assume a strictly defensive position.[152] I once or twice terribly repulsed the enemy but my orders peremptorily forbad pursuit. I had to keep up the spirit of the men by starting the rumour that McClellan was in Richmond. I am sure I thought he would be there that day. In the night going to Gen. McClellan's Headquarters he asked me what about our Corps. I told him that with a few strong divisions we could attack and drive the enemy. He said he hadnt a man for us.

Fox said that the night before the evacuation of Yorktown he staid [in] McClellan's tent. McC. said he expected to bag 18,000 of them. You wont bag one replied Tucker. And he didnt.[153]

Hooker says "Marcy sometimes sent important orders which McClellan never saw. On one occasion when I had advanced my pickets very near Richmond, I received an order through Heintzelman, 'Let Genl Hooker return from his brilliant reconnaissance, we cannot afford to lose his division.' I did not see how my division could be lost as in that country there was no cutting me off. I started back however & soon met McClellan himself who asked me what it meant, my withdrawal. I showed him his own order. He said he had never seen it, and I ordered my men back. I returned over the swamp and held my position for weeks afterwards.

Hooker and Butterfield both agree as to the terrible defeat the rebels suffered at Malvern and the inefficiency which suffered them to escape without injury. They say there was a corps, fresh and unharmed, which might have pursued the rebels and entered Richmond in triumph. (Franklin's)[154]

Wise and H. talked about California, hydraulic mining &c. Hooker asked me very anxiously about our relations with France. He seems very eager to raise an army on the Pacific coast for a fight with a foreign nation. His eye brightened as he talked of it.[155]

Hooker drank very little, not more than the rest who were all abstemious, yet what little he drank made his cheek hot and red & his eye brighter. I can easily ~~see~~ understand how the stories of his drunkenness have grown, if so little affects him as I have seen. He was looking very well tonight. A tall and statuesque form—grand fighting head and grizzled russet hair—red florid cheeks and bright blue eyes, forming a fine contrast with Butterfield who sat opposite, A small stout compact man with a closely chiselled Greek face and heavy black mustache—like Eugene

Beauharnais ~~in the pictures I have seen~~. Both very handsome and very different.[156]

10 September 1863, Thursday

A despatch came yesterday morning from Rosecrans written in a most querulous and discouraged tone, saying to Halleck that his orders warning Rosecrans agst a junction of Johnston & Bragg were too late: the junction could not be prevented: he must fight both: Gen Burnside's movement was independent of his: he knew nothing and expected nothing from him: The gravest apprehensions were justifiable: they were the legitimate consequences of Halleck's orders: all that could now be done was for Burnside to close in on his (R's) left and throw forward his right to threaten the enemy while he (R) caught the enemy in his grip & either strangled him or perished in the attempt.[157]

The President read it with a quiet smile. He said he did not believe the story of Johnston's junction. Johnston was watching Mobile. Rosecrans was a little excited. In the afternoon a despatch in a better tone came from Rosecrans. He intimated that the prospect was the enemy would leave Chattanooga without a fight.

This morning the despatches confirmed the last view, justified, as usual, the President's instinct, and proved that Rosecrans was a little stampeded.

Frank Blair was in my ~~office~~ room today. I congratulated him on his new position of leader of the Copperheads in the next Congress & asked what arrangement he would make with Ferndo Wood. He said he would drive him out of the party.[158]

George Opdyke called to say that though the President had treated him very cavalierly when he last visited him he wanted to thank him for his recent admirable letter to the Springfield Convention.[159]

I dined tonight at Wormley's, with Hooker, Butterfield, Fox, Wise, and Col. Rush of Philadela.[160] Early in the dinner we began to talk about England and the retribution to come for her insults and injuries when this war is over. Everybody had something to say. Fox said, "When the time comes, a publication will be made of insults and wrongs on every sea—of ports closed to us and opened to the enemy—of flags dipped to them and insultingly immovable to us—of courtesies ostentatiously shown them and brutally denied us—that will make the blood of every American boil in his brain-pan. We shall have men enough when this thing is over."

"We will be the greatest military power on earth" said Hooker "greatest in numbers, in capability, in dash, in spirit, in intelligence of the soldiery. These fine fellows who have gotten a taste of campaigning in the last three years will not go back to plowing, and spinning and trading, and hewing wood and drawing water. They are spoiled for that and shaped for better work. If they can find no war to their hand, they will filibuster."

"Pleasant fields in Canada," suggested one "very like Normandy!"

"A Prince of the blood Royal will not save them in that day however much DArcy McGee may put faith in him."[161]

"In the Patriot War said Hooker, when I was in command on our border there, the picked troops came over & deserted in squads. They had to place native recruits at last in all exposed places. They can never keep an English army together on our soil. They will desert and colonize."[162]

"We will make no fight on Canada," said Fox, "that will fall of itself. But we will cast our eyes at Bermuda at Nassau at the Islands that infest our coast, nurseries of treason & piracy against us, by whose aid England has been at war with us & we at peace with her. We have found it is not good for these possessions to lie so near for our discomfort. When we come together again, the rebel leaders dispersed & exiled—the army scattered—the people weary and reconciled & only waiting for an outside quarrell to bind them closer together, we will turn to these Islands and we will say 'Get out of this! Go you to your own place.' And it will be the worse for them if they hesitate to go."

Wise. "As our war draws near its close the British Legation sometimes speak of the horrors of war. 'How very distressing it is, to be sure.' 'Nothing of the kind. We are getting the hang of the game and rather like it.' Which occasions vague uneasiness."

Hooker says "Our war has developed no great cavalry officer. Stoneman has good points but does not fulfill his early promise. Pleasanton is splendid, enterprising and brave—but full of mannerisms and weaknesses. Buford is far superior to any others in all the qualities of a great rider. But none of them approach the ideal."[163]

Speaking of Lee, he expressed himself slightingly of Lees abilities. He says he was never much respected in the Army. In Mexico he was surpassed by all his Lieutenants. In the cavalry he was held in no esteem. He was regarded very highly by Genl. Scott. He was a courtier and readily recommended himself by his insinuating manner to the General whose petulant and arrogant temper has driven of late years all officers of spirit and self respect away from him.

"Look at all his staff officers—sleek and comfortable and respectable and obsequious: Townsend Cullum Hamilton Wright &c.[164]

"The strength of the rebel Army rests on the broad shoulders of Longstreet. He is the brain of Lee as Stonewall Jackson was his right arm. Before every battle he has been advised with. After every battle Lee may be found in *his* tent. He is a weak man and little of a soldier. He naturally rests on Longstreet who is a soldier, born."[165]

~~Rush spoke this evening rather contemptuously of Dr Kane and to my surprise, everybody agreed with him. He seems to be considered by these people, at least, as a reckless romancer and adventurer, with little but rhetoric to recommend him. I cannot think but that injustice is done him—perhaps in both praise and blame.~~[166]
~~Fox has a most wonderful story about "Kane's remains."~~

Fox was more than usually funny tonight. After dinner he said how delightful are the usages of society on the coast of Africa. There when you dine with a native prince, the etiquette is to appear naked; free from the contingencies of bursting buttons."

He says one of his brother officers once made a present to a native King of a cocked hat a green velvet waistcoat and a skillet. On dining with him the next day, the grateful host appeared in the cocked hat with the flaps drawn down like elephants ears over his chops, the green velvet waistcoat pulled to bursting over his stomach the tense hide bulging out below like the ~~swell~~ base of a Corinthian ~~pediment~~ column, the second button left open to display his umbilical development, ~~his testicles stored in the skillet and his male organ fastened to its handle, the whole apparatus~~ the skillet being moored around his loins by cowhide thongs.

~~His yarn about the Bay of Fundy & the sentinel pig is immense. I asked him if the pig would run from a sow-wester.~~

Wise gave a ridiculous account of a Breakfast given to some American officers by a Mexican Colonel. This started a vein of Mexican reminiscence. Fox recounted his march with a detachment of sailors to Tabasco, his overload—his scanty raiment when arrived there—his plunder of a trombone & the way he lost it—(a serious mistake, I suggested, taking a trombone for loot:) Perry's answer to a Mexican flag of truce, &c. & Wise gave an account of the only time Halleck ever smelt gunpowder.[167]

11 SEPTEMBER 1863, FRIDAY

Today the President wrote a letter to Andrew Johnson telling him now is the time to reorganize the loyal government of Tennessee. But it must be so done that the friends and not the enemies of the Union should be in the ascendant. That the toil of liberating Tennessee would be purposeless and futile if the struggle ended by putting Gov Johnson down & Gov Harris up. This must not be. Exclude from the Govt. those who cannot be trusted for the Union and you will be recognized by the government here as the Republican govt. guaranteed to the States and protected from invasion of internal tumult.[168]

In connection with the question of time, the President cannot tell who will be the next occupant of his place or what he will do. Present action is therefore important.

He has heard that Johnson has lately declared for emancipation in Tennessee and says God Bless him. Incorporate emancipation in the new state Govt. Constitution and there will be no such word as fail in the case.

Arming negroes he thinks will be advantageous in every way.

17 SEPTEMBER 1863, THURSDAY

I went to Philadelphia to assist at the wedding of Becky Stewart to a fine young fellow named Grant.

I met at the Union League Rooms Geo H Boker & at her father's house Mrs LeRoy. One of the most lovable of men & most lovely of women. The loyalty of a truly patriotic Philadelphian is of that magnificent and uncompromising character such as is not seen elsewhere. It is carried into every incident of life.[169]

Passed the evening partly in Wayne McVeagh's room (Chairman, State

Central Committee) partly in General Butler's. McVeagh does not seem entirely easy about the result in Pennsylvania. He wanted everybody to beg Butler to make more speeches & specially wanted Cameron to come out strong for Curtin which he has not yet done. He thought the chief dangers were—the solid Irish vote— the chill and discouragement of the draft— the proclamation of Habeas Corpus—& such.[170]

Butler talked of the folly of the Irish casting their vote as a solidarity— as having a tendency to rouse against them the bitter prejudices of race & religion & overwhelming them.

[27 SEPTEMBER 1863, SUNDAY]

Sunday morning, the 20th of September the President showed me Rosecrans despatch of the day before detailing the first day's fighting & promising a complete victory on the next day. The Presdt. was a little uneasy over the promise, and very uneasy that Burnside was not within supporting distance.

The next morning he came into my bedroom before I was up, & sitting down on my bed said "Well, Rosecrans has been whipped, as I feared. I have feared it for several days. I believe I feel trouble in the air before it comes. Rosecrans says we have met with a serious disaster—extent not ascertained. Burnside instead of obeying the orders which were given him on the 14th & going to Rosecrans has gone up on a foolish affair to Jonesboro to capture a party of guerrillas who are there."[171]

Day by day the news brightened up. Thomas held his own magnificently & virtually whipped the enemy opposed to him. The scattered divisions came together—the enemy halted—Rosecrans established himself again at Chattanooga. The stampede seemed to be over.[172]

On Wednesday night, the 23rd coming home I found on my table some interesting despatches from the Rebel papers which I thought the President would like to read. They contained pretty full accounts of rebel losses in the late battles: Among other things chronicling the death of B. Hardin Helm Mrs. L's brother in law who spent some time with the family here and was made a paymaster by the President.[173] I took them over to the War Department to give them to an orderly to carry to the President. I found there the Sec. of War who was just starting to the Soldiers' Home to request the President to come to the Department to attend a council to be held there that night rendered expedient, as he said, by recent despatches from Chattanooga.

While I was in the room they were endeavoring to decipher an intricate message from Rosecrans giving reasons for the failure of the battle. The Secy. says "I know the reasons well enough. Rosecrans ran away from his fighting men and did not stop for 13 miles." A moment after he broke in "No, they need not shuffle it off on McCook. He is not much of a soldier. I never was in favor of him for a Major Genl. But he is not accountable for this business. He & Crittenden both made pretty good time away from the fight to Chattanooga, but Rosecrans beat them both"[174]

I went out to the Soldiers Home, through a splendid moonlight, & found the ~~Tycoon~~ President abed. I delivered my message to him as he ~~robed~~ dressed himself & he was considerably disturbed. I assured him as far as I could that it meant nothing serious, but he thought otherwise, as it was the first time Stanton had ever sent for him. When he got in however we found a despatch from Rosecrans stating that he could hold Chattanooga against double his number: could not be taken until after a great battle: his stampede evidently over.

They came together to discuss the practicability of reinforcing ~~Rosey~~ Rosecrans from Meade. Present A Lincoln, Halleck, Stanton, Seward, Chase, Watson & Hardie: and for a while McCallum. It was resolved to do it. The 11th and 12th Corps were selected for the purpose, Hooker to be placed in command of both. Finished the evening with a supper by Stanton at 1 o'clock where few ate.[175]

On the morning of the 26th Gen Howard 11th corps came in as he was passing through town. A fine handsome thoughtful looking New Englander: and Graham came at same time, an exchanged prisoner, whom the rebs captured at Gettysburg—later in the evening came Slocum 12th Corps. He said he would call in the morning. He did so Sunday morning accompanied by Governor Seward. The result of the visit, a request by the President to Genl Rosecrans urging him to take Slocum from Hooker's force and give Hooker some corresponding force. Slocum does not seem to me a very large man. He seems peevish, irritable, fretful. Hooker says he is all that on account of his digestive apparatus being out of repair. Hooker does not speak unkindly of him; ~~I believe he blackguards~~ while he never mentions Hooker but to attack him.[176]

Tonight (Sep. 27) I rode out to the Soldiers Home with Hooker. The

President, who has been spending the evening at the War Dept. arranging some plan by which Burnside may be allowed to continue his occupation and protection of East Tennessee, went out at 9 oclock & Hooker who wanted to take leave went out afterwards, picking me up on the street. He does not specially approve of the campaign down there. He thinks we might force them to fight at disadvantage, instead of allowing them to continually choose the battleground. Does not think much can be made by lengthening Rosecrans' line indefinitely into Georgia. Atlanta is a good thing on account of its railroads & store houses & factories. But a long line weakens an army by constant details while the enemy falling back gradually keeps his army intact till the itinerary equalizes the opposing forces.[177]

Hooker goes in the morning. I hope they will give him a fair show. Slocum's hostility is very regrettable. Hooker is a fine fellow. The President says "Whenever trouble arises I can always rely upon Hooker's magnanimity." The President this morning asked him to write to him. I told him if he did not wish to write to the ~~Tycoon~~ President he might write to me. I wish ~~to God~~ I was able to go with him. But Nicolay is in the mountains getting beef on his bones and I am a prisoner here. With Rosecrans, Sherman, Burnside & Hooker, they will have a magnificent army there in a few days & some great fighting if Bragg does not run. Deserters say A. P. Hill is coming. I dont believe that.[178]

28 SEPTEMBER 1863, MONDAY

The Missouri Radicals are here, staying at Willard's. They are making up their case with a great deal of care and have not yet waited upon the President. Hawkins Taylor is very anxious for the President to meet them on a friendly basis. He says he has been in Missouri the past season & knows the state of affairs: that these people are really the President's friends: that the Conservatives are only waiting a favorable opportunity to pronounce against him: that these radicals will certainly carry the state in the next election: and that to use their own expression "It is for the President to decide whether he will ride in their wagon or not." I had previously been a good deal impressed with the fact that the Blairs were not the safest guides about Missouri matters, and that the surest reliance could be placed on men who were passionately devoted to the principle which the Republican party represents and upholds. The "Mo Repn" devoted to the interest of the Conservatives in Missouri and of the Copperheads in Illinois, seems to me a significant indication of the ultimate tendencies of those people. In that sense I have spoken to the President several times & have urged others to speak to him. He gets the greater part of his information from the Blairs & the Bates people who do not seem to me entirely impartial. Noble fellows they are though I have no sympathy with the radical abuse of them. They stood by Freedom in a dark hour and cannot be excommunicated now by any eleventh hour converts. Hawkins Taylor had a talk with him yesterday morning & came out very much disheartened. He thinks there is no hope of an agreement.[179]

I dined yesterday with Cartter & Fisher at Lamon's. Cartter was very much exercised about the matter. He thinks the most momentous political issues depend upon the manner in which the Presdt. receives this delegation. He talked as usual in his coarse arrogant and brilliant way about the matter. He says Chase is about giving up his Presidential aspirations. Stanton has none & is for Lincoln. That everyone is beginning to recognize that he is to save us if we are saved in the next election & he therefore hopes to have the Transmississippi States right when the time comes. I told him that I had said so much as already to appear partizan and advised him to speak for himself: to which he seemed disinclined.[180]

29 SEPTEMBER 1863, TUESDAY

I Had a little talk with the Presdt. today about the Missourians. He says that they come he supposes to demand principally the removal of Schofield—and if they can show that Schofield has done anything wrong & has interfered to their disadvantage with State politics—or has so acted as to damage the cause of the Union and good order their case is made.[181] But on the contrary he (A. L.) thinks that it will be found that Schofield is a firm competent energetic & eminently fair man, and that he has incurred their ill will by refusing to take sides with them in their local politics: that he (A L) does not think it in the province of a military commander to interfere with the local politics or to influence elections actively in one way or another.

I told him the impression derived from talking with people from there was that there were two great parties in Missouri, the Secession sympathizing Democrats & the Radicals—that the Union Conservatives were too small to reckon—that the Radicals would carry the State and it would be well not to alienate them if it could be avoided, especially as their principles were in fact ours and their objects substantially the same as ours. He seemed fully to recognize this and other things in the same strain.

He suddenly said, These people will come here claiming to be my best friends, but let me show you a letter from Joe Hay." He showed me one from Uncle Joe, saying that Drake had recently in a speech a[t] La Grange denounced him for a tyrannical interference with the convention through his agent Schofield, referring of course to the letter he wrote Schofield in June in reply to S's telegram earnestly soliciting from him some statement of his views, in favor of gradual emancipation and promising that the power of the general government would not be used against the slaveowners for the time being provided they adopted an ordinance of Emancipation—stating at the same time that he hoped the time of consummation would be short and a provision be made against sales into permanent slavery in the meantime. He said after rereading his own letter, "I believe that to be right & I will stand by it."[182]

He said "John, I think I understand this matter perfectly and I cannot do anything contrary to my convictions to please these men, earnest and powerful as they may be."

Today came to the Executive Mansion an assembly of cold-water men & cold water women to make a temperance speech at the ~~Tycoon~~ President & receive a response. They filed into the East Room looking blue & thin in the keen autumnal air; Cooper, my coachman, who was about half tight, gazing at them with an air of complacent contempt and mild wonder. Three blue-skinned damsels ~~did~~ personated Love, Purity, & Fidelity in Red White & Blue gowns. A few Invalid soldiers stumped along in the dismal procession. They made a long speech at the ~~Tycoon~~ President in which they called Intemperance the cause of our defeats. He could not see it, as the rebels drink more & worse whiskey than we do. They filed off drearily to a collation of cold water & green apples, & then home to mulligrubs.[183]

30 September 1863, Wednesday

The Missourians spent rather more than two hours with the President this morning. They discharged their speech at him which Drake read as pompously as if it were full of matter instead of wind, and then had desultory talk for a great while. The President never appeared to better advantage in the world. Though He knows how immense is the danger to himself from the unreasoning anger of that committee, he never cringed to them for an instant. He stood where he thought he was right and crushed them with his candid logic. I was with those people all the while till today. They trifled with a great cause unpardonably. The personal character of the men, too, ill sustained their attitude. They are gone and I suppose have virtually failed.[184]

1 OCTOBER 1863, THURSDAY

Dined with Hanscom — birthday Went to the Depot. Met Gus. Spent the evening raging around. Saw the Capitol by night. It never looked finer.[185]

2 OCTOBER 1863, FRIDAY

Got up at Daybreak. Washington to Relay House. Soldiers — to Harper's Ferry — the broken spans — the shelving river bed — the journey — women who entered cars — Supper. Hot car. Sleeping car.

3 OCTOBER 1863, SATURDAY

Benwood. Old German & Young Yankee women. Bellaire. Late train. Soldiers. Vallandigham discussion. Old Copperhead and his troubles — Young soldier too much for him.

Neil House. Met Brough & Galloway at supper. They manifestly feel very good over the prospect in this state. McCoy was talking like an ass about the sure thing in Pa. They have an awful fight in that state. Curtin is an incubus but they hope to carry him by God's grace.[186]

4 OCTOBER 1863, SUNDAY

Went to the Episcopal Church this morning, A. L. & I.[187] In the evening had a talk with Brough. He says they are going to carry the State by not less than 25,000 on the Home Vote and vastly greater on the soldiers. The Canvass is one of singular energy and vigor. The Vallandighams are giving it up now however. They are spending no money and importing no men. I told him I thought they were diverting men and money into Pennsylvania. He said it was probable. He said he had been this morning doing the personal electioneering business among the Dutch around here. Our peo-

~~ple had given them up, but they were coming right of themselves. They would say to him, "Johnny if you aint elected it wont be de fault of Schenkenheimer's brewery" &c.~~

~~He was very anxious about Pennsylvania and seemed much gratified by the cheering news from Forney and especially Cameron. He was not personally friendly with Cameron but thought him one of the most sagacious of men.~~

~~He says Prof McCoy, after a good deal of indirect boring came at him flat-footed this evening urging the absolute necessity of uniting on Gen. Butler as our Presidential candidate. He snubbed McC. severely: saying one war at a time.~~

~~He says that when he heard he was nominated he sent a despatch to Tod asking him to assure the President that the change in nominee inferred argued no blame of either State or national administration and that there should be no difference in the attitude of Ohio towards the general government.[188]~~

~~He says he was nominated against his earnest protest. He was in favor of Tod.~~

~~Governor Dennison came in late this evening. He spoke also of the earnestness and passion of this canvass — gave illustrations of it. He said that the people at large were beginning to appreciate the importance of this struggle as the fore-runner of the Presidential contest: that he had conversed much with leading men in different localities and he found a widespread and constantly increasing concurrence of sentiment in favor of the reelection of Mr. Lincoln. He requested me to say as much to him: That throughout the West so far as he knew the feeling was quietly assuming the same aspect: in New York it seemed to be the same.~~

8 OCTOBER 1863, THURSDAY, WARSAW, ILLINOIS

~~My birthday and my sister Mary was married today and started off to Cairo with her husband.[189]~~

13 OCTOBER 1863, TUESDAY, SPRINGFIELD

~~Saw Cullom & M. Hay. They are not so unfriendly to A. L. as I had been led to suppose. They were in a terrible miff about the appointment of Mark Delahay to the Judgeship in Kansas. They had recommended Jack~~

~~Grimshaw who is outraged at being beaten by Delahay. Still they seem as~~
~~friendly as ever to the President in spite of what they call his faults. Judge~~
~~Logan whom we had been led to give up is not at all copperish.~~[190]

14 OCTOBER 1863, WEDNESDAY

~~Great rejoicing over the Ohio & Pennsylvania elections.~~[191]

17 OCTOBER 1863, SATURDAY, NEW YORK

Saw Marston. He says if Chase would pay a little attention to his damned old paper mill in Washington instead of running around the country electioneering, the finances of the country would be better off.[192]

Denison says C. is working like a beaver—that he sent a special confidential agent to N. Y. the other day. Came to Denison who would not talk with him, saying he was pledged to Lincoln. Says there is a persistent fight between Opdyke and Barney, Chase being with Opdyke as he thinks O. is for him. Says Andrews & Barney are both very inefficient though good men.[193]

Says he is investigating a great and disgraceful fraud perpetrated by Henry B. Stanton. He has been clearing goods for the Southern ports and cancelling their bonds-against-running-blockade, for fees paid in hand. It is a most painful affair, as he has been one of the loudest and most uncompromising Anti Slavery men. His wife has also been very prominent in the Women's Loyal League. Stanton is the chief fugleman of Mr Chase in the Custom House.[194]

D—— says the whole thing is one way in the State of N. Y. Evarts says it is so in Vermont.[195]

[Inserted into the diary is a copy, in Hay's hand, of a letter from Lincoln to Halleck:]

Washington, October 16, 1863

Major General Halleck

I do not believe Lee can have over sixty thousand effective men. Longstreet's corps would not be sent away to bring an equal force back upon the same road. And there is no other direction for them to have come from. Doubtless in making the present movement Lee gathered in all available scraps and added them to Hill's & Ewell's Corps; but that is all. And he made the movement in the belief that *four* corps had left. Gen. Meade; and General Meade's apparently avoiding a collision with him, has confirmed him in that belief. If Gen. Meade can now attack him on a field no worse than equal for us, and will do so with all the skill and courage, which he his officers & men possess, the honor will be his if he succeeds, and the blame mine if he fails.

Yours truly

A. Lincoln

18 OCTOBER 1863, SUNDAY

I arrived in Washington today after an absence of a little more than two weeks.

On presenting myself to the President this morning, I told him what Govr. Dennison had told me. He rejoined by telling me that Gov D had been here and repeated what he had said to me.

I gave him my impression of the ~~unmanly~~ conduct of Mr. C in ~~trying to cut under~~ acting in the way he is doing, instancing what Denison of N. Y. had related. He said "it was very bad taste, but that he had determined to shut his eyes to all these performances: that Chase made a good Secretary and that he would keep him where he is: if he becomes Presdt., all right. I hope we may never have a worse man. I have all along clearly seen his plan of strengthening himself. Whenever he says [sees] that an important matter is troubling me, if I am compelled to decide it in a way to give offense to a man of some influence he always ranges himself in opposition to me and persuades the victim that he has been hardly dealt by and that he (C) would have arranged it very differently. It was so with Gen. Fremont—with Genl. Hunter when I annulled his hasty proclamation—with Gen. Butler when he was recalled from New Orleans—with these Missouri people when they called the other day. I am entirely indifferent as to his success or failure in these schemes, so long as he does his duty as the head of the Treasury Department."[196]

He talked of the Missouri matter and read to me the letter he had written Drake for the Committee. As it will probably be published I forbear synopsis. ~~It is a superb affair,~~ His attitude is perfectly just and frank, courteous but immoveable. He will not be bullied even by his friends. He tries to reason with those infuriated people. The world will hear him if they do not. He read to me a letter which he has today written to Governor Gamble, who it seems, is anxious to have the Presdt. espouse his side of the quarrel and to recognize him as the State Government and use the Federal authority to crush out the Radicals, who, he says, meditate Revolution and civil war in Missouri. The President answering says he will be at all times ready to extend to Missouri the protection guaranteed by the Constitution against domestic violence, whenever he (the Pres.) shall see cause to suspect such violence as imminent. He does not so regard it at present. He thinks the instructions given to Genl. Schofield cover the case.[197]

We got into this vein of talk through my telling him what Joe Gillespie says and what I myself observed, of the tendency of public opinion in the West, almost universally in favor of the Radicals as against the Conservatives in Missouri.[198]

Talking of the military Situation he says Lee probably came up the other day thinking our army weaker than it is and finding his mistake from the fight at Bristow is holding off at present. Rosecrans is all right though somewhat bothered about his supplies.[199]

Tonight as I came in from Dinner the ~~Tycoon~~ President said a despatch had just come in from Meade, in which he says that the enemy has disappeared from in front of him but that he does not know where he is—that he has probably gone in the direction of the Rappahannock.[200]

~~Kent says Count Gurowski has broken with the Tribune Bureau here. He drew a revolver in a furious rage on Hill one evening. Hill wrote him a note forbidding him the office—sent it to him by a messenger who says Adam G. read it carefully & scribbled on the envelope, "I have no time to read this. I have resolved to have nothing more to do with you."~~[201]

19 OCTOBER 1863, MONDAY

The President told me this morning that Rosecrans was to be removed from command of the army at Chattanooga.[202] Thomas is to take his original army and Grant to command the whole force, including Hooker's and Burnside's reinforcements. He says Rosecrans has seemed to lose spirit and nerve since the battle of Chicamauga. I told him that I believed Thomas would fail in attack, like Meade and others. The *vis inertia* which prevents those fellows from running when attacked will prevent them from moving in the initiative.

Dining in company with T. J. Coffey today he says Covode is still in a bewildered state trying to understand why he was beaten for the nomination for Governor & why Bill Mann did not make a better use of the $1000 dollars he gave him to buy delegates. Coffey claims a sort of proprietorship in Covode as he sent him to Congress first.[203]

Coffey says A. L. will be renominated by acclamation.

20 OCTOBER 1863, TUESDAY

Sickles came to my room this morning.[204] He thinks Lee should have been attacked on his last advance. He says the Army of the Potomac has made the usual mistake of waiting for a perfectly sure thing.

He thinks Grant and Rosecrans have won their great successes by disregarding the warnings and the maxims of the books and plunging ahead. The enemy are not prepared for desperate enterprises on our part. They think we can and will proceed deliberately and upon ascertained chances: while hunger and destitution impel them into quick and unexpected dashes. So Chattanooga fell. They had not apprehended an attack there at that time. They argued that the length of the line the broken character of the country and such considerations would keep us quiet for the present. But Rosecrans dashing up ahead spoiled their theory.

I spoke of a Western Brigade plunging over an open field under the direct fire of an earthwork — crossing a slough — cutting through an abattis — and storming the work successfully — thus performing what had been called by good regular officers four impossibilities. Battles are won and campaigns frequently decided by the accomplishment of what seems impossible or absurd.

Andrews says French was very drunk the other day when Sickles went down to the Army & was complaining of political generals cutting in and taking all the credit away from men who had been in service thirty years.[205]

I could not help thinking how much happier Sickles was today sitting curled up in a boyish attitude on my sofa or stumping around my room on his one leg talking pleasantly the while, in the broad sunshine of fame and popular favor, than ever before. He has wiped out by his magnificent record all old stains and stands even in his youth sure of an honored and useful life. One leg is a cheap price to pay for so much of the praise of men and the approval of his own soul conscience.

(good thing about Dug Wallack light at the Serenade)

Dined with Wise and Fox. Wise announced his discovery of the authorship of Miles O'Reilly. Fox seemed a little annoyed. Wise enjoys the articles.[206]

After everybody had gone, Wise spoke sadly about Dahlgren: said he had applied to come home & will probably come. If so he will scarcely go back. Rowan will succeed him, "a fine fellow," Wise says "with the coolness of a hero & the ferocity of a wolf. Dahlgren has been in wretched health, dyspeptic, distraight and overworked. His brain seems to be a little affected. He seems to have lost his continuity of thought. His despatches have lost coherence. The business of the fleet is in chaos. He confides nothing to his officers; sometimes even calls a council of war, & when they come tells them not to talk or he cant sleep. His delicate organization seems giving way under the strain of his position."[207]

Dupont is acting badly, trying to cherish a grievance against the Navy, for which there is no reason as he was relieved at his own request.

I said it seemed as if the Lord was managing this thing so that no vast and overshadowing success of any soldier or sailor should occur, to endanger the new liberty of the people.

"And that nothing that walks on two legs shall hereafter be sold in this land" added Wise, which surprised me as I had not expected to see him yet enrolled among the grand army of the Abolitionists.

Today I induced the President to ~~write~~ sign a letter I wrote to Col. Rowland approving his proposed National Rifle Corps. I think Rowland himself rather a humbug but his idea is a good one.[208]

Fox said today that he was always glad to hear of the rebels getting more arms—that he wanted their whole ablebodied population involved in this business—so that after we whip them they will be whipped finally.

21 OCTOBER 1863, WEDNESDAY

Grow and Usher and the Virginians Chandler and Bowden were in my room this morning and in the other end was Governor Parker of New Jersey and Provost Marshal General Fry. Grow and one of the Virginians began pitching into Seymour and Parker calling them traitors so far as they were not cowards. It seemed likely that there would be a row. Parker was discreetly deaf.[209]

Bibb came in this morning with a couple of very intelligent East Tennesseans. They talked in a very friendly way with the President. I never saw him more at ease than he is with those first rate patriots of the border. He is of them really. They stood up before a map of the Mountain Country and talked war for a good while. They were urging upon the President the importance of a raid through Georgia and North Carolina to cut the Weldon line of railway which will at once isolate the Army of Virginia.[210]

They were full of admiration for the President's way of doing things, and especially for that farsighted military instinct which caused him to recommend last year and urge ineffectually upon Congress the building of a railroad from Louisville to Knoxville and Chattanooga.[211]

Dined with Rogers & Taylor at Wise.[212] Spent evening at Chase's. Pretty Katie spoke a little spitefully about Rosecrans' removal. Her father's old game.

22 OCTOBER 1863, THURSDAY

I spoke to the President today about Blair—his Rockville speech and the action of the Union League of Philadelphia leaving out his name in resolutions electing the Cabinet honorary members of the League. He says Blair is anxious to run Swann and beat Winter Davis. The President on the contrary says that as Davis is the nominee of the Union convention & as we have recognized him as our candidate it would be mean to do anything against him now.[213]

Things in Maryland are badly mixed. The unconditional Union people are not entirely acting in concert. Thomas seems acceptable to every one. Cresswell is going to make a good man. But Schenck is complicating the canvass with an embarrassing element, that of forcible negro enlistments. The President is in favor of the voluntary enlistment of negroes with the consent of their masters & on payment of the price. But Schenck's favorite way (or rather Birney's whom Schenck approves) is to take a ~~file~~ squad of soldiers into a neighborhood, & carry off into the army all the ablebodied darkies they can find without asking master or slave to consent. Hence results like the case of White & Sothoron. "The fact is," the ~~Tycoon~~ President observes, "Schenck is wider across the head in the region of the ears, & loves fight for its own sake, better than I do."[214]

~~Went to the Theatre with Miss Chase. Saw there at Chase's Robert Dale Owen, who is about to go West. The play was "The Pearl of Savoy" and was exquisitely done. It made the statuesque Kate cry like a baby.~~[215]

I dined with Wise. Winthrop, Chandler & some others present. State Rights were severely attacked and Chandler defended them rather lamely I thought, though I am prejudiced. I think that pestilent doctrine has been only fruitful of harm for the last half century and I thank God that this war has [bruised?] its head forever.

23 OCTOBER 1863, FRIDAY

Reverdy Johnson and Dr Stone were talking this morning in my room.[216] They both have relations & affiliations in the South. They get letters of the general hopeless look of the Rebel cause. They think if the President will withdraw his proclamation the South would at once come back to the Union as soon as they could arrange the necessary machinery. Stone said if he did so he would be elected Presdt. by acclamation & Reverdy said if he did not, he was ruined Blind and childish groping after a fact which has been buried. Puerile babble over a ghost of an institution which is as ~~odorously defunct~~ flagrantly dead as was Lazarus.

Schenck & Piatt came in. Piatt defends flatly the forcible enlistment of negroes. Says it will be a most popular measure among the people of Maryland, & unpopular only among the slaveholders & rebel sympathizers. He says that this man Sothoron is a recruiting agent for the rebels & that he would have been in the jug if they had got him as they expected before the murder.[217]

~~Dined at Wise's & after dinner read the Miles OReilly dinner to Fox & Wise. Spent the evening at General Hunters. Heard some almost incredible accounts of Mr K's silliness.~~[218]

24 OCTOBER 1863, SATURDAY

This morning the President said that Dana has continually been telegraphing of Rosecrans anxiety for food but Thomas now telegraphs that there is no trouble on that score. I asked what Dana thought about Rosecrans. He said he agreed that Rosecrans was for the present completely broken down. The President says he is "confused and stunned like a duck hit on the head," ever since Chickamauga.[219]

I saw last night Charlie Dahlgren the Admiral's son who is just from the South. He says you can see the double line of piles in Charleston Harbor at low water and the buoys which designate the torpedoes. That there is but one channell left from Charleston which runs just under the guns of fort Johnson.[220]

Oct. 29. Smith says Com. Ammen went beyond Sumter in a picket boat & saw no piles. *Au contraire.*)

The Admiral has leave of absence but a letter comes from him last night stating that he is entirely well again and fuller of fight than I have seen him before. He denounces the newspapers and says if they hound him on to attack before he is ready they will be the first to denounce him if he fails. Altogether it seems as if we must admit that his career at Port Royal is up to this point a failure, as Gen Terry & Colonel Hawley said this morning at Breakfast. They were very bitter & I thought unjust. I hope Smith will come down here & give me some idea of the way army men feel about the matter.[221]

25 OCTOBER 1863, SUNDAY

Terry and Hawley were here this afternoon and I presented them to the President. They said in answer to his inquiry why Charleston was not shelled that they preferred to save their fire for service against Johnson & Moultrie when the navy moves, rather than burst their guns now by throwing a few Shell into the city. A very sensible conclusion as it appears to me. They had a long talk & came away much pleased with the Tycoon.[222]

Pet Halsted walked up with me. He says the President won over Ames and Brandegee by his friendly candid manner and the fair way in which he met their complaints and requests. He seems to think that Chase is going to pack the Convention.[223]

Puleston came in after Pet had gone, drank a glass of wine and talked. He gave a most graphic account of the way Curtin received the news of Little Mac's letter (against his election as Governor.) Et tu Brute was not a circumstance.[224]

He also gave a very funny account of the way Chase effusively cultivated him the other day, "with Presidency glaring out of both eyes" said the wily Doctor. "Poor devil, he has no more show than that Chair." which remains to be seen.

~~Chase yesterday asked for his young clerk Plantz to be made District Attorney of Florida. A nomination so weak that its purpose is most obvious. I gave the [President my?] impressions about it & he has determined to appoint Ferry of Illinois tomorrow.~~[225]

26 OCTOBER 1863, MONDAY

~~Which he did. Today gave Cutts his reprimand which I attach to this page: rather the mildest cussing on record. The poor devil seems heartbroken. He can scarcely stare one in the face~~

~~The President must pardon & restore Hutton also or seem to side with sneaks and skulkers.~~[226]

Executive Mansion

Washington, October 26, 1863

Although what I am now to say is to be in form a reprimand, it is not intended to add a pang to what you have already suffered upon the subject to which it relates. You have too much of life yet before you, and have shown too much of promise as an officer, for your future to be lightly surrendered. You were convicted of two offences. One of them, not of great enormity, and yet greatly to be avoided, I feel sure you are in no danger of repeating. The other you are not so well assured against. The advice of a father to his son, "Beware of entrance to a quarrel, but being in, bear it that the opposed may beware of thee, is good & yet not the best. Quarrell not at all. No man resolved to make the most of himself can spare time for personal contention. Still less can he afford to take all the consequences including the vitiating of his temper & the loss of self control. Yield larger things to which you can show no more than equal right; and yield lesser ones though clearly yr own. Better give yr. path to a dog than be bitten by him in contesting for the right. Even killing the dog would not cure the bite.

In the mood indicated deal henceforth with your fellow men, and especially with your brother officers; and even the unpleasant events you are passing from will not have been profitless to you.[227]

Sent the Sanitary Fair the autograph of the Proclamation and wrote Boker letter (dated 24) accepting the gold medal and honorary membership of the Philadela Union League.[228]

~~Dined with Fox and Wise. Afterwards visited a wonderful telegraph man named Beardsley & finished the evening with Canterbury & initiating those two innocent youths into the Harveyan mysteries of stewed oysters.~~[229]

27 OCTOBER 1863, TUESDAY

~~I went with Lamon & C. Butler of this town to the races today.~~ *~~Butler won without any special trouble in 2.'30" @ 2.'34".~~*[230]

~~Charley Boteler is an average Washingtonian in some things and much better in others. He spoke most kindly of Lamon's personal popularity with the people here. Says he could be elected Mayor. He spoke also most kindly and respectfully of the President, seeming to regard him as necessarily his own successor. Straws.~~

~~Dined at Wise's with Fox and Capt. Ritchie—a fine handsome young fellow perfectly ignorant of politics but with the most fresh and delightful feelings of patriotism and honor and fine anger at things mean and false. He also seemed to believe thoroughly in the President. As everybody else but those who fear and those who envy.~~[231]

28 OCTOBER 1863, WEDNESDAY

The President today wrote a letter to Schofield in relation [to] his alleged arming of returned rebels in Missouri, in which he said that the government here had done the same thing frequently. He orders Schofield to give attention to the matter, if things are wrong, right them; protect the polls from any interference by either citizens or soldiers.[232]

The President added, "I believe, after all, those Radicals will carry the state & I do not object to it. They are nearer to me than the other side, in thought and sentiment, though bitterly hostile personally. They are utterly lawless—the unhandiest devils ~~fellows~~ in the world to deal with—but after all their faces are set Zionwards."[233]

Lt. Col Smith, A. A. G Dept. of the South, spent the afternoon & evening with me. He thinks Dahlgren is dreadfully broken in health & spirit. That except in the event of the Navy forcing their way in, the army's work is done. That now the only practicable advance is by sapping along the left bank of the Stono, with the gunboats covering our left flank.[234]

Benham has gotten a friend Prof Martin to submit a plan through Sumner of an approach by way of Dewee's Inlet to the North side of the city which Smith says is wholly impracticable by reason of preparations of the enemy.[235]

29 OCTOBER 1863, THURSDAY

I Went down to Willard's today & got from Palmer who is here a free ticket to New York and back for Walt. Whitman the poet who is going to New York to electioneer and vote for the Union ticket.[236]

Saw Garfield & Hunter. Hunter is just starting for the West on a tour of inspection. I would give my chances for ———— to go with him but Nicolay still stays in the sunset & I am here with a ball and chain on my leg.[237]

The President tonight wrote letters to several of the more prominent Senators & [   ] of the Republican States urging them to take care of a supposed plot of Gen. Etheridge.[238]

This crazy Tennessean, who was kindly taken up by the Republicans & made clerk of the House, has turned malignantly Copperhead and now hopes to retain his clerkship by copper votes. His plan for securing to the opposition the organization of the House is to take advantage of a foolish little law passed in the hurry of the concluding days of the last session (approved March 3, 1863) making certain specific requirements for credentials; and to throw out those state delegations which are principally Republican. He will of course post those Governors whose delegations are a majority Democratic & will leave in ignorance those who have a Republican preponderance in their delegation. This matter was suggested to the Presdt. some days ago by a man named Briggs who came with a great show of mystery which I thought humbug and had two audiences of the Presdt.[239] The President has taken occasion to checkmate any such rascality by sending to some of the Governors a specific form gotten up by himself which will cover the case. The members are to bring their ordinary certificates and these supplemental ones are to be procured by their Senators or some such and brought on in case of any such question being made.

Garfield was with the President today. ~~He speaks with much enthusiasm of Steedman at Chickamauga.~~[240] He always mentions Rosecrans with kindness, even tenderness & says he is a man of such fixed convictions as to be frequently unreasonable in holding to them. At the battle of Chickamauga he became convinced that the field was lost & that his place was in the rear. It really seemed so. But when Garfield heard the firing steadily resumed on the left where Thomas was engaged he was convinced that the left still stood & urged Rosecrans to stay & save the field. The General would not listen to such a suggestion & when Garfield begged permission himself to stay & join the battle on the left Rosecrans parted with him as if never expecting to see him again.

I told the ~~Tycoon~~ President that Chase would try to make capital out of this Rosecrans business he laughed & said "I suppose he will, like the blue-bottle fly, lay his eggs in every rotten spot he can find." He seems much amused at Chase's mad hunt after the Presidency. He says it may win. He hopes the country will never do worse.[241]

I said he should not by making all Chase's appointments make himself *particeps criminis.*[242]

He laughed on & said he was sorry the thing had begun, for though the matter did not annoy him his friends insisted that it ought to. He has appointed Ferry tax Comr. for Tennessee & has promised Plantz the District Attorneyship of Florida. ~~I told him Plantz went down with but two ideas, to steal money for himself and votes for Chase.~~ He thinks the matter a devilish good joke. He prefers letting Chase have his own way in these sneaking tricks than getting into a snarl with him by refusing him what he asks.

Wise says that at the time the President made up his mind to provision Fort Sumter he sent Wise to New York to make the necessary preparations. They were to be made quietly. Therefore he got Aspinwall to provide a ship & applied to C H Marshall to provision her. He declined saying it would certainly inaugurate civil war and the publication of the fact would prevent the negotiation of a loan on any terms.[243]

I went tonight to Willards: found there Palmer, Webster, Murphy, Smalley and other New York Republicans. They have been working like beavers & seem in fine feather. They say they shall carry the state without doubt. They have sent home 10,000 men from the army to vote. They say every facility has been afforded them. Surgeon General Barnes has acted they say "like a trump" exerting himself to carry out their wishes. A wonderful change for Barnes, who formerly rejoiced in a very copperish head.[244]

30 OCTOBER 1863, FRIDAY

Dennison came this morning to urge the sending of Rosecrans to Missouri.[245]

Theodore Tilton sends an abusive editorial in the Independent & a letter stating he meant it in no unkindliness.[246]

I spent the evening at Dahlgrens—took Col. Ned Smith up with me. There were there the Duchess Lucignano and Captain de Lacy of the Italian Army, Miss Dahlgren Miss Maury & Mrs. Goddard.[247]

The President & Mrs Lincoln went to see Fanchon.[248] About midnight the President came in. I told him about Dennison's note and asked if D——— had not always been a Chase man. He said "Yes until recently but he seems now anxious for my reelection."

I said Opdyke was expected here today & told the President the story of Palmer and Opdyke. He went on and gave me the whole history of the visit they made to Springfield Barney Opdyke & Hogeboom—of the appointment of Barney—of the way Opdyke rode him—of his final protest & the break.[249]

I said "Opdyke now was determined to have the Custom House cleaned out"[250]

"He will have a good time doing it"

He went on telling the history of the Senate raid on Seward—how he had & could have no adviser on that subject & must work it out by himself—how he thought deeply on the matter—& it occurred to him that the way to settle it was to force certain men to say to the Senators *Here* what they would not say elsewhere. He confronted the Senate & the Cabinet. He gave the whole history of the affair of Seward & his conduct & the assembled Cabinet listened & confirmed all he said.

"I do not now see how it could have been done better. I am sure it was right. If I had yielded to that storm & dismissed Seward the thing would all have slumped over one way & we should have been left with a scanty handful of supporters. When Chase sent in his resignation I saw that the game was in my own hands & I put it through. When I had settled this important business at last with much labor & to entire satisfaction into my room one day walked D. D. Field & George Opdyke and began a new attack upon me to force me to remove Seward. For once in my life I rather gave my temper the rein and I talked to those men pretty Damned plainly. Opdyke may be right in being cool to me. I may have given him reason this morning."[251]

I wish they would stop thrusting that subject of the Presidency into my face. I dont want to hear anything about it. The Republican of today has an offensive paragraph in regard to an alleged nomination of me by the mass meeting in New York last night.

Received a more than usually Asinine letter from Stoddard who is in New York stock Jobbing & writes to me pretending he is working for the election.[252]

1 NOVEMBER 1863, SUNDAY

Spent the Sunday on the Potomac with Wise Fox Ammen Ives Horwitz Faxon Chad.[253]

This evening Genl. Schenck, accompanied by Genl. Garfield & Judge Kelley came in to insist upon some order which would prevent disloyal people from voting at the ensuing Maryland election. Before going into the President's room (Kelley & Garfield sitting with me in the ante room) Kelley spoke very bitterly of Blair's working against the Union party in Maryland.[254]

After they were gone I handed the President Blair's Rockville speech, telling him I had read it carefully, and saving a few intemperate and unwise personal expressions against leading Republicans which might better have been omitted, I saw nothing in the speech which could have given rise to such violent criticism.[255]

"Really" says the President "the controversy between the two sets of men, represented by him and by Mr. Sumner is one of mere form and little else. I do not think Mr Blair would agree that the states in rebellion are to be permitted to come at once into the political family & renew the very performances which have already so bedeviled us. I do not think Mr. Sumner would insist that when the loyal people of a state obtain the supremacy in their councils & are ready to assume the direction of their own affairs, that they should be excluded. I do not understand Mr. Blair to admit that

Jefferson Davis may take his seat in Congress again as a Representative of his people; I do not understand Mr Sumner to assert that John Minor Botts may not.[256] So far as I understand Mr Sumner he seems in favor of Congress taking from the Executive the power it at present exercises over insurrectionary districts, and assuming it to itself. But when the vital question arises as to the right and privilege of the people of these states to govern themselves, I apprehend there will be little difference among loyal men. The question at once is presented in whom this power is vested. And the practical matter for decision is how to keep the rebellious populations from overwhelming and outvoting the loyal minority."

I asked him if Blair was really opposed to our Union ticket in Maryland. He said he did not know anything about it—had never asked: he says Crisfield plainly told him he was opposed to the Administration.[257]

I spoke of Fox having said that Union men must divide on the question of the Blair and Sumner theories & that I could see no necessity for it. He agreed. He says Montgomery Blair came to him today to say that Frank has no idea or intention of running for Speaker—that Frank wishes to know what the President desires him to do & he will do it. The President will write to Frank his ideas of the best thing to do: for Frank to come here at opening of Congress: say publicly he is not candidate for Speaker: assist in organization of the House on Union basis & then go back to the field.

If Frank Blair does that, it will be the best thing for his own fame he has recently done. He is a glorious fellow & it is pitiable to see him the pet of traitors or lukewarm loyalists in Mo, and attacked abused and vilified by his old friends and adherents.

I was pleased to learn from the President tonight that the Eleventh Corps did specially well in Hooker's night battle on the Tennessee.[258]

2 NOVEMBER 1863, MONDAY

This morning I met Kelley at Willard's at Breakfast. He resumed the subject of his last nights talk about Blair. He says there is a combination on foot to make Blair Speaker and Etheridge Clerk: That Pendleton was already out of the field: and that Etheridge was betting money liberally on Blair.[259] I told him Blair was not a party to that arrangement or any such. As he seemed to insinuate his fears that the administration favored some such thing I told him I was for Colfax all the time & I believed the President was decidedly though he would think it highly indecorous for him to interfere in the matter.

Kelley says that he has no part in any Presidential intrigue: that he would prefer Abraham Lincoln for his own successor to any one: that he would be grieved if by the course of the Government itself he should be forced into an attitude of seeming hostility.

I came up and told Presdt. the wrong and injurious impressions Kelley had & he asked to see Kelley. I found him closeted with Garfield & Whitelaw Reid, who seemed a little disgruntled at my abrupt requisition. He came up with me talking in his effusive and intensely egotistic way about the canvass he had been making & speaking most bitterly of Blairs Rockville Speech. He went in and talked an hour with the President.[260]

After him came Schenck and the President fixed up a letter to Bradford about Schenck's election order, in which while he guaranteed to all loyal people the right of voting for whom they pleased he strongly intimates that the loyalty of the candidates is not a sufficient safeguard—that men elected by disloyal votes are not wholly to be trusted.[261]

I saw Sam: Wilkeson today. He tells me he assisted at a somewhat formal conference of political people yesterday and the unanimous conclusion was that the Union nominee for the next Presidency must be Abraham Lincoln. And that as a necessary condition of reelection a reorganization of the cabinet must be made. The feeling of the country on this matter demands it. He laid his finger mysteriously on his lips and flitted like an elderly owl into the Treasury Department.[262]

The President says Butler has been tendered Foster's Department while Foster goes to relieve Burnside, who resigns. It is not yet known whether Butler will accept.[263]

I asked about Rosecrans. The President says he sees no immediate prospect of assigning him to command: that he had thought, when the trouble and row of this election in Missouri is over, and the matter will not be misconstrued, of sending Rosecrans to Missouri and Schofield into the field. He says that it was because of Grant's opposition that Rosecrans is not in the Army of the Cumberland: when it was decided to place Grant in command of the whole Military division, two sets of orders were made out, one contemplating Rosecrans' retention of the command of his own army & the other his relief. Grant was to determine that question for himself. He said at once that he preferred Rosecrans should be relieved—that he (R) never would obey orders. This consideration of course involves a doubt as to whether Rosecrans should be placed in command of a district from which Grant must to a certain extent derive supplies & reinforcements, on occasion.

Tonight Schenck sent for copies of the correspondence between the Presdt. and Bradford. The ~~Tycoon~~ President came into ~~my~~ his room with the despatch in his hands, clad in an overcoat pure & simple reaching to his knees & sleepily fumbled for the papers in his desk till he found them & travelled back to bed. I took the ~~screeds~~ letters to the telegraph office & sent them off about midnight.[264]

3 NOVEMBER 1863, TUESDAY

Judge Cartter was in my room this morning talking about Butler. "I am glad he is going there. He will have N. C. in the Union before frost is out of the ground. He is the smartest damned rascal that ever lived. He grovelled in the dirt for years, cutting under everybody in the race of degradation till they got tired of following him; rolled himself in the dust, eating dirt, vainly working to get lower; and when he rose from his wallowing & shook from him the filth of his life's contamination, he stood head & shoulders above everybody."

"At the Charleston convention he went out of sight; the Devil got ashamed to own him."

He says Butler assigns as a reason for his former proslavery record that he wanted to run the thing into the ground & disgust his own party. Credat Judaeus.

Passed the evening in the telegraph office reading the returns. Found on arriving there that Stanton and the President were a little dubious about the result. But they afterwards discovered an error in their calculations which corrected evidently gave them the state. Sanford's last telegram assured them of success.[265]

Stanton said the disheartening thing in the affair was that there seemed to be no patriotic principle left in the Democratic party: the whole organization voting, as solidly as usual, against the country.

4 November 1863, Wednesday

Very anxious all day about Maryland. ~~Dined with Plantz and Stickney.~~[266]

5 November 1863, Thursday

Maryland all right. Nicolay returned this morning from the West.[267] We spent the evening at a small party given by Mrs Goddard for the Duchess of Lucignano.

I rode in the afternoon over to Georgetown Heights with A. S.

7 November 1863, Saturday

The President passed the morning in disposing of cases of Courts Martial with the Judge Advocate Genl.

Gen Butler called this morning to report on his way to assume command at Ft Monroe. Nicolay & I spent the evening at Sec. Chases.

8 November 1863, Sunday

The President tells me that Meade is at last after the enemy and that Grant will attack tomorrow.[268]

Went with Mrs Ames to Gardner's gallery & were soon joined by Nico & the Prest. We had a great many pictures taken. Some of the Presdt. the best I have seen. Nico & I immortalized ourselves by having ourselves done in group with the Presdt.

In the evening Seward came in. He feels much easier about his son. He is very easy and confident now about affairs. He says N. Y. is safe for the Presidential election by a much larger majority: that the crowd that follows power have come over: that the Copperhead spirit is crushed and humbled. He says the Democrats lost their leaders when Toombs & Davis & Breckenridge forsook them and went South: that their new leaders, the Seymours Vallandighams & Woods are now whipped and routed.[269] So that they have nothing left. The Democratic leaders are either ruined by the war or have taken the right shoot & have saved themselves from the ruin of their party by coming out on the right side.

No party can survive an opposition to a war. The Revolutionary heroes were political oracles till 1812 and afterwards the soldiers of the latter war succeeded to their honors. They were a small & exclusive class But we are hereafter a nation of soldiers. These people will be trying to forget years hence that they ever opposed this war. I had to carry affidavits to prove I had nothing to do with the Hartford Convention. Now that party that gained eminence by the folly of the Federalists in opposing the war have the chalice commended to their own lips.

He told the Democratic party how they might have saved themselves & their organization & with it the coming presidential election—by being more loyal and earnest in support of the Administration than the Republican party—which would not be hard, the Lord knows.

Hill Lamon tonight read us a slip from the Chicago Tribune in which they very strongly advocate A. L. for his own successor, an utterance, Hill says, stimulated by the prospect of a new Administration paper being started in Chicago pledged against grumbling.

Spent the evening at Butler's rooms at Willard's. Nice wife & very pretty daughter. Butler went away early in the evening after a discharge of bile at Mercier.[270]

9 NOVEMBER 1863, MONDAY

Spent the evening at the theatre with the President Mrs Lincoln, Mrs Hunter Cameron and Nicolay. J Wilkes Booth was doing the "Marble Heart." Rather tame than otherwise.[271]

10 NOVEMBER 1863, TUESDAY

Went to Mt. Vernon with an excursion I had gotten up for Miss Chase's bridesmaids. The party was Mrs Ames Mrs Lander, Miss N. Chase, Miss Nichols, Miss Skinner, Albrecht & Bates, Capt. Ives, Johnson, Ritchie, who backed out before starting Nicolay, Maj. Garrard & myself.[272]

In the evening called to see Mrs Goddard and the duchess Lucignano.

11 NOVEMBER 1863, WEDNESDAY

Went to the Capitol this afternoon & looked at some pictures.

In the evening went to the theatre with Ulric Dahlgren Stahel Kent &

Kirkland to see Wilkes Booth in Romeo. Wheatly took all the honors away as Mercutio. Went to Harveys & afterwards to Willard's ~~and drank a good deal~~. Dahlgren was very funny by the onelegged enterprise he displayed in making a night of it.[273]

Finished the evening by a serenade of Miss Chase by the band of 17th Infantry.

12 NOVEMBER 1863, THURSDAY

Genl. Schenck came in this morning with Davis Cresswell Evans Hoffman & others of the Maryland Emancipationists.[274] He is a little severe on Bradford & Reverdy Johnson for their recent demonstrations in Maryland. Told a very good story on Corwin & Congressional service.

Hanscom had a long yarn to tell me this morning about Chase's complicity with the enormous jobbing in the Treasury Dept.

In the evening Miss Chase & Govr. Sprague's wedding. A very brilliant looking party. Kate looked tired out and languid especially at the close of the evening when I went into the bridal chamber to say Goodnight. She had lost all her old severity & formal stiffness of manner, & seemed to think she had *arrived*. McDowell Stahel Schenck Stoneman Cameron and other present. The President came for a few minutes.[275]

18 NOVEMBER 1863, WEDNESDAY

We started from Washington to go to the Consecration of the Soldiers' Cemetery at Gettysburg. On our train were the President Seward Usher & Blair: Nicolay & Myself: Mercier & Admiral Reynaud; Bertinatti & Capt. Isola & Lt. Martinez & Cora: Mrs Wise: Wayne McVeagh: McDougal of Canada and one or two others.[276] We had a pleasant sort of a trip. At Baltimore Schenck's staff joined us.

Just before we arrived at Gettysburg the President got into a little talk with McVeagh about Missouri affairs. McV. talked radicalism until he learned that he was talking recklessly. The President disavowed any knowledge of the Edwards case, said that Bates said to him, as indeed he said to me, that Edwards was inefficient and must be removed for that reason.[277]

At Gettysburg the President went to Mr. Wills who expected him and our party broke like a drop of quicksilver spilt. McVeagh young Stanton & I foraged around for a while—walked out to the College got a chafing dish of oysters then some supper and finally loafing around to the Court House where Lamon was holding a meeting of Marshals, we found Forney and went around to his place Mr. Fahnestocks and drank a little whiskey with him. He had been drinking a good deal during the day and was getting to feel a little ugly and dangerous. He was particularly bitter on Montgomery Blair. McVeagh was telling him that he pitched into the ~~Tycoon~~ President coming up and told him some truths. He said the President got a good deal of that from time to time and needed it.[278]

He says "Hay you are a fortunate man. You have kept yourself aloof from your office. I know an old fellow now seventy who was Private Secretary to Madison. He has lived ever since on its recollection. He thought there was something solemn and memorable in it. Hay has laughed through his term."

He talked very strangely referring to the affectionate and loyal support which he and Curtin had given to the President in Pennsylvania: with references from himself and others to the favors that had been shown the Cameron party whom they regard as their natural enemies. Forney seems identified fully now with the Curtin interest, though when Curtin was nominated he called him a heavy weight to carry and said that Cameron's foolish attack nominated him.[279]

We went out after a while following the music to hear the serenades. The President appeared at the door said half a dozen words meaning nothing & went in.[280] Seward who was staying around the corner at Harper's was called out and spoke so indistinctly that I did not hear a word of what he was saying. Forney and McVeagh were still growling about Blair.

We went back to Forney's room having picked up Nicolay and drank more whiskey. Nicolay sung his little song of the "Three Thieves" and we then sung John Brown. At last we proposed that Forney should make a speech and two or three started out Shannon and Behan and Nicolay to get a band to serenade him.[281] I staid with him. So did Stanton and McVeagh. He still growled quietly and I thought he was going to do something imprudent. He said if I speak, I will speak my mind. The music sounded in the street and the fuglers came rushing up imploring him to come down. He smiled quietly told them to keep cool and asked "are the recorders there." "I suppose so of course" shouted the fugler. "Ascertain" said the imperturbable Forney. "Hay, we'll take a drink." They shouted and begged him to come down The thing would be a failure—it would be his fault &c. "Are the recorders congenial?" he calmly insisted on knowing.

Somebody commended prudence He said sternly "I am always prudent."
I walked down stairs with him.

The crowd was large and clamorous. The fuglers stood by the door in
an agony. The reporters squatted at a little stand in the entry. Forney stood
on the Threshold, John Young & I by him.[282] The crowd shouted as the
door opened. Forney said "My friends, these are the first hearty cheers I
have heard tonight. You gave no such cheers to your President down the
street. Do you know what you owe to that Great man? You owe your country—you owe your name as American citizens."

He went on blackguarding the crowd for their apathy & then diverged
to his own record saying he had been for Lincoln in his heart in 1860—that
open advocacy was not as effectual as the course he took—dividing the
most corrupt organization that ever existed—the proslavery Dem. Party.
He dwelt at length on this question and then went back to the eulogy of
the President that great, wonderful mysterious inexplicable man: who
holds in his single hands the reins of the republic: who keeps his own counsels: who does his own purpose in his own way no matter what temporiz-
ing minister in his cabinet sets himself up in opposition to the progress of
the age.

And very much of this.

After him Wayne McVeagh made a most touching and beautiful speech
of five minutes and Judge Shannon of Pittsburg spoke effectively and ac-
ceptably to the people.

"That speech must not be written out yet" says Young. He will see further about it, when he gets sober," as we went up stairs. We sang John
Brown and went home

[19 NOVEMBER 1863, THURSDAY]

In the morning I got a beast and rode out with the President's suite to
the Cemetery in the procession. The procession formed itself in an or-
phanly sort of way & moved out with very little help from anybody & after
a little delay Mr. Everett took his place on the stand—And Mr Stockton
made a prayer which thought it was an oration[283]—and Mr Everett spoke
as he always does perfectly—and the President in a firm free way, with
more grace than is his wont said his half dozen ~~words~~ lines of consecration and the music wailed and we went home through crowded and cheering streets. And all the particulars are in the daily papers.

I met Genl. Cameron after coming in and he McV. and I went down to dinner on board the railroad U. C. R. R. car. I was more than usually struck by the intimate, jovial relations that exist between men that hate and detest each other as cordially as do those Pennsylvania politicians. We came home the night of the 19th.

20 NOVEMBER 1863, FRIDAY

The President called me today & read the following letter which he had written in answer to one from Chandler of Michigan blackguarding Seward Weed Blair & entreating him to stand firm and other trash which lunatics of that sort think is earnest and radical, the immediate cause of this righteous outburst being a paragraph from some newspaper stating that Morgan & Weed were in Washington urging upon the President a conservative policy for his Message.[284]

Ex. Man.
Washn.
Nov. 20, 1863

Hon Z Chandler

My Dear Sir

Your letter of the 15th marked "*private*" was received today. I have seen Govr. Morgan & Thurlow Weed separately but not together, within the last ten days; but neither of them mentioned the forthcoming message or said anything so far as I can remember, which brought the thought of the message to my mind.

I am very glad the elections this autumn have gone favorably and that I have not by native depravity, or under evil influences, done anything bad enough to prevent the good result.

I hope to stand firm enough to not go backward, and yet not go forward fast enough to wreck the country's cause.

Yours truly,

He has also written a short letter to Mr Everett in reply to one from Mr E. containing (both letters) mutual congratulations & civilities about the Gettysburg business.[285]

21 November 1863, Saturday

Schuyler Colfax was here last night. He is very sanguine about the Speakership: in fact almost absolutely certain about it. ~~He says Blair~~ He was talking to the President this evening about the matter Nicolay & I being present. He says there is some fear that Gen Etheridge may attempt some outrageous swindle for the purpose of throwing out the Maryland votes by Gov. Bradford's aid. But does not think it will succeed.[286]

He then related an interview between himself and Montgomery Blair. He had heard Blair was against him & so said he "I went to see Blair about it. He said he was against me. I said I was glad to know where he stood: that I remembered two years ago when Frank was a candidate, when I could have been elected I declined in Frank's favor and worked for him— that M. B. then assured me that I should have their lifelong gratitude: that if this was a specimen of it I would give them a receipt in full. He said matters had changed since then—that I was now running as a Chase candidate. I said I was not running as a Presidential candidate at all: that the Presidential question should not be mixed up with the current questions of the day. That I did not call on him except to ascertain his position and to tell him he was free from that debt of lifelong gratitude. Now what I would not say to him, I will say to you, Mr. President.[287]

"Dont say anything to me you do not wish to say" said the ~~Tycoon~~ President.

Said Schuyler "I wish only to say that wherever I have been this summer I have ~~heard nothing but~~ seen the evidences of a very powerful popular feeling in your favor and that I think it will continue unless you do something to check it in your message or public utterances or acts this winter.

After a while Nicolay & I left them & they talked for an hour or so longer. Colfax came out and talked freely for a while. He does not fully commit himself but he talks fairly enough and I think will be all right in the coming fight.

22 November 1863, Sunday

Judd was in our rooms this morning We had a good deal of talk about things in general. He is restless and unhappy in Europe. He feels so thoroughly at home in our politics that it seems a banishment to be out of the whirl.[288]

He was recalling with immense delight his two great political feats of getting the Convention at Chicago & then seating the Convention.

This evening Seward read to the President a despatch from Cash. Clay in which he discussed the whole field of American politics—European diplomacy—and the naval improvements of the century. This man is certainly the most wonderful ass of the age. He recently sent a despatch to Seward criticizing in his usual abusive and arrogant style the late Oration of Sumner on Foreign Relations, concluding in regular diplomatic style by saying "you will read this to Mr. Sumner and if he desires it, give him a copy."[289]

Seward says "It is saddening to think of the effect of prosperity on such a man. Had not we succeeded and he prospered he would always have been known as a brave sincere selfsacrificing and eloquent orator. I went all the way to Kentucky to see and to encourage him. It is prosperity that has developed that fearful underlying vanity that poisons his whole character."

I asked Mr Seward if he had heard of the three Revolutions of Matamoras of which we have been talking today.[290] He said "Yes, I have received a despatch about it from Govr. Banks. I am surprised that a man so sagacious and cautious should have been on the point of doing so imprudent a thing."

"He was about to fire on them, then?" said the Presdt.

"Yes" said Seward "Our consul at Matamoras asked for protection and he brought his guns to bear on the castle for that purpose. I wrote to him at once that that would be war. That if our consul wanted protection he must come to Brownsville for it. Firing upon the town would involve us in a war with the Lord knows who.

"Or rather" said the ~~Tycoon~~ President "the Lord knows who not."

I happened to mention the Proclamation of Emancipation and Seward said "One half the world are continually busying themselves for the purpose of accomplishing Proclamations & Declarations of War &c which they leave to the other half to carry out. Purposes can usually better be accomplished without proclamations. And failures are less signal when not preceded by sounding promises.

The slave states seem inclined to save us any further trouble in that way" he continued. "Their best men are making up their minds that the thing is dead. Bramlette has written an admirable letter in answer to some slaveholders who ask him how he a proslavery man can support a war whose result will be the abolition of slavery. He tells them the war must be prosecuted no matter what the result: that it will probably be the destruction of slavery & he will not fight against it nor greatly care to see the institution ended."[291]

The President added, as another cheering incident from Kentucky, that Jerry Boyle had asked for permission to enlist three thousand negroes for teamsters paying them wages and promising them freedom.[292]

The President is very anxious about Burnside.[293]

23 NOVEMBER 1863, MONDAY

Got news tonight of Grant's advance on the enemy at Chattanooga & Thomas success. The President who had been a little despondent abt Grant took heart again.

Nicolay went tonight to New York.

24 NOVEMBER 1863, TUESDAY

A very remarkable editorial appeared this morning in the Baltimore American under the title, "Shall the Gulf States be allowed to retain a remnant of slavery?", arguing that as there has been a very large increase of the number of slaves in the South which I add here.[294] I took it in to the President to show it to him. He said he did not entirely agree with that view. He thinks that the enormous influx of slave population into the Gulf states does not strengthen slavery in them. He says, "It creates in those states a vast preponderance of the population of a servile and oppressed class. It fearfully imperils the lives and safety of the ruling class. Now, the slaves are quiet, choosing rather to wait for the deliverance they hope from us, rather than endanger their lives by a frantic struggle for freedom. The society of the Southern states is now constituted on a basis entirely military. It would be easier now than formerly, to repress a rising of unarmed and uneducated slaves. But if they should succeed in secession the Gulf states would be more endangered than ever. The slaves, despairing of liberty through us would take the matter into their own hands, and no longer opposed by the government of the United States they would succeed. When the Democrats of Tennessee continually asserted in their canvass of 56 that Fremont's election would free the negroes, though they did not believe it themselves, their slaves did: and as soon as the news of Fremont's defeat came to the plantations the disappointment of the slaves flashed into insurrection.

Casey & Webster of Md. were in my room today.[295] It is the most encouraging thing in the world in consideration of the thick complications of the time to see these slave state fellows thoroughly emancipated from the influence of a lifelong superstition in relation to this Mud God Slavery. Casey has some good ideas about reconstruction, which are the result of careful observation. He says that some of the bitterest rebels are beginning to acquiesce in the necessity of submission. That having submitted themselves, it is a point of honor to preach that doctrine, both to justify themselves & induce others to do likewise: and men soon begin to believe what they pertinaciously preach.

He explains the attitude of Kentucky on the slavery question by showing how in all the other border states, the element of enterprise and energy remains in them or comes to them. But in Kentucky the flower of her life has gone out to Illinois & Indiana & Missouri—Her young ambitious liberal men—and left the decayed branches of old proslavery houses still there supreme. Yet even in those dry bones there is agitation and a man may today talk freely in a way that would have insured a tarry-feathery outfit a year or two ago.

Tonight the President said he was much relieved at hearing from Foster that there was firing at Knoxville yesterday (Nov. 23d). He said anything showing Burnside was not overwhelmed was cheering: Like Sallie Carter when she heard one of her children squall would say "There goes one of my young uns, not dead yet, bless the Lord."[296]

26 NOVEMBER 1863, THURSDAY

Thanksgiving Day to which Grant's despatches this morning give glorious significance.[297]

I heard a sermon from Dr. Hall in which he argued that our national troubles originated from a spirit of anarchy—that the affliction will not have been in vain if the war begets reverence for law.[298]

The President quite unwell.[299]

I took tea at Wise's. Mr. Everett is there.

Coming home had some talk with Sec'y Watson. He says the rebels steal the stores we send our prisoners at Richmond. He also read to me the despatches just received from Dana giving a glowing account of that miraculous charge up Mission Ridge. It was Titanic.

27 NOVEMBER 1863, FRIDAY

I dined today at Wise's with Mr. Everett. He is a very delightful old gentleman in his personal and family relations. His talk to his grandchildren was very winning and graceful.

28 NOVEMBER 1863, SATURDAY

The Secretary of State came in this morning and gave me his contribution to the President's Message, relating exclusively to foreign affairs.

He then said he had a matter to submit, which was strictly confidential. "I saw a great while ago that the President was being urged to do many things which were to redound to the benefit of other men, he taking the responsibility and the risk. I preferred to leave to these men the attitude they coveted, of running before and shouting for the coming events: I preferred to stay behind, to do with and for the President what seemed best, to share with him the criticism and the risk and to leave the glory to him and to God.

Among other measures to unite good men and to divide the opposition was the Loyal League Associations of the country. I saw very early that they would be valuable in bringing over to our side the honest War Democrats and I therefore encouraged them as far as possible with my influence and my money. Soon I discovered a wheel within this enterprise—a secret Know Nothing Masonic order with signs and pass words. They asked me for money. They sent to me from California for charters. Not to make trouble I complied with all requests. You will see for what purpose this machine is being used." Here he handed me a scrap of paper on which was scrawled in Thurlow Weed's handwriting "Loyal Leagues, into which Odd Fellows and Know Nothings rush, are fixing to control delegate appointments for Mr. Chase." Seward, still scribbling said "If you want to be cheated, join a secret society. They are all swindles. If I have an idiosyncrasy, it is a hatred of Secrets. The Consul at London tells me that he has received trustworthy information of an alliance between France and the Rebels: But his sources of information being secret he cannot give his authority. I answer asking him what right he has to have a secret from the President, concerning public affairs, and directing him to lay his information, whatever it may be before the American Minister at London."[300]

He handed me a paper upon which he had copied this extract. "The more I reflect, the less I am inclined to trust the Pa proposition. The public men of that state are queer."

I am to give both to the Presdt.

Wayne McVeagh was here this morning. I took him into my private room and we wet our whistles. And talked politics. Wayne is very bitter against Blair: especially for having insulted Curtin by removing a Postmaster for favoring his election and assigning that as the only reason for doing so. Correy Walborn's sister being appd. in his place at Middletown. (It seems on investigation that Blair did not assign any such reason for his action; but alleged that the P. M. was removed (as he was appointed) at the request of Gen. Cameron.)[301] Wayne says the President will be reelected *if* he turns Blair out of the Cabinet, but with that dead weight we cant carry Pennsylvania. He says Chase is at work night and day, laying pipe.

Bowen tells me that Chase sent for Tilton and manipulated him "all a summer's day" to get his influence in the Independent for him. But Tilton vain and shallow as he is, was disgusted, and went home and wrote a strong Lincoln article.[302]

Defrees gives some amusing incidents of his energetic electioneering.[303]

I sat by Gen. Spinner today at dinner. He says Fernando Wood sought an interview with the Secretary of the Treasury today and talked with him in private. The Secretary says he gave in his adhesion and announced his intention of supporting the administration in all its war measures—"and the Secretary sucked it all in" added the General.

Sunset Cox, it is said, is also now on the war path, and all the foul birds that have [been] croaking treason all the summer, are flapping their unclean wings about holy places and trying to roost under the National Aegis.

[9 December 1863, Wednesday]

The exciting canvass for Speaker closed on Saturday night 5th December, by Washburne withdrawing and Colfax being nominated by acclamation. All day Sunday there was great excitement about Etheridge's course of action. He seemed at the close to grow nervous and shaky to lose the defiant air with which he had started out and to assume a complaining and injured tone—saying he was only obeying the law—he did not see the reason why the Republicans should be so vindictive against him.[304]

The President sent for Colfax. I went for him and as we were riding up from the National I referred to the attempts which were making to identify him with the Chase interest. He characterized them as unjust and unfounded and said that with as much justice Washburne could be called the Grant candidate.[305]

Lovejoy was in my room a good part of Sunday morning in his finest vein. He avows the deepest faith in A. L. and the firmest adherence, though there is nothing subservient about it. He made a mauvaise plaisanterie about Miss Dickinson which considering the man and the day was startling. Lovejoy says he is going in, and is going to vote, and if it comes to a question of muscle he can whip Etheridge.[306]

Monday morning the 7th, we went up expecting a taste of a scrimmage but were disappointed. Etheridge was very quiet and reasonable. He left off a large number of names but entertained the motion to put them on the rolls when it was made, contrary to the protest of J. C. Allen of Illinois. Everything went on properly then. The vote was taken showing 20 majority on the side of the Government, Odell and Stuart and Morrison and a few others of whom better things were expected voting wrong. When this was over Washburne nominated Colfax for Speaker and a round of applause burst from the galleries. Pendleton nominated Cox and a shower of hisses came from the critics above. A singular contrast with the voices of the celestials a few years ago.[307]

Colfax was elected & made a neat speech, & we went home.

On Tuesday 8th the house organized and the joint committees waited on the President, but Usher had changed the rhetoric of his paragraph in the Message, spoiled eight pages of matter & forced the Message over till the next day.

Wednesday we went up with the document and it was read. We watched the effect with great anxiety.[308]

Whatever may be the results or the verdict of history the immediate effect of this paper is something wonderful. I never have seen such an effect produced by a public document. Men acted as if the Millennium had come. Chandler was delighted, Sumner was beaming, while at the other political pole Dixon & Reverdy Johnson said it was highly satisfactory.[309] Forney said "We only wanted a leader to speak the bold word. It is done and all can follow. I shall speak in my two papers tomorrow in a way to make these Presidential aspirants squirm." Henry Wilson came to me and laying his broad palms on my shoulders said "The President has struck another great blow. Tell him from me God Bless him."

In the House the effect was the same. Boutwell was looking over it quietly & saying, It is a very able and shrewd paper. It has great points of popularity: & it is right." Lovejoy seemed to see on the mountains the feet of one bringing good tidings. He said it was glorious. I shall live he said to see slavery ended in America" Garfield says, quietly, as he says things, "The President has struck a great blow for the country and himself." Kellogg of Michigan was superlatively ~~enthused~~ enthusiastic. He said "The President is the only man. He is the great man of the century. There is none like him in the world. He sees more widely and more clearly than anybody."[310]

Judd was there watching with his glittering eyes the effect of his great leaders word. He was satisfied with the look of things. Said Lovejoy, Some of Lincoln's friends disagreed with him for saying 'a house divided &c.' "I did" said Judd. "I told him if we had seen the speech we would have cut that out." "Would you" said Lincoln. "In five years he is vindicated."[311]

Henry T. Blow said, "God Bless Old Abe. I am one of the Radicals who have always believed in the President." He went on to talk with me about the feeling of the Missouri Radicals. That they must be reconciled to the President. That they are natural allies. That they have nowhere to go out of the Republican party, that a little proper treatment would heal all trouble as already a better feeling is developing. He thinks the promotion of Osterhaus would have a good effect.[312]

Horace Greeley went so far as to say it was "Devilish good!"[313]

All day the tide of congratulation ran on. Many called to pay their personal respects. All seemed to be frankly enthusiastic. Gurley of Iowa came and spent several hours talking matters over. He says there are but two or three points that can prevent the renomination of Mr Lincoln: Gen Halleck: the Missouri business: Blair may be the weapons which in the hands of the Radical and reckless German element, may succeed in packing a convention against him.[314]

In the evening Judd & Usher and Nicolay and I were talking politics and blackguarding our friends in the Council Chamber. A great deal had been said about the folly of the Edwards-Bates letter—the Rockville Blair Speech—&c. when the President came in. They at once opened on him and after some talk he settled down to give his ideas about the Blair business: he said

"The Blairs have to an unusual degree the spirit of clan. Their family is a close corporation. Frank is their hope and pride. They have a way of going with a rush for anything they undertake: especially have Montgomery and the Old Gentleman. When this war first began they could think of nothing but Fremont: they expected everything from him and upon their earnest solicitation he was made a general and sent to Mo. I thought well of Fremont. Even now I think well of his impulses. I only think he is the prey of wicked and designing men and I think he has absolutely no military capacity. He went to Missouri the pet and protégé of the Blairs. At first they corresponded with him and with Frank, who was with him, fully and confidently thinking his plans and his efforts wd. accomplish great things for the country. At last the tone of Frank's letters changed. It was a change from confidence to doubt and uncertainty. They were pervaded with a tone of sincere sorrow, and of fear that Fremont would fail. Montgomery showed them to me and we were both grieved at the prospect. Soon came the news that Fremont had issued his Emancipation order and had set up a bureau of Abolition giving free papers and occupying his time apparently with little else. At last, at my suggestion, Montgomery Blair went to Missouri to look at and talk over matters. He went as the friend of Fremont. I sent him as Fremont's friend. He passed on the way Mrs. Fremont coming to see me. She sought an audience with me at midnight and taxed me so violently with many things that I had to exercise all the awkward tact I have to avoid quarrelling with her. She surprised me by asking why their enemy Monty Blair had been sent to Missouri? She more than once intimated that if Gen Fremont should conclude to try conclusions with me he could set up for himself."[315]

(Judd says "it is pretty clearly proven that Fremont had at that time concluded that the Union was definitely destroyed and that he should set up an independent Government as soon as he took Memphis and organized his army.")

"The next we heard was that Fremont had arrested Frank Blair and the rupture has since never been healed.

"During Fremont's time the Missouri Democrat which had always been Blair's organ was bought up by Fremont and turned against Frank Blair.

This took away from Frank, after his final break with Fremont, the bulk of the strength which had always elected him. This left him ashore. To be elected in this state of things he must seek for votes outside of the Republican organization. He had pretty hard trimming and cutting to do this consistently. It is this necessity as it appears to me, of finding some ground for Frank to stand on that accounts for the present somewhat anomalous position of the Blairs in politics."

Judd. "The opinion of people who read your Message today is that on that platform two of your Ministers must walk the plank—Blair and Bates."[316]

Lincoln. "Both of these men acquiesced in it without objection. The only member of the Cabinet who objected to it was Mr. Chase."

The Grand Council of the Union League met tonight and did nothing of moment.[317]

The Officers of the Russian Fleet were entertained tonight by the Sec of the Navy. They have vast absorbent powers and are fiendishly ugly. I grieve to say Mme Lissovski is not an exception.[318]

10 DECEMBER 1863, THURSDAY

Tonight the President talking with Arnold and me, told a magnificent Western law story about a steam doctor's Bill.[319]

Joe Forrest came in while we were talking and gave some of the comments upon the Message. Dickey says it is a "damned cunning trick—a trap." Florence says it is "very ingenious: admirably calculated to deceive."[320] The plainness and simplicity of the thing puzzles and confounds them. They are trying very hard to make a mystery of it and roll up a devil in its folds.

Sumner speaks of the Message with great gratification. It satisfies his idea of proper reconstruction without insisting on the adoption of his peculiar theories. The President repeated what he has often said before that there is no essential contest between loyal men on this subject if they consider it reasonably. The only question is who constitute the State? When that is decided the solution of subsequent questions is easy.[321]

He says that he wrote in the Message originally that he considered the discussion as to whether a state has been at any time out of the Union as vain and profitless. We know that they were, we trust they shall be in the Union. It does not greatly matter whether in the meantime they shall be considered to have be[en] in or out. But he afterwards considered that the

4th Section 4th Article of the constitution empowers him to grant protection to states *in* the Union and it will not do ever to admit that these states
have at any time be[en] out. So he erased that sentence as possibly suggestive of evil. He preferred he said to stand firmly based on the constitution rather [than] to work in the air."[322]

Talking about the Missouri matter he said: I know these Radical men
have in them the stuff which must save the state and on which we must
mainly rely. They are absolutely uncorrosive by the virus of secession. It
cannot touch or taint them. While the Conservatives, in casting about for
votes to carry through their plans, are tempted to affiliate with those whose
record is not clear. If one side *must* be crushed out & the other cherished
there could be no doubt which side we would choose as fuller of hope for
the future. We would have to side with the Radicals.

But just there is where their wrong begins. They insist that I shall hold
and treat Governor Gamble and his supporters—men appointed by loyal
people of Mo. as reps. of Mo. loyalty—and who have done their whole duty
in the war faithfully & promptly—who when they have disagreed with me
have been silent and kept about the good work—that I shall treat these
men as copperheads and enemies to the Govt. This is simply monstrous."

I talked to these people in this way when they came to me this fall. I saw
that their attack on Gamble was malicious. They moved against him by
flank attacks from different sides of the same question. They accused him
of enlisting rebel soldiers among the enrolled militia: and of exempting all
the rebels and forcing Union men to do the duty: all this in the blindness
of passion. I told them they were endangering the election of Senator: that
I thought their duty was to elect Henderson and Gratz Brown: and nothing has happened in our politics which has pleased me more than that
incident.[323]

He spoke of the newborn fury of some of these men—of Drake stumping against Rollins in '56 on the ground that R. was an abolitionist—of ci-
devant rebels coming here in the radical convention.[324] Not that he
objected to penitent rebels being radical: he was glad of it: but fair play: let
not the pot make injurious reference to the black base of the kettle: he was
in favor of short statutes of limitations.

In reply to a remark of Arnold's about the improved condition of things
in Kentucky & the necessity of still greater improvement and the good disposition of the Kentucky Congressmen, the President said he had for a long
time been aware that the Kentuckians were not regarding in good faith the

Proclamation of Emancipation and the laws of Congress but were treating as slaves the escaped freedmen from Alabama & Mississippi: that this must be ended as soon as his hands grew a little less full.[325]

Horace Greeley wrote a letter today to Nicolay commending the Message.[326]

~~I went to the theatre & saw the pretty lithe Webbs. The Muskovites were in the proscenium boxes and were disgustingly tight and demonstrative.~~[327]

Forney said Yesterday he should nominate the President today in his two papers. He has thought better of it. The leader in the Chronicle this morning ends amusingly. It looks as if the closing sentence had been emasculated. I think he probably corrected it cutting out all positive recommendation, after it was set up.

The Union League Convention seems to be going on right. They re-elected their present officers today, who are generally Lincoln men.

General Augur today reports that numbers of men are coming to him to take the oath prescribed in the Proclamation of Amnesty.[328] A very rapid working of the machine.

11 DECEMBER 1863, FRIDAY

Hawkins Taylor began again this morning on his unending theme the Missouri business He says there is an industrious effort making to combine and solidify the whole German vote against the President on those questions—Halleck—Blair—Bates.

He says Chase has lost strength by not insisting on the removal of all the Conservative office holders in Missouri.

12 DECEMBER 1863, SATURDAY

~~Nicolay & I went to the~~ [theatre to] ~~see the Webb girls.~~

I met at the Theatre S. S. Cox, who was speaking of the statesmanship and success of Govr. Seward, attributing much to the bonhommie and affability of his manners. He says Seward sent for him the other day and asked him if he wanted to retain his place on the Committee Foreign relations, & if he wished to designate what gentlemen on the democratic side should be associated with him, promising to speak to Colfax for him. This frank kindliness seemed to have won Cox over very much personally. Seward is unquestionably gaining in popularity very fast. Mercier said of him the other day "Il est tres sage." The diplomatic body have all apparently stopped ~~blackguarding~~ abusing him and those who do not like have been forced to respect.

13 DECEMBER 1863, SUNDAY

The President speaking today about Missouri matters said he had heard some things of Schofield which had very much displeased him: That While Washburne was in Missouri he saw or thought he saw that Schofield was working rather energetically in the politics of the State, and that he approached Schofield and proposed that he should use his influence to harmonize the conflicting elements so as to elect one of each wing, Gratz Brown and Henderson. Schofield reply was that he would not consent to the election of Gratz Brown.

Again when Gratz Brown was about coming to Washington he sent a friend to Schofield to say that he would not oppose his confirmation if he S would so far as his influence extended, agree to a convention of Missouri to make necessary alterations in her State Constitution. Schofield's reply as reported by Brown to the President, was that he would not consent to a State Convention. These things the President says are obviously transcendent of his instructions and must not be permitted. He has sent for Schofield to come to Washington and explain these grave matters.[329]

The President is inclined to put Rosecrans in Schofields place and to give to Gen Curtis the Department of Kansas. But Halleck and Stanton stand in his way and he has to use the strong hand so often with those impracticable gentlemen, that he avoids it when he can.[330]

These Kansas people are a queer lot. Delahay is here all alive with the idea that there is a Chase conspiracy about the President of which Pomeroy is one of the head devils, while Pomeroy swears by the President night & morning. Jim Lane told Champ. Vaughn he was for the President's action in the Schofield case & requested him to so tell Schofield.[331] Yet he raised a deuce of a bobbery in the Union League Convention about the same matter, still disclaiming any personal hostility to the President in the matter.

~~I talked with Ray this morning to try to get Reid removed from his functions as Correspondent of the Western Assd Press. He is so outrageously unfair to the President and so servilely devoted to Mr. Chase.~~[332]

Tonight Hackett arrived and spent the evening with the President. The conversation at first took a professional turn, the ~~Tycoon~~ President showing a very intimate knowledge of those plays of Shakespeare where Falstaff figures. He was particularly anxious to know why one of the best scenes in the play that where Falstaff & Prince Hal alternately assume the character of the King is omitted in the representation. Hackett says it is admirable to read but ineffective on stage. That there is generally nothing sufficiently distinctive about the actor who plays Henry to make an imitation striking.[333]

Hackett plays with stuffing of India Rubber says Shakespeare refers to it when he says "How now! Blown Jack" Hackett is a very amusing and garrulous talker. He had some good reminiscences of Houston, Crockett (the former he admires, the latter he thinks a dull man), McCarty and Prentiss.[334]

Sickles and Wadsworth were in the room part of the evening.

I visited Mrs L. Her sister, Mrs Gen. Helm is with her just arrived from Secessia.[335]

[18 DECEMBER 1863, FRIDAY]

Tuesday December 15th The President took Swett Nicolay & me to Fords with him to see Falstaff in Henry IV. Dixon came in after a while. Hackett was most admirable. The President criticised H's reading of a passage where Hackett said, "Mainly *thrust* at me" the President thinking it should read "mainly thrust at *me*." I told the Presdt. I tho't he was wrong, that "mainly" merely meant "strongly" "fiercely."[336]

The Presdt. thinks the dying speech of Hotspur an unnatural and unworthy thing—as who does not.

Thursday the Presdt. went to see the Merry Wives & Friday to Bayard Taylor.[337]

One morning this week I went to the State Department to get Gantts pardon to send to him by Gen Rice. Found Seward very busy over the complications arising from the "Chesapeake" Piracy. He said Sumner had just come in & said with great glee, "This proves my position to be correct that England was wrong in conceding belligerency to these people." "Of course" said Seward "but how the Devil does that help the matter." Sumner was delighted to have his theory vindicated even by such trouble.[338]

19 DECEMBER 1863, SATURDAY

There was a reception this morning to the Officers of the Russian fleet at the Executive Mansion There were present by invitation: Supreme

Court, Cabinet, Diplomatic body, Congress, Officers of the Army & Navy. ~~Seward has just received another idiotic despatch from Cash Clay abusing the Emperor Napoleon like a pickpocket.~~

I went tonight to Gen. Jessups to a rehearsal of private theatricals—a little farce, "Game of Roulette." Mrs Davenport, Misses Jessup Ramsay Loring & Hetzel. Kennedy, Malet & Hueage of the English Legation there.[339] I took a part in rehearsal but declined permanent situation. Left early & went to a supper party at Col Barnes' acting Surgeon General.

20 DECEMBER 1863, SUNDAY

Gen Buford's funeral. Nicolay & I spent an hour with Gardner leaving our shadows on his glass.

23 DECEMBER 1863, WEDNESDAY

I took to the Senate today the nomination of Schofield as Major General. The President had previously spoken to some of the Senators about it. He is anxious that Schofield shd. be confirmed so as to arrange this Missouri matter properly. I told Sherman Wilson Harris and Doolittle. Senator Foote also agreed to do all he could to put the matter properly through. But on the nomination being read in Executive session Howard of Michigan objected to its consideration and it was postponed. Sherman and Doolittle tell me it will certainly go through when it is regularly taken up.[340]

Lane came up to see the President about it, and told him this. Lane is very anxious to have the Kansas part of the plan at once carried out.

Morgan says that Gratz Brown gave to Sumner to present to the Senate the radical protest against Schofield's confirmation, and that Sumner presented it today. The President sent for Sumner but he was not at his lodgings.

The President is very much disappointed at Brown. After three interviews with him he understood that Brown would not oppose the confirmation. It is rather a mean dodge to get Sumner to do it in his stead.

Brown and Henderson both agree on Rosecrans. The Presdt. thinks he will get on very well for the Present, besides doing a good thing in the very sending.

General Banks writes the President a letter saying that Shepley and Durant & Co claim exclusive charge of the quasi civil administration of affairs in Louisiana: that with proper management Louisiana can be made a free state in sixty days, with as little trouble as it would take to make and execute a dog law in Massachusetts. The President writes him in reply.[341]

Ex Man,
Wash
Dec. 24, 1863

M. G. Banks:

Yours of the 6th inst. has been recd. and fully considered. I deeply regret to have said or done anything which cd give you pain or uneasiness. I have all while intended you to be *master* as well in regard to reorganizing State government for La, as in regard to the military matters of the Dept & hence my letters on reconstruction have been nearly, if not quite all addressed to you. My error has been that it did not occur to me that Gov Shepley or any one else wd. set up a claim to act independen[t]ly of you, & hence I said nothing expressly upon the point. Language has not been guarded at a pt where no danger was thot of. I now tell you that in evy dispute with whomsoever you are master. Gov She[ple]y was appd to *assist* the Comr. of the Dept. and not to thwart him or act independ[entl]y of him. Instructions have been given directly to him, merely to spare you detail labor, and not to supercede yr. authority. This, in its liability to be misconstrued, it now seems was an error in us. But it is past. I now distinctly tell you that you are master of all, and that I wish you to take the case as you find it, & give us a free State reorg[anizatio]n of L[ouisian]a in the shortest poss[ible] time. What I say here is to have a reasonable construction. I do not mean that you are to withdraw fr. Texas, or abandon any other military measure, which you may deem important. Nor do I mean that you are to throw away available work already done, for reconstruct[io]n, or that war is to be made upon Govr. Shepley, or any one else, unless it be found that they will not cooperate with you, in [which] case, & in all cases you are master while you remain in command of the Dept.

My thanks for yr successful & valuable operations in Texas.

Yours as ever

A Lincoln

Gen. Banks, writing to the Presdt. under date N. O. 16 Dec. answers the Presdt.'s letter of the 5th more at length saying he is impelled to make certain statements for the information of the Presdt. that he is only in partial command in N. O. "There are not less than *four* distinct Govts. here, claiming and exercising original and independent powers, based upon instructions received directly fr. Washn, and recognizing no other authority than their own. They claim and exercise civil & military powers. Sometimes to the very serious injury of the public service. It cannot be necessary that such conflicting authority shd. exist and it certainly cannot be exercised consistently with the interests of yr. administration. If it be necessary I have nothing to say; but in that event the separate powers shd be distinctly defined: if not, the power of yr. Govt. shd. be concentrated somewhere so that somebody shd. be responsible for the results. I have never asked increase of authority, but as yr. letter implies a responsibility in some matters, which I did not understand were committed to me, I think it my duty to you personally and to your Government officially to represent my position and the difficulties I encounter in other relations than those referred to in my letter of the 6th Inst. which relates to the reconstruction of the State Govt. in Louisiana only."

I Relates incident of the civil authorities seizing a vessel which he was loading for the Texas expedition, which he afterwards had to retake forcibly occasioning trouble and delay & a reprimand fr. the Court to officer executing his (B's) order.

II The circumstances attending the recapture of the steamer "Leviathan." The unpopularity of Military Power in the Court. The Judge of the Court Mr. Durell & his financial operations—Dist Atty crazy.[342]

III The Dist. Court of one of the City Dist[ricts, of which] there are 6, recently decided that the Mil. Authority hd no power here agst judicial decree: that the Courts were established by the Mil. Govt. in pursuance of powers recd fr. Washn. & that no Mil. order cd. stand agst. judgment of these local Courts.

IV City Courts assuming authority of all offenses of soldiers or officers & abolition of the Courts.

V Police in the hands of civil authority & ill-disposed towards the army.

VI The 6000 families supported by Charity still on our hands & the funds which supported them taken possession of by the Treasury Dept.

VII Mil. Governor assumes the granting of the Passes.

VIII Gen. Halleck has already informed Gen. B that his authority is supreme. But he does not wish to be wasting his time & strength in quarrelling with these people. Let powers of the difft. officers be more closely defined, or concentrated into single hands with direct responsibilities. Specially what is called the "State Govt." be lifted out of its ruts.

A year since he assumed command: the improvement so manifest as to give him consolation for suffering & labor.

Apologizes for trespassing, but hopes that the near approach of peace & the restoration of the country fr. its greatest peril will serve as an anodyne for all suffering & sorrow.

The Prest in answer repeats what he said in letter of Decr. 24.

The President tonight had a dream.

He was in a party of plain people and as it became known who he was they began to comment on his appearance. One of them said, "He is a very common-looking man." The President replied "The Lord prefers Common-looking people: ~~are the best in the world:~~ that is the reason he ~~the Lord~~ makes so many of them."[343]

~~Waking, he remembered it, and told it as rather a neat thing.~~

24 DECEMBER 1863, THURSDAY

Last night Nicolay went to Philadelphia to spend Christmas with Kelley. K. rather surprised us the other day at dinner by saying, in the course of a tirade against Blair, "This man calls himself the distinctive friend of Lincoln & says that the opposition to him is oppn. to the Presdt. "No man shall go from my district to the Convention who is not pledged to Lincoln first last & all the time. I honor and admire Mr. Chase; Lincoln out of the way, I should be proud to support him. But the Lord has given us this man to keep as long as we can."[344]

O'Neill of Philada. said something very similar to me the other day.[345]

I dined today with S. S Cox. He spoke of Greeley's foolish Chase explosion the other night at Wendell Phillips Cooper Institute meeting & said Chase was working night and day.[346] He has gotten nearly the whole strength of the New England States. If there is any effort made in Ohio, he can be beaten there. He has little strength in his own State.

I asked him whom his party would nominate. C. "General McClellan.

We will run McClellan. He is our best ticket. He lost some prestige by his Woodward letter. But it was necessary. He never could have gotten the nomination without it."[347]

You dont agree with the Herald on Grant?[348]

C. "Grant belongs to the Republicans. We cant take him after his letter to Washburne. But for that we might have taken him. The Republicans wont take him either. They have got his influence and have no further use for him."[349]

If I were a soldier I should much prefer commanding the U. S. Army for life, to four years in the Executive Mansion. I think Grant would."

C. "So would McClellan I know."

I met him again tonight in the Theatre. He says he is getting tired of Washington. He wants to spend a few years in Europe. He will go if McClellan is the next Presdt.: thinks he will anyhow. Says it is delightful to be in the minority you are not bored by your people for offices. "Glad you like it" quoth I, "We will try to keep you so."

25 December 1863, Friday

A lonesome sort of Christmas. I breakfasted, dined and supped alone. Went to the Theatre & saw Macbeth alone. Came home and slept alone.

The President today got up a plan for extending to the people of the rebellious districts the practical benefits of his proclamation. He is to send record books to various points to receive subscriptions to the oath, for which certificates will be given to the man taking the oath. He has also prepared a placard himself giving notice of the opening of the books and the nature of the oath required.[350]

He sent the first of these books to Pierpoint to use in Virginia.[351] The Second he will probably send to Arkansas.

The Presdt. was greatly amused at Greeley's hasty Chase explosion and its elaborate explanation in the Tribune. He defended Govr. Chase from Phillips unjust attacks, saying that he thought Chase's banking system rested on a sound basis of principle, that is, causing the Capital of the country to become interested in the sustaining of the national credit. That this was the principal financial measure of Mr. Chase in which he (L) had taken an especial interest. Mr. C. had frequently consulted him in regard to it. He had generally delegated to Mr C. exclusive control of those matters falling within the purview of his dept. This matter he had shared in, to some extent.[352]

Usher said that there had been some symptoms of antagonism developed by the bankers of N. Y. against the proposed system of National Banks and that Mr Hutton backed by Cisco & others would put the matter through.[353]

The President read to us a paper he had written last summer during the days of bitterest opposition to the draft, arguing its constitutionality and expediency. He was a little curious to know what could have been the grounds taken by the Sup. Court of Pa in deciding otherwise. The matter seemed so clear to him that he wondered how there could be any other side to it.[354]

28 DECEMBER 1863, MONDAY

The President yesterday went down the river to Pt. Lookout to visit Gen. Marston. He returned about dusk. He says that Gen M. represents a strong feeling of attachment to the Union or rather disgust for the rebellion existing among his prisoners—a good many of whom are Northern men & foreigners the victims of conscription: from one-third to one-half ask that they may not be exchanged and about one half of this number desire to enter our army, having, poor devils, nowhere else to go & nothing else to do. The Bill just introduced in the Rebel Congress which will probably become a law, holding permanently all soldiers now in the army, will doubtless greatly increase the disaffection.

Peck was here this evening. The Indiana State Convention meets in Mass Assembly of the people on the 22nd of February to nominate delegates to the Union Convention for Presidential selection. P. does not understand this clearly. He will cause the Illinois Convention to be called two days before, if it is thought advisable. Morton is a trickster & has been bitten himself by the White House Gad-fly. I recd. tonight letters from Paige & Stickney asking me to come down to Florida and be their Representative in Congress.[355]

Talked with the President about the matter of the reconstruction of Florida. He wants me to take one of his Oath books down to Pt. Lookout and get the matter going there and after that he will appoint me a Commissioner to go to Florida and engineer the business there. By their meeting at St. Augustine the other day there seems a prospect of getting the state under way early next Spring. I will go down & form my plans after I get there, as to my own course.[356]

29 DECEMBER 1863, TUESDAY

~~Cam tells a good story on D. Yates. D. had been very tight all evening & at last told C. that he intended to be next Presdt. and in that case he would make C. a Q Master.~~

31 DECEMBER 1863, THURSDAY

Spent the evening at Forney's. There was quite a gathering of political people early in the evening which thinned as the night wore on. Shortly after 11 oclock Gen. Martindale issued a military order that no man should leave the room this year.[357] Forney made several very ebrious little speeches. He talked a great deal about the President. The love of the people for him: his unconscious greatness: the vast power he wields and the vast opportunity afforded to a diseased ambition. "If the old man knew the loving thoughts and prayers that are rising for him tonight from Millions of hearts, the unconditional confidence and the loyalty to his person that is felt throughout this land, he could do or be anything he wished. But thank God he is incapable of abusing this trust, and the freedom of our institutions render impossible a devotion to any man at variance with the spirit of our government.

He said "He was for Lincoln because he couldnt help it"

When any one asks who are you are for Presdt. he says Nobody. Not for Lincoln, he never asked me & dont want me. When I go to see him he asks me what is the last good joke I have heard.

"Lincoln is the most truly progressive man of the age, because he always moves in conjunction with propitious circumstances, not waiting to be dragged by the force of events or wasting strength in premature struggles with them."

Some Treasury people were there who winced with all the sensibility their copious libations had left them.

He made a dead set at me and demanded the administration policy for the coming year. I said a half dozen words expressing the hope that the rest of the fight should be like Hooker's battle at Lookout Mt. above the clouds. The mists of prejudice and passion and popular indecision seemed at last beneath our feet, and we might hope to finish the business in the higher sunshine.

We sung a good deal of John Brown and a little of other things. ~~I dined at Butlers with Grover Philp Eastman & Young. Grover is a most amusing blackguard with a queer history.~~[358]

4

1864

1 JANUARY 1864, FRIDAY

I DID NOT ATTEND THE RECEPTION TODAY, LABORING ALL THE morning under a great disgust.

I left Willards yesterday & went to live at Club today.[1]

[2–4 JANUARY 1864, SATURDAY–MONDAY]

Point Lookout

The President and Secretary of War today Jan. 2, 1864 commissioned me to go down to Lookout Point and deliver to Gen. Marston the book of oaths and the accompanying blanks and explain to him the mode in which they are to be used. Gen Butler was ordered by telegraph to meet me there and consult as to the manner of carrying out the Presidents plan for pardoning and enlisting the repentant rebels. I bore a letter for Gen. Butler's instruction.[2]

I went on board a little tug at the 7th Street wharf, and rattled and rustled through the ice to Alexandria where I got on board the Clyde most palatial of steam tugs: fitted up with a very pretty cabin and berths heated by steam and altogether sybaritic in its appointments.

The day was bitterly cold and the wind was malignant on the Potomac. I shut myself up in my gorgeous little cabin and scribbled and read and slept all day. The Captain thought best to lay to for a while in the night, so we put in at Smith's creek and arrived at Point Lookout in the early morning. I went to the headquarters of the General accompanied by a young officer who asked my name & got it. I felt little interest in his patronymic & it is now gone into the oblivion of those ante Agamemnona. It was so cold that nobody was stirring. A furry horse was crouching by the wall. "Hello Billy! Cold, Aint it?" said my companion Billy was indignantly silent. We stumbled on, over the frozen ground, past the long line of cottages that line the beach built by the crazy proprietor of the land who hoped to make here a great wateringplace which would draw the beauty & fashion of the country away from ~~Cape May~~ Long Branch & make Newport a Ranz des Vaches. We came up to a snug looking frame house, which had been the dwelling of the adventurous lunatic. A tall young man with enormous blond mustaches and a general up-too-early air about him, hove in sight and my guide & friend introduced me. "Yes I have heard of you Mr Hale. I got a despatch from the General saying you would be here. When did you arrive Mr. Kay? Rather cold weather. Any ice on the River Mr. Day?" All this in a voice like the rumbling of distant thunder, measured & severe, and with a manner of preternatural solemnity. "The General will soon be up Mr Hayes" my mild insinuations as to my agnomen having brought him that near to my christening, at last.

He disappeared and coming back, beckoned me out. I followed him across the little entry into a room opposite. There stood in the attitude in which if Comfort ever were deified the statues should be posed—parted coat-tails—a broad plenilunar base exposed to the grateful warmth of the pine wood fire—a hearty Yankee gentleman, clean shaven—smug and rosy—to whom I was presented & who said laconically, "Sit there," pointing to a warm seat by a well spread breakfast table. I had an appetite engendered by a day and night of river air and I ate breakfast, till the intelligent contraband who served us caught the infection and plied me with pork steaks till hunger cried quarter. The General told a good yarn on a contraband soldier who complained of a white man abusing him. "I doesnt objick to de pussonal cuffin, but he must speck de unicorn."

The General's flock are a queer lot. Dirty, ragged, yet jolly. Most of them are still rebellious but many are tired and ready to quit while some are actuated by a fierce desire to get out of the prison and by going into our army avenge the wrongs of their forced service in the rebel ranks.[3]

They are great traders. A stray onion—a lucky treasure-trove of a piece of coal—is a capital for extensive operations in Confederate trash. They sell and gamble away their names with utter recklessness. They have the easy carelessness of a Frenchman about their patronymics. They sell their names when drawn for a detail to work, a great prize in the monotonous life of every day. A smallpox patient sells his place on the sick list to a friend who thinks the path to Dixie easier from the hospital than the Camp. The traffic in names on the morning of Gen. Butler's detail of 500 for exchange was as lively as Wall Street on days when Taurus climbs the Zenith or the "Coal Hole" when gold is tumbling ten percent an hour.

They live in a 30 acre lot fenced around by themselves. They put up the fence with great glee saying "they would fence out the D——d Yankees & keep respectable."

Rather a pleasant place on a pleasant day is Pt. Lookout. Today it was dreary and cold. I could not but think of the winter life of the sanguine lunatic who built the little village intended for the summer home of beauty & chivalry & destined for the malodorous abode of the diseases and the unfragrant belongings of a great Hospital in busy War times.

My little boat got frightened at the blow that freshened in the evening and I sent her up to snooze the night away in Smith's creek.

In the dusk of the evening Gen Butler came clattering into the room where Marston & I were sitting, followed by a couple of aides. We had some hasty talk about business: he told me how he was administering the oath at Norfolk:[4] how popular it was growing: children cried for it: how he hated the Jews: how heavily he laid his hand on them: "A nation that the Lord had been trying to make something of for three thousand years & had so far utterly failed." "King John knew how to deal with them—fried them in swine's fat."

After drinking cider we went down to the Hudson City the general's flagship: His wife niece and excessively pretty daughter: tall statuesque & fair and named by a happy prophecy of the blond beauty of her maturity Blanche, were there at tea. I sent my little webfooted sulky word to get home as she could and sailed with the Butlers for Baltimore.

At night after the ladies had gone off to bed—they all said *retired* but I suppose it meant the same thing in the end—we began to talk about some queer matters. Butler had some odd stories about physical sympathies: he talked also about the Hebrew jurisprudence & showed a singular acquaintance with biblical studies: his occasional references to anatomy & physiology evidently surprised the surgeon to whom he respectfully deferred from time to time. He talked till it grew late & we dispersed to bed. I slept on the guards; a pleasant bed-room but chilly & listened till I slept to the cold & shuddering roar of the water under the wheels.

At Baltimore we took a special car & came home. I sat with the Genl. all the way and talked with him about many matters: Richmond & its long immunity. He says, he can take an Army within thirty miles of Richmond without a skirmish & supply them there without any trouble: from that point the enemy can either be forced to fight in the open field south of the city or submit to be starved into surrender.[5]

He was very severe on McClellan for his action about the New Orleans expedition. He says that before the Expn. was resolved on by the Prest. McC. said it wd. require 50,000 men: after it was resolved on he said 5,000 wd. be enough. He said he did not like to attack McC. nil nisi bonum &c but he might have to exploit that matter sometime.[6]

I told him of the night of October 21.[7]

He gave me some very dramatic incidents of his recent action in Fortress Monroe smoking out adventurers & confidence men, testing his detectives and matters of that sort. He makes more business in that sleepy little Department than any one wd. have dreamed was in it.

~~His good joke on Ould with the female captive. Two for one~~.[8]

Copy of letter to Gen. Butler

> Executive Mansion
> Washington
> Jan 2, 1863 [1864]

Major Genl. Butler

The Secretary of War and myself have concluded to discharge of the prisoners at Point Lookout, the following classes:

1. Those who will take the oath prescribed in the Proclamation of Dec. 8th and by the consent of Gen. Marston will enlist in our service.

2. Those who will take the oath and be discharged and whose homes lie safely within our military lines.

I send by Mr Hay this letter and a blank book, and some other blanks, the way of using which I propose for him to explain verbally, better than I can in writing.

> Yours very truly,

> A Lincoln

8 January 1864, Friday

Nicolay and I visited tonight the Secretaries of the Interior and of the Treasury. Usher talked about the vacancy occasioned by the death of Caleb B Smith. Said he understood Smith to be for him, when he was asking it for himself. Otto is an admirable man for the place but Usher does not want to lose him from the Department.[9]

We found at Chase's a most amusing little toy, "the Plantation Break-down." the Secretary and his daughter were busily engaged exhibiting it to some grave and reverend old fellows who are here at the meeting of the Society of Arts & Sciences. In the course of conversation the Secretary said to me, "It is singularly instructive to meet so often as we do in life and in history, instances of vaulting ambition, meanness and treachery failing after enormous exertions and integrity and honesty march straight in triumph to its purpose." ~~untouched by~~

A noble sentiment Mr Secretary.

9 January 1864, Saturday

Cameron has written to the President that the entire Union force of the Pa. Legislature, House and Senate have subscribed a request that the President will allow himself to be reelected, and that they intend visiting Washington to present it. He says "I have kept my promise."[10]

The indications all look that way. The loud Lincoln men, who are useful only as weather guages to show the natural drift of things, are laboring hard to prove themselves the original friends of the Prest. Mark Delahay is ~~gassing~~ talking eternally about the Chase plot to ruin him and Lincoln. He says Pomeroy is to be at the head of the New Fremont party that is soon to be placed in commission: And much of this. On the other hand Wayne McVeagh who dined with me today says that the struggle now seems to get ahead of each other in the nomination. The New Hampshire occurrence startled the Union League of Philadela. They saw their thunder stolen from their own arsenals. They fear their own endorsement will be passé before long and are now casting about to get some arrangement for putting him in nomination at once.[11]

Wayne told a very funny story about Forney & Cameron in conversation about politics on the train, Forney bibulously insisting that if he had beaten Cameron for the Senate there would have been no war.[12]

13 JANUARY 1864, WEDNESDAY

I received today my commn. as A A G from the War Department & accepted it taking the oath of allegiance before Notary Callan.[13]
Made a visit or two.
Went into the ~~Tycoon's~~ President's room and announced myself ready to start.[14]
"Great good luck and God's blessing go with you John."
How long will you stay One month or six months
Sleeping car experiences. Small Israelite. Sharp practice.

14 JANUARY 1864, THURSDAY, NEW YORK

Custom House politics. Mrs J. Wood in evening.[15]

15 JANUARY 1864, FRIDAY

On board the Fulton. The embarkation of the 54th Boys—variety of complexions—redheads—filing into their places on deck—singing whistling smoking and dancing—eating candy & chewing tobacco.[16] Jolly little cuss round rosy & halfwhite, singing

Oh John Brown dey hung him
Were gwine to jine de Union Army
Oh John Brown dey hung him,
We're gwine Dixie's land.

Way down by James' River
Old Massa's grave is made
And he or me is sure to fill it
When he meets de black Brigade

Were gwine to trabbel to de souf
To smack de rebels in de mouf

I leff my wife in Richmond Street
Im gwine to jine &c

And towards de Souf I turn my feet
Im gwine

Sung by a tall cadaverous fellow

Now in de Southern Section
Dey rose a insurrection
And so all de country is a flamin
But were gwine to put em down
With the sword of Ole John Brown
Or come back by de happy land of Canaan.

Oh Oh Oh
Listen to me now

De Fifty-fourth boys is a coming
God Bless de whole Capoodle
Of de fighting Yankee Doodle
And save em in de happy land o' Canaan.

"Twist yr. gun so when you come to a present."
Desperate effort and dead failure.
"I aint a going to twist my smoothbore into a rifle."

Gold watch and clustered seals of the Orderly Sergeant.

At two oclock the Captain decides that he cannot sail for the fog and
the passengers dispersed for a few hours furlough on shore.

"Off for Charleston early in the morning"
Rosedale in the evening—

16 JANUARY 1864, SATURDAY

A still cold blowy day. Saltatory exercise among the colored forecastlers.
Frantic little cuss beaten in dancing wants to bet $50 on the victor. Chorus
of friends—"hasnt begun to dance.

17 January 1864, Sunday

The morning services. the Chaplain His efforts to convince the young fellows on board that they were totally & utterly depraved without a singular good impulse or quality.

Evening services.

18 January 1864, Monday

A little commissary trying all day to persuade me he had smallpox.
De profundis
Hide blushing glory, hide Pultowa's day.

19 January 1864, Tuesday

A cold raw day. Passed Charleston early in the morning. Fort Sumter lit up by a passing weft of sunshine. A shot fired from Cummings point as we passed. The weather—demoralized by Yankee contact—growing so cold as to drive passengers below stairs to Euchre

20 January 1864, Wednesday, Hilton Head, S. C.

On arriving at Hilton Head yesterday afternoon, I found that Gen. Gillmore's Headquarters were now at Hilton Head. I went on shore, met Col. Smith & made an appointment to be presented to Gen. G. later.[17] Took tea at the Port Royal House & was told by the gentlemanly proprietor that I had better forage on my friends for a bed. Was presented to the Genl. & delivered my letter to General G.

> Exec Mans
> Washingtn
> Jan 13, 1864

Major General Gillmore

I understand an effort is being made by some worthy gentlemen to reconstruct a loyal state Government in Florida. Florida is in your department & it is not unlikely that you may be there in person. I have given Mr. Hay a Commission of Major and sent him to you with some blank books and other blanks, to aid in the reconstruction. He will explain as to the manner using blanks, and also my general views on the subject. It is desirable for all to cooperate; but if irreconcilable differences of opinion shall arise, you are master. I wish the thing done in the most speedy way possible, so that when done it lie within the range late proclamation on the subject. The detail labor of course will have to be done by others; but I shall be greatly obliged if you will give it such general supervision as you can find consistent with your more strictly military duties.

Yours very truly,

A Lincoln

He seemed perplexed rather & evidently thought he was expected to undertake some immediate military operation to effect the occupation & reconstruction. He dwelt on the deficiency of transportation in the Dept. & the immobility of his force for purposes of land attack. He has only now after great efforts succeeded in mounting a regt. of infantry for Cavalry service, &c &c

I told him it was not the President's intention to do anything to embarrass his military operations—that all I wished from him was an order directing me to go to Florida & open my books of record for the oaths: as preliminary to future proceedings.

He said we would speak farther of it. Meanwhile I will wait for my papers, delayed at New York.

Spent the evening with Col Smith & Genl. Turner, & slept on a cot, my feet hanging like icicles over its lower end.[18]

Major Dorman of Florida came in this morning. He is rather severe on the measures initiated by our friends the Tax Collectors to reconstruct the State. He says the people of the state, if they can be reached and protected are ready to come back: but the movement must come from the people: and the state must be occupied by our troops. That he knows all about them & can do more than any one for this purpose: and asked me to take tea with him.[19]

Mr Browne, of Salem, was at dinner. He is on his way to Florida & took letters for me to Stickney & Latta. He believes very thoroughly in Stickney: says he is going to redeem the State.[20]

Tea at Dorman's. I heard a great deal of very entertaining reminiscence fr. himself & wife about the early days of secession in Florida. One especially dramatic passage by the lady of the reception of the news of the fall of Sumter.

Coming back was taken to guard house for being dressed en citoyen.[21]

21 JANUARY 1864, THURSDAY

Steamer Cosmopolitan sailed for the North today.[22] Spent the day in writing to A. L. J. G. N. A. L. H. C. E. H. C. D. C. & A. M. S.

The General directed me to say to the President that he would cordially cooperate in carrying out the President's wishes.

I had considerable talk with the Genl. this evening. He spoke of his dispersing the Secesh Convention at Frankfort, &c Meriwether.[23] He says "I hope we will get enough voters out of the Territory already in our hands in Florida: if not, we will occupy some more territory."

He seems frankly and sincerely anxious that the Presidents intentions shall be fully carried out.

I spent evening at Morgans & Bartons.[24]

Talking with Gen. Turner, he said, "An officer may plot and plan and figure forever: without result: what is needed is for a man to stand by & say 'Go in.'"

He says Dahlgren lost caste with the sailors for being sea-sick. He stood it as long as he could but had to yield to it or die.

After Ammen had made his reconnaissance, Dahlgren seemed struck with new idea: said "We can go in any time: whenever we please: but must not go in without a plan: must get up plan first." This to Terry.[25]

Turner says Dahlgren never seemed to have plan: accepted readily any suggestion made by Gen G. Never suggested modification or change.

Father French and the Telegraph trip.

22 JANUARY 1864, FRIDAY

Morning in the Photograph Gallery—

Wrote a letter to Gen Banks asking authority to open book at Key West.[26]

Rode in the afternoon Col. Ellwell's horse, with Smith & Turner.[27]
Called on Dr Craven in the evening He had a dead hawk a beautiful creature. And many sea-shells.
Drank whiskey-punches in Turner's room till it grew late. Talked about ghosts.

23 January 1864, Saturday

The Fulton sails today for the North.

[24 January 1864, Sunday]

Saturday night I went on board the Ben De Ford with the Genl. to visit Folly & Morris Islands. Col Jackson Major Brooks, Capt Reese, & Frothingham were the party.[28]

In the morning we were at Pawnee Landing, Folly River. We mounted & rode to Gen. Terry's Headquarters—saw model of Fort Wagner—Terry joined Gillmore & we went up the beach to Lt. House inlet—saw the scene of the crossing by Strong—crossed & went in ambulance to Wagner. Spent some time there.[29]

From Wagner we walked up to Gregg leaving our ambulance.[30] Saw the mortar batteries before getting there. From Gregg had a good view of Ft Sumter—silent as the grave—flag flying over it—a great flag flying over the battery on Sullivan's Island. The city too, was spread out before us like a map. Everything very silent. A ship lying silent at the wharf. No sign of life in Ripley Johnson or Pinkney.

Saw Major Ames & Lt. Michie.[31] Walked back to Wagner. Fragments of shell strewn everywhere over the island—the light sand blows and obliterates the traces of our approaches on Wagner

Going back visited Fort Shaw.

Went to see Admiral Dahlgren and went to the "Bendy" for dinner.

From Pawnee Landing you can see the signal station whence Gen. Gillmore communicated with Strong in his crossing of Lt House Inlet. The camps of the colored troops &c on the other side of Coles & Kiawah Islands.

A queer little acting ensign was on board, Cocker, promoted for gallantry & addicted to drink.

25 JANUARY 1864, MONDAY

Went with Dr. Craven & F. a shell hunting. A first rate crew of negro boatsmen. Jim jolly & merry—July guttural and given to whiskey. The boys clamored for promises of eating & drinking. Dr. cautious & negative. Started, I at tiller. Narrowly escaped being run down by a Steamer loaded with refugees & then across the harbor keeping nose well up to the west for the heavy tide was running out. Shooting seagulls. Landed at Navy Dock Bay point. Dr. went up to water the whiskey. I walked over the dock to kick at XV in. shells. Meanwhile Darkies skedaddled. Dr. came back in a rage. Threatened condign vengeance. Anger diverted by crowd of birds on shore. Loaded up. I took gun & brought one down. Little darks ran & chased it tumbling over & over on the sand. Crew came back & Dr. forgetting rage said "Tumble in bullies."

Off again. Shot a sea gull who fell in shallow water, couldnt get at him, ran aground. Made for the bar in front: couldnt reach it. Dr. waded ashore: we made a detour for him Came back on the shoulders of July & swinging his scoopnet. The next bar: a bold shore slipped from the boat on dry land. Lunched. "Craven Island."

Off again—made for Phillips Island shore. Jim carried the party on shore. I took the gun & after much maneuvering killed 2 crows at a shot. Loafed on the sand till Dr. who had been visible at a distance grubbing like an overgrown woodchuck hove in range & shouted "Eureka I have found a bed of clams."

Off again. More whiskey. Jim had to take 3 drinks & thereafter inexorably "no more." ~~Many unsuccessful attempts~~ Out towards the path within the bars, grounded. July got out & wandered vaguely into the distance towards the south looking like a gigantic crane. Water continually getting shoaled. Jim at last got out & walked the other way—up to his knees in a moment. we followed Jim & called for July. We next tried to get into a little inlet that seemed to run inside the bar, got into it found it landlocked.

July rising to the requirements of the occasion, says "well row back de way we come." A leader found, accepted by unanimous suffrage of the crew. We rowed back outside the breakers & came into the wharf just as the sun was sinking behind the pines.

Negro songs.

1

One morning as I was a walking along
I met Ole Satan wid his head hung down
Colloquy. Ax me whare I gwine
I told him I was gwine to glory
Met a lion in the way & never turn back

2

Jerusalem in the morning

3

A singular chorus dramatic in form describing Jacob's wrestling with the angel.

26 January 1864, Tuesday

A Quiet day. In the evening I went up to Beaufort Breakfasted with Gen Saxton & returned[32]

27 January 1864, Wednesday

The Atlantic arrived this morning fr the North vice the Arago transferred to New Orleans & brought my books & my whiskey.[33]
I am happy—modifiedly, as a worm must be.

31 January 1864, Sunday

The 62d Regt. veterans reenlisting went down to the Atlantic this morning with all possible pomp & circumstance escorted by two brigades who formed on the two sides of the prin. Street: between them came the veterans, bearing palmettos, palm canes mementos of all sorts and a few leading pets dogs cats birds squirrels, tattered & stained flags.[34] The change in bearing—they go home men and soldiers. The music especially enlivening Band played "sweet home"
Marching home up the beach—the black Regt. 8th U. S.[35]
The sand trodden level as a floor—Army shoes—

Headquarters Dept of the South
H. H. S. C.
Feb. 1 1864.

Colonel:[36]

This will be handed to you by Maj. J. H. A A G who is ordered to Fla for the purpose indicated in Genl. Orders No 16. C. S. fr. these Hdqrs. You will afford him all necessary facilities in execution of those orders. Maj. H. on leaving (F or St. A) will transfer to you the instructions under which he is acting which you will carry out in his absence.

Very Res

YObt Se

No transportation Cant get off today.
Ethiopian entertainment at Sayer's until bedtime

1 AND 2 FEBRUARY 1864, MONDAY AND TUESDAY

Evening of Feb 1st Gen Turner & I got on board a noisy little tug at Wharf which took us to the Ben De Ford. We went up stairs & drank a few whiskey punches & then to sleep.

In the morning found ourselves off Stono—tide too low to let us over the bar—were rowed ashore—Gen Terry, Turner & I.

Stopped at lower end of Folly for an Ambulance—rode to Gen Terry's Headquarters & took horses to ride to Lt. House Inlet—crossed in a boat & walked up to Col. Davis'. Col. D. full of a plan for capturing Sumter Garrison.[37]

We went in ambulance to Wagner. The sound of firing had been heard all the morning. It grew more frequent & Davis told us it was directed at a stranded Blockade runner—Just as we got in sight of Wagner, a white smoke appeared in the clear air (the fog had lifted suddenly) and a sharp crack was heard. It seemed as if a celestial pop corn had been born in the ether. There's a shell from Simkins, said Turner. We went on & there were more of them. As we got to Wagner, We got out & sent the Ambulance to a place of safety under the walls. They were just making ready to discharge a gt gun fr. Wagner. The Gens clapped hands to their ears. The gun was fired & the black globe went screaming close to the ground over the island, over the harbor, landing and bursting near the helpless Blockade Runner stranded half way from Ft. Beauregard to Fort Moultrie.[38] We walked up the beach. Heretofore we had from time to time seen little knots of men gathered to look at the fight, but now the beach was deserted—once in a while you wd. see a fellow crouching below a sandhill keeping a sharp lookout. We soon came to Batteries Seymour Barton & Chatfield which were firing vigorously.

We mounted the parapet & took a good look at the steamer. She was already a good deal damaged by our shell amidships.

The enemies fire was getting pretty warm. They had the range perfectly. Most of the shell burst in or over the works, but the men were so well protected that all the time we were there but 3 were hit & they were said to be imprudent. The men dodged & broke to cover at the flashing of the enemies' batteries. But the officers exposed themselves with perfect insouciance.

The shells had singular voices. Some screamed frightfully: some had a regular musical note like Chu-chu-wachu-wachu-*brrr* and each of the fragments a wicked little whistle of its own. Many struck in the black marshy mud behind us burying themselves & casting a malodorous shower into the air—others burrowed in the sand. One struck the face of Chatfield while I was standing on the parapet with a heavy thud—& a moment afterward threw a cloud of sand into the air. I often saw in the air a shell bursting—fierce jagged white lines darting out first, like javelins—then the flowering of the awful bud into full bloom—all in the dead silence of the upper air—then the crack & the whistle of the fragments.

Col Drayton took us to see the great 300 pder Parrot.[39] At a very little distance an ugly looking hole where a shell had just burst—beside the gun traces in the sand of hasty trampling & wagon wheels—dark stains soaking into the sand—a poor fellow had just had his leg taken off by a piece of a shell.

I saw them putting a crushed and mangled man into an ambulance. He was still & pale—The driver started off a merry trot. A captain said "Dm you, drive that thing slower."

Two or three young fellows were playing with their horses in the parade.

The horses joining in the fun threw riders over their heads & started off

The illstarred boat got badly pounded. Her machinery & works battered in. She seemed sinking before we left. The navy were off nearly two miles but still made passable shooting—their ricochet shots however were generally failures.

With a good glass we could see a good many anxious spectators on the rebel side.

Chatfield to Boat 2600 yds. Wagner to B 3000 Monitors = 2 miles.

We walked back on the beach to Wagner. A shell exploded close behind us. I made a bad dodge.

Walked all over Wagner & got a synthetic view of the whole affair. Saw great many loafers laying low.

They were mounting a gun in Wagner

Came back to Terry's Hdquarters. He had sent a puzzling despatch to his brother, *Envoyer Acheter du Ouiskie pour moi* It had gone through. We took nips & went.

Got on B. D. & started home. There was some very lively firing on Coles & James islands. Pawnee & Mortar schooner against their batteries.

Captain shot a seagull with a musket.

I read Hannah Thurston[40]

Got home at 9 or ten at night

3 FEBRUARY 1864, WEDNESDAY

Passed part of the morning in Engineer offices with Maj Abot.[41]

Took long ride this afternoon Turner & Heath Pope's Seabrooks, Ft. Mitchell Eliots Draytons The woods were on fire. The smell of burning resin—the mad leaping of the flame up the leafy trees &c The flames as we passed were near the smallpox tent

Party tonight. I dont go

4 FEBRUARY 1864, THURSDAY

Gen Seymour today had a review of the corps which is to invade Florida. 6000 men, black & white infantry, Artillery & Mted Inftry.[42]

In the evening Gen. G explained to me his plan & gave me this letter to take to

Headquarters, Dept of the South,
A A G's O
H. H. S. C.
Feb 4, 1864.

My Dear Sir

Yr note of yesterday is received. I did hope the railroad would not be disturbed by the enemy for 2 or 3 days to come. As they have commenced their work I must inaugurate mine, although not quite ready.

Yr. offer to aid me is accepted promptly & thankfully. Please confer with Col. Guss & secure success in the following named project viz.

To have R.R. track on Jacksonville & Tallahassee Route & also on Fernandina and Cedar Keys route torn up at and beyond Baldwin in several places on Saturday next after the train comes in from the West.[43]

I shall land a force at Jacksonville by noon. Major Hay, Assistant A G will deliver this & explain details

(Endorsed)

Col Guss will please furnish Major Hay every possible facility for carrying out the project referred to in the within letter to Judge Stickney. I will be at Fernandina perhaps tomorrow night but nothing should wait for me.

Q. A. Gillmore.

5 FEBRUARY 1864, FRIDAY

A bad time coming down, a foul wind dead ahead all the way delaying us badly. The captain put in at St. Andrews thinking it Fernandina.

Arrived at F. at 3½ oclock. I immediately went to see Judge Stickney delivered my letter. We concluded to proceed at once to the mouth of the St. John's. The captain the pilot & Capt. McGowan revenue service declared it impossible to go over the bar tonight.[44] Ordered him to be in readiness at daylight. Went on board Cuyahoga & dined.

Met at Col. Guss' after dinner Maj. Brooks and told him the whole thing—he agreed with me that all possible efforts must be made to carry out Gen. G's wishes. We went to see Mr. Alsop[45] & after discussing matters fully, it was resolved:

1. To send three trusty men over land to the line beyond Baldwin, cut that & return

2. For Brooks & Alsop to go down to the mouth of the St. John's & select some trusty negroes to go up Trout Creek & do the same thing.

Went down to Col. Guss to order light house lit up with candles, in case Gen. Gillmore shd. be outside the bar & to let out the Island City: to find Private Roberts a Florida refugee to report to Brooks: & to give him suggestion (1).

To the Island City & then back to Judge Stickneys where I was mortified to find the Judge had given up his bed to me & left the house for the night.

6 FEBRUARY 1864, SATURDAY

Opened my book in an office over Robinson's Store, sent out my posters & sat like a spider. A few men straggled in and swore. One hesitating cuss who evidently feared he was going to be tricked into the army swore, but dallied so on the signing that I shut the book & told him to make up his mind before calling again.[46]

Went to dinner at J. S. Capt. McGowan was there. While we were drinking our coffee an orderly came for me & handed a note from G. G. to Col Guss, saying the expedn wd. not be at mouth St. John's till Sunday morning, wants the road kept broken until then, if train caught. I jumped on the orderly's tacky & galloped down. Found that Guss had detailed an officer to go down, but I thought I had better go myself. I got on board the Harriet Weed. The Captain was very fearful we could not get off the bar before night. If a Captain says he is afraid his boat cant do a given thing in a given time you may be sure it cant near do it. So I resigned myself to a miserable afternoon and night. To my surprise I was not seasick—we had a heavy sea running landwise & a stiff breeze blowing off shore. Mysterious dispensation. Arrived off mouth St. John's about 6½. night foggy around the edges & sullenly clear above—the stars shorn of their beams. Blew our whistle thrice—fired our guns—no use: the shore obdurately silent & sulkily foggy. Officers peering at the shore desperately anxious to make themselves believe they saw something. No use: cast anchor & turned in.

The Pilot Boy broken down. Pretty story about her—
The Una—Push & be damned—as we called men in Alabama & her end

She could go—11 knots—in a heavy dew—Old Billy could turn her in a pint of water—steady her head & swing her tail around—She went to pieces off Cape Fear, lost her stern wheel & went to pieces—towed for a while by a gunboat—Old Billy found her going to pieces—put off crew—set her on fire—made a line fast to himself & was dragged up nearly drowned.

[7 FEBRUARY 1864, SUNDAY]

The night passed well enough with occasional interruptions of jolly mariners coming in to announce various misadventures—once the seacock was open and the mate thought the boat was sinking, and various climatic changes were duly announced—drifted into the bar & anchor coming loose &c

In the morning we found we were not off St. John's but Nassau: as the fog lifted we saw the hard clear line of the land before us. The sun was on the horizon but invisible: the flush of dawn rosy in the east: the delicate grey line of clouds hanging above the sea like a string of pearls on the neck of Aurora. In the far south one or two sails, and behind us the Neptune wallowing on with a load of horses, keeping close to our stern, afraid to lose us.

Then there was swearing, loud and deep. "It is too by God Jesus Christly bad."

Soon hove in sight the Island City. I saw Brooks on the hurricane deck: hailed: he came over in the I. C.'s metal boat: I got in & went back: found him and Alsop happy over the good look of their work. The Floridians were pleased at the prospect. (As Alsop was making a hole in the belt of one of the fellows, the knife dropped & stuck in the ground: That's lucky the man said, very earnestly.)

While we were at Breakfast the Captain came in excitedly saying a steamer was coming up with ensign at the fore. We hailed her. "Gen. Seymour on board?" We went on a little way & held a council. Captain says "them longlegged boats cant get in without us" we concluded to go back. The I. C. "draws no more water'n a herrin."

The Captains shibboleth

Get the two lights in range then keep the red one ahead to the Southard of the white light till you come to the black buoy: leave that on yr port bow: hug the reef till you pass 'twixt the spar & the barrel buoy & then straight into the harbor."

We concluded to go back: hailed the Ben De Ford crowded with soldiers & towing a schooner loaded with commissary stores, & told her to follow us. We got over the bar & looking back saw the unhappy Bendy stuck. Looking at her paddles we saw them reversed & flying very lively but in vain: she was checked: We started to give her a tow but the Harriet Weed passing by we delegated to her the labor of love & went on to turn into the right path a couple of truant propellers who were plunging madly at the North Breakers. I watched the Bendy. Suddenly I saw the Harriet casting off her tow & coming away in a great disgust. The Bendy had treated her shamefully—tearing off her after cabin & exposing her paddles to the general scorn. She flew about in a fine feminine rage—now seeming resolved to stave in her ungallant consort & now to rush for his schooner in tow & steal his commissary stores.

We went calmly on our way leading in the Delaware. Suddenly the Captain rushed forward exclaiming bitterly against the mendacity of human nature. "That fellow told us he drew 8 feet & there he is aground in 10 ft water. Give us a cast of the lead there" "¼ less 2" "There"

The Delaware was evidently in for it. When we got near enough we listened to her prayer & gave her a tow while the Harriet Weed, good-hearted & placable took charge of the schooner in tow & carried it off to deep water beyond the bar. The horses in the schooner seemed miserably content. We could do nothing with the Delaware. We told them so & the Bendy & made an arrangement for lighting & helping them off in the afternoon. Then we went into the harbor surrounded already by the foaming cream of the breakers.

We found a little ruinous village inside the harbor.

Gen. Seymour was just making off up the river. We learned from him that Gen Gillmore wld be here tonight. We gave him our cook for pilot and the liberating expedition sailed splendidly up the river in single file.

Thus deserted, we suddenly took the resolution of loading up with troops & starting for Jacksonville.[47] The captain received the order with plucky joyfulness & we went ~~alongside~~ the Delaware. The Captain whose time this morning was passed in unintelligible howls at the passing vessels, again intimated that he wanted to get off.

We made arrangements to take off some 400 of 115th N. Y. & went to dinner pending that inveigling Col Barton commanding the Brigade to come across the raging flood in a boat attached to a hawser which he did with his usual dig & grace.

The troops came over very slowly & with singular awkwardness. Two little darkeys George Washington & Nero came over in loving companionship.

One fellow scrambled down & jumped up saying "Now I pity the first rebel I see." Some grumbled at being compelled to change.

Our load on board we started for the River again—our pilot Canto presiding in the wheel house. We passed grounded vessels now & then At every unusual view or occurrence the men would pour on one side of the vessell till she careened: then trimming, they would over-trim.

We arrived at Jacksonville as night closed in. I went immediately to Gen. Seymour's quarters to report: passed over the wharf, through an arch of a great building & up a queer looking street to Sandersons where I found him, surrounded by all the improvised state of military authority. The room he occupied was almost filled with officers just landed & reporting for duty and along one side was a row of citizen prisoners, in various stages of decrepitude, caught in the town. The General was asking them questions whose purport they did not seem to understand & exacting their promise, on word of honor, not to do various hostile acts—which they could not have done to save their lives. He finally ordered a general jail delivery and the confused Floridians limped & shuffled away, not seeming clearly to see why they were caught or why discharged.—I reported & introduced Alsop & started to return to the bar.

The streets were full of troops & horses & wagons. Large stores had been suddenly appropriated & were filled with cavalry & artillery properties. Great masses of forage were discharging from the transports. Bodies of men were still coming out of the black hulks on the dock. Everything seemed chaotic but really full of order and symmetry.

I went back to my boat & found the soldiers pouring out. We soon disgorged, & started away again. We met from time to time as we proceeded down the River, the boats we had passed this afternoon hard aground

I record today, for future mortification, and as a preventive of possible pride & vainglory the fact that 1st this day I have not washed my face 2nd I ate an onion for breakfast—Decency, avaunt! I am henceforth a loafer.

I went on board the Monohassett to consult with Maj. Brooks and staid there all night. The phosphorescent gleam of the water was wonderfully fine.

8 FEBRUARY 1864, MONDAY

At early dawn I woke up & roused the Major. We got Canto off the I. C. & sent him to the Hunter & ordered the Monohassett to follow us out—the Harriet Weed steaming ahead—having gone out at daybreak and snaked in a grounded schooner.

We got to the Bendeford who was badly aground & found alongside the Cosmopolitan. I ran out to speak some other vessells—among them the Saxon 11½ ft draft loaded with Cold. troops. ordered Monohassett to take em on board.

We boarded the Cosmopolitan: Genl G & staff at Breakfast: got letters & then took boat to pull to the I C.

A mutinous & gabby Portlander on the boat dried up by Major B. Breakfasted and gave orders for the Hunter & Weed to lighten the Bendy

I then started for Fernandina. A clear & very beautiful day. We steamed into Amelia river a little after 12 M.

I gave to Col. Guss my books and papers for Fernandina. Dined with Stickney & packed my valise for the Campaign. I am afraid my memorandum is substantially at an end—I have put on a coat with an insufficient pocket. On events so trifling hinge consequences so vast.

I made ready & started out of the Harbor at 3.30 P.M. As we were clearing the bar we met the Nellie Baker steaming in; the indomitable Brooks in the foreground & ordered us back. When we got to Fernandina the Major explained the matter.

Took Tea with Guss. after tea a lively discussion of plan by Sears Freeman Guss Brooks.[48] The contrabands were called in.

Prince Wild & Abner (who got fighting mad at the intimation that somebody was a better oyster raker than him) and Billy Blue (who went away in disgrace because he hadnt rafted furd'n Callahan's *flatform*) and old Prince, the true prince, who carried his patent of nobility in the crown of his hat in the shape of his portrait by our Special Artist on the spot. They were queer talkers: very correct and graphic ideas of distance and locality: a singular tendency to run off into difuseness & irrelevant incident: their admiring and confident indorsement of each other: The recusant Cassio or Cudjo Martin who said hed be ——d if he'd come: all these were very amusing & graphic to see & hear.

Sears told a good story of Hatto Gordon the member from Nassau &

his circus picture: And his reply to the landlord's request for attention to his little bill.

At ten the council came to a conclusion & I went to my boat & found there Stickney & Rivington waiting. We hailed the Brig Perry, got a cutter, & after being hailed on the river more than a sufficiency, we went over the side of the Nelly B. There was no place to sleep so we slept no place in particular but loafed about premises. A stalwart Lt. walked dreamily over the damp floors barefoot & attempted, in reply to my mild remonstrance against so ruinous a practice to show that because he once slept in a frozen blanket, his present unshod perambulation was eminently sanitary. Aghast at his logic I begged a blanket of Major Place and courted Sleep.[49]

9 FEBRUARY 1864, TUESDAY

Woke with a frowsy sense of having passed a bad night—some neat lunatic proposes a wash and others with sleepy meekness accede. We wash & breakfast.

The sun rises strangely here. A few degrees above the horizon, a purple blot appears gathering strength gradually to shoulder its way through the heavy mists of the morning, and coming out at last coppery opaque & with a dull glimmer like a new suit of the old school. New suns & new babies always have that red blush as if they were unbared unawares before a gazing world; the mauvaise honte of nature.[50]

On the way down I met the John Adams & ordered her to Fernandina. The Captain thought foul scorn of my shouted mandate and demanded literam scriptam.[51] I gave it & he steamed away.

As we entered the harbor of St. Johns we saw that the Ben Deford was gone. Great was the rejoicing in the camp of the righteous.

(The Soldier & the dogs

We took in tow an Engineer Schooner & loafed slowly up stream. Remington stood in the bow hailing with boyish shouts of recognition the estates of his friends & acquaintances & his own.

We came to Jacksonville, gay with flags & busy with shipping, at noon. I landed & found no Genl. no staff no means of information. Ignorance the densest. Met Dorman who took me to Mrs ~~Taylor's~~. I saw in a few moments' glance the wretched story of two years. A lady well bred & refined, dressed worse than a bound girl on a country farm. A pretty young girl, with a dirty and ragged gown that did not hide her trim ancles and fine legs. A white haired, heavy eyed, slow speaking old young man. A type of thousands of homes, where punishment of giant crimes has lit on humble innocents.[52]

I put on my seven leaguers & rode with Reese & Place in the afternoon around the pickets. Reese selected points for fortifications. We saw two negro regiments one at dress parade gay with banners, one in camp, fragrant with salt horse. Some firing in the front—with ultimate intentions of mutton or fresh pork. As we came home we saw a train going to provision Gen Gillmores advance—a pretty dandy walking in the silent street— & some blue bellied Vandals making themselves agreeable to one of the few remaining families.

Moved to the Ben Deford & tea. After tea went with Reese & Stickney to get a map from Judge Burritt. Cordial reception. Flowering Jessamines— law library—& cautious talk. We came back and talked some politics with Dorman & Stickney & went to bed.

A mail goes tonight to Hilton Head. I wrote A. L. H. C D C, H H, A. M. S., Jno G N A. L. & Smith

10 FEBRUARY 1864, WEDNESDAY

Walked out to the suburbs early in the morning with Reese and Stickney to see the work built by Gen Wrights engineers in our former occupation—now demolished.[53] Saw our first yaller dog in Florida— ~~diabetic~~ and burr-haunted—Back to Breakfast, tithes of mint & Jessamine on the way.

Yesterday I had a number of copies of the Proclamation posted through the town The few citizens gathered around—the lettered reading, the unlettered listening with something that looked like a ghost of interest

Rode out with Reese and Place & Walker to place the works for defense of the town.[54] One by the site of Wright's work. One small battery looking down the Panama road and another if necessary by an old Church (which must be removed) which will dominate the Panama Road and the crossing at the Cemetery. We rode out beyond our furthest pickets unquestioned. The troops had evidently been foraging in the woods. We saw in one place the carcass of a cow & in another the head of a hog, neatly relieved, looking as if that much had just grown out of the ground. We rode on till we came to a little settlement. Saw a newborn calf, heard the baying of dogs: the cackling of poultry: rode up to the house fragrant with applebloom. No soul near. Everything in order: As if that instant occupied. Called: no one answered. they were probably hidden in the bushes. Evident traces of some refinement in the house: books on the centre table &c. We rode away leaving the strange solitude. Surrounded the [work?] Some beautiful specimens of Southern Flora. Came out on Cemetery road, but couldnt cross the causeway as bridge was gone. Passed a Hebrew graveyard D. C. 5619 & coming home again saw a negro sergeant copying the Proclamation

At 2½ P.M. General Gillmore & Staff came clattering into the cabin of the Ben Deford. They seemed greatly elated by the success of the expedition & were full of Col. Henry's achievement in the capture of the artillery beyond Camp Finegan.[55]

In the afternoon Lt. Michie came in with his railroad train from Baldwin. He had 4 mules for locomotive who had a playful habit of humping themselves & casting off their riders. He had a young woman on board to whom he showed the usual courtesy of RR Conductors

11 February 1864, Thursday

By direction of Gen G I went to the prisoners confined in the guard house read to them the Procn. & said I had come to inform them "of the Executive act & extend to you its benefits. I have in my possession a book for the record of oaths. I have certificates entitling signing book to benefits of the act. If you sign you will be released & allowed to return to your homes if they are not &c. If not you will be sent north as prisoners of war, for exchange. By signing it you will entitle yourself to all yr rights as citizens of the U. S.

It is a matter for yr. own choice. There is to be neither force or persuasion used in the matter. It is a matter which you must decide for yrselves.

There has been some doubt expressed as to whether you will be protected. I am authorized to promise that you will be. The ocupn permanent. Men enough.

Inducement is peace & protection & reestablishment of yr. State Govt.

When I had finished the little I had to say they crowded around me asking innumerable questions. I got away & had an office fixed up in the quartermaster's block & waited for my flock. They soon came: a dirty swarm of grey coats & filed into the room, escorted by a negro guard. Fate had done its worst for the poor devils. Even a nigger guard didnt seem to excite a feeling of resentment. They stood for a moment in awkward attitudes along the wall. I could not but think that the Provost had made a mistake & sent me his whole family; As Alsop said he thought 8 or 10 of them could be induced to take the oath of allegiance. But I soon found they had come up in good earnest to sign their names. They opened again in a chorus of questions which I answered as I could. At last a big goodnatured fellow said "There's questions enough. Lets take the oath." They all stood up in line & held up their hands while I read the oath. As I concluded, the negro sergeant came up, saluted, & said "Dere's one dat didnt hole up his hand."

They began to sign—some still stuck and asked questions—Some wrote good hands, but most bad. Nearly half made their mark.

The captured crew of the St. Mary's came in.[56] said they were aliens & owed no allegiance, & I sent them suddenly back to the guardhouse.

I sent in the evening (in the Cosmopolitan's cutter) Judge Alsop over to the west bank of the river to see Sheriff Bowden a very intelligent cracker who is said to be loyal.

(February 12. Alsop returns saying that Bowden will follow him at once & take the oath of allegiance.)

Feb. 11—*continued* The General received today a despatch from Seymour saying that Henry fell into an ambush at the South Fork of the St. Mary's & lost 25 in killed & wounded. The enemy got away with slight loss. Seymour is informed & seems to believe that there is a large rebel force at Lake City, larger than his own.

The General gives no opinion. He says "Seymour has positive orders not to get whipped"

Ate apples till it grew late & went to bed.

12 FEBRUARY 1864, FRIDAY

Received orders from the General to go to St. Augustine with despatches for Col. Osborne to move his force except two companies to Picolata. (Seymour asked last night for the "54th Mass without delay. One co. is enough for St. Augustine) "Cool for a subordinate" said Q. A.) I went over to Halliwell & transferred my blasphemy business to him & made ready at once to go on the Helen Getty, ~~Judge Stickney going with me~~. I concluded to go by way of Fernandina to get near my "base of supplies" & to see if my goods had come fr. H H. I turned out of the boat the pilgrims of Port Royal, who growlingly filed over the gangplank.[57]

My first days operations in Jacksonville were such as to give very great encouragement. I enrolled in all 60 names—some of them men of substance and influence. The fact that more than 50 per cent of the prisoners of war were eager to desert & get out of the service shows how the spirit of the common people is broken. Everybody seemed tired of the war. Peace on any terms was what they wanted. They have no care for the political questions involved. Most of them had not read the oath & when I insisted on their learning what it was they would say listlessly "Yes I guess I'll take it." Some of the more intelligent cursed their politicians & especially South Carolina, but most looked hopefully to the prospect of having a government to protect them after the anarchy of the few years past. There was little of what might be called loyalty. But what I build my hopes on is the evident weariness of the war & anxiety for peace.

The leading man of the town Judge Burritt is deeply exercised about the reconstruction. He has ~~prayed worshipped~~ courted so long the triple-headed cerberus, the World the Flesh & the Devil that he finds it very hard to shift to a new object an exhaustive devotion. He hangs like Mahomet's coffin beyond loyalty & rebellion. Between the Gillmore who is here & the Finegan that may return he knows not how to choose. If he is true to Gillmore he may get cotton. If he is false to Finegan he may stretch hemp.

He has given Dinner to Swift & tea to Dorman & has powerful allies at Headquarters. But Quincy not knowing much law has an awkward directness that insists that a man must be loyal or disloyal. So over the head of the Judge hangs like a Damocles sabre my awful oath. I think he will, like the juggler of Siva, conclude to swallow it.

I wrote orders yesterday for Montgomery to take 3 companies of his regt & try to capture the rebel pickets at Doctor's Lake & Green Cove. The Expn. started last night.

Feb 12 at noon we got to the mouth of the river and the rough line of breakers on the bar deterred the pilot from attempting the passage. The pilot being an absolute autocrat we ungraciously assented and watched the porpoises for the rest of the afternoon.

In the evening Major Brooks came in with Col. Sammis.[58] They had left the Island City hard aground between the Two Sisters, with Prince on board, & had come to us in a boat. I started to take Brooks to Jacksonville malgre the protest of the Pilot. The moon, young but vigorous was just in the zenith & I thought he could make it. But he whined about it, & soon ran the nose of Miss Getty into the Marsh near Yellow Bluffs. I told him to anchor & Brooks told him to be d——d. He obeyed me, postponing consideration of Brooks order.

We had a raw oyster, & wd. have gone to bed but found the saloon like a small Tophet, Stickney breathing stertorously in the thick air. Brooks opened all the doors & windows as I found on going down about 11 after spending an hour or two on deck. I shut part up & wrapped myself in my blanket.

13 FEBRUARY 1864, SATURDAY

Got up white with blanket & we steamed down to the mouth of the river. There waited until the day grew late & we impatient. It was half past ten oclock when we started for the basin & Haskell boarded us fr. a vessel which he had just brought over the bar. The Bar was very difficult since the blow. The channell had shifted badly & there was only 9½ feet on the bar. We turned the Achilles back. We got safely over & sent Haskell to the Beaufort. We made a quick run to Fernandina getting there a little after 3 oclock.

Spent the evening at Captain Sears. Heard some music. Returned with Lt. Tallcott. Found cabin full of [smoke?].

Brown & Sears. The altercation

14 FEBRUARY 1864, SUNDAY

We steamed out of the Harbor of Fernandina as the sun was rising. Struck about noon a school of whales—great shining black or dirty grey monsters with backs like hills & flukes like weavers' beams. I fired at one and missed him & felt unhappy.

Canis Marinus suddenly spoke at dinner with his mouth full of pudding Why, today's Valentine's day.

Sunday & St. V's Day. The cabin boy combed his locks & greased them in honor of the day. The skipper shaved & brushed his few remaining hairs "to the place where the hair didnt grow." Its gentle influences breathed in bay rum & bloomed in fine linen.

We took our pilot on board at 2½ & came in over the bar barked at by breakers on either hand. Past the hulk of the Jeff Davis—now used as a target by our guns & a place to take sheepshead by the idle & the piscatory.

Went to Papy's, to deposit our baggage.[59] Took a walk to our orange grove with the present keeper. The magnificent show of the bitter sweets & the promise of the fruited year. Lemons. Citron guava, plum peach & fig in plenty and pomegranate.

Called on Col Osborne & delivered the orders.[60] Col says he has but 250 men available for the purpose designated. I shall send the Getty to the Genl to let him know the state of the case & meanwhile order Osborn to get ready to move.

15 February 1864, Monday

Got the Helen Getty off at 10½ this morning. Established my office in the Dist Atty's office of the U. S. Court Room. After dinner swore a few persons.

Walked out to see the Johnson property. It looks very promising—a few wet places, but susceptible of much culture.

Two or three crackers came in & took a swear. They were recounting some queer experiences. One of them described Dickinson's men coming after him—his hiding in the bushes—his dismay at hearing one say "let's build a fire"—his relief at the reply "No, the whole woods is full of Yankee Cavalry & they wd. be down on us in ten minutes. His candid statement that he was studying up what tale to tell if they caught him.[61]

A fat young deserter loafed in & gave his story. Had got off on a 7 days to Green Cove & came in here. Was contentedly staying in the guardhouse till he could be discharged. Vowed his intention of taking the oath.

~~Walked around town to look at some property. Everyone seems to know just what I have done.~~[62]

Went to Miss Mathers in the evening, & from there to a little birthday toot of Major Hooper's at Col. Osborne. Mrs. Raymond there & Amy, the sweetest child in all the world.

16 February 1864, Tuesday

Dined at Mrs. Gardner's who has a beautiful avenue of orange trees. Received a good many signatures. The Colonel Recd. orders to take the

24th Mass. to Jacksonville. Leaving Col. Otis here.[63] I think I will go with them & get thence to Fernandina.

In the evening Mr. Oliveros came in & spent the shank thereof.[64] He is a shrewd old fellow without education or refinement but full of practical hard sense. He gave a short lecture on orange culture which is just now specially interesting to ~~Stickney and~~ me. The pruning, the manuring which blackens the leaves & strengthens the shoots—(the full-grown tree needs none, as the falling leaves perform that office) and many things else. He gave a most humorous account of the effect of muck manure on a farm near here, producing enormous turnips which afterward became the nursery of early watermelons which sold lucratively—the trick of a northern man he added simply. Indeed I find among these people everywhere a quiet & almost unconscious admission of the superiority of the North. A Northern house—a Northern farm—a Northern apparatus of any kind.

Oliveros gave a singularly candid account of the way he came to leave this country & his return, the Govt. [Copinge?] having threatened to shut him up in the fort "till his bones rotted" if he wouldnt go wrecking with Captain Martinelli.

We got him to talking politics & it seemed he wd. never stop. He had very little to say of recent affairs: his heart was in the past. If we asked him how any one stood on the great questions he wd. say "He is a good Whig"—or "a bitter Democrat."

17 FEBRUARY 1864, WEDNESDAY

Today in anticipation of the Hunter going I gave up my business to Col. Otis.

Hunter did not go in the morning. Capo says "I takes him out but he not like a lay out all night. All same so. He go out early morning so soon as see & he git to Jacksonwill tree oclock tomorrow."

Yesterday I met in the Plaza, Buff. with his friend Pareitti. He introduced him as "one of our strong Union men." Pareitti cringed & grinned, & shook my fist with snaky fingers. They have here a very uncommon breed of scoundrels. The greatest liars & most fawning stab-you-in-the-back rascals you could find unhung in any southern climate. Buff. tells his constituents that any one signing my oath signs his death warrant: & fawns snakily on every one with army buttons. He shall sign my oath himself or vote nevermore.

Today made an arrangement with Biddlecom to take care of our property here: he receiving $25 a month & a fourth of the oranges. ~~I walked around with him to see my houses. They very much need repair.~~

Mrs. Papy, Oliveros Daughter, gave me a splendid sweet orange

Went out to Old Oliveros place in the afternoon. He was busy working pretended not to see us till we were upon him. He showed us over his nursery & we then went with him to his house where he has some superb orange & citron trees. He showed as a compliment to his sagacity a dissected orange tree, & "bofe of em died."

Got my baggage on board & slept till six oclock in the morning.

18 February 1864, Thursday

When Cap. Alley waked me up & we went on board the Hunter, Capo came up stairs swearing fearfully.[65] He had lost his way down stairs & said he must have pilot to show him the way over the vessell.

Breakfast & sudden disappearance of the breakfasters. Each one assigning some special dish as the cause of his undoing. The true cause, the rolls.

We arrived at Jacksonville about dusk. I went out to loaf & met some of the 24th-sters whom I joined & we went to Col. Hartwell's quarters.[66] There we learned that a military execution was about to take place. Four negroes had Committed a rape on a woman in the neighborhood. After a while we heard dead march sounding & a regt marching by. Going out I saw the 55th in line in open square. Went in. In middle of the square a gallows was erected. It was light enough to define gallows clearly against the sky. A cart drove in & after pulling & hauling & swearing was backed under the gallows: the poor devil stood upright apparently engrossed by the trivial details: wanted more rope, &c. His sentence was read, the noose adjusted he said a few words to the crowd & the cart beginning to move he jumped up & tried to break his neck but failed & gasped & jerked & struggled dreadfully. His stertorous breathing could have been heard over the square. A man jumped up to his shoulders & hung on him swinging— No Effect: Another man got on: he still gasped: At last they raised him up

& jerked him down hard: & he ceased struggling & after a while the crowd dispersed.

We foraged for supper

19 FEBRUARY 1864, FRIDAY

I got my baggage on board the Price & filled up the time to ten oclock in tramping around. I passed by the hanging place & saw the poor devil still fluttering his rags in the wind—his head horribly oblique, his eyes staring wide his mouth open & his blackened tongue protruding. A curious crowd of negroes boys & crackers lingered around him, some who had been there last night taking a permanent station near him & detailing with intense relish to those less favored the hideous show of the night before.

Found the work by the old redoubt pretty well advanced and the one by the church staked off ready to begin.

Went to examine Record book & found a large no of citizens had signed, some of position and influence.

Got on board & started down the river about ten. Cold & raw on deck. Went below. A group of river men & one or two cracker deserters were sitting around the fire talking about the hanging. They described many styles—the favorite being that where a falling weight jerks the culprit up—then the Cuban garote where "one turn of the screw gives a click & yr. neck's broke." To all this talk the deserter listened with a breathless interest. One of the river men says with jocular delicacy "I guess you'll git hung when they ketch you." which did not seem to reassure him much.

They talked of their deaths affecting their life assurances with the greatest interest &c.

A rebel on shore waved a little white flag but we could not stop

We got to the mouth of the Harbor & went to the Ben Deford & spent the afternoon. I boarded the Haughton got Place to tea & gassed the evening.

20 FEBRUARY 1864, SATURDAY

No chance of getting out this morning. Visited Cosmopolitan, Gen Hunter, and went ashore & looked over ruins of Mayport-Mills.

Dined on board the Pawnee.

[twelve illegible lines]

21 FEBRUARY 1864, SUNDAY

Got over the bar this morning soon after day. Bingham woke me up with the miserable news of Henry's death, loss of 7 pieces, capture of 400 wounded & our total repulse, about 7 miles beyond Sanderson.[67] He has despatches from Turner to Gillmore.

Arrived at H. H. about 9½ after a good run of 14½ hours. Delivered our news to Gen. Gillmore. The Genl. was much shocked. He said "This comes of disobeying orders." He dwelt on this for some time. He said afterwards "I should rather he had lost these men in obedience to orders than in disobedience."[68]

Seymour has seemed very unsteady and queer since the beginning of this campaign. He has been subject to violent alternations of timidity & rashness now declaring Florida loyalty was all bosh—now lauding it as the purest article extant, now insisting that Beauregard was in his front with the whole Confederacy & now asserting that he could whip all the rebels in Florida with a good Brigade. He was ordered to fortify St. Mary's & Baldwin but pushed out beyond Sanderson instead & got severely punished.[69]

Bingham is going around the Head giving a terribly stampeded account of the affair.

22 FEBRUARY 1864, MONDAY

"Peconic" comes in this morning & reports Simmons Hamilton Meyrick Dunbar & McRae wounded. Col. Fribley killed.[70] Seymour in one despatch says "it is doubtful whether we can get in all our wounded": in another states that they are on the way in.

Gen. Vogdes was at breakfast this morning & I suppose will supercede Seymour.[71]

The Gen. G wrote today a letter to Turner in which he tells him what reinforcements are coming & what is best to be done. Two Brigades are going down, Ames & Fosters.[72] Jacksonville is to be held unless holding it involves a defeat.

Seymours "advance and consequent repulse" is characterized as "unauthorized & ill-timed" Frothingham has been sent down with the letter.

There was a ball tonight at Beaufort—gotten up by the young officers there in honor of the 22nd. Gen. G. went up for a few moments to lend his influence to counteract the gloom which was overspreading the camp. We got there early & loafed about till the dancing began. The room was exquisitely decorated. Several very clever pictures, eagles &c were done on the walls with magnolia leaves, & flags of all nations from the Navy &c.

I left with Gen. G & went on board the Hospital Ship: filled with wounded: went through the hold & up stairs where the artillery boys were. Saw many desperately wounded Col. Reed mortally, clutching at bed clothes & passing garments, picked up bed and all & carried away, picking out his clothes from a pile by the shoulder straps—"Major? no, Lt Col. Hamilton Myrick Dodge & Eddy, all very chipper & jolly.[73] Myrick shot in toes & hat (like a parenthesis) & sabre—Hamilton between seat & saddle & in forearm. Myrick proposed to Hamilton "to go to party. I'll do the dancing & you the hugging."

Suddenly Gen. Saxton who had been much moved by Reeds appearance, started off up to the ball. He arrived during a moment's pause in the [Lanciers?]. He stamped his foot. Let the music stop." Which it did. "The Ball cannot go on. Lights be out in half an hour" A friend of the Genl. asked "can we eat supper?" "Anyone who has the heart to eat at such a time" All had a heart of that peculiar construction for all ate. He came back glowing with the triumph of a generous action performed & asked us up to his house, where we drank champagne & whiskey & ate cake. Coming out found the grumbling feasters & went to Hilton Head abt 2 oclock.

23 FEBRUARY 1864, TUESDAY

Wrote to Nicolay an account of the matter in morning.
Rode Turners Horse in afternoon
The wounded officers came down & were stowed away in the quarters. Hamilton still indomitable. His nephew Sergeant Sessions, badly wounded with him. Myrick Dodge & Eddy holding court in Reese's tent.

24 FEBRUARY 1864, WEDNESDAY

Rode out with Turner who returned last night & represents Seymour as plucky & defiant. He brought his troops off the field splendidly according to all accounts.[74]

25 February 1864, Thursday

Craven spent the evening with us, talking about professional matters: trepanning two sergeants—one of whom the Dr. said "they are holding him in bed till he dies & he's an awful while pegging out." He gave a most ludicrous account of Dr Muzzy's Morphine-Belladonna escapade. Muzz took the Morphine by mistake for Quinine: then in defiance of Craven's advice, ate breakfast, relying on his great specific Belladonna to counteract it. Chewed Belladonna till he grew heavy & stertorous (nose itched, began scratching the back of the *neck.*): opened eye & saw he was poisoned: had him trotted around deck of Deford till got to Pulaski: there tumbled him into boat & went ashore: then pitched him into wheelbarrow & detailed two sergeants to spank him: pumped him out & put him in soak mucilage from the scenery at Theatre Barton & poured into him laudanum to counteract the counteragent.

Maj. Mulford had a picture taken of the wheelbarrow scene.[75] Lt. Col. Shoulder strap exposed—& wanted it sent to Muzzy as a good joke.

Dont like Hamilton's restless nervousness. A bad sign in the forehead. A[n]guish. Slippers a bad thing to wear.

Frothingham & I spent an hour at the Port Royal House with the Stickneys & Rivington.

26 February 1864, Friday

Admiral Dahlgren called on the Genl this morning[76]

28 February 1864, Sunday

The Arago came in this morning. The papers of the 23rd & 24th attack my coming here as a political trick. Q A G is much troubled at it. ~~I proposed to leave the department~~ [   ][77]

I had some talk with Turner. He thinks I had better stay. He gave me in full his idea of the present campaign.

This is Gen. G's birth day. He called us all together & we drank a glass of wine with him. He said to me in the hurry of preparation for going "What day is this?" "28." My birthday. I must open a basket of wine before

I go. We had a pleasant half-hour. The Gen hailed Jackson Frothingh and Henshaw. Henshaw whimsically disgusted.

We got on the Dictator at midnight.[78] The General's horse lost over-board—swimming around miserably snorting boats pulling after her. Couldnt find her.

Heard some of Henshaw's stories & went to bed.

29 FEBRUARY 1864, MONDAY

This morning as we neared Fernandina I persuaded the General to go on to Jacksonville & send boat back here for us. We landed. I summoned Col Guss to the General Arsenal.

Headache & misery in the afterday.

[several illegible lines]

Heard some queer incidents about the physical breakdown of the wounded officers. [two illegible lines]

1 MARCH 1864, TUESDAY

I opened my book this morning & got a few more names. Some refused to sign, on the ground that they were not repentant rebels: or that it was in Stickney's office. ~~I wrote to Biddlecom & sent him fees. Drew on [   ] for one thousand dollars.~~ The Dictator came in this afternoon & reported to me for orders. I will start for Key West in morning—

Henshaw sends a note asking me for Amour de Dieu to send him some gin from Key West.

2 MARCH 1864, WEDNESDAY

Island City got off very early this morning, leaving all the passengers behind but Alsop who rose with the lark.

The Dictator not coaled: the Captain cocking his weather eye sharply at the troubled Northeast sky.

A few crackers this morning varied the monotony of the guardhouse by coming in & taking a swear at the book.

I read Epes Sargent's farrago of stale sentiment & frantic balderdash which has been so lucky as to be the first out & has beguiled from the asinine public much greenback.[79]

We got on board the Dictator this evening for an early start. The wind moans ominously around the stateroom doors presaging a rough day tomorrow. We shall see.

3 MARCH 1864, THURSDAY

We went out to the Bar & passed it. I heard the sea hammering on the guards and turned over for another nap. Came back to Fernandina. The sea was very heavy: a steady line of breakers rolling in over the bar, without a break in 3 fathom water.

I went on shore. About noon came in the Peconic fr. Hilton Head with Judge Fraser.[80]

I walked out to the light House with Morrill & climbed to the top. The windows were broken & the place looked ruinous. "The 9th Maine" says the quiet Pennsylvanian who kept the light. "No such thing" shouted Private Morrill 9th Maine, "10th Connecticut.[81]

A varied panorama below my eyes: an immense dry marsh below bordered by wooded hills sloping off into the fields that girdled the town: a rivulet cutting it like the wavy streak I have seen in Calicoes: in front the white capped sea & to the right a dirty sky: bluegray and threatening.

M. had speculation in his eye. A dyke—a few drains—hay galore & $100 an acre.

I came back to boat: being late I teaed with subordinates: talking about weather: thought it squally.

I spent part of evening on board the Peconic. [ ] for a little while till I got opportunity to talk to Judge Fraser, who seems sincere & candid man with clear views. He thinks the time is not yet come for Florida.

I am very sure that we cannot now get the President's 10th & that to alter the suffrage law for a bare tithe would not give us the moral force we want. The people of the interior would be indignant against such a snap-judgment taken by incomers & would be jealous & sullen.

Dr Gross is on board. ~~Underwood tells a queer joke about him in the wheelhouse tight & roused by the swaying wheel to playing pilot. The results. "ring the bell, go ahead." Vessel rammed against wharf. "Wants me to run machine?"~~

~~Stickney said today, looking at States which have declared for Lincoln, "No power on earth can prevent his election.~~

4 MARCH 1864, FRIDAY

Judge Fraser seems to be a strong Lincoln man. He has very firm views about the way in which he thinks the State should be brought back into the Union—
We took a walk to the Light House this morning. ~~The girls had a tough time getting down and up stairs through hole a foot square.~~
I walked in the afternoon with Miss F. to the earth work guarding the city—coming back bought turnips.
We started for the bar at two P.M. The captain not liking the look of the weather we returned.
Gen. Gillmore & staff came in on Monohasset at dark. ~~We had a great time the staff people. Henshaw, being disposed by [   ] & the neglect of the young people told some good stories, "Rachel Elliott prepared for judgment" among others. I brought them to my room & they drank much whiskey & we went to bed late.~~

5 MARCH 1864, SATURDAY

Went to bed last night in the hazy state indicated in the last entry. Did not get up until tea today "In bunco tutissimus ibis"[82] There has been quite a heavy swell. Tonight the phosphorescent show is the finest I have yet seen. A broad track of glory follows the ship. By the sides abaft the wheels the rushing waves are splendid silver flecked here and there with jets of flame; while outside the silvery trouble the startled fish darting from our track mark the blue waters with curves & splashes of white radiance. Occasionally across our path drifts a broad blotch of luminous brilliancy—a school of fishes brightening the populous waters.

6 MARCH 1864, SUNDAY

A beautiful Sunday. The purest Southern day. The air cool but cherishing and kindly. The distant shore fringed with Palms & cocoanuts. The sea a miracle of color. On the one hand a bright vivid green: on the other a deep dark blue: flecked by floating shadows cast by the vagrant clouds that loaf in the liquid sky.

Passed Hillsboro & New River Inlet in the morning & made Cape Florida at noon. We struck out seaward there skirting the inner edge of the gulf stream where the pure emerald of the water was marred by the darker waves of the Gulf. Lighter around the vessel grew the pale green of the sea; more vivid and brilliant the shine inshore. When we passed the shoals off the Cape & took our southerly course outside the reefs ~~which we were henceforth to keep~~ I thought I had never seen so splendid a prodigality of Coloring in any marine picture. On our left towards the horizon rolled the dark azure of the Gulf Stream: before us and to our right as far as the distant shore the vivid emerald of these strange Floridian waters, the darker vegetation of the Coral Keys throwing its pale beauty into finer relief, while the sunny skies were flushed with a faint auroral radiance of pearl & pink, such as tinges the polished lips of the seashells of this coast.

Leaning over the starboard rail, gazing with a lazy enjoyment at this scene of enchantment, at the fairy islands scattered like a chain of gems on the bosom of this transcendent sea, bathed in the emerald ripples and basking in the rosy effulgence of the cherishing sky; the white sails flitting through the quiet inlets; the soft breeze causing the sunny waters to sparkle and the trees to wave: I ~~could not but~~ thought that here were the Isles of the Blessed: within the magic ring of these happy islands, the syrens were singing, and the Naiads were twining their flowing hair with sprays of the coral. Anchored in everlasting calm far from the malice of the sky or the troubling eyes of men, they sported through the tranquil years of the unending summer, in the sacred idleness of the immortals.

My friend Canis Marinus begged to differ. He said "there's the Rugged Keys: full o' mud-torkles & rattle snakes: them little boats is full of Conks—come up for to sponge."

At dusk we came to anchor off Indian Key—a rather famous place where a horticultural lunatic lived planted & died. We rowed ashore. As we neared the Island, a gruff voice hailed us, "Who are you?" "Reed" shouted our pilot which seemed satisfactory. We scraped heavily on the coral bottom as we went in, and brought up at a rickety old wharf. There had once been a rather lively place here. Large Buildings fitted up for Hospital purposes in the old wars. Now occupied by Capt. Bethel & a family of spongers. We asked for fish. Bethel said it was *Sabbath*: caught no fish today. Asked for Cocoanuts. Said hadnt any gathered. Pretty ugly job gathering on 'em in the night. Our little purser volunteered for the service & he Stickney & I went out. He & I scaled alternate trees & sent down the heavy clusters. We plunged into a tangled abattis of some thorny thing they called [Manilla?]: which scratched & pierced like the devil.

We came in bearing our spoils & found the whole family in the great barn like room of the store. White-headed—apathetic—open-mouthed—silent—indolent and stupid. We bought sponges & shells of them galore & went back to our ship.

Bethel came after us for a newspaper & a gass with Reed. They talked about wrecks & the profits thereof—of weddings & elopements—of crops & wealth at intervals of ten minutes between interlocutions. Brains hardening into an unlovely mould in a lonely life on one of these coral islands.

7 MARCH 1864, MONDAY

We steamed away as it grew light and arrived at Key West about noon. The Key lies bathed in the quiet ripples of the pale green water whitened by the coral. So bright green that I cannot describe the gemlike shine of the distant waters. The seagulls that soar above the sea have their white breasts & inside wings splendidly stained with green by the reflection of the gleaming water.

I went ashore, and after several inquiries found that Gen. W. lived ½ a mile from the dock. I went to a Hotel to inquire about a carriage & was referred to a Jew druggist, who pointed to a bay rat hitched to a shay in front of his door: & implored me for the pure love of God to be back by Two. I drove out by the beach to the barracks: passed 2 black sentries & found the General's Adjutant Capt. Bowers & soon thereafter, Genl. W. I was expected: Gen. Banks orders having arrived some time ago. I arranged my matters in half an hour.[83]

Going back to the boat saw Plantz & went ashore with him & Stickney & Browne to get a noted Spanish drink which he called champarao. From which henceforward all good angels guard me. It tasted like Paragoric debased by association with vitriol. I went off with a goodnatured party named Rawson & took the taste out of my mouth with Champagne & sat down to write letters to Banks & Hahn & glorify over the Louisiana elections.

In the evening Stickney & I went out to see a "popular nigger" named

Sandy. Some young "Knavies" were there. They chatted a moment, ordered some sapadillos (which taste like Castile soap & rotten apples) & then went away saying they were going to see the ladies—Whereat Sandy chuckled & guffawed to the imminent danger of his supper which he had been eating quietly sensibly refusing to let our entrance disturb him.

Sandy talked mostly of his influential friends, "Captains & Colonels & them things" & gingerly of the rebellious & fugacious. S. asked him if he were bothered much. "No! not sence I broke dat fellers jaw in tree pieces— I blieve he was a rebel. A passel 'em: a dozen, sar, come to debbil me: dey tore down my fence panels & I went out to see. I aint feared a nobody. But a man got to be lively whan he's fighting a passel: its a busy time of the year den: I hit one of em & he straightened out like a log: broke his jaw in tree pieces: & de rest dey run. I nebber complains: de officers dey got dere hands full: must not trouble bout every little tittle: Is a darkey sort of person. I takes off hat to everybody: but dey got to luff me alone."

I went to see Judge Boynton: found Admiral Bailey there. Boynton is the jolliest invalid I have ever met. Blackguards his doctors in the most refreshing way & damns the undertakers grinning about the door. His irrepressible vivacity & elasticity & consequent imprudence retards his recovery.[84]

8 March 1864, Tuesday

I walked around the town this morning—met several of the citizens who said they were pure & disinterested & other people were unscrupulous scamps—seems the usual topic of conversation here with strangers within their gates. The town looks more like the tropics than anything I have yet seen. The cocoanut trees are the special feature of the streets: every yard is distinguished by their huge fanlike branches.

I have loafed nearly all day on deck looking with unsatisfied eyes on the beauty of this water. Filled with gunboats blockaders & clumsy schooners & white men of war's boats flashing through the pale waves.

Took dinner, in company with Brown and Stickney, with Plantz, Dist. Atty. A very nice dinner—my first experience of fried plantains. Capt. Bowers came in to invite me to dine with the General tomorrow. Declined as I hope to be off by noon.

Passed a half hour talking politics with Mr. Howe, collector of the Port.[85]

9 MARCH 1864, WEDNESDAY

(The only hold I have on days of the week & month is this notebook.)

I Went this morning early to pay me parting compliments to Admiral & General. They both had a story of a victory at Jacksonville which I think improbable.

I found a very decent darky with a very decent buggy belonging to a v. d. Dr Sweet & they, all together, took me riding to my engagements. The only blot of decency on the Key West escutcheon. Otherwise they a race of thieves & a degeneration of vipers.

We cast off about noon and night came upon us before we had made Indian Key which was to be our anchorage for the night, as we wanted to be in the Lee of Alligator Bank & reef to avoid the fresh gale now blowing in the gulf. We all stood widelegged and anxious on the forecastle as men will about little things on ship—Joe heaving the lead—the Captain leaning to the breeze his alpaca coat bagging like a [seedy?] balloon—old Reed confident and oracular—till Strong who had been hanging like a pointer dog over the rail sung out "Light Ho! 4 Pts on the Port Bow." This was old Bethel & we at once knew where we were. We anchored and lay there quietly.

I finished my poem begun today on Leaving Key West ("Northward")

10 MARCH 1864, THURSDAY

Sailed away early in the morning and passed Cape Florida at noon. Made Jupiter Light at six oclock in the evening.

I burnt my face badly by dozing in the sun. Covered it with Glycerin & felt uncomfortable & unpresentable.

11 MARCH 1864, FRIDAY

Early this morning as we had passed Jupiter Inlet, a little smack ran across our bow. On her stern was painted Hannah of Nassau. We hailed her, she came alongside and said she was bound from Nassau to Key West: Had had rough weather in the gulf. We thought her a blockade runner She was manned by two ragged white men and one negro who all seemed badly frightened. I suppose she was a blockade runner but as she was utterly valueless to us, as we could not tow her without swamping her, as we could not spare men from our crew to manage her I gave orders to let her go. There was some grumbling, but I ~~shut~~ quieted it ~~up~~.[86]

It is cool & cloudy & a souwester is blowing.

Later the wind freshened to a sort of gale and a heavy shower fell.

We reached Fernandina between four & five entering the muddy water of this coast soon after dinner. We found there had been a heavy hailstorm here this morning.

[illegible line]

12 March 1864, Saturday

A fine day. Got away from Fernandina at 5½ A.M. and arrived at Hilton Head at 3 P.M. The General read Stickney's letter and directed me to send to Fernandina for him.

Sanger & Suter came in and staid late & sang songs & drank whiskey.

I saw today a ~~blackguardly~~ savage article in the World or News about me.[87]

I was much shocked at hearing today of Ulric Dahlgren's death. A great future cut off and a good fellow gone.[88]

13 March 1864, Sunday

Dined at Beaufort today with Dr. Clymer. A good time. Coming back I first heard Ralph Trembly play the Jewsharp, a miraculous performance.[89]

Gen. Vogdes expects to be placed in command in Florida. He gave me this morning in extenso his views of our campaign here and the strategy of the coming year in whole field. The object here being, *illo teste* to occupy points now held & thence make careful incursions into the interior, getting supplies & harrassing the enemy: and away fr. here, to take Richmond & the line of the James River with 150,000 men and then increase the army of the South to 80,000 or so & take Augusta Georgia. He thinks the enemy's plan is to fight and damage Grant as much as possible & then to reinforce Lee & slip Meade and raid into Maryland & Pennsylvania. He estimates enemy's present force 150,000 & the amount which will be raised in every way 200,000 more. I think he overestimates the enemy.

16 MARCH 1864, WEDNESDAY

Party last night in the Commissary building.[90]

17 MARCH 1864, THURSDAY

I breakfasted on board the Arago like a fighting cock.

I read from Gen. Gillmore's letter book that

on Decem. 22 1863, Gen. Halleck informs Gen G. that he is authorized by the Sec. of War to undertake any expedition he chooses with the force at his disposal.

Jan. 14. Gen G. writes to the Sec of War that he intends to occupy the West Bank of the St. John's & to revive trade and business in that region, & on the

15th Jan 1864 He says the same thing to Gen. Halleck.

I arrived at H. H. Jan 19, 1864

on the 22nd of January Halleck writes that as an outlet for cotton & a place for recruiting the expedn. may pay. As a purely military measure he don't think much of it.

And on the 31st Jan. Gen Gillmore writes to Halleck showing that the purposes of the expedn. are

1st To afford an opening for trade

2nd to cut off largely enemies supplies & railroad facilities,

3d to obtain recruits

4th to comply with wishes of the loyal citizens & enable them under protection to organize the state Govt.

It is this last expression, an evident afterthought, added after the rest was penned, which Gen. Halleck has used so much to the disadvantage of the expedition, of Gen. Gillmore the President and myself.

I spoke to the General about it: he said he added that clause to show Gen. Halleck that the expedition wd. incidentally favor the reconstruction of the State, and wd. thereby advance the cause which the Prest. has at heart.

I could not but be struck with the honor and loyalty and soldierly candor at the bottom of a blunder so great, as that of supposing that a cause wd find favor in Gen. Halleck's eyes, because it advanced the cause which the Prest. has at heart.

18 March 1864, Friday

The day is windy and cold. A large party went riding on the beach. Passed the smallpox camp telling the ladies it was Camp Variola. "Who is in command?" "Col. Petit verole."[91]

At night went to the Theatre: saw the Idiot Witness & Boots at Swan.[92]

After the Theatre had many fellows in my room & drank liquors various & copious. After that in Sanger's room. Still more whiskey. A very sociable crowd at midnight.

19 March 1864, Saturday

This morning was waked up by demands for whiskey to sober on. Music at quarters.

I went to say Good Bye to Hamilton. He is getting quite despondent. He torments himself with all the little knowledge of surgery he has, until he has grown very morbid & low. He thinks he must lose his arm & fears his system is too much reduced to stand the shock.

The General tells me he intends to ask of the War Department permission to take the 10th Army Corps away from here and lead it in the field himself. Halleck has asked him how many troops he can spare reserving enough for purely defensive operations. He says he can spare 8 or 9000. Now the effective force of the 10th Corps is 11,000 men, & the troops composing it are such as have been longest in the Dept. and the Medical director advises that they be moved first. Gen. Gillmore will make this application by today's steamer.[93]

We got on board at about 4 oclock & soon after weighed anchor. We lay in the Stream until Gen Gillmore boarded us in a tug & gave me despatches for Halleck & Cullum of the tenor aforesaid.

I assumed command making Capt. Burger Adjt. & Executive Officer.[94] A few men quietly tight on smuggled liquors About midnight found a man on deck furiously drunk: had him put in irons and triced to the Jackstaff. Sergeants begging for him, good quiet fellow, & that style.

P. S. Same man drunk and tied up next night. Told him I would let him go, if he would preach. See me d——d first.

20 MARCH 1864, SUNDAY

A very fine day—clear & cool. Service below stairs in morning—on deck afternoon & prayermeeting in the cabin. I read George Sand's "Mare au Diable."[95]

21 MARCH 1864, MONDAY

A miserable day—strong head wind blowing—everybody (I look at matters subjectively) sea-sick. I lay on my back and read Dickens accounts of his own misery coming over here.[96]

22 MARCH 1864, TUESDAY

"And the second was like unto it."
I read Eleanor's Victory" —one of Miss Braddon's impossible unsexed women, whom even marrying a good man dont cure.[97]

23 MARCH 1864, WEDNESDAY

Lay to soon after midnight. A full attendance at breakfast. Three inches of snow on deck—a cold raw day. Effeminate Southerners of six months standing, shivering like Italian Greyhounds.[98]

Our sick woman obstinately refuses to die & grows almost well as the time approaches for her to get home

My family grew uproariously happy as they drew near home.

We drove to the Hotel & played soldier like young idiots coming home from School. The Shops were sutlers—the Butchers commissaries &c.

I went to the Custom House & talked awhile with D. He has a plan by which through ——— he can exploit the ——— and get ——— off the track. Le jeu vaut-il la chandelle?[99]

Brother [Charlie] very sick: went to him. Found him still consumed by rage military. Uniform on a table, foils on the wall. His last fancy the 11th Indiana. Talked matter over.

Reported [   ] to Dix, dined & started for Washington. After preposterous supper at midnight adjourned with Greene to sleeping car. Arrived at Washington halfpast 6.

24 March 1864, Thursday

I Arrived at Washington this morning finding Nicolay in bed at 7 oclock in the morning. We talked over matters for a little while & I got some ideas of the situation from him.

After breakfast I talked with the President. There was no special necessity of presenting my papers as I found he thoroughly understood the state of affairs in Florida and did not seem in the least annoyed by the newspaper falsehoods about the matter. Gen. Halleck, I learn has continually given out that the expedition was the Presidents & not his (Halleck's). So Fox tells me. The President said he has not seen Gillmores letters to Halleck but said he had learned from Stanton that they had nothing to bear out Halleck's assertion. I suppose Halleck is badly bilious about Grant. Grant the Prest. says is Commander in Chief & Halleck is now nothing but a staff officer. In fact says the President "when McClellan seemed incompetent to the work of handling an army & we sent for Halleck to take command he stipulated that it should be with the full power and responsibility of Commander in Chief. He ran it on that basis till Pope's defeat: but ever since that event, He has shrunk from responsibility whenever it was possible"[100]

The Radicals are acting very ugly. Gratz Brown says they will beat Lincoln in any case. Peck says they have no voting strength.[101]

The President looks favorably on Gen: Gillmore's plan of coming north with the 10th Corps but no decision will be made until Grant returns. He advised me to go down to the Army of the Potomac and talk things over with the Genl. who is now at Culpepper: or wait till he comes here & go down to Fort Monroe with him. I fear I cant as Nicolay is going away.[102]

25 March 1864, Friday

Spent part of last evening talking with Secretary Chase. He seems deeply interested just now in negro [voting?], believing it to be the best thing for the slave states & the surest safeguard against a rebel reaction after the war. I mentioned my plan for a convention in Florida which he heartily approved.

A bad Day—rain & wind & weather. Nicolay goes to New York tonight.

Blair talking about the Missouri muddle spoke of the Presidents lais-
sez-faire policy with the radicals there, as resembling the Irishman's with
the skunk: "let him alone and the d——d little thing will stink itself to
death."

Hawkins Taylor says that Jim Lane will beat Carney on his election &
that Pomeroy has ripped up his own bowels by his recent course.[103]

26 MARCH 1864, SATURDAY

Colonel Webster is here, very anxious to have the Marylanders in the
army allowed to come home and vote. He says the vote will be very close
& without the soldiers, the state may be lost.[104] Stanton says the troops
must not leave on the eve of action.

Frank H. Underwood came in this morning to get a recn. to Gillmore
to allow him to saw mill at Jacksonville.

Grant writes a despatch fr. Hd Qrs of the Army suggesting a very extensive Spring Campaign. That Shreveport being taken by Banks he should
then move against Mobile. Rosecrans & Steele should reinforce him in this
as heavily as possible and if necessary Sherman add something to his force.
That Gillmore should keep what he has in the South holding all his available force mobilized to assist Grant when he begins to operate against
Lee.[105]

Seward says Wykoff is in town to sell out the Herald to the highest bid-
der. S. is bored by him but will not see him.[106]

27 MARCH 1864, SUNDAY

I Had a little talk with Stanton this morning. He says Gillmore has
rather lost in popular favor recently but without any merited blame: that
he had done all he promised. He is a little severe on the Navy.

He speaks very freely in favor of the President on the Prestial fight.

~~I went to church & was badly bored.~~

Saw General Grant: a quiet, self possessed and strong sense looking man. He pleased me by the prompt way in which he heard what I had to say about Gillmore & answered.

Dined with Sumner at the Hoopers. S. says that matters look well with France—that Drouyn de L'Huys sent for Dayton the other day & said Max. wd. not affiliate with the rebels.[107]

General Hunter was in my room today. He is very anxious to go into the field. They have offered him one or two administrative departments but he will not accept them. He wants to fight.[108]

He spent a great while with Grant in the West. He has a very good opinion of him. He says he is a cool man: industrious, discreet and enterprising: able to hold his own plans and purposes and profit by the errors of the enemy.

> Executive Mansion,
> Washington,
> March 27, 1864

My Dear General [Gillmore]

I have spoken with the President the Secretary of War & General Cullum about the matter of the detachment of the 10th Corps from the Department. It seemed eminently practicable to the President & was not viewed unfavorably by either of the others.

Today, General Grant came to Washington for a few hours. By the permission of the President I called upon him and told him the whole of the circumstances as detailed by yourself to me, and repeated to him the expression of your desire that the 10th Corps be preserved intact, and led by you in the field. He seemed ~~much~~ pleased by the suggestion, & said that while without the expression of your willingness to lead a corps in the field, he would not have given an order for you to do so, he would be very glad to have the benefit of your services thus voluntarily tendered: & said that he would write to you at once to make such arrangements ~~in the Department~~ as will ~~release the 10th Corps from active duty &~~ enable you to concentrate and organize the 10th Corps so in readiness ~~that it may be ready at any time~~ that it may be moved where it is required.[109]

30 MARCH 1864, WEDNESDAY

I spent the early part of this evening at Mr. Welles: a very large infusion of fogy there: fine old fellows with nine stripes on the coat sleeve. All the Admirals and Commodores on the Wilkes Court-Martial were there: Mrs General Grant also. I went from there to Forneys, where a party was assembled to meet Forrest. I got there late; after the toasting & speeching of the great Edwin was over, but heard some recitations from him & McCullough and from Dan Dougherty of Philadelphia who was by far the cleverest and brightest of the party: his Spring Garden reminiscences were full of character. Dougherty toasted Sickles who responded—first paying a most graceful compliment to Forrest as a representative of American genius, (the old fellow surlily eyeing him, with his head abased like a Buffalo Bull) then went off into the general issues of the war: saying by nature habit & education he was a sympathizer with rebels & rebellions: that he had studied this thing at its beginning but that this was different from all other rebellions in the fact that it was a reaction against liberty—conspiracy of the strong vs the weak: of privilege against freedom, of Aristocracy vs Democracy. He concluded by expressing his belief that the nation would come out of the struggle stronger than ever before purified & strengthened, with its only element of discord eliminated.[110]

Once or twice during Sickles careful little speech, Forrest applauded. Forney was delighted, & clinched the thing by referring to it in a little speech—claiming Forrest as one of us.

31 MARCH 1864, THURSDAY

A ball at National: very neat little thing. I was congratulated by chuckleheaded boys who have been a week or two in the service, on being "one of us." Johnson & Kinney had a dirty little muss.[111]

I adjourned to the Patent office about 2 in the morning & saw the fag end of the dance there—clouds of dust & crowds of demi monde & base mechanicals. A small policeman in constant hot water guarding the entrance to the hats—&c

2 APRIL 1864, SATURDAY

The Kentucky Congressmen in my room with Rousseau. Enter Jim Lane, Rousseau addressing him with Kentucky cordiality; after Jim goes

Rousseau turns to his friends evidently pluming himself on the magnanimity which he displayed in speaking to James.[112]

They talked on about men and things. Sumner was discussed: "Why" said Rousseau "let him come out to Kentucky & see our different way of living & he wd. never be satisfied again with the mean and low life of New England. He wd. find such a noble freehearted hospitality there that he cd. never bear his life at home again. There is nothing now to take him to Boston: so he always spends his vacations here. It wd. be different if he visited Kentucky once." Clay quietly extinguished the argument by saying "he has been at Ky and at my house: & here he scarcely knows me."

3 April 1864, Sunday

Dined at Lamons, & spent part of the evening with Lorings. The oldsters veering round to the heavy patriotic & the youngster still vehemently secesh.

4 and 5 April 1864, Monday and Tuesday

Der Freischutz at Grover's, & April 5th Martha. The President and Mrs. Lincoln attended. On the 4th the President wrote a political letter to Hodges of Ky which will be published in due time. The radicals will attack him like drabs on the strength of it.[113]

7 April 1864, Thursday

Tonight Private Theatricals at Maunsell B. Fields.[114] Seward, Chase, Stanton, were there, with their families. Major Hetzel recently dismissed [from] the service played a Gens d'Armes in a Majors uniform.

13 April 1864, Wednesday

My Dear Halpine,

I thank you for yr. kind & most unjust letter. I did call at your lair on Bleecker Street and you were not at home—nor was M. le General. I am too old a Soldier to pass thro yr. camp without reporting.

I thank you for offering to set me right with the pensive public. But the game is not worth so bright a candle. The original lie in the Herald was dirty enough & the subsequent commentaries were more than usually nasty. But the Tycoon never minded it in the least and as for me, at my age, the more abuse I get in newspapers the better for me. I shall run for constable some day on the strength of my gory exploits in Florida.[115]

I am stationed here for present. I fear I shall not get away soon again. I have a great deal to do. It is the best work that I can do if I must stay here.[116]

24 APRIL 1864, SUNDAY

Today the President loafing into my room picked up a paper and read the Richmond Examiners recent attack on Jeff. Davis. It amused him. "Why" said he "the Examiner seems abt. as fond of Jeff as the World is of me."[117]

Ives has returned to the Navy Yard: was here this morning.

E. Lyulph Stanley son of Lord Stanley has been here for a week.[118] I took him over to Arlington & showed him the African. He asked more questions than I ever dreamed of in similar circumstances. He applied a drastic suction to every contraband he met with & came back with brain and note-book crammed with instructive miscellany. He has been exhausting everybody the same way: till his coming is dreaded like that of the schoolmaster by his idle flock. He is a most intelligent gentleman—courteous & ready—a contrast to most Englishmen in his freedom from conceit & prejudice.

He leaves town today. I gave him my autograph book: we exchanged Cartes "like two young shepherds very friendly & pastoral. Tonight Gen. Burnside came up with me from Willards to see the President. They talked about the opening campaign more than anything else. The despatch of Admiral Lee that had just been recd. containing the news of the fall of Plymouth, Burnside thot bogus.[119]

He gave some interesting reminiscences of the siege of Knoxville.[120] (Tad laughing enormously whenever he saw his father's eye twinkle, though not seeing clearly why).

Burnside & Sigel are the only ones in motion in accordance with the order for a general movement on the 23d.

25 April 1864, Monday

This morning Burnside came in with Foster a fine handsome fellow who *looks* like a soldier at least & seemed to think the Plymouth matter was more serious than he considered it last night.[121]

If I can get away during this campaign, I think I will go either with Burnside or Gillmore.

[27 April 1864, Wednesday]

On the evening of the *25th* Fox who had been frequently telegraphed by Butler to come down to Ft. Monroe determined to go & asked me to go with him. We started from the Navy Yard at 5:30, passing Willards while Burnsides splendid column was moving down 14th Street across the Long Bridge into Virginia.[122] This is the finest looking & best appointed force I have ever yet seen. A little gorgeous & showy, reminding one of the early regiments who went shining down to Bull Run & the Peninsula as if to a pic-nic. The 3d N. J. Cavalry looked fine and yellow in their new cloaks & gold braided [   ]. The officers looked so superbly outlandish that it surprised one to hear them speaking, in a Yankee accent, pure American, as Cash Clay calls it. The black regiments looked well & marched better than others: As in fact they always do.

We went down the river among the twilight "shadders" and got some fish and dined off shad roe and shad. Fox had brought with him some of his choice Oolong tea. He told us of a present that a Chinese grandee once made to the crew of a ship he was on of a chest apiece of their fine tea that the crew not liking sold for common tea & the officers drank gradually growing to like it until one day a tea-taster came in and smelling the exquisite bouquet exclaimed that they were drinking a tea which would impoverish a millionaire to use habitually.

We got to Fortress Monroe in the morning & Welles & I visited the "Iroquois," Capt. Raymond Rodgers, while Fox went to see the General. Coming ashore we skirmished for some time about the walls of the Fortress before we could find the right entrance. We went in: saw Schaffer and Kent who was loafing around with an air intensely ennuyeé, and who said "There are plenty of indications here which to a green hand wd. ~~indicate~~ presage an early movement: but we blasé fellows dont seem to see it: we are familiar with large promise & scanty performance.[123]

Joined Butler & Fox on the ramparts. Butler said he was walking there for the first time in several months: preferring to take necessary exercise on horseback. He spoke highly of the negro troops—especially of their walking powers: they start off & trot slouchingly without wasting any muscle in grace of action, he said illustrating the shuffling step on the ramparts bending his knees & dragging his feet over the oniony grass.[124] He spoke of the delight with which Bob Ould ate the good dinners he got while at the fort—saying that one breakfast he got at Shaffers wd. have cost $2000 in Richmond.

At Gen. Butler's suggestion we went to the Rip-Raps. On the way to the boat we met Gens. Vogdes, Foster & Kautz, whose troops are at Yorktown, where is also Turner and Terry. The Rip-Raps is a flattened ellipse—a splendid piece of masonry so far to which two more stories are to be added—one being already completed. The old wall, whose sinking caused the change & delay in the fort's construction is still to be seen, the roughness & imperfect workmanship contrasting sharply with the finish & magnificence of the work of today. Butler is anxious to be allowed to fire at the work from Old Point to test its strength before the building goes any farther. He told me of a remarkable shot that was made from Ft. Wool—(Ripraps) at the rebel flagstaff sewalls point.[125]

We went back joined by Admiral Lee & Capt. Barnes and started up to Luncheon. Major Davis was good enough to give us somewhat to sustain life, a better luncheon than one cd. easily get in Washington. We called on Madame la Generale a most courteous and kindly lady and then loafed awaiting the issue of the conference of General Secretary & Admiral. My own enterprise was a failure, owing to Gillmore's not having arrived and Turner having gone to Yorktown.[126]

I had a good deal of talk with Schaffer, One of "the best staff a man was ever blessed with—Strong Turner Shaffer & Weitzell" as Butler says. Schaffer is sanguine about the coming movement. "We will fasten our teeth" he says "on Lee's line of supplies & he must leave his positions to come and beat us off," relying on Grant's not being the man to let that be done quietly.[127]

We went up to Yorktown, accompanied by Admiral Lee: Met there Capt. Babcock & visited Baldy Smith who returned to the Cabin of the "Baltimore" and passed several hours in conference.[128]

Fox seemed troubled sorely by the prospect. He fears the details have not been sufficiently studied: that the forces are to bulge ahead and get badly handled: that they rely on help from the Navy in places where the Navy cannot possibly help—but rather "will be as useless as an elephant with his trunk unscrewed & his tusks unshipped." That going up the James between the precipitous banks a few riflemen on the banks will produce a panic that nothing can remedy. He seemed surprised that the Navy shd. not have been informed of the intended movement until today: or that Grant shd. have sanctioned & concluded that G. must be letting the thing slide on without suggestion from him, to squelch it before it was consummated, or relying upon his other plans might have given this column up to the fate of a reconnaissance in force which will have accomplished its object if it diverts from *his* front a force large enough to destroy it.

We arrived off the Arsenal at 4½ on the 27th and finding our way barred by a grounded schooner we got upon the wharf & walked to the avenue. We ate shad & fired vainly at vagrant birds on the way up the river.

28 APRIL 1864, THURSDAY

Had considerable talk with the Prest. this evening. He understands that the day arranged for Grants movement is to be the 2nd prx—Monday. Sherman has asked for a little more time—says that he cant fully come up to his part in the programme before the 5th. Sigel is at work on his.[129]

The stories of Grant's quarrelling with the Secretary of War are gratuitous lies. Grant quarrels with no one.

The Prest. tells a queer story of Meigs. When McClellan lay at Harrison's Landing, Meigs came one night to the President & waked him up at Soldier's Home to urge upon him the immediate flight of the Army from that point—the men to get away on transports & the *horses to be killed* as they cd not be saved. Thus often" says the Prest. "I who am not a specially brave man have had to sustain the sinking courage of these professional fighters in critical times.[130]

"When it was proposed to station Halleck here in general command, he insisted, to use his own language on the appt. of a General-in-Chief who shd. be held responsible for results. We appointed him & all went well enough until after Pope's defeat when he broke down—nerve and pluck all gone—and has ever since evaded all possible responsibility—little more since that than a first-rate clerk.[131]

Granville Moody was here this evening & told a good story abt. Andy Johnson & his fearful excitement when Buell was proposing to give up Nashville to the enemy.[132] He found him walking up & down the room supported by two friends. "Moody I'm glad to see you" he said. The 2 friends left & he & Moody were alone. "We're *sold* Moody—Were *sold*" fiercely reiterating. He's a traitor Moody" and such. At last suddenly "Pray! Moody!" And they knelt down & prayed Andy joining in the responses like the Methodists. After they had done he said, "Moody I feel better. Moody I am not a Christian—no church—but I believe in God—in the bible—all of it—Moody—but *I'll be damned if Nashville shall be given up.*

The Prest. was much amused by a story I told him of Gurowski.

The venomous old count says, "I *despise* the Anti-Lincoln Republicans. I say I go against Lincoln, for he is no fit for be President: di say di for one term (holding up one dirty finger) [bimeby?] di beat Lincoln, den di for two term (holding up two unclean digits): di is cowards and *Ass!*"

A despatch just recd. from Cameron stating that the Harrisburgh [convention] had elected Lincoln delegates to Baltimore properly instructed.[133]

The President assents to my going to the field for this campaign if I can be spared from here.

Jim Lane came in a few days ago with a telegram announcing his complete victory over the Carney-Pomeroy men—the happiest fellow out of jail. He read over the list of elected delegates to Baltimore, himself & Wilder being among them, and added "All vindictive friends of the President." The adjective is especially felicitous.[134]

30 APRIL 1864, SATURDAY

The President this morning read me his letter to Gen. Grant, an admirable one, full of kindness & dignity at once. It must be very grateful to Grant on the eve of battle.[135]

Fry's nomn. which has been delayed for several days was signed today. Fry has been removing Provost Marshals without consultation & has stirred up hot water in Pennsylvania. I warned him of the trouble he was causing & he said the Secretary had authorized him to make removals where he saw fit.[136]

Fox now thinks that Butler and Lee are moving in the dark. That their destination will be changed at the last moment. He thought the movements down there were inexplicable on any other theory. He told Halleck so, on arriving here at which he grinned, & said they had not got their orders yet.

I Heard at Blair's last night a singular story of a young fellow of good family named Koon of Phila. marrying a Soubrette a notre dame de Corinthe—Sophie Gimber.

Tonight came in Swett and Lamon anxious about their line of stocks. Well might they be!

The President came loafing in as it grew late and talked about the reception which his Hodges letter has met with. He seemed rather gratified that the Tribune was in the main inspired by a kindly spirit in its criticism. He thought of & found & gave to me to decipher Greeley's letter to him of the 29th July, 1861.[137] This most remarkable letter still retains for me its wonderful interest as the most insane specimen of pusillanimity that I have ever read. When I had finished reading Nicolay said "That wd. be nuts to the Herald. Bennett wd. willingly give $10,000.00 for that." To which the Prest., tying the red tape round the package, answered "I need $10,000 very much but he could not have it for many times that."

The President has been powerfully reminded, by General Grants present movements and plans, of his (Presidents) old suggestion so constantly made and as constantly neglected, to Buell & Halleck et al to move at once upon the enemy's whole line so as to bring into action to our advantage our great superiority in numbers.[138] Otherwise by interior lines & control of the interior railroad system the enemy can shift their men rapidly from one point to another as they may be required. In this concerted movement however, great superiority of numbers must tell: As the enemy however successful where he concentrates must necessarily weaken other portions of his line and lose important position. This idea of his own, the Prest. recognized with especial pleasure when Grant said it was his intention to make all the line useful—those not fighting could help the fighting. "Those not skinning can hold a leg" added his distinguished interlocutor.

It seems that Banks' unhappy Red River Expedition was undertaken at the order & under the plan of Gen. Sherman, who having lived at Alexandria had a nervous anxiety to repossess the country. Grant assented from his confidence in Sherman & Halleck fell into the plan. Had not this wasteful enterprise been begun Banks wd. now be thundering at the gates of Mobile & withdrawing a considerable Army from Sherman's front at Chattanooga.

Sherman has asked for an extension from the 2nd to the 5th to complete his preparations ~~vs~~ against Dalton. He says that Thomas' and Schofield's Armies will be within one day's march of Dalton by tonight, and that McPherson will be on time.[139]

A little after midnight as I was writing those last lines, the President came into the office laughing, with a volume of Hood's works in his hand to show Nicolay & me the little Caricature "An unfortunate Bee-ing," seemingly utterly unconscious that he with his short shirt hanging about his long legs & setting out behind like the tail feathers of an enormous ostrich was infinitely funnier than anything in the book he was laughing at. What a man it is! Occupied all day with matters of vast moment, deeply anxious about the fate of the greatest army of the world, with his own fame & future hanging on the events of the passing hour, he yet has such a wealth of simple bonhommie & good fellow ship that he gets out of bed & perambulates the house in his shirt to find us that we may share with him the fun of one of poor Hoods queer little conceits.[140]

5 MAY 1864, THURSDAY

Last evening Grant telegraphed that he was across the Rapidan dating 1.30 P.M. & wished Butler to be so informed.[141] Butler said the evening before "I am ordered to move at 8 A.M. tomorrow & shall obey the order."

This evening while I was sitting in the Prst's room, came in Green Clay Smith & Ashley. They were talking about some matters which drifted into politics. Smith said nothing cd. beat Lincoln. Ashley did not give in his adhesion, but denounced the Fremont-Cleveland movement as foolish and ruinous: he said that Fremont was in New York personally soliciting signers to the Cleveland call: that he sent for him (Ashley) & he wd. not go to see him: that Fremont was an ass &c.[142] That when he was a candidate in '56 at first no one imagined he was going to be elected: he was nominated because they did not want to damage a better man by having him beaten: but that before the canvass ended they feared F. would be President: A. says he has a natural affinity for scoundrels. A. seems to be inclined to support the regular nominees, but I suppose he will make up his mind on that point after the convention meets. I never see him now without thinking of *Prof Ashley the Great Biologizer*. A great fine animal nature—unabashed cheek and a cheery manner are good stock in trade for a mesmerist. The long-haired vegetarians always make a sad hash of it when they attempt it.

9 May 1864, Monday

Received today the first despatches from Grant.[143]

The President thinks very highly of what Grant has done. He was talking about it today with me and said "How near we have been to this thing before and failed. I believe if any other General had been at the Head of that army it would have now been on this side of the Rapidan. It is the dogged pertinacity of Grant that wins." It is said that Meade observed to Grant that the enemy seemed inclined to make a Kilkenny cat fight of the affair, & Grant answered, "~~We have~~ Our cat has the longest tail."

13 May 1864, Friday

Early this morning Nesmith came in with Ingalls spread eagle despatch—which "Nez" in the worst possible taste published in the papers[144]—Seward and the President in the room together reading telegrams. Nesmith on hearing that Grant had said "I will fight it out on this line if it takes all summer" told an awful backwoods story which is a miracle of pertinency.

Jim Lane came into my room this morning and said the President must now chiefly guard against assassination. I poohpoohed him & said that while every prominent man was more or less exposed to the attacks of maniacs, no foresight could guard against them. He replied by saying that he had by his caution & vigilance prevented his own assassination when a reward of one hundred thousand dollars had been offered for his head. Bruce, who was sitting near, who has lost his contest in the House & who consequently is disposed to take rather cynical views of things, observed, when Lane had left, that he was probably anxious to convince the President that his life was very precious to *him* (L).

14 May 1864, Saturday

Carney has written a very impertinent letter to the President in relation to troops for Kansas which the President today in a very characteristic letter answers & nullifies.[145]

Kelley was here this morning. He is much disgusted with the recent foolish and injurious action of Anna Dickinson. He says also that Miller McKim and other distinguished radical abolitionists are entirely satisfied that the President is (in Kelly's words) "the wisest radical of them all," which accounts for Garrisons speech at the recent anniversary.[146]

The President came in last night in his shirt & told us of the retirement of the enemy from his works at Spotsylvania & our pursuit. I complimented him on the amount of underpinning he still has left & he said he weighed 180 pds. Important if true.

Pomeroy has recently asked an audience of the President for the purpose of getting some offices. He is getting starved out during the last few months of dignified hostility and evidently wants to come down. He did not get any.

I have not known the President so affected by a personal loss since the death of Baker, as by the death of General Wadsworth. While deeply regretting the loss of Sedgwick he added, "Sedgwick's devotion and earnestness were professional.[147] But no man has given himself up to the war with such self sacrificing patriotism as Genl. Wadsworth. He went into the service not wishing or expecting great success or distinction in his military career & profoundly indifferent to popular applause, actuated only by a sense of duty which he neither evaded nor sought to evade"

20 May 1864, Friday

Last evening I spent at Charles Eames where we went to drink tea with Mrs Julia Ward Howe, who has been reading some very remarkable essays here during the past week. One on "Moral Trigonometry" whatever that may mean: one on the French revolution which she calls by the somewhat affected title Equalities. This evening she read again; a practical discourse on Life full of admirable promptings and suggestions. She is rather the most remarkable woman I have ever met: she carries the greatest head piece without getting top heavy.[148]

I spent the latter part of the evening at Chase's to hear Teresa Carreno play the piano: A wonderful child: babyish, infantile with a child's smile & a man's power over the keys.[149] The company was rather noticeable for the absence of uniforms—my buttons showing in solitary splendor.

The company to hear Mrs. Howe was oddly composed. Lorings—Julians—Ashleys Chase Philp &c

21 MAY 1864, SATURDAY

Jim Lane brot up today & introduced Mr. Fishback the new Senator from Arkansas—a rather decent looking person ~~from the West~~. The Congressional delegation from there was lying about my office in an orphaned sort of way most of the morning oppressively patronized by Stoddard who wants them to recommend him for Marshal of the State.[150]

Music on the grounds in the afternoon. Some good women & some not so good. I passed the early part of the evening in Georgetown, & the latter part at the Theatre where I saw Bouci's Relief of Lacknow a very telling sensation play.[151]

22 MAY 1864, SUNDAY

Grant has marched by the left flank down the left bank of the Mattapony to Bowling Green & Lee has shifted his position to meet him there. The town is full of silly rumors that Lee is skedaddled & such trash.

Butler is turning out much as I thought he would—perfectly useless & incapable for campaigning. He quarrels with Gillmore & Smith & makes rather a nuisance of himself.[152]

I said to the President today that I thought Butler was the only man in the army in whom power would be dangerous. McClellan was too timid & vacillating to usurp: Grant was too sound and cool headed & too unselfish: Banks also: Fremont would be dangerous if he had more ability & energy.

"Yes" says the Ancient "he is like Jim Jett's brother Jim used to say that his brother was the ~~damdest~~ biggest scoundrel that ever lived but in the infinite mercy of Providence he was also the ~~damdest~~ biggest fool.

~~The Germans seem inclined to cut up rough, about the removal of Sigel from Command in the Shenandoah. They are heaping up wrath against themselves by their clannish impertinence in politics.~~[153]

24 MAY 1864, TUESDAY

I yesterday discovered that Doolittle and Randall were urging the appt. of R's brother for the Tax Comn. in Fla. I arranged it to have R. go to Louisiana & Smith to Fla. I feared trouble in Fla if Randall went down, from the legacy of the Reed matter.[154]

Doolittle is a fine instance of the result of industry, steadiness of mind & common sense applied to politics. He attends rigorously to his business: is a leading man in his party and yet finds a great deal of time for literary culture and improvement. During the last year he has become quite proficient in French. He thinks very small beer of the "Dutch Revolt." Gurowski says if Lincoln is nominated, he will take the stump.

I saved the life of a poor devil at Ft. Monroe today: two innocent little sisters came down begging it: the Judge A. G. made a favorable report & we put him in jail[155]

Seward and Cameron spent the evening with the President. Seward has prepared the answer to Winter Davis' guerilla Resn. and it will go up tomorrow. It seems perfectly satisfactory to the Prest. & Nicolay. I think it will subject the Admn. to a good deal of rancorous and foolish attack at this time. Davis' Resn. though expressing the feelings of almost every American citizen was introduced from the worst motives; still these motives can not be gracefully explained by our government to France.[156]

Despatches from Dana & Grant show them making fine time. Warren has been behaving finely at the crossing of the North Anna. Things look better than it was rumoured with Butler. Meigs & Barnard say he can hold his position with 10,000 men.[157]

31 MAY 1864, TUESDAY

Despatches from Grant show the country apparently clear of the enemy to the Chickahominy. I hope the evil portent of that stream may not avail against our little Western General.

Stager telegraphs today that the Cleveland Convention, which has been rather a small affair every way, has adjourned after nominating Fremont and Cochrane.[158]

Cochrane came down here some time ago & volunteered to the President the information that he was going up to Cleveland to try to forestall and break up that bolting institution.

1 JUNE 1864, WEDNESDAY

Ashley was in my room this morning, talking to E. C. Ingersoll, & saying that he wrote to all his counties urging the endorsement of the President.[159] An old ~~fellow~~ Preacher who opposed Lincoln's endorsement on the ground that he had not crushed the rebellion in three years was met & ~~squelched~~ silenced by the suggestion that the Lord had not crushed the devil in a much longer time.

5 JUNE 1864, SUNDAY

For a day or two the House has been full of patriots on the way to Baltimore who wish to pay their respects & engrave on the expectant mind of the ~~Tycoon~~ President, their images, in view of future contingencies. Among the genuine delegations have come some of the bogus & the irregular ones. Cuthbert Bullitt is here with Louisiana in his trowsers pocket. He has passed thro' New York & has gotten considerably stampeded by the talk of the trading pettifoggers of politics there. He feels uneasy in his seat.[160]

The South Carolina delegation came in yesterday. The Prest. says "let them in." "They are a swindle," I said. "They wont swindle me" quoth the ~~Tycoon~~ President. They filed in: A few sutlers, cotton-dealers and negroes, presented a petition & retired.[161]

Florida sends two delegations: neither will get in. Each attacks the others as unprincipled tricksters.[162]

Lamon hurt himself badly yesterday by falling from his carriage on the pavement. I went to see him this morning, found him bruised, but plucky. Says he intends to go to Baltimore tomorrow. Says he feels inclined to go for Cameron for Vice Prest. on personal grounds. Says he thinks Lincoln rather prefers Johnson or some War Democrat as calculated to give more strength to the ticket.

Nicolay started over today in company with Cameron.

Puleston dined with me at the Club. He says very many of the New Yorkers are talking Grant. Says Penna. wd. prefer Hancock for Vice.[163]

Whitely (reporter of the Herald says Chase told him the other day that
he now for the first time in his life agreed with the N. Y. Herald in politics.
It is thought that he may in the hope of obtaining preferment from Grant
(if the popular will points to Grant) advocate him for Prest. in oppn. to
Lincoln. The Post Correspt. pledges him however to the Baltimore Nominee.

Talking with Swett tonight found he was running Holt for Vice Prest. I
suggested to him that two Kentuckians from adjoining states was rather
crowding his ticket.

~~I spent part of the Evening at Lorings where I met all there is left of that
magnificent young fellow Col. Bartlett. Then went down to Eames: saw
Count Gurowski come into the parlor & go growling out because I was
there & then talked to the male Eames who thinks I ought to write verses
and get married. Then went to Philp, Bibliopole where were some hetero-
geneous foreigners musicians singers & vagrom people & passed the rest
of the evening pleasantly with music and potables.~~[164]

6 JUNE 1864, MONDAY

House full of delegates: Steve Hurlbut here from the West.[165]

Got a letter from Nicolay at Baltimore—answered by mail & telegraph.[166] The President positively refuses to give even a confidential suggestion in regard to Vice Prest. Platform or organization.

Every body comes back from Convention tired but sober. Nicolay says
it was a very quiet convention. Little drinking—little quarrelling—an
earnest intention to simply register the expressed will of the people and go
home. They were intolerant of speeches—remorselessly coughed down the
crack orators of the party.

[15 JUNE 1864, WEDNESDAY][167]

L. Washn. June 10, Friday 1864 at 5.20 on Balt & O RR: arrived in Eutaw
House at 7.30 about: supper: left at 9.30 bought ticket for Harrisburgh,
Pittsburg, Mingo, Columbus, Cincinnati, Vincennes, St. Louis, $28. Har-
risburgh abt. midnight. Pittsburg noon of Saturday. Breakfast Altoona:
dinner Pittsburg. Tea. Caddy's, which means, I think, Cadiz. Cars very

crowded & malodorous. Soldiers & beggars vigorously scratching—some natty & clean talking coolly abt. their fights: not so much bosh as earlier in the war.

A woman caring for a wounded boy with a miraculous patience all night & all day without moving from her place. He was a mere child badly wounded fretful & petulant but her patience never for an instant of the 18 hours gave way. She held him in her arms all that time not sleeping & leaving her seat to eat. They arrived at Pittsburg & met the friends awaiting them.

Took a sleeping car at Mingo Station that kept to Cincinnati, where arrived a good deal behind time at 10 oclock—Bathed dressed & breakfasted—Met Hapgood & went to church Dull sermon & no beauty. Visited Ned: Andn. & Mrs. Pendleton & found Ned out & Mrs. P in Europe.[168]

We approached Cincinnati along the Ohio from the East—a very godforsaken looking scene. A Cincinnatian sitting by me was earnestly protesting that this was not a favorable view of the city.

Young Larz Anderson called to answer my card to his brother—asked me to tea & to see the town with him—sorry I could not. The 6th Ohio, a pet Regt. commanded by Nick. Anderson, comes home tomorrow & they are to have a fine reception.[169]

Left Cincinnati 6 P.M. 12th June Sunday. Supper at Seymour, 10.40. Breakfast at Odin 8. St. Louis at 11 oclock A.M. 13th June. Lindell Hotel.[170]

Reported to Genl. R at once. He received me cordially invited me to dine with him at 5½ and to talk business at 7.

I loafed diffused through the city until evening. Saw Gr who gives a disheartening acct. of the corruption in cotton & trade regulations.

Dined with the Genl. & Maj. Bond at 5½.[171] The Genl. was chatty & pleasant. The dinner as bad as hotels do. Adjourned to Generals room: & he sat down to talk seating himself in a remarkable combination chair which was equally adapted to work & leisure. Offered me a cigar which I declined

He said long-necked fellows like me did not need them: he had a tendency to fulness of habit which they kept down He began to talk: freely & loudly but soon threw a glance over his shoulder, lowered his voice & drew his chair nearer.

We talked for a couple of hours until S came in & after some further talk

I went over to S's room & read papers with him for another hour: returning to the Genl. & finishing the evening with him. Found here when I returned Gov Hall & Mr. Saunders.[172] They were talking about the guerrillas:

The General talking about his own posn. to me said I get my heartiest support fr. Rads though I take no sides in politics. The Rads seem to know I am in sympathy without words."

He is very severe on [   ] and somewhat on [   ]. He says S has exerted himself to crush harry & thwart him in every possible way & that the latter has made some statements & authorized others, that are false and injurious. Lookout Valley, &c.

It is said Hillyer made a fortune in cotton and is now in N. Y. fighting for Grant. Rawlins is on the [   ].[173]

Thomas (R says) is the [   ]. He detailed the circumstances of Thomas action at Murfreesboro & after Chickamauga, in reference to assuming command. He says that Sherman says on Grants authority that Grant did not know why Rosecrans was removed: It was in answer to R's inquiry abt the common rumor that G had requested it

R's intelligent contraband gave us a remarkable brew called the [   ] cocktail, a thick syrup of sugar & poured carefully over it so as not to mix some good spirits. The final effect is eminently satisfactory

Came to Springfield in the Tuesday 14th day train. Missed Charlie on the way who was going down to see me. Staid all day. He arrived in evening & I staid all night with him. Left Sf on the 15th 10.15 train for Columbus. Will shape course then according to morning telegram.

[17 JUNE 1864, FRIDAY]

Thursday night June 9 the President came into my room just before bed-time and said that Rosecrans had been sending despatches requesting that an officer of his staff might be sent to Washington to lay before the Prest. matters of great importance in regard to a conspiracy to overthrow the government. He asked for this permission on account of the outrage committed upon Major Bond of his Staff who was some time ago Court-martialed for coming to Washington under General Rosecrans' orders. Recently Gov. Yates has joined in Rosecrans' request asking that Sanderson shall be sent for. "If it is a matter of such overwhelming importance," said the President "I dont think Sanderson is the proper person to whom to entrust it. I am inclined to think that the object of the General is to force me into a conflict with the Secretary of War and to make me overrule him in this matter. This at present I am not inclined to do. I have concluded to send you out there to talk it over with Rosecrans and to ascertain just what he has. I would like you to start tomorrow."[174]

He gave me, in the morning before I was out of bed, this note to deliver to Rosecrans.

Executive Mansion.
Washington
June 10, 1864

Major General Rosecrans

Major John Hay, the bearer, is one of my Private Secretaries, to whom please communicate in writing or verbally, anything you would think proper to say to me.

Yours truly

A. Lincoln.

Friday afternoon June 10, I left Washington and passed through Harrisburgh at midnight, Pittsburgh noon of the 11th, through Mingo, Cadiz, to Cincinnati where I arrived on Sunday morning. I washed my face and went out, saw a plain old church covered with ivy and congratulated myself that there I would find some decent people worshipping God comme il faut:[175] and was horribly bored for my worldliness. After dinner, where I met a rascally looking Jew who was dining with a gorgeous lovette, and who insisted on knowing me & recognizing me from a picture in Harpers Weekly—I strolled out to make visits. The Anderson's were not at home, except young Larz. I plunged into the bosom of a peaceful family and demanded to see the wife of a quiet gentleman on the ground that she was a young lady now travelling in Europe. He commiserated my wild and agitated demeanor and asked me to dinner.

I left Cincinnati Sunday evening & came to St. Louis about 11 oclock Monday morning. The road is a very pleasant one, though rather slow. I sat and wrote rhymes in the same compartment with a brace of whiskey smugglers.

I reported to General Rosecrans immediately upon my arrival. After waiting some time in an ante room full of officers, among them Gen Davidson—a young nervous active looking man—Gen. Ewing whom I had known before a man of great coolness and steadiness of judgement: Rosecrans came out and took me to his room.[176] I presented my letter; he read it, & nodded "All right—got something to show you—too important to talk about—busy just now—this orderly business—keep me till 4 oclock—dine with us at the Lindell—½ past five—then talk matter over at my room there: Hay, where were you born? How long have you been with the President? &c." And I went away. He is a fine hearty abrupt sort of talker, heavy-whiskered blond, keen eyes, with light brows and lashes, head shunted forward a little: legs a little unsteady in walk.

We dined at the Lindell quietly at 6 oclock, Rosecrans, Major Bond and I. The General was chatty and sociable; told some old Army stories: and drank very little wine. The dinner had nothing to tempt one out of frugality in diet: being up to the average badness of hotel dinners.

From the dining room I went to his private room. He issued orders to his intelligent contraband to admit no one. He seated himself in a queer combination chair he had—which let you lounge or forced you to a rigid pose of business as you desired—and offered me a cigar. "No? Longnecked fellows like you dont need them. Men of my temperament derive advantage from them as a sedative and as a preventer of corpulence." He puffed away & began to talk, in a loud easy tone at first, which he soon lowered, casting a glance over his shoulder and moving his chair nearer.

There is a secret conspiracy on foot against the government carried forward by a society called the Order of American Knights or to use their initials—O. A. K. The head of the order, styled the high-priest, is in the North Vallandigham and in the South, Sterling Price. Its objects are in the North, to exert an injurious effect upon public feeling, to resist the arrest of its members to oppose the war in all possible ways: in the border States to join with returned rebels and guerrilla parties to plunder, murder, and persecute Union men and to give to rebel invasion all possible information and timely aid. He said that in Missouri they had carefully investigated the matter by means of secret service men who had taken the oaths and they had found that many recent massacres were directly chargeable to them: that the whole order was in a state of intense activity—that they numbered in Missouri 13,000 sworn members: in Illinois 140,000. In Ohio & Indiana almost as large numbers and in Kentucky a very large and formidable organization:[177]

That the present objective point was the return and the protection of Vallandigham. He intends, on dit [it is said], that the district convention in his district in Ohio shall elect him a delegate to the Chicago Convention. That he is to be elected and come over from Canada & take his seat, and if the Government should see fit to rearrest him, then his followers are to unite to resist the officers and protect him at all hazards.

A convocation of the order was held at Windsor, Canada, in the month of April under his personal supervision: to this came delegates from every part of the country. It is not definitely known what was done there.

The Grand Commander of the order for the State of Missouri is Hunt, the Belgian Consul whose exequatur was recently revoked on account of his pleading his consular privilege against enrollment. For a long time Rosecrans had been informed that treasonable meetings and practices were carried on under the mask of this fellow's consular office. He set his spies to watching him. One of them gained Hunt's confidence by exhibiting to him forged credentials from Sterling Price and thus obtained from him copies of their books of ritual and organization. He also followed Hunt on a journey he made from St. Louis and ascertained that he went directly to Windsor for a Conference with Vallandigham. On such evidence as this he was arrested. The day I arrived in St. Louis R. recd. a despatch from the Sec. of War, directing him to release Hunt and give him up his papers. He answered protesting against the order and requesting that it be withheld until my arrival in Washington. R. says the order resulted from a lying despatch sent by one Johnston, a St. Louis secessionist, a brother of Joe.[178]

An important part of the plot in the border states is the protection and encouragement and organization of rebels from Kirby Smiths & other armies coming North as spies or as pretended deserters.[179] Some coming out of the bush as the Missourians phrase it with Grass in their hair & the oath in their pocket—to plunder steal persecute and kill, and stand ready for insurrection and revolt.

Rosecrans has made some arrests and has alarmed the leaders in St.

Louis Some of them fled at the first intimation of trouble: among them George Washington Wiley, &c.

This is the substance of what Rosecrans told me in the course of the evening. Later, Sanderson came in and added some things to R's recital. He laid special stress on the disclosures made by one ~~Captain~~ Lieutenant Rolla on the staff of Forrest, a woman who has served in disguise throughout the war. She has been attached to Forrest in all his campaigns except the last, being then a prisoner. She has served as chief ordnance officer and had made several trips to St. Louis, coming in the dress of a woman and succeeding through the influence of the order in getting everything needed, purchased and sent over the lines. While recently a prisoner at Fort Pillow, a spy, a pretended refugee, approached her and said that Forrest sent him to her to tell her to keep up heart—that he would soon be there to rescue her: that she disclosed this fact to the Comdt. that he removed her before the massacre took [place]. She now alleges that she has no wish to return to the rebel service: pretends to be very grateful for the kindness shown her by Sanderson in her sickness and imprisonment: and talks and writes pretty freely about the subject in hand. Sanderson says he surprised her into an involuntary admission of her knowledge of the order by giving her some of the signs, stroking his beard shading his eyes with his hand, &c. She asserts, as in fact all do that death is the penalty of disclosure, and it is this consideration more than any other that causes Rosecrans' attempt to envelope the matter in such profound mystery.[180]

I went over to Sanderson's office and he read to me his voluminous report to Rosecrans in regard to the workings of the order and showed me some few documents, among them a letter from Vallandigham to the Abbé McMaster dated June 1 in which he at first complains that the "orders issued" are not properly executed—hints at a scarcity of funds—expresses himself a little dubious as to his own action in relation to the Chicago convention—and concludes by referring to the "Household of Faith.[181]

We went back and finished the evening at Rosecrans' rooms. I said I would go back to Washington & lay the matter before the President as it had been presented to me and I thought he would look upon it as I did, as a matter of importance. I did not make any suggestions: I did not even ask for a copy of Sanderson's report or any of the papers in the case 1. because my instructions placed me in a purely receptive attitude & 2nd because I saw in both R. & S. a disposition to insist on Sanderson's coming to Washington in person to discuss the matter without the intervention of the Secretary of War. Two or three motives influenced this, no doubt. Rosecrans is bitterly hostile to Stanton: he is full of the idea that S. has wronged him & is continually seeking opportunities to thwart and humiliate him: then Sandn. himself is rather proud of his work in ferretting out this business and is not unwilling to come to Washn. & impress the Prest. with the same sense: then they wish a programme for future operations determined, & finally they want money for the secret service fund.

Gen. Rosecrans wrote a letter to the President Monday night which I took on Tuesday morning & started back to Washington.[182]

R. talked about many things with perfect freedom and frankness. He told me about Thomas' conduct on being assigned command after Perryville and again after Chickamauga: that Thomas told him R. that if R were removed from command of the Army of the Cumberland, he did not wish to remain in it. That he (R) persuaded him to accept the command[183]

He says further that Sherman informed him on Grants authority that he Grant did not know why Rosecrans was removed: (In one sense this is true. Grant had nothing to do with the supercession of R by himself. But he did object to having R in the same department with him saying he would not obey orders, & he has since repeated the same criticism upon him.

I had bad luck coming back. I missed a day at Springfield, a connection at Harrisburgh and one at Baltimore, leaving Philadelphia five minutes after the President and arriving at Washington almost as many hours behind him. I saw him at once and gave him the impressions I have recorded above. The situation of affairs had been a good deal changed in my transit by the Avatar of Vallandigham in Ohio. The President seemed not overwell pleased that Rosecrans had not sent all the necessary papers by me, reiterating his want of confidence in Sanderson, declining to be made a party to a quarrel between Stanton and Rosecrans, and stating in reply to Rosecrans' suggestion of the importance of the greatest secrecy, that a secret which had already been confided to Yates Morton Brough Bramlette & their respective circles of officers could scarcely be worth the keeping now. He treats the Northern section of the conspiracy as not especially worth regarding, holding it a mere political organization, with about as much of malice and as much of puerility as the Knights of the Golden Circle.[184]

About Vallandigham himself, he says that the question for the Government to decide is whether it can afford to disregard the contempt of authority & breach of discipline displayed in Vallandigham's unauthorized return: for the rest, it cannot but result in benefit to the Union cause to have so violent and indiscreet a man go to Chicago as a firebrand to his own party. The President had some time ago seriously thought of annulling the sentence of exile but had been too much occupied to do it. Fernando Wood said to him on one occasion that he could do nothing more politic than to bring Val. back: in that case he could promise him two democratic candidates for President this year. "These war democrats" said F. W. "are scoundrelly hypocrites: they want to oppose you & favor the war at once which is nonsense. There are but two sides in this fight: yours & mine—war & peace. You will succeed while the war lasts, I expect, but we shall succeed when the war is over. I intend to keep my record clear for the future."[185]

The President said one thing in which I differ from him. He says "The opposition politicians are so blinded with rage seeing themselves unable to control the politics of the country that they may be able to manage the Chicago convention for some violent end, but they cannot transfer the people, the honest though misguided masses to the same course" I said "I thought the reverse to be true: that the sharp managers would go to Chicago to try to do some clever and prudent thing such as nominate Grant without platform: but that the barefooted Democracy from the heads of the hollows who are now clearly for peace would carry everything in the Convention before them. As it was at Cleveland; the New York politicians who came out to ~~fugle~~ intrigue for Grant could not get a hearing. They were as a feather in the wind in the midst of that blast of German fanaticism. I think my idea is sustained by the action of the Illinois Convention which endorses Val. on his return & pledges the party strength to protect him. In the stress of this war politics have drifted out of the hands of politicians & are now more than ever subject to genuine popular currents."[186]

The President said he would take the matter into consideration and would write tomorrow the 18th to Brough & Heintzelman about Val. and to Rosecrans at an early day.[187]

18 JUNE 1864, SATURDAY

The Illinois copps. are troubled about the Val. apparition. Billy Morrison said to me this morning "How much did you fellows give Fernandywud for importing that fellow."[188] Joe Forrest tells me that Allen is also uneasy about it.

I spent the evening at Sewards. He began by asking me if Val. had come back by consent of the Government. I said I thought it too marked an exercise of good sense to be ascribed to the Administration. I considered it a visible interposition of Divine Providence agst. the harmonious Democracy." He said V's friends seem to be preparing for a war with the Govt on his account: that we probably will not oblige them until some thing more decisive comes from Grant or Sherman. That of course the Government must take cognizance of the matter in time. I told him his Belgian Consul Hunt had been arrested on account of complicity with the conspiracy which thus results, and that an order fr. Washn. had gone forward for his release. He seemed surprised at this: said [Blondell?] had represented that Hunt had been arrested for pleading his consular privilege agst. the enrollment: and that Rosecrans had not denied that this was the case. But that if Hunt had been guilty of these treasonable practices he must be held and tried for them.[189]

Later in the evening talking to his dog He said "Midge, what do you conclude about the Major? Did you ever notice that the dog is the only animal that gains his impressions of the persons he meets by studying their faces? The other day I was driving pretty rapidly; a large Newfoundland dog lay in the street, taking his dolce far niente; he had just time to get out of the way by a movement which was unpleasantly hurried. Instead of attacking the horses, or us who were in the carriage, he addressed himself to the driver, who was farther from him than either, as the cause of the trouble; defied him with a loud voice, and dared him to come down and have it out in a fair fight. No man could have acted with more discretion & spirit.

21 JUNE 1864, TUESDAY

Today the President started down the river with Fox to have a talk with Gen Grant and Admiral Lee.[190]

General Gillmore arrived at Willard's today. He is very much cut up by Butler's mean and ungenerous blow in ordering him to the rear in the midst of a campaign like this. Brooks says that Butler has quarrelled with every general officer who has been thrown in contact with him.[191] Wright Terry &c. Wright is especially severe upon him. Wright had been ordered by Butler, who was very far in the rear, to take a position which had been ascertained by reconnaisance to be enfiladed from both sides by the enemies' batteries. Wright sent a despatch to Butler announcing his readiness to move and adding this statement of fact. Butler replied "I ordered you to fight: you answer with an argument." Wright appealed at once to Meade to relieve him from Butler's command. An insult like that from a man who never smelt powder to one who has been in half the battles of the war, is almost incredible.

Butler's whole course down there seems marked by the two faults which seem inseparable from civilian generals, (excepting those who have a natural aptitude for military affairs, which B. has not): too great rashness & too great timidity in constant alternation. His ignorance of war leads him constantly to require impossibilities from his subordinates and to fear impossibilities from the enemy.

23 JUNE 1864, THURSDAY

The President arrived today from the front, sunburnt and fagged but still refreshed and cheered. He found the army in fine health good position and good spirits; Grant quietly confident: he says quoting the Richmond papers, it may be a long summer's day before he does his work but that he is as sure of doing it as he is of anything in the world. Sheridan is now on a raid, the purpose of which is to sever the connection at junction of the Lynchburg & Danville R.R.'s at Burke's, While the Army is swinging around to the south of Petersburg and taking possession of the roads in that direction.[192]

Grant says he is not sufficiently acquainted with Hunter to say with certainty whether it is possible to destroy him: but that he has confidence in him that he will not be badly beaten. When McPherson or Sherman or Sheridan or Wilson is gone on any outside expedition he feels perfectly secure about them knowing that while they are liable to any of the ordinary mischances of War there is no danger of their being whipped in any but a legitimate way.[193]

Brooks says of Grant that he seems to arrive at his conclusions without any intermediate reasoning process—giving his orders with the greatest rapidity & with great detail. Uses the theoretical staff officers very little.

24 June 1864, Friday

Today a resolution came from the Senate asking information about War and Treasury Orders concerning exportation of arms to Mexico. I did not like to act without consulting Seward, so took the paper to him, asking if it would be well to send copies to Secs. War & Treasury or not. He said "Yes: send the Resolution to the Secretary of War, a copy to the Secretary of the Treasury asking reports from them and then when the reports are in ———

(Did you ever hear Webster's recipe for cooking a cod? He was a great fisherman & fond of cod. Some one once asking him the best way to prepare a cod for the table, he said "Denude your cod of his scales—cut him open carefully—put him in a pot of cold water—heat it until your fork can pass easily through the fish—take him out—spread good fresh butter over him liberally—sprinkle salt on the butter—pepper on the salt—and—send for George Ashmun and me.")

When the reports are in let me see them."

He got up, stumped around the room enjoying his joke for awhile, then said, "Our friends are very anxious to get into a war with France, using this Mexican business for that purpose.[194] They dont consider that England and France would surely be together in that event. France has the whip hand of England completely. England got out of the Mexican business into which she had been deceived by France, by virtue of our having nothing to do with it. They have since been kept apart by good management, and our people are laboring to unite them again by making war on France. Worse than that, instead of doing something effective, if we must fight, they are for making mouths and shaking fists at France warning & threatening and inducing her to prepare for our attack when it comes."

Carpenter, the artist, who is painting the picture of the "Reading of the Proclamation" says that Seward protested earnestly against that act being taken as the central and crowning act of the Administration. He says slavery was destroyed years ago: the formation of the Republican party destroyed slavery: the anti slavery acts of this administration are merely incidental. Their great work is the preservation of the Union and in that, the saving of popular government for the World. The scene which should have been taken was the Cabinet Meeting in the Navy Department when it was resolved to relieve Fort Sumter. That was the significant act of the administration: The act which determined the fact that Republican institutions were worth fighting for.[195]

25 June 1864, Saturday

Gen. Gillmore called to take leave of the President this morning: he goes to New York. He told me another incident of Butler's brutality. Col Serrell, Gillmore's Engineer officer was engaged under Butler's order building a little field work that a sergeant could have superintended as well While Gillmore had an extensive line of works in process of construction, G. asked for Serrell to return. Butler replied "If Gen. Gillmore feels himself incompetent to execute the duties devolving upon him, he can ask the assistance of Gen. Weitzel or Col. Comstock." Gillmore returned the despatch for "the correction of a mistake in it" & Butler quietly put it in his pocket.[196]

Fox, who has an old grudge against Gillmore for becoming popular by his operations on Morris Island instead of Dahlgren, abuses both Gillmore & Butler.[197] Says B. is an elephant on the hands of the authorities. My only hope is that he will quarrel with Grant & be sent to Ft. Monroe.

30 June 1864, Thursday

This morning, the President sent for me saying "When does the Senate meet today?"

"Eleven oclock."

"I wish you to be there when they meet. It is a big fish. Mr. Chase has resigned & I have accepted his resignation. I thought I could not stand it any longer."

"Is it about the Field matter?"[198]

"Yes."

"Who is to be his successor?"

"Dave Tod. He is my friend, with a big head full of brains."[199]

"Has he the skill and experience necessary for such a place?"

"He made a good Governor, and has made a fortune for himself. I am willing to trust him."

I arrived at the Senate door while the Chaplain was praying. When he ceased I delivered the message and went back to the Executive Mansion.

In an hour the excitement rolled up our way. Mr. Hooper came in, much excited. He feared the effect on our finances. He says it is not about the Field matter because Cisco has withdrawn his resignation. Ashmun looks at it coolly, does not think the bottom has fallen out. *Washburne does.* I never knew a man more stampeded. He says it is a great disaster: At this time, ruinous; this time of military unsuccess, financial weakness, Congressional hesitation on question of conscription & imminent famine in the West. Chittenden came over to say that there was a movement for a general resignation in the Department: that he would stay until Tod came and got things started, although intending for some time past to resign as soon as possible.[200]

In the afternoon I talked over the matter with the President. He said that Chase was perfectly unyielding in this whole matter of Field's appointment: That Morgan objected so earnestly to Field that he could not appoint him without embarrassment & so told the Secretary requesting him to agree to the appointment of Gregory Blatchford or Hillhouse or some other good man that would not be obnoxious to the Senators: the Secretary still insisted, but added that possibly Mr. Cisco would withdraw his resignation: the President answered that he could not appoint Mr. Field but wd. wait Mr. Cisco's action. Yesterday evening a letter came from the Secretary announcing first the intelligence that Mr. Cisco had withdrawn his resignation. This was most welcome news to the President. He thought the whole matter was happily disposed of. Without waiting to read further he put the letter in his pocket & went at his other work. Several hours later wishing to write a congratulatory word to the Secretary he took the papers from his pocket, and found to his bitter disappointment the resignation of the Secretary. He made up his mind to accept it. It meant "You have been acting very badly. Unless you say you are sorry, & ask me to stay & agree that I shall be absolute and that you shall have nothing, no matter how you beg for it, I will go." The President thought, one or the other must resign. Mr. Chase elected to do so.[201]

The Finance Committee to whom was referred the nomination of Tod came down in a body to talk to the President; he says, "Fessenden was frightened, Conness was mad, Sherman thought we could not have gotten on together much longer anyhow, Cowan & Van Winkle did not seem to care anything about it." They not only protested against any change but objected to Tod as too little known and experienced for the place. The President told them that he had not much personal acquaintance with Tod; had nominated him on account of the high opinion he had formed of him while Governor of Ohio: but that the Senate had the duty & responsibility of considering & passing upon the question of fitness, in which they must be entirely untrammelled. He could not in justice to himself or Tod withdraw the nomination.[202]

Mr. Hooper talked with me for some time this afternoon. He says that he feels very nervous & cut up about today's work. That he had been for some time of the opinion that Mr. Chase did not see his way entirely clear to raising the money necessary: that this supplementary demand sent in at the close of the session, after everything had been granted which he had asked looked like an intention to throw an anchor to windward in case he was refused, that he might say, "if you had given me what I asked &c" Like McClellan on the Peninsula continually asking for reinforcements which did not exist: "I (H) woke up this morning feeling a little vexed that Mr. Chase had done this at this time, attempting to throw unfair responsibilities upon Congress: but now this comes to relieve him of all responsibility in the most remarkable manner: I would not have lifted the responsibility from him for any thing. It may be that Tod knows so little of the work before him that he will accept. It is an enormous work and the future is troubled. You have the great practical problem regularly recurring, to raise one-hundred millions a month: I do not clearly see how it is to be done. This talent of finance is a very special one: in its larger sense entirely distinct from banking. The bankers generally attack Mr. Chase. Chase has the faculty of using the knowledge and experience of others to the best advantage: that has sufficed him hitherto; but a point has been reached where he does not clearly see what comes next: and at this point the President allows him to step from under his load." Hooper did not seem to anticipate any fall in securities or rise in gold but rather the contrary, thinking that gold must go down anyhow.[203]

Fox is the only man who seems to be jolly over it Fox & Rush Plumley, the two antipodes. Plumley said when he heard of it, "That is right—the judgements of God are sure." Fox says Morgan says a weight has been lifted from the financial heart.[204]

In Congress and on the street there is a general feeling of depression and gloom. It looks like a piece of ratting on the part of Chase, to some: like a triumph of the Blairs, to other idiots: like a dangerous symptom of general decay and break-up of the administration to most. I cannot help regarding the financial future with foreboding. For some months the feeling has grown upon me, and this incident convinces me that Chase is anxious to stand from under the ruin.

Harrington is acting.[205] The little man was astounded this morning at his appointment. He is in a constant twitter occasionally subdued by a vague sense of dignity and responsibility suddenly enveloping him. He rises to the level of the occasion by opening his eyes like saucers pursing his lips & speaking in a basso profundo.

Tonight the aspect of affairs is changed by Tod's declining by telegraph on account of bad health. I, thinking the Senate might hold an executive session tonight & reject him, thought it well to go up & inform them, to which the President assented. I told Fessenden who told everybody and the comment was universal "Not such a fool as I thought he was" "Shows his sense."

Hooper thinks that this imbroglio will slough off from the Union party a large and disastrous slice.

If the President has made a mistake (as I think he has) in allowing Chase to shirk his post of duty, Chase's leaving at this time is little less than a crime.

1 JULY 1864, FRIDAY

I went in at ~~eleven~~ half past ten this morning to see the President: he gave me a nomination: he said "I have determined to appoint Fessenden himself." I said "Fessenden is in my room waiting to see you."

"Send him in & go at once to the Senate."[206]

I delivered the message to the Senate & it was instantly confirmed: the executive session not lasting more than a minute: & returned to my office. There I met Abe. Wakeman in high glee.[207] He thought it a great thing to do: that henceforward the fifty thousand treasury agents would be friends of the President instead of enemies. I could not help pouring some cold water on his enthusiasm.

Going to the Senate as usual early this afternoon I saw several who seemed very well pleased. At the house it was still better. Washburne said,

"This appointment of Fessenden is received with great éclat. The only fear is that he will not accept. The general feeling in Congress is in favor of Boutwell in case Fessenden declines. If the President cares for any expression from Congress a very strong one could be sent up for Boutwell." Coe of New York was here about the Gold Bill which was repealed today. He visited the President & was by him set upon Fessenden to aid in insisting on his accepting the place. The President said so to Howe and to Diven & to Ashmun and others.[208] A strong delegation of Congress waited upon Fessenden today to add their request that he would accept.

The President says "It is very singular, considering that this appointment of F's is so popular when made, that no one ever mentioned his name to me for that place. Thinking over the matter two or three points occurred to me. *First* he knows the ropes thoroughly: as Chairman of the Senate Committee on Finance he knows as much of this special subject as Mr. Chase. *2nd* he is a man possessing a national reputation and the confidence of the country. *3d* He is a radical—without the petulant and vicious fretfulness of many radicals. On the other hand I considered the objections: the Vice President & Sec Treasury coming from the same small state—though I thought little of that: then that Fessenden from the state of his health is of rather a quick & irritable temper: but in this respect he should be pleased with this incident; for, while for some time he has been running in rather a pocket of bad luck—such as failure to renominate Mr. Hamlin which makes possible a contest between him & the V. P. the most popular man in Maine for the election which is now imminent—& the fact of his recent spat in the Senate where Trumbull told him his ill-temper had left him no friends—this thing has developed a sudden & very gratifying manifestation of good feeling in his appointment, his instant confirmation, the earnest entreaties of every body that he may accept & all that. It cannot but be very grateful to his feelings. This morning he came into this room just as you left it. He sat down & began to talk about other things. I could not help being amused by seeing him sitting there so unconscious and you on your way to the Capitol. He at last began to speak of this matter, rather supporting McCulloch for Secretary. I answered 'Mr. Fessenden I have nominated you for that place. Mr. Hay has just taken the nomination to the Senate' 'But it hasn't reached there—you must withdraw it—I cant accept.' 'If you decline' I replied 'you must do it in open day: for I shall not recall the nomination.' We talkd about it for some time and he went away less decided in his refusal. I hope from the long delay, that he is making up his mind to accept. If he would only consent to accept & stay here and help me for a little while, I think he would be in no hurry to go."[209]

The President yesterday told me he had a plan for relieving us to a certain extent financially: for the government to take it into its own hands the whole cotton trade and buy all that offered: take it to New York, sell for Gold, & buy up its own greenbacks." Harrington talked somewhat the same doctrine to me last night.[210]

I am glad the President has sloughed off that idea of colonization. I have always thought it a hideous & barbarous humbug & the thievery of Pomeroy and Kock have about converted him to the same belief. Mitchell says Usher allows Pomeroy to have the records of the Chiriqui matters away from the Department to cook up his fraudulent accounts by. If so, Usher ought to be hamstrung[211]

The President says, what Chase ought to do is to help his successor through his installation as he professed himself willing to do in his letter to me: go home without making any fight and wait for a good thing hereafter, such as a vacancy on the Supreme Bench or some such matter.[212]

This evening I referred to Wilkeson's blackguardly misstatements in todays Tribune & asked if I might not prepare a true statement of facts to counteract the effects of these falsehoods; he answered "Let 'em wriggle."[213]

4 JULY 1864, MONDAY

Today Congress adjourned at noon. I was in the House for a few minutes before the close. They read the declaration of Independence there in spite of the protest of Sunset Cox that it was an insurrectionary document & would give aid & comfort to the rebellion.

In the Presidents room we were pretty busy signing & reporting bills. Sumner was in a state of intense anxiety about the Reconstruction Bill of Winter Davis. Boutwell also expressed his fear that it would be pocketed. Chandler came in and asked if it was signed "No." He said it would make a terrible record for us to fight if it were vetoed: the President talked to him a moment. He said Mr. Chandler, this bill was placed before me a few minutes before Congress adjourns. It is a matter of too much importance to be swallowed in that way." "If it is vetoed it will damage us fearfully in the North West. It may not in Illinois, it will in Michigan and Ohio. The important point is that one prohibiting slavery in the reconstructed states."[214]

Prest. "That is the point on which I doubt the authority of Congress to act"

Chandler. "It is no more than you have done yourself"

President. "I conceive that I may in an emergency do things on military grounds which cannot be done constitutionally by Congress."

Chandler. "Mr. President I cannot controvert yr. position by argument, I can only say I deeply regret it."

Exit Chandler.

The President continued, "I do not see how any of us now can deny and contradict all we have always said, that congress has no constitutional power over slavery in the states." Mr. Fessenden, who had just come into the room, said "I agree with you there, sir. I even had my doubts as to the constitutional efficacy of your own decree of emancipation, in such cases where it has not been carried into effect by the actual advance of the army."[215]

Prest. This bill and this position of these gentlemen seems to me to make the fatal admission (in asserting that the insurrectionary states are no longer states in the Union) that states whenever they please may of their own motion dissolve their connection with the Union. Now we cannot survive that admission I am convinced. If that be true I am not President, these gentlemen are not Congress. I have laboriously endeavored to avoid that question ever since it first began to be mooted & thus to avoid confusion and disturbance in our own counsels. It was to obviate this question that I earnestly favored the movement for an amendment to the Constitution abolishing slavery, which passed the Senate and failed in the House. I thought it much better, if it were possible, to restore the Union without the necessity of a violent quarrel among its friends, as to whether certain states have been in or out of the Union during the war: a merely metaphysical question and one unnecessary to be forced into discussion."[216]

Seward Usher and Fessenden seemed entirely in accord with this.

After we left the Capitol I said I did not think Chandler, man of the people and personally popular as he was had any definite comprehension of popular currents and influence—that he was out of the way now especially—that I did not think people would bolt their ticket on a question of metaphysics.

The Prest. answered, "If they choose to make a point upon this I do not doubt that they can do harm. They have never been friendly to me & I dont know that this will make any special difference as to that. At all events, I must keep some consciousness of being somewhere near right: I must keep some standard of principle fixed within myself."

Stanton talking about Harpers Ferry was thinking of sending for Alex. McCook to take command there.[217] I suggested Gillmore who is on a visit to his family at New York. Mr. Seward concurred thinking Gillmore the best man.

The President thinks with decent management we destroy any enemy who crosses the Potomac. Stanton says he would be sure of that if he could rely entirely upon Hunter.[218]

5 JULY 1864, TUESDAY

I went this morning to get places at the Canterbury. I found the lower boxes taken, but they told me at the office that G. C. S. had taken the one I wanted would probably not occupy it as he generally sat on the stage. I went down to the National to see him about it, was directed to his room & went there alone. Mr. Goodloe his nephew opened the door & on my telling what I wanted he asked me into the room where there were 3 Canterbury girls.[219] We had some Bourbon whiskey which the sprightly ladies drank like little men ~~One of them, overcome by her emotions, retiring for ten minutes or so with Goodloe & then came back to be joked by the envious others.~~

I dined with Malet Kennedy & Bob L and went to the Canterbury in the evening. The room was hot and we took off our coats & sat comfortably in the box. Smith's was occupied but I saw him sitting in the flies, fanning the legs of a dancing girl. The show was the Bushwhackers of the Potomac, filthy & not funny except in its burlesque of Beau Hickman.[220] There is a sentinel discovered pacing in front of the Capitol by moonlight. He is quickly shot by the heavy man, the Bushwhacker, who informs the audience that another yankee has gone to his long home—that he (the B.) has a Union wife & "cherishes a lustful passion" for his sister: both these ladies coming on the stage opportunely he kills the one & requests the other to fly with him—She objects and a miserable hangdog creature comes on the scene in the garb of a lieutenant who of course points his finger in defiance at the bushwhacker who sneaks off saying he will have revenge. We then have a haunted hut & an apparition of Washington—a flash ball—an indecent scene in which some African gypsies strip Beau Hickman's trousers from him—a few bloody fights & a final apotheosis of everybody who has been killed in the play, while the bloody Bushwhacker of course dies miserably.

There was a pic-nic yesterday, in the Presidents grounds, of the negroes of Washington. They were very neatly & carefully dressed very quietly & decently behaved: the young fellows buckishly & the young girls like ill bred boarding school maids. There were many of both sexes, perfectly white and blue-eyed.

7 JULY 1864, THURSDAY

Today I went to the Attorney General to talk over the matter of Chamberlins reappointment which has lapsed by the adjournment. The old judge was not in the best humor: in the first place, he considered his dignity infringed by the fact that neither Fraser nor Chamberlin had ever sent a line of report to him:[221] second he did not think a court could have any show of jurisdiction then in the power of the army. He talked a long while and very earnestly in deprecation of the present overriding of law and of judicial procedure in the military departments: the leasing of cotton plantations by Treasury agents & all that class of affairs. He seems in a decided and growing frame of discontent at the way things are going. The President says Judge Bates is persuaded and tries to persuade him that the Baltimore Convention was thoroughly Anti Lincoln & though forced to nominate him did every thing else in the interest of the opposition. The worthy old gentleman feels that he has fallen on evil times.

8 JULY 1864, FRIDAY

B. L. & I visited the Sewards last evening for a little while. The Secretary had the New York Tribune in his hand giving the reasons of Mr. Chase's resignation: simply enough stated; that he wanted to appoint Mr. Field, & the President desired him to select some other man on account of the political opposition to Mr. Field: but he states disingenuously that he resigned because the President refused him an interview, thus showing a want of confidence in him. The Secretary ~~went on to say~~ said that this statement was absurd, as nobody ever wanted to see the President who did not—that there was never a man so accessible to all sorts of proper and improper persons. He then continued his comments on the matter very severely adverting to Chase's iron and unbending obstinacy in the matter of appointments and in matters strictly within the scope of the President's authority.[222]

10 JULY 1864, SUNDAY

A rather quiet day in spite of Wallace's defeat and the nearness of the enemy. The usual flight of rumors but no special excitement.[223]

I spent the evening—an hour at General Wright's, whose wife and daughter were waiting for their soldier and sure that the Capital would be safe when he got here—and an hour after at Malet's where were several Britons. When I got home I found Mr. Whiton had been there had stampeded the servants by leaving a message for me suggesting that Mr. Lincoln should have a gunboat in readiness to leave in the morning as the enemy was in force within five miles. I went to bed.[224]

A little after midnight R. T. L. came into my room & got into bed: Saying Stanton had sent out for them all to come in.[225]

11 JULY 1864, MONDAY

The President concluded to desert his tormentors today & travel around the defenses. Gillmore arrived & reported. Wright & staff also came in.

At three oclock P.M. the President came in bringing the news that the enemy's advance was at Ft. Stevens on the 7th Street road. He was in the Fort when it was first attacked, standing upon the parapet. A soldier roughly ordered him to get down or he would have his head knocked off. I can see a couple of columns of smoke just north of the White House. It is thought to be Silver Spring in flames.—I was at Mr. Blairs this evening; Fox says Gen Wright tells him that Silver Spring is not burnt.[226]

The President is in very good feather this evening. He seems not in the least concerned about the safety of Washington. With him the only concern seems to be whether we can bag or destroy this force in our front.

Part of Canby's troops are here. Gillmore has been placed in command of them. Aleck McCook is in charge of the defences.[227] There is a great plenty of Generals. Meigs has gone out for a spurt.

12 JULY 1864, TUESDAY

The President seemed in a pleasant and confident humor today. The news from Sherman if confirmed is good—that the enemy intend to desert Atlanta.

The President again made the tour of the fortifications; was again under fire at Ft. Stevens: a man was shot at his side.[228]

The militia of the District are offering their services and the Department clerks are also enrolling themselves. In Judge Lewis office, 87 men enlisted and organized themselves in 15 minutes.[229]

Last night the President's guard of Bucktails was sent to the front.[230]

Mr. Britton A. Hill called this evening, in great trepidation and said he was apprehensive of a sudden attack on the Navy Yard.[231]

13 JULY 1864, WEDNESDAY

The news this morning would seem to indicate that the enemy is retiring from every point.

The President thinks we should push our whole column right up the river road & cut off as many as possible of the retreating raiders.

There seems to be no head about this whole affair. Halleck hates responsibility: hates to give orders. Wright Gillmore & McCook must of course report to somebody & await somebody's order which they dont get.

I rode out to the front this morning, R. T. L. & I. We visited Wright's Headquarters first. On our way out we found the road full of black men and women who had come out to see the fun & had been turned back by the hard hearted guard.

At Crystal Spring we met young Capt. O. W. Holmes, Wright's A. D. C. He joined us and we proceeded through the encampment, which was stretched in a loafer like gipsy style among the trees—the Artillery ready to move, the Infantry diffused through the brush—dirty careless soldierly in all else—every variety of style and manner among officers. We went to Ft. Stevens & had a good view from the parapet of the battlefield of yesterday. Then went to McCook's headquarters ~~and drank lager beer~~. The room was full of regulars from the bureaus at Washington.

We took a ride over to the Qr Mr's Hdqrs and lunched under the trees with Gen. Rucker. Young Welles who had been ordered to bury the rebel dead got a squad of fifty contrabands under an old sapper & miner & we started for the field.[232] Going down the road in advance of our squad we came to the toll gate & looking back saw them halted half way up the road. Sent an orderly back who returned with information that they had stopped to speak to an old acquaintance. They came on & charged on a pile of picks and shovels. The Comr. Sapper then gave the order to those who were to carry the stretchers, "Chief mourners, to the rear as pall bearers. Get out yr. pocket hankerchers."

We soon came to the orchard through which our troops marched. The trees were riddled to pieces with musketry. It was here that our heavy loss took place.

We skirted around fences & country roads for an hour until I got tired ~~of the fun~~ and came home.

There were a few prisoners brought in to McCook: ragged & dirty but apparently hearty & well-fed of late. Most of them expressed themselves anxious to get out of the army. Said they had been watching for a chance, &c &c.

14 July 1864, Thursday

Nothing of importance yet. This evening as the President started to the Soldiers' Home I asked him ~~quid nunc~~ "what news?" & he said, "Wright telegraphs that he thinks the enemy are all across the Potomac but that he has halted & sent out an infantry reconnaissance, for fear he might come across the rebels & catch some of them." The Chief is evidently disgusted.

15 July 1864, Friday

Last night failing to get away, I went over to Georgetown to inquire after the health of Miss A. B. Her father told me she was dying. Coming back, the streets were full of marching & shouting—said to be Ord's men and the Qr Mrs. Department people.[233]

This morning got up early and started for the cars; too late; leave on the

11.15 train. Am ordered by President to see Greeley & ask if he has done anything about the President's letter.

[CA. 21 JULY 1864]

On the 8th day of July 1864 the President received the following letter and enclosures from the Hon. Horace Greeley (A). I handed them to him & read them, though Greeley's letter being copied in another hand was more intelligible than the philosopher's usual scrawl. The next day 9th the President wrote to G. as follows (B). I telegraphed to G. the same day. Here the matter rested until the morning of the 15th when the President received the letter from G. marked (C). When the letter arrived, Prt. was at the War Department. I read it to him; he seemed vexed that there should be such delay. He walked with me over to the Executive Mansion & wrote the letter (D) for me to take to New York. I started that morning at 11.15, going by way of Baltimore, around by Boat to Perryville & thence by rail, the vilest route known to travel. Got into N. Y. at six oclock the 16th Saturday & while I was washing my face came up G.s card. I went down to the parlor delivered the letter (D) to him. He didnt like it, evidently: Thought he was the worst man that could be taken for the purpose: that as soon as he arrived there, the newspapers would be full of it: that he would be abused & blackguarded &c &c. Then he said if the President insisted on his going he would go, but he must have an absolute safeconduct for four persons, saying the President's letter wd. not protect him against our own officers. This seemed to me reasonable & I had even presented the matter to the President in the same way. I wrote the despatch marked (E) & sent it to Washington. About noon came the answer marked (F).[234] I then wrote the safe-conduct marked (G) & took it to the Tribune Office. I left the names blank & was going to let G fill them up but he said "no" in his peculiar querulous tone "I wont write a word. I expect to be pitched into everywhere for this—but I cant help it. I was going to write a safeconduct for "H. G. & four others" but he wd not permit it. "I want no safeconduct. If they will catch me & put me in Ft. Lafaytte it will suit me first rate" I wrote the names in & gave it to him. "I will start tonight" said he. "I shall expect to be in Washington Tuesday morning, if they will come."

He was all along opposed to the President proposing terms. He was in favor of some palaver any how—wanted them to propose terms which we could not accept—if no better—for us to go to the country on—wanted the government to appear anxious for peace & yet [was?] strenuous in demanding as our ultimatum proper terms.

As I left his office, Mr. Chase entered.

I went back to Washington, arriving there Monday morning. A few hours after I arrived, a despatch came from G. as follows (H) I took it to the President. He told me a few minutes afterwards to hold myself in readiness to start if it became necessary—that he had a word to say to Mr. Seward in regard to the matter. In the afternoon he handed me the note marked (I) & told me to go to the Falls, see Greeley & deliver that note & to say further that if the ~~they~~ Commissioners wished to send any communications to Richmond for the purpose indicated, they might be sent through Washington, subject to the inspection of the Government & the answer from Richmond should be sent to them under the same conditions. Provided, that if there was any thing either way objectionable to the Government in the despatches sent, they wd. be returned to the parties sending them without disclosure.[235]

I went over to see Seward—he repeated about the same thing adding that I had better request the Comn. to omit any official style which it would compromise our Govt. to transmit—that they could waive it in an unofficial communication among themselves & not thereby estop themselves of any claim.

I left Washington Monday evening—arrived in New York too late Tuesday: took the evening Tuesday train & arrived at Niagara Wednesday morning at 11½. Saw G. at once at the International Hotel. He was evidently a good deal cut up at what he ~~seemed to consider~~ called the President's great mistake in refusing to enter at once into negotiations without conditions. He thinks it would be an enormous help to us in politics & finance to have even a semblance of negotiation going on—that the people would hail with acclaim such a harbinger of peace. He especially regretted that the President should have as he said shown his hand first. That he should have waited their terms—if they were acceptable, closed with them—if they were not gone before the country on them.

I of course combatted these views saying that I thought the wisest way was to make our stand on what the moral sentiment of the country and the world wd. demand as indispensable & in all things else offering to deal in a frank liberal & magnanimous spirit as the President has done—that the two points he insists on are such points—that he could not treat with these men—who have no power: that he could do no more than offer to treat with any who came properly empowered. I did not see how he could do more.

Mr. Greeley did not wish to go over. He had all along declined seeing these people & did not wish to give any handle to talk He thought it better that I should myself go over alone & deliver the letter. I really thought so to—but I understood the Prest. & Seward to think otherwise so I felt I must insist on G's going over as a witness to the interview. We got a carriage & started over.

We got to the Clifton House & met George Saunders at the door I wrote G.s name on my card & sent it up to Holcombe, Clay being out of town at St. Kate's.[236]

Sanders is a seedy looking rebel with grizzled whiskers & a flavor of old clo'. He came up & talked a few commonplaces with G. as we stood by the counter. Our arrival, Greeleys well known person created a good deal of interest: the barroom rapidly filling with the curious & the halls blooming suddenly with wide eyed & pretty women. We went up to Holcombe's room, where he was breakfasting or lunching—tea & toasting at all events. He was a tall solemn spare false looking man with false teeth false eyes & false hair.

Mr. Greeley said "Major Hay has come from the President of the United States to deliver you a communication in writing & to add a verbal message with which he has been entrusted." I handed the note & told him what the President & Seward had told me to say.

~~He said "Mr. Clay is now back at St. Catherines. I will telegraph~~ & I added that I would be the bearer of anything they chose to send by me to Washington or if they chose to wait it could go as well by mail.

He said "Mr. Clay is now absent at St. Catherines. I will telegraph to him at once & inform you in the morning."

We got up to go. He shook hands with Greeley who "hoped to meet him again," with me & we went down to our carriages. Sanders was on the piazza. He again accosted Greeley—made some remark about the fine view from the House—& said "I wanted old Bennett to come up but he was afraid to come."[237] Greeley answd. "I expect to be blackguarded for what I have done &c. I am not allowed to explain. But all I have done has been done under instructions."

We got in & rode away. As soon as the whole thing was over, G. recovered his spirits & said he was glad he had come—& was very chatty & agreeable on the way back & at dinner.

After dinner I thought I wd. go down to Buffalo & spend the night. Went down with young Dorsheimer formerly of Fremonts staff.[238] I found him also deeply regretting that the President had not hauled these fellows into a negotiation neck & ear without terms. He gave me some details of what G. had before talked about—the political campaign these fellows are engineering up here. He says Clay is to write a letter giving three points on which if the Democracy carry the fall elections the South will stop the war & come back into the Union. These are

1st Restoration of the Union

2 Assumption of Conf Debt

3 Restriction of slavery to its present limits & ackt. of de facto emancipation. On this platform it is thought Judge Nelson will run.[239]

Spent night of the 20th & morning of the 21st at Buffalo.

Coming back to the Falls & finding nothing from the Rebs I wrote

International Hotel,
July 21, 1864

Major Hay would respectfully inquire whether Prof Holcombe & other gentlemen associated with him desire to send by ~~Major Hay~~ him to Washington any messages in reference to the Communication delivered by him on yesterday; & in that case, when he may expect to be favored with such ~~reply~~ messages

[AFTER 22 JULY 1864]

It seems necessary to make some additional statement of facts in relation to the late proceedings at Niagara Falls in the interest of peace.[240]

In the early part of this month, Mr. Horace Greeley received from a source which he considered entitled to credit the intelligence that there was in Canada a commission sent by Jefferson Davis to try to arrange terms of peace with the United States. This information came from a man attached to the so-called commission with whom Mr. Greeley had formerly held relations of intimate friendship. He at once communicated to the President the information of which he had thus become possessed, adding his own emphatic assurance of its trustworthiness.

The President, anxious for peace and unwilling that any opportunity should be neglected which if embraced might lead to the consummation so earnestly desired, at once requested Mr. Greeley to proceed directly to Niagara Falls, and if it could be ascertained that any such authorized commission existed to bring them at once to a conference at Washington. Armed with the President's safeguard for Clement C. Clay, Professor J. P. Holcombe, Jacob Thompson and George N. Sanders, Mr. Greeley proceeded to the Falls, and in his unpublished letter of the 17th July invited the commissioners "as duly accredited from Richmond, bearers of propositions looking to the establishment of peace" to visit Washington in company with him, under the safe-conduct of the President.

This frank and liberal offer at once developed the character of these Southern adventurers. As long as they had only to deal with Democratic politicians, and manage the Chicago Convention, they were ambassadors to all intents and purposes, with full powers to treat and negotiate. But as soon as they were invited to Washington by an authorized agent of the President they discovered that they had no credentials whatever; they were simply highly intelligent gentlemen, "thoroughly informed, travelling for sanitary purposes and prepared to lend a hand to their friends in the Presidential contest." They added, however, that if their bogus government at Richmond only knew what a brilliant offer had been made, they, or some other party, would at once be empowered to come to Washington as proposed.

Mr. Greeley communicated this to the President by telegraph. Still determined that nothing should be left undone to bring about the desired negotiations, the President wrote the memorandum of the 18th, announcing that he was at all times ready and willing to meet and second a movement for peace from the South, only insisting upon those terms which he thought demanded by the national honor, and the moral sentiment of the country and the world. This paper he gave to Major. Hay, A. A. G., and Acting Private Secretary, with orders for him to deliver it, in company with Mr. Greeley, to the so-called commissioners at the Clifton House, and further to state to them that if they desired to make any communication to Richmond for the purpose of obtaining consent to act in the way indicated, our Government would transmit such communication to its destination, and convey also the answer thereto, back to them. Provided always, that there should be nothing in the despatches either way, objectionable to the Government, in which case the despatch containing the obnoxious passages should be returned to its source without publicity, if desired.

Major Hay on arriving at Niagara the morning of the 20th saw Mr. Greeley and drove over with him to the Clifton House. Their names were presented by Mr. Sanders to Professor Holcombe and they went at once to his apartments. Major Hay delivered the note of the President and added the verbal message given above. Mr. Holcombe, after reading the note, said that Mr. Clay was not then at the Falls, having gone to St. Catherine's to pass the day; that he would at once telegraph for him and that after considering the matter, they would send a reply, if they had anything to send, to Major Hay at the international Hotel. Mr. Greeley and Hay then took leave and went back to the American side. Mr. Greeley returned to New York the same afternoon, Major Hay remaining at the Falls to await the reply of Messrs. Clay and Holcombe.

At this juncture, an odd, half-witted adventurer named Jewett who had been employed by Mr. Greeley to fetch and carry messages to and from the Clifton House, as being a person whose flitting back and forth would be least likely to attract attention, having in some manner gained the confidence and insinuated himself into the favor of the rebel emissaries, induced them to entrust to him the copy of their letter of the 21st for delivery to Mr. Greeley, which he placed in the mail having previously made a copy for publication.[241] Major Hay having waited all day for the communication he had been promised in the morning, addressed a note to Mr. Holcombe making inquiries as to the delay and was informed by him that the letter in question had already been transmitted to Mr. Greeley. A note was simultaneously received from Mr. Jewett conveying the same information, and intimating that if Major Hay had seen fit to show said Jewett a proper consideration, he would have received this interesting intelligence earlier. Major Hay set out at once for Washington, profoundly impressed with the importance of making the acquaintance of Jewett as soon as possible.

23 SEPTEMBER 1864, FRIDAY

Senator Harlan thinks that Bennett's support is so important especially considered as to its bearing on the soldier vote that it would pay to offer him a foreign mission for it, & so told me.[242] Forney has also had a man talking to the cannie Scot who asked plumply "Will I be a welcome visitor at the White House if I support Mr. Lincoln?" What a horrible question for a man to be able to ask? I think he is too pitchy to touch. So thinks the Prest. apparently: it is probable that Bennett will stay about as he is, thoroughly neutral, balancing carefully until the October elections & will then declare for the side which he thinks will win. It is better in many respects to let him alone.

24 SEPTEMBER 1864, SATURDAY

This morning I asked the President if the report of the resignation of Blair were true.[243]

He said it was.

"Has Dennison been appointed to succeed him."[244]

"I have telegraphed to him today—have as yet received no answer."[245]

"What is Mr. Blair going to do?"

"He is going up to Maryland to make speeches. If he will devote himself to the success of the national cause without exhibiting bad temper towards his opponents, he can set the Blair family up again."

"Winter Davis is taking the stump also. I doubt if his advocacy of you will be hearty enough to be effective."

"If he and the rest can succeed in carrying the state for emancipation, I shall be very willing to lose the electoral vote."[246]

25 SEPTEMBER 1864, SUNDAY

Yesterday Nicolay who has been several days in New York, telegraphed to the President that Thurlow Weed had gone to Canada & asking if he, N, had better return. I answered he had better amuse himself there for a day or two. This morning a letter came in the same sense. The President when I showed it him said "I think I know where Mr. W. has gone. I think he has gone to Vermont, not Canada. I will tell you what he is trying to do. I have not as yet told anybody.

Some time ago, the Governor of Vermont came to see me "on business of importance," he said. I fixed an hour & he came. His name is Smith. He is, though you wouldnt think it, a cousin of Baldy Smith. Baldy is large, blonde, florid. The Governor is a little dark phystey sort of man. This is the story he told me, giving General Baldy Smith as his authority.²⁴⁷

When General McClellan was here at Washington, Baldy Smith was very intimate with him. They had been together at West Point & friends.²⁴⁸ McClellan had asked for promotion for Baldy from the President & got it. They were close and confidential friends. When they went down to the Peninsula their same intimate relations continued, the General talking freely with Smith about all his plans and prospects: until one day Fernando Wood & one other politician from New York appeared in Camp & passed some days with McClellan. From the day that this took place, Smith saw or thought he saw that McClellan was treating him with unusual coolness & reserve. After a little while he mentioned this to McC. who after some talk told Baldy he had something to show him. He told him that these people who had recently visited him, had been urging him to stand as an opposition candidate for President: that he had thought the thing over, and had concluded to accept their propositions & had written them a letter (which he had not yet sent) giving his idea of the proper way of conducting the war, so as to conciliate and impress the people of the South with the idea that our armies were intended merely to ~~improve~~ execute the laws and protect their property &c., & pledging himself to conduct the war in that inefficient conciliatory style. This letter he read to Baldy, who after the reading was finished said earnestly "General, do you not see that looks like treason: & that it will ruin you and all of us." After some further talk the General destroyed the letter in Baldy's presence, and thanked him heartily for his frank & friendly counsel. After this he was again taken into the intimate confidence of McClellan. Immediately after the battle of Antietam Wood & his familiar came again & saw the General, and again Baldy saw an immediate estrangement on the part of McClellan. He seemed to be anxious to get his intimate friends out of the way and to avoid opportunities of private conversation with them. Baldy he particularly kept employed on reconnoisaances and such work. One night Smith was returning from some duty he had been performing & seeing a light in McClellan's tent he went in to report. Several persons were there. He reported & was about to withdraw when the General requested him to remain. After every one was gone he told him those men had been there again and had renewed their proposition about the Presidency—that this time he had agreed to their proposition and had written them a letter acceding to their terms and pledging himself to carry on the war in the sense already indicated. This letter he read then and there to Baldy Smith.

Immediately thereafter Baldy Smith applied to be transferred from that army.

At very nearly the same time other prominent men were asked the same, Franklin Burnside and others.

Now that letter must be in the possession of Fernando Wood, and it will not be impossible to get it. Mr. Weed has, I think, gone to Vermont to see the Smiths' about it."

I was very much surprised at the story & expressed my surprise. I said I had always thought that McClellan's fault was a constitutional weakness and timidity which prevented him from active and timely exertion, instead of any such deeplaid scheme of treachery & ambition.

The President replied "After the battle of Antietam, I went up to the field to try to get him to move & came back thinking he would move at once. But when I got home he began to argue why he ought not to move. I peremptorily ordered him to advance. It was 19 days before he put a man over the river. It was 9 days longer before he got his army across and then he stopped again, delaying on little pretexts of wanting this and that. I began to fear he was playing false—that he did not want to hurt the enemy. I saw how he could intercept the enemy on the way to Richmond. I determined to make that the test. If he let them get away I would remove him. He did so & I relieved him.[249]

I dismissed Major Key for his silly treasonable talk because I feared it was staff talk & I wanted an example.[250]

"The letter of Buell furnishes another evidence in support of that theory. And the story you have heard Neill tell about Seymour's first visit to McClellan all tallies with this story."[251]

I went over to talk with Fox about Wilmington. I asked when operations wd. begin there, wanting to go as a volunteer. He says we hope to take it in October. Porter is gone to the West to hurry up his business there & put up the shutters & shut up shop & will then return and organize the expedition. Fox took Gillmore down to Grant for the land operations but Grant simply said he would assign an officer to that duty when the time came; Fox thinks Weitzel. The Army have to take the town this time—the Navy forced to be secondary by the shoal water.[252]

It is a most important thing. Fox says in scripture phrase the rebellion is sustained "not by what entereth into their ports but by what proceedeth out." The rebel credit will collapse the day their cotton supply is stopped.

26 SEPTEMBER 1864, MONDAY

Blair has gone into Maryland stumping. He was very much surprised when he got the President's note.[253] He had thought the opposition to him was dying out. He behaves very handsomely and is doing his utmost. He speaks in New York Tuesday night.

Blair in spite of some temporary indiscretions is a good and true man and a most valuable public officer. He stood with the President against the whole Cabinet in favor of reinforcing Fort Sumter.[254] He stood by Fremont in his Emancipation decree though yielding when the President revoked it. He approved the Proclamation of January 1863 and the Amnesty Proclamation & has stood like a brother beside the President always. What have injured him are his violent personal antagonisms and indiscretions. He made a bitter and vindictive fight on the Radicals of Missouri, though ceasing at the request of the Prest. He talked with indecorous severity of Mr. Chase & with unbecoming harshness of Stanton, saying on Street corners, "this man is a liar, that man is a thief." He made needlessly enemies among public men who have pursued him fiercely in turn. Whitelaw Reid said today that Hoffman was going to placard all over Maryland this fall "Your time has come." I said "He wont do anything of the kind & moreover Montgomery Blair will do more to carry Emancipation in Maryland than anyone of those who ~~blackguard~~ abuse him."

Nicolay got home this morning looking rather ill. I wish he would start off & get hearty again, coming back in time to let me off to Wilmington.

He says Weed said he was on the track of the letter & hoped to get it. ~~The object of N's trip was to see Weed who has a plan for getting campaign money out of Cotton — teterrima fons malorum — N says it wont do.~~[255]

Forney writes a tight and enthusiastic letter claiming Pennsylvania by 50,000.[256]

Nicolay thinks we will carry New York. The New Jersey men promise their state & the Kentuckians pluckily swear they will be on hand with theirs.

29 SEPTEMBER 1864, THURSDAY

Blair was introduced to the great War Meeting Tuesday night by Curtis Noyes. In the beginning of B's Speech he said his own father suggested the propriety of his resignation to the President.[257]

Webster has just returned here from the North. He says New York is absolutely safe: that Weed is advising his friends to bet: that Dean Richmond is despondent—saying the Democratic party are half traitors.[258]

Things looked very blue a month ago. A meeting was held in New York (to which Geo Wilkes refers) of Union men opposed to Lincoln & it was resolved that he should be requested to withdraw from the canvass. But Atlanta & the response of the country to Chicago infamy set matters right.[259] Weed says they sent for him to come & join them. He replied that his only objection to Mr. Lincoln was his favor to such fellows as they & that he shd. not join them against him. He also says that Ben. Butler in his last visit to New York spent several hours with him trying to get him to go in for him (Butler) on a new Buffalo or Cincinnati supplementary convention ticket. W. told him the question lay between Lincoln and McClellan.

Grant is moving on Lee. This morning early the Prest. telegraphed to Grant expressing his anxiety that Lee should not reinforce Early against Sheridan. Grant answered that he had taken measures to prevent it by attacking Lee himself. He is moving in two columns, Ord South, & Birney North of the James. Stanton was much excited on hearing the news & said "he will be in Richmond tonight." "No" said the President. "Halleck! what do you think?" Halleck answered that he wd. not be surprised if he got either Richmond or Petersburg by the maneuver.[260]

Gold was at 201 & fell to 96 on the news of Grant's being in motion.

Today Hooker leaves for the West. He takes charge of the Dept. administered by Heintzelman. Heintzelman is busily engaged canvassing for McClellan & the President kindly takes off his hands the additional burden of military duty.

2 OCTOBER 1864, SUNDAY

Today I received a letter from Wm. N. Grover saying certain of his friends had agreed to press his name for Judge of the District Court Western Missouri in place of Judge Welles. He adds however that in case Judge Bates Attorney General should desire the appointment he would not stand in his way, believing that Bates appointment would be very advantageous & satisfactory to the Union people of the State. He requested me to make this known both to Mr. Bates & the President. I read his letter to the President, at the same time referred to the recent indiscreet announcement made by Cameron, that in the event of a reelection the Prest. wd. call around him fresh & earnest men. He said "they need not be especially savage about a change. There are now only 3 left of the original Cabinet with the Government."[261] He added that he rather thought he would appoint Mr. Bates to the vacant judgeship if he desired it. He said he would be troubled to fill his place in the Cabinet from Missouri especially from among the Radicals. I thought it would not be necessary to confine himself to Missouri: that he might do better farther South, by taking Mr. Holt from Kentucky.

He did not seem to have thought of that before. But said at once "that would do very well. That would be an excellent appointment. I question if I could do better than that. . . . I had always thought, though I had never mentioned it to any one, that if a vacancy should occur on the Supreme Bench in any southern District, I would appoint him. . . . But giving him a place in the Cabinet would not hinder that."[262]

I told him I should show Grover's letter to Judge Bates, to which he assented.

7 OCTOBER 1864, FRIDAY

I showed Bates the letter today: he said some friends of his had previously spoken to him in the same sense, that he was friendly to Grover, thought well of him as a gentleman and a lawyer, and knew of no one whom he would sooner see appointed. That he would not take the office himself in any case. That he had earnest antagonisms in that state: he was fighting those Radicals there that stood to him in the relation of enemies of law and order. There is no such thing as an honest and patriotic American Radical: Some of the transcendental Red Republican Germans were honest enough in their moonstruck theorizing: but the Americans impudently and dishonestly arrogate to themselves the title of unconditional loyalty, when the whole spirit of their faction is contempt of and opposition to law. . . . While the present state of things continues in Missouri, there is no need of a Court—so says Judge Treat & I agree with him.[263]

Mr. Nicolay has gone West to try to find some way of pacifying the Missouri muddle. ~~He started [ ] evening~~. McKee has been here to have the Post Office changed. Carl Schurz writes advising the same.[264]

8 OCTOBER 1864, SATURDAY

Today I got a letter from Grover protesting against an assessment which has been levied upon him by Jim Lane's advisory committee, & sending me instead a hundred dollars. I gave it to Harlan with an explanation which seemed unnecessary to him, as he said there was a general doubt as to Lane's entire fitness as a disbursing officer.[265]

Last night Swinton of the Times was in my room several hours.[266] He says Raymond went away a good deal discouraged about money matters.

Halpine is working for the County Clerkship & will get it if the newspapers are worth anything.[267]

General Banks arrived yesterday morning.[268] I visited him and his wife at Willards last night.

9 OCTOBER 1864, SUNDAY

Governor Dennison and General Banks spent a little while in my room this morning. Banks says there is no city on the continent more salubrious than New Orleans, properly cared for as it has been during our occupancy. The city is now thoroughly loyal, thoroughly in harmony with the country at large, in spite of all that has been said to the contrary. The national airs are forever sounding in the schools and streets: the national bunting floating in the air. Society is running now in loyal channells: the secession element must breathe loyal air or perish. When Banks went there the prominent resident families would invite officers to their houses on condition that they should not wear their uniform. When Gen. Grant came down from Vicksburg, only our officers families & a few of the poorer classes attended his receptions. Banks says that all this is changed. At his receptions & those of his prominent associates in command, the best society of the city crowded his drawing rooms.

The loyal feeling of common nationality has done much to break up the exclusion and demarcation existing between the French and American classes; the town is more American than ever before. The organization of the fire companies, which was formerly in rebel hands has especially felt the influence of this change of sentiment until now that enormous organization can be relied upon thoroughly in the interests of the Government. In very many cases, it is not so much a change of sentiment and conviction, as a more intelligent perception of interests and probabilities. They see the experiment of rebellion has failed, that the national cause will triumph and that free labor affords to them a brighter and more progressive future. But still insist, many of them, that slavery was best for the negro, that secession was constitutional and other such worn out maxims of the past.

I referred to the humiliating fact that while abroad the world was recognizing the fact of the rehabilitation of Louisiana and the convincing proof it afforded of the entire feasibility of the national plan of a permanent and conquered peace on the basis of freedom, there were many men and journals in the North, esteemed able and patriotic, who labored to prove that all this work was a failure. I referred to the Evng Post and others. He replied that the foundation of those attacks in the E. P. was neither honesty nor patriotism, but unsuccessful pecuniary projects—something I had not heard of before.[269]

Cameron telegraphed last night that the magnificent demonstration in Philadelphia was the certain augury of victory on Tuesday. Thurlow Weed says he is easy about Pennsylvania but anxious about Indiana.[270] Defrees writes under date October 5 from Indiana that he thinks the state will be ours by a small majority. Illinoisans generally claim Illinois.

The President is fighting today to get time to write a letter to the Baltimore meeting but is crowded as usual by visitors[271]

P. S. Wrote the letter. I changed the word "posted" to "informed"[272]

10 OCTOBER 1864, MONDAY

Kelley was here before breakfast. He says he will carry his district by 2000 which will grow to 4000 by November. He says we shall carry the state in spite of Cameron who is trying to manage the campaign with a view to elect himself Senator. He charges C. with working to defeat McClure. He says that Childs a strong friend of Cameron is trying to defeat him (K) because he wont declare for Cameron as Secretary of War instead of Stanton.[273]

Washburne tells me that Kelley wants Judge Lewis made Sec. Interior in place of Usher to keep Cameron out of the Cabinet.

Kelley is getting more and more infatuated with himself. He told today a dull anecdote for the purpose of bringing in what some one said of him. "You Judge Kelley with your splendid voice your fine address, your fervid & impassioned eloquence, are one of the most dangerous men of the time."

Yet the old fellow has fine abilities and is devoted to the good cause of equal rights.

11 OCTOBER 1864, TUESDAY

~~Newell handed me this morning an estimate from A. Cummings giving 18,900 as the probable majority on the home vote in Pennsylvania.~~[274]
~~Thurlow Weed writes anxiously on the subject of the Navy vote. The President has been with Seward & Welles this morning and arranged about it.~~[275]
~~Morgan writes about Vanderbilts medal. I went over to the State Department & set the thing going. Leutze is to make the design.~~[276]
I showed the President today W. E. Dodge's letter to Judge Davis complaining of the effect of the Niagara manifesto & asking the President to explain it away, &, says the Prest. "lose ten times as much on the other side." I got to discussing the matter with Dorsheimer who dined with me today & who has been talking somewhat freely with Holcombe. I told him I thought the President was right: that if he had shown any backtrack inclinations in that matter our people wd. have lost heart and faith in the cause: that there was really no opportunity at that time for honorable peace: that an attempt coupled with the reception of Commissioners at Washington would have excited the vague hopes of the country & a failure which was inevitable wd. have occasioned a disastrous relapse, which wd. have demoralized public sentiment so as to have risked this canvass & campaign. So it was better to meet them on the threshold & let them and the world know where we stood.[277]

When Joe Medill wrote me an impertinent letter (hoping I wd. read it to the President which hope was fallacious) denouncing the Niagara note of the President I cd. not but think how loudmouthed wd. have been his denunciation of Lincoln's recreancy to principle if he had not made the condition of which these croakers now complain.

Montgomery Blair was here for a while this afternoon. He gives a most graphic picture of the fight in Maryland for the Mayoralty & Winter Davis' plottings & plannings, Swanns speech last night &c.

I was mentioning old Mr. Blairs very calm and discreet letter of October 5 to the Prest. today contrasting it with Montgomery's indiscretions, & the President said "Yes, they remind me of He was sitting in a barroom among strangers who were telling of some affair in which his father, as they said, had been tricked in a trade, and he said 'That's a lie!' Some sensation. 'What do you mean?' 'Why, the old man aint so easy tricked. You can fool the boys but ye cant the old man.'"[278]

At 3 oclock came despatches from Puleston saying they would give a moderate but decided majority for the Administration & we wd. gain 4 or more Congressmen.[279]

At Eight oclock the President went over to the War Department to watch for despatches.[280] I went with him. We found the building in a state of preparation for siege. Stanton had locked the doors and taken the keys upstairs, so that it was impossible even to send a card to him. A Shivering messenger was pacing to and fro in the moonlight over the withered leaves, who catching sight of the President took us around by the Navy Department & conducted us into the War Office by a side door.

The first despatch we received contained the welcome intelligence of the election of Eggleston and Hays in the Cincinnati districts. This was from Stager, at Cleveland, who also promised considerable gains in Indiana, made good a few minutes after by a statement of 400 gain in Noble County. Then came in a despatch from Sandford stating we had 2500 in the City of Philadelphia and that leading Democrats had given up the state. Then Shellabarger was seen to be crowding Sam Cox very hard in the Columbus District in some places increasing Brough's colossal vote of last year.[281]

The President in a lull of despatches took from his pocket the Nasby Papers and read several chapters of the experiences of the saint & martyr Petroleum V. They were immensely amusing. Stanton and Dana enjoyed them scarcely less than the President who read on *con amore* until 9 oclock. At this time I went to Seward's to keep my engagement. I found there Banks and his wife Cols. Clark & Wilson Asta Buruaga & Madame, The New Orleans people and a young Briton who was nephew to the Earl of Dorset, somebody said & who wd. like to enter our Army before we finish this thing up.[282] Dennison was also there. We broke up very early. Dennison & I went back to the Department.

~~We found the good Indiana news had become better and the Pennsylvania had begun to be streaked with lean. Before long the despatches announced with some certainty of tone that Morton was elected by a safe working majority. The scattering reports from Pennsylvania showed about~~

~~equal gains and losses. But the estimates and flyers all claimed gains on the Congressmen. A despatch from Puleston says "we have gained 4 or five or even 6 Congm. I am going to New York to sleep a few days." Not a word came from any authorized source. Cameron and the State Committee silent as the grave. It was suggested that Cameron had gone home to Harrisburgh to vote. It looked a little ominous his silence. The President telegraphed to him but got no answer.~~[283]

Reports began to come in from the Hospitals and camps in the vicinity, the Ohio troops about ten to one for Union and the Pennsylvanians ~~about~~ less than three to one. Carver Hospital by which Stanton & Lincoln pass every day on their way to the country gave the heaviest opposition vote—about one out of three. Lincoln says "Thats hard on us Stanton—they know us better than the others." Co K, 150 P. V. the Presidents personal escort voted 63 to 11 Union.

~~An enthusiastic despatch announcing 30,000 for Morton came in, signed McKim. "Who is that?" "A Quartermaster of mine," said Stanton "he was sent there to announce that. By the way" he added "a very healthy sentiment is growing up among the Quartermasters. Allen is attending all the Republican meetings, so is Myers. A nephew of Broughs that I placed at Louisville & made a Colonel, I reduced to a Captain and ordered him South the other day.... He was caught betting against Morton" A murmur of adhesion filled the apartment.~~[284]

I suggested to the Secretary what Dorsheimer had told me about Dandy's Regiment being all for McClellan. I added that Dandy wanted promotion. "He will get it" said the Secretary, puffing a long blue spiral wreath of smoke from his stern lips. Colonel Dandy's dream of stars passed away in that smoke.[285]

They spoke of McClernand's manifest and seemed glad to be rid of him. A vain irritable overbearing exacting man who is possessed of the monomania that it was a mere clerical error which placed Grant's name and not his in the Commission of the Lieutenant General.[286]

Washburne read an amusing letter about Scates, saying that the old fellow was declaring in favor of revolution in case McClellan is elected.[287] He has gone crazy in the fiery exuberance of his young Republican zeal. These new converts put us old originals to the blush.

I am deeply thankful for the result in Indiana. I believe it saves Illinois in November. I believe it rescues Indiana from sedition & civil war. A copperhead Governor would have afforded a grand central rallying point for that lurking treason whose existence Carrington has already so clearly demonstrated which growing bolder by the popular seal and sanction wd have dared to lift its head from the dust and measure strength with the Government. The defection of the Executive Governments of those two great States Illinois & Indiana, from the general administration would have been disastrous and paralyzing. I should have been willing to sacrifice something in Pennsylvania to avert that calamity. I said as much to the President. He said he was anxious about Pennsylvania because of her enormous weight and influence which, cast definitely into the scale, wd. ~~have closed~~ close the campaign & left the people free to look again with their whole hearts to the cause of the country.[288]

12 October 1864, Wednesday

~~This morning made arrangements with Mr. Harrington and Secretary Fessenden to have a Revenue Cutter send along the Blockading Squadron to pick up the votes.~~

~~A committee is here bothering about the New York Navy Yard saying it is used against us. The President told me to say to Fox that (he the Prest. must be relieved in this matter. Something must be done to satisfy these people. Fox says everything possible is done: that the dissatisfied cannot even agree among themselves & that if they can poll the yard the Dept. stands ready to turn out any man hostile to the Administration.~~[289]

~~The indefinite claims of last nights Pennsylvania despatches are not borne out by this mornings details. The home vote will be very close & we may need the soldier vote after all to give us a clear majority.~~

13 October 1864, Thursday

Last night Chief Justice Taney went home to his fathers. The elections carried him off, said Banks this morning.

Already (before his poor old clay is cold) they are beginning to canvass vigorously for his successor. Chase men say the place is promised to their *magnifico*, as crazy old Gurowski styles him.

I talked with the President one moment. He says he does not think he will make the appointment immediately. He will be, he says, rather "shut pan" in the matter at present.[290]

14 OCTOBER 1864, FRIDAY

Judge Lewis talked to me this morning earnestly against Chase for that place. He says he is not a man of enlarged legal or financial knowledge; that his supreme selfishness has gradually narrowed and contracted his views of things in General; that his ignorance of men, & many other things that I knew before &c &c.

He says he thinks Chase really desired, toward the end of his continuance in office to injure and as far as possible destroy the influence and popularity of the Administration. By his constant denunciation of the extravagance of expenditure, his clamor against the inefficiency of other departments, his personal tone of slighting comment upon every act of the President, and more than all by his steady & persistent attempts to make the taxes more & more burdensome upon the people, (having increased his demands from $150,000,000 to $300,000,000 in the face of Lewis' and Morrills representations) he clearly indicated his desire to excite popular discontents and grumblings against the Government.[291]

His selfishness, continued the Judge, blinded him utterly to the character of the flatterers who surrounded. (I gave him some instances of this.) Lewis says that Field, for whom he gave up his place expressed himself as relieved by his absence.

Pennsylvanians returning from their voting furloughs almost all accuse Cameron of having botched the canvass badly.

6 NOVEMBER 1864, SUNDAY

~~Marshal Murray came from New York today to get the release of a blockade runner, recd. by Weed. Forney writes to have a fellow released from Old Capitol. The President sent me to Stanton about it. I found him sick in bed. But he made the necessary orders. We spoke of Jim Brady's recent foolish somerset back into the mud of Copperheadism. He ascribed it to Brady's envy & jealousy of the recent magnificent movement of the War Democrats.~~[292]
~~He seemed thoroughly sick & tired of the constant jobs that people were asking for, under pretence that they are to aid the election; & heartily wished for Tuesday to come and go to end the nuisance of them.~~

7 November 1864, Monday

Talking with the President a day or two ago about Sherman he told me that Sherman was inclined to let Hood run his gait for a while, while he overran the Gulf States in Hoods rear. Grant seems rather inclined to have Sherman strike and destroy Hood now, before going South but gives no orders in the case.

~~Spent Sunday evening with the Lorings. They are bitterly despondent: and with a most wonderful assurance, talk about *our* frauds.~~

~~Bartlett writes to President that Mrs. J. G. B. has become an earnest Lincolnite. Poor Mcs Visiting these people and compromising himself to them has been of no avail and must be terribly humiliating to a man so wellbred as McC. is.~~[293]

8 November 1864, Tuesday

The House has been still and almost deserted today. Every body in Washington, not at home voting seems ashamed of it and stays away from the President.

I was talking with him today. He said "It is a little singular that I who am not a vindictive man, should have always been before the people for election in canvasses marked for their bitterness: always but once: When I came to Congress it was a quiet time: But always besides that the contests in which I have been prominent have been marked with great rancor."

At noon Butler sent a despatch simply saying, "The quietest city ever seen."

Butler was sent to New York by Stanton. The President had nothing to do with it. Thurlow Weed was nervous about his coming, thought it would harm us and even as late as Sunday wrote saying that ~~it~~ Butler's presence was on the whole injurious, in spite of his admirable General Order.[294]

Hoffman sent a very cheering despatch giving a rose-coloured estimate of the forenoon's voting in Baltimore.[295] "I shall be glad if that holds," said the President "because I had rather feared that in the increased vote over that on the Constitution, the increase would rather be against us."

During the afternoon few despatches were received.

At night, at seven oclock we started over to the War Department to

spend the evening. Just as we started we received the first gun from Indianapolis, showing a majority of 8000 there, a gain of 1500 over Morton's
vote. The vote itself seemed an enormous one for a town of that size and
can only be accounted for by considering the great influx since the war of
voting men from the country into the state centres where a great deal of
Army business is done. There was less significance in this vote on account
of the October victory which had disheartened the enemy and destroyed
their incentive to work.

The night was rainy steamy and dark. We splashed through the grounds
to the side door of the War Department where a soaked and smoking sentinel was standing in his own vapor with his huddled up frame covered
with a rubber cloak. Inside a half-dozen idle orderlies: up stairs the clerks
of the telegraph. As the President entered they handed him a despatch from
Forney claiming ten thousand Union Majority in Philadelphia. "Forney is
a little excitable." Another comes from Felton, Baltimore, giving us "15,000
in the city, 5000 in the State. All hail, Free Maryland." That is superb. A
message from Rice to Fox followed instantly by one from Sumner to Lincoln claiming Boston by 5000 and Rice's & Hooper's elections by majorities of 4000 apiece. A magnificent advance on the chilly dozens of 1862.[296]

Eckert came in shaking the rain from his cloak, with trowsers very dis-
reputably muddy. We sternly demanded an explanation. He had slipped
he said & tumbled prone, crossing the street. He had done it watching a
fellow-being ahead and chuckling at his uncertain footing: Which reminded the Tycoon, of course. The President said "For such an awkward
fellow, I am pretty sure-footed. It used to take a pretty dextrous man to
throw me. I remember, the evening of the day in 1858, that decided the contest for the Senate between Mr. Douglas and myself, was something like
this, dark, rainy & gloomy. I had been reading the returns, and had ascertained that we had lost the Legislature and started to go home. The path
had been worn hog-backed & was slippering. My foot slipped from under
me, knocking the other one out of the way, but I recovered myself & lit
square: and I said to myself, '*It's a slip and not a fall.*'"

The President sent over the first fruits to Mrs. Lincoln. He said "She is
more anxious than I."[297]

We went into the Secretary's room. Mr. Welles and Fox soon came in.
They were especially happy over the election of Rice regarding it as a great

triumph for the Navy Department. Says Fox "There are two fellows that have been specially malignant to us, and retribution has come upon them both, Hale and Winter Davis." "You have more of that feeling of personal resentment than I," said Lincoln. "Perhaps I may have too little of it, but I never thought it paid. A man has not time to spend half his life in quarrels. If any man ceases to attack me, I never remember the past against him. It has seemed to me recently that Winter Davis was growing more sensible to his own true interests and has ceased wasting his time by attacking me. I hope for his own good he has. He has been very malicious against me but has only injured himself by it. His conduct has been very strange to me. I came here, his friend, wishing to continue so. I had heard nothing but good of him; he was the cousin of my intimate friend Judge Davis. But he had scarcely been elected when I began to learn of his attacking me on all possible occasions. It is very much the same with Hickman. I was much disappointed that he failed to be my friend. But my greatest disappointment of all has been with Grimes. Before I came here, I certainly expected to rely upon Grimes more than any other one man in the Senate. I like him very much. He is a great strong fellow. He is a valuable friend, a dangerous enemy. He carries too many guns not be respected in any point of view. But he got wrong against me, I do not clearly know how, and has always been cool and almost hostile to me. I am glad he has always been the friend of the Navy and generally of the Administration."[298]

Despatches kept coming in all the evening showing a splendid triumph in Indiana showing steady small gains all over Pennsylvania, enough to give a fair majority this time on the home vote. Guesses from New York and Albany which boiled down to about the estimated majority against us in the city 35,000 and left the result in the state still doubtful.

A despatch from Butler was picked up & sent by Sanford saying that the City had gone 35000 McC & the State 40,000. This looked impossible. The state had been carefully canvassed & such a result was impossible except in view of some monstrous and undreamed of frauds. After a while another came from Sanford correcting former one & giving us the 40000 in the State.

Sanford's despatches all the evening continued most jubilant: Especially when he announced that most startling majority of 80,000 in Massachusetts.

General Eaton came in and waited for news with us. I had not before known he was with us. His denunciations of Seymour were especially hearty & vigorous.[299]

Towards midnight we had supper, provided by Eckert. The President went awkwardly and hospitably to work shovelling out the fried oysters. He was most agreeable and genial all the evening in fact. Fox was abusing the coffee for being so hot—saying quaintly, it kept hot all the way down to the bottom of the cup as a piece of ice staid cold till you finished eating it.

We got later in the evening a scattering despatch from the West, giving us Michigan, one from Foy promising Missouri certainly, but a loss in the first District from that miserable split of Knox & Johnson, one promising Delaware, and one, too good for ready credence, saying Raymond & Dodge & Darling had been elected in New York City.[300]

Capt. Thomas came up with a band about half past two, and made some music ~~and a small hifalute~~. The President answered from the window with rather unusual dignity and effect & we came home. I wrote out the speech & sent it to Hanscom.[301]

W. H. L. came to my room to talk over the Chief Justiceship; he goes in for Stanton & thinks, as I am inclined to think, that the President cannot afford to place an enemy in a position so momentous for good or evil.[302]

He took a glass of whiskey and then refusing my offer of a bed went out & rolling himself up in his cloak lay down at the President's door; passing the night in that attitude of touching and dumb fidelity with a small arsenal of pistols & bowie knives around him. In the morning he went away leaving my blankets at my door, before I or the President were awake.

9 NOVEMBER 1864, WEDNESDAY

Mr. Dana came this morning to ask the President to come over to the War Department, Mr. Stanton being unable to come to the Ex. Mansion. They are to consult in regard to some suggestions of Butler's, who wants to grab & incarcerate some gold gamblers. The President dont like to sully victory by any harshness.

Montgomery Blair came in this morning. He returned from his Kentucky trip in time to vote at home. He is very bitter against the Davis clique, (whats left of it) and foolishly I think confounds the War Department and the Treasury as parties to the Winter Davis conspiracy against the President. He spoke with pleasant sarcasm of the miscalculation that has left Reverdy Johnson out in the cold, & gave an account of his "being taken by the insolent foe" in the Blue Grass Region. He says he stands as yet by what he has said, that Lincoln will get an unanimous electoral vote. The soldier vote in Kentucky he thinks will save the state if the guerillas have allowed the country people peace enough to have an election.

2 o'clock: Hoffman just reports a splendid sett of Majorities in Maryland reaching an aggregate of 10,000.

Webster brings a despatch from Hastings (Albany Knickerbocker) saying we will have the state by 5,000.[303]

Swett sends a desponding despatch in which he virtually gives up the State, charging it to Frauds and the demoralizing influence of Seymour's military patronage.[304]

11 NOVEMBER 1864, FRIDAY

This morning Nicolay sent a ~~superb~~ dispatch from Illinois giving us 25000 majority and 10 Congressmen which we take to mean Wentworth Farnsworth Washburne Cook Ingersoll Harding Cullom Bromwell Kuykendall, and Moulton at Large, leaving the Copperheads Thornton Morrison Ross and Marshall.[305]

At the meeting of the Cabinet today, the President took out a paper from his desk and said, "Gentlemen do you remember last summer I asked you all to sign your names to the back of a paper of which I did not show you the inside? This is it. Now, Mr Hay, see if you can get this open without tearing it!" He had pasted it up in so singular style that it required some cutting to get it open. He then read as follows:

> Executive Mansion
> Washington
> Aug. 23, 1864.

This morning, as for some days past, it seems exceedingly probable that this Administration will not be re-elected. Then it will be my duty to so cooperate with the President elect, as to save the Union between the election and the inauguration; as he will have secured his election on such ground that he cannot possibly save it afterwards.

> A Lincoln.

This was indorsed:

William H. Seward
W. P. Fessenden
Edwin M Stanton
Gideon Welles
Edw. Bates
M Blair
JP Usher
August 23, 1864

The President said "you will remember that this was written at a time (6 days before the Chicago nominating convention) when as yet we had no adversary, and seemed to have no friends. I then solemnly resolved on the course of action indicated above. I resolved, in case of the election of General McClellan being certain that he would be the Candidate, that I would see him and talk matters over with him. I would say, 'General, the election has demonstrated that you are stronger, have more influence with the American people than I. Now let us together, you with your influence and I with all the executive power of the Government, try to save the country. You raise as many troops as you possibly can for this final trial, and I will devote all my energies to assisting and finishing the war.'"

Seward said, "And the General would answer you '*Yes, Yes*'; and the next day when you saw him again & pressed these views upon him he would say 'Yes—yes' & so on forever and would have done nothing at all."

"At least" added Lincoln "I should have done my duty and have stood clear before my own conscience."

~~Seward was abusing Forney today for a report of his (S's) remarks last night at the serenade, which appeared horribly butchered in the Chronicle, in which S.s Biblical lore is sadly out at the elbows.~~

The speech of the President at the two last Serenades are very highly spoken of. The first I wrote after the fact, to prevent the "loyal Pennsylvanians" getting a swing at it themselves. The second one, last night, the President himself wrote late in the evening and read it from the window. "Not very graceful" he said "but I am growing old enough not to care much for the manner of doing things.[306]

Today I got a letter from Raymond breathing fire and vengeance against the Custom House which came so near destroying him in his District. I read it to the President. He answered that it was the spirit of such letters as that that created the faction and malignity of which Raymond complained.

It seems utterly impossible for the President to conceive of the possibility of any good resulting from a rigorous and exemplary course of punishing political dereliction. His favorite expression is "I am in favor of short statutes of limitations in politics."

[16 NOVEMBER 1864, WEDNESDAY]

12th November 1864, I started for Grant's Headquarters. We left the Navy Yard at 2 oclock in the afternoon. The Party consisted of Fox, Dyer, Wise, M Blair, Pyne, Ives, Forbes, Ives, Tom Welles Foster a chinese-English merchant & Reid of the Gazette.[307] The day was sad blowy bleak and a little wet.

We dined and some played cards and all went to bed. When we got up in the morning we were at Hampton Roads. We made no stay there but after communicating with the Admiral, D D Porter, we started up the James River, he following in his Flagship the Malvern. He overtook us about noon or a little after, & came on board, with Captain Steadman of the Navy.[308] Porter is a good-looking lively man ~~of a little less than medium height~~, a ready offhand talker; a man not impressing me as of a high order of talent—like the McCooks rather: a hale fellow: a slight dash of the rowdy.

In the afternoon, we passed by the island of Jamestown. On the low flat marshy island where our first colony landed, there now remains nothing but ruins. An old church has left a solitary tower as its representative. A group of chimneys mark the spot of another large building. On the other side of the river there is high fine rolling land. One cannot but wonder at the taste or judgement that selected that pestilential site in preference to those breezy hills. They probably wished to be nearer their boats & also thought a river was a handy thing to have between them and the gentle savages that infested the shores of the James.

Fort Powhatan we saw also—where a battalion of negroes flaxed out Fitz Hugh's command of F. F. V.s.[309]

We arrived at City Point at 3 oclock. There are very few troops there but quite a large fleet lying in the river.

We went ashore; walked through the frame building standing in place of that blown up by the late fearful explosion. We climbed the steep hill whose difficulty is mainly removed by the neat stairs that Yankee care has built since our occupation of the point. At the top of the Hill we found a young sentry who halted us & would not let us go further: till Porter throwing himself on his dignity which he does not use often said Let the General know that Admiral Porter & Mr. Fox are here to see him. He evidently impressed the sentry for he said after an instant's hesitation "Go ahead. I reckon its all right."

A common little wall tent being indicated, we went up to beard the General. At our first knock, he came to the door. He looked neater & more careful in his dress than usual; his hair was combed his coat on & his shirt clean, his long boots blackened till they shone. Every body was presented.

After the conference was over, we went back to the boat: the General accompanied us. We started down the river and soon had dinner. During dinner Porter talked in very indecent terms of abuse of Banks, saying that the fleet got ahead of the army & stole the cotton which the army intended to steal. He spoke of some articles which had appeared in the papers criticising his action & said he could stand the criticism as long as he had his pockets full of prize money.

After dinner we all gathered around Grant who led the conversation for an hour or so. He thinks the rebels are about to the end of their tether & said "I hope we will give them a blow this winter that will hasten their end."

He was down on the Massachusetts idea of buying out of the draft by filling their quota with recruits at $300.00 from among the contrabands in Sherman's army. "Sherman's head is level on that question" he said in reply to some strictures of Mr. Forbes. "He knows he can get all these negroes that are worth having anyhow & he prefers to get them that way rather than to fill up the quota of a distant state and thus diminish the fruits of the draft." Sherman does not think so hopefully of negro troops, as do many other generals. Grant himself says they are admirable soldiers in many respects: quick and docile in instruction and very subordinate: good in a charge: excellent in fatigue duty. He says he does not think that an army of them could have stood the week's pounding at the Wilderness and Spotsylvania as our men did: "in fact no other troops in the world could have done it," he added.

Grant is strongly of the belief that the rebel army is making its last grand rally: that they have reinforced to the extent of about 30000 men in Virginia, Lee getting 20000 and Early getting 10,000. He does not think they can sensibly increase their armies further. He says that he does not think they can recover from the blow he hopes to give them this winter.

He is deeply impressed with the vast importance and significance of the late Presidential election. The point which impressed him most powerfully was that which I regarded as the critical one—the pivotal centre of our history—the quiet and orderly character of the whole affair. No bloodshed or riot—few frauds and those detected and punished in an exemplary manner. It proves our worthiness of free institutions, and our capability of preserving them without running into anarchy or despotism.[310]

Grant remained with us until nearly one oclock at night Monday morning & then went to his own boat the "Martin" to sleep till day. Babcock Dunn and Badeau of his staff were with him.[311]

In the morning we were at the Roads again. Breakfasted and went on shore. Ives and I visited Mrs. Stackpole and Miss Motley.[312]

Porter before leaving us for his flagship the Malvern off Newport News Sunday night invited us to Luncheon at 12. We went. There was quite a large party. Mrs. Porter was present.

Ives & I wishing to see the Florida took one of the Malvern's boats and went on board. Comr. Beardsley, in command of the prize, showed her to us. She is a dirty looking beast: the worst kept craft I ever saw.[313]

Some of her officers were still on board, among them Emory's boy Tom. Some of our people had committed the folly of asking him to take the oath of allegiance: the privilege of refusing gave him a sense of importance to which he had no right.[314]

There was a very fine display made by the sailors and Marines of the fleet in a review and drill in Landing. Some fifty boats crews were going through their evolutions at once. The boats were gay with flags.[315]

We left Fort Monroe at 3 & ½ and arrived at Washington Tuesday morning the 15th at 7 A.M.

17 NOVEMBER 1864, THURSDAY

Ives came in in the evening, and he and I went over to Wise's. I found there Benton of the Army ordnance, Wise Aulick and Jeffers of the Navy. They were discussing the project of which the President spoke to me some time ago, as having been suggested by Butler, that of exploding a great quantity of powder between the enemy's forts at the mouth of the Cape Fear River for the purpose of dismantling them. The late occurrences at Erith in England were discussed at Length together with all the few events in history bearing on the point. All seemed to think there was something in it but no one seemed to me to speak with conviction. This morning Gillmore was in my room for a while, & I spoke of the matter to him. He gave it no credit whatever: said Col. Tighlman had such fancies which came to nothing: that to produce any considerable wave a fabulous amount of powder would be required: but concluded by saying that the whole question was as yet unascertained and dependent upon experiment; that a shock *might* be produced which would unship all the guns and give the fleet time to sail in.[316]

Dana gave the President today a letter from General Dix

18 December 1864, Sunday

This morning Blair came into the office and talked a good while about the Presidents singular policy of favoring his enemies and crushing out his friends. He says that although he has elected every body in Maryland, his own people are getting disheartened and demoralized fearing that they are not recognized as the friends of the Administration, and that Senator Hicks who is to be appointed Collector of the Port to make room for Blair in the Senate, is finessing with the factious opposition lest he should be rejected when before the Senate for confirmation & it is suspected that he may throw himself into the hands of the Anti-Lincoln Davis faction, as really the stronger party.[317]

Blair denounces nearly everybody as Lincoln's malignant enemies. He says Chase is—which nobody doubts—that Seward and Stanton are in league against Lincoln. That Stanton went into the Cabinet to break down the Administration by thwarting McClellan & that Seward was in cahoot with him. That Seward was last fall coquetting with the Copperheads to run as their candidate for the Presidency against Lincoln on the platform of the Crittenden Resolutions. I asked him what gave him that idea. He said he was in correspondence with Barlow about McClellan: that he told Barlow that if McClellan would withdraw himself from politics & would make that sort of an announcement, he had no doubt the President would assign him to a command—which he could not do so long as McC. held so prominent a position of political antagonism to the administration. Barlow answered that McCs position was identical with that of "the leading member of the government" and quoted from a letter "lying before him" to that effect. Blair says this letter was Sewards. He claims to have *exposed* Seward in this way to the President & also to the Barlow crowd. He says he made known to them Seward's duplicity & treachery & thus prevented their offering him the Democratic candidacy—which, he says excited against him the bitter enmity of Seward & Weed and their party.[318]

And much more of the same sort.

When the President came in, he called Blair and Banks into his office meeting them in the hall.

They immediately began to talk about Ashleys Bill in regard to states in insurrection. The President had been reading it carefully & said that he liked it with the exception of one or two things which he thought rather calculated to conceal a feature which might be objectionable to some. The first was that under the provisions of that bill negroes would be made jurors & voters under the temporary governments. "Yes, said Banks, that is to be stricken out and the qualification white male citizens of the U. S. is to be restored. What you refer to would be a fatal objection to the Bill. It would simply throw the Government into the hands of the blacks, as the white people under that arrangement would refuse to vote."[319]

"The second said the President is the declaration that all persons heretofore held in slavery are declared free. This is explained by some to be not a prohibition of slavery by Congress but a mere assurance of freedom to persons actually then [free] in accordance with the proclamation of Emancipation. In that point of view it is not objectionable though I think it would have been preferable to so express it[320]

The President and General Banks spoke very favorably, with these qualifications of Ashley's bill. Banks is especially anxious that the Bill may pass and receive the approval of the President. He regards it as merely concurring in the Presidents own action in the one important case of Louisiana and recommending an observance of the same policy in other cases. He does not regard it, nor does the President, as laying down any cast iron policy in the matter. Louisiana being admitted & this bill passed, the President is not estopped by it from recognizing and urging Congress to recognize another state of the South coming in with constitution & conditions entirely dissimilar. Banks thinks that the object of Congress in passing the Bill at all is merely to assert their conviction that they have a right to pass such a law in concurrence with the executive action. They want a hand in the reconstruction. It is unquestionably the prerogative of Congress to decide as to qualifications of its own members: that branch of the subject is exclusively their own. It does not seem wise therefore to make a fight upon a question purely immaterial, that is, whether this bill is a necessary one or not, and thereby lose the positive gain of this endorsement of the President's policy in the admission of Louisiana, and the assistance of that state in carrying the constitutional amendment prohibiting slavery.

Blair talked more than both Lincoln and Banks, and somewhat vehemently attacked the radicals in the house and senate who are at work upon this measure accusing them of interested motives and hostility to Lincoln. The President said "It is much better not to be led from the region of reason into that of hot blood, by imputing to public men motives which they do not avow."[321]

Appendix
Notes
Index

Appendix

Speech to the Citizens of Florida

Citizens of Florida.[1] I shall only occupy a few minutes of your time this evening and will then give way to others who are better qualified to address you by years experience and an intimate acquaintance with your wants. I see around me those whose devotion to yr own best interests and the interests of the country—which are in fact identical has been signalized by toil danger and wounds. These men can speak by authority, sure of respectful audience and credit. I can only say simply what I am sent to you for.

It is pretty well established by this time, on both sides of the lines of the Union armies, that the Rebellion set on foot for the purpose of destroying popular government on this continent has failed of its purpose. Its history has been full of surprises. Its originators thought at first that there would be no fighting at all: that a bold front and a quick arm would carry the thing through to completion with trifling expense, and no more bloodshed than characterizes the annual tumult and riots of election time. Mr. Davis in his recent message to the Richmond Congress says this more plainly than it has been said before. He said it appeared incredible at the outset of the contest that the Northern people would sacrifice blood treasure and liberty in the subjugation of the South, as he is pleased to style it, the ~~liberation of the South as I know the Northern voters before God consider their work.~~ I need not tell you how this fancy has been realized. The people of the North are ahead of their legislators & abreast of their Executive Officers in demanding the unstinted prosecution of the war to the end of an honorable peace.

Another chimera was that our fighting would have to be done at home. That the soldiers of the Union marching Southward to sustain the constitution and enforce the laws would have to fight their bitterest battles within their own borders. There was some justification for this hope in the infamous and craven utterances of Northern men. ~~I know that~~ many who considered themselves leaders of public sentiment gave reason to Southern leaders to believe that the fight would never reach the Southern border but that it would rage and die in the bosom of our own states. Franklin Pierce was a shining ~~example~~ mouthpiece of that craven prophecy in New Hampshire.[2] Governor Seymour, crouching in abject terror of the coming storm, repeated it in [Tweddle?] Hall. It was echoed by lesser scoundrels in Pennsylvania and died away in the rattle and hiss of crawling reptiles on the prairies of Southern Illinois & Ohio.

I will do the brains of some of these men the justice to believe that they knew they were lying, for many when the war burst hastened to retrace their steps and take place in line with their people. The loudest secessionist in Illinois, one who had sworn to do his part to make the valleys of Egypt [southern Illinois] a sepulcher for any Abolitionists who should march from the North was among the first to beg from the President a commission for his son in the Abolition Army. And the lesser lights followed suit rapidly.

How the expectations of these people of a divided North have been met let the recent elections answer. Never in the history of American politics has such unanimity been seen before. Those acts of the Govt. which have been most severely criticised the so called arbitrary arrests, upon military authority have been fully endorsed. The bitter partizan ~~attacks, initiated by~~ combination who found their first exponent in a cabal at Albany and another in a carpet bag delegation from Ohio, denouncing the government with revolution and overthrow because of the banishment of that pestilent agitator C. L. Vallandigham, repelled & foiled at the time by the unanswerable logic of the President has been utterly defeated & put to shame by the recent verdict of the people of Ohio, who decide with the unquestioned authority of 100,000 Majority that the hands of the Government shall be upheld while acting in accordance with that loftiest maxim of ancient judicial wisdom, The safety of the ~~people~~ Commonwealth is the highest law. The ~~melancholy~~ utter failure of all attempts to cripple the government by resisting the draft, by force as in New York, where the arm of the law crushed to the earth the demon of revolt, and drove back to their underground slums & cellars the howling apostles of the New Gospel of peace; and by a corrupt judiciary as in Pennsylvania, where the people in the exercise of their high discretion hurled from power the disloyal court that dared to trifle with their dearest interests;[3] (these failures) must have convinced every one candid man that any hope based on northern divisions or dissentions is utterly vain and unfounded. The country is as true, in the shock of this great contest as the beaten anvil to the stroke. The shafts of envy & malice & partizan hate launched against it, are as harmless, as the beams of the Arctic moonlight striking & shivering on the intact bulk of an iceberg.

Who believes that the rebellion could have lasted so long but in the hopes of a divided North? And who could have been so wild as to have even planned it but in the hope of a United South? But we see both hopes equally & surely blasted. We see the North welded together more firmly than ever before in the fierce heat of this trial. And we see the structure of Southern society and the sisterhood of the Southern States shaken in [sunder?] by the shock that but strengthened the North. The rebellion broke out with brilliant prospects in the border states. Carried away by the frenzy caught from the contagion of a kindred institution, the fiery spirits of the border, eager for change, threw themselves into the contest with a vigor and alacrity to which for a time equal energy & enterprise was not opposed by cooler heads and more loyal hearts, who still adhered to the Union. The military organizations of most of the border states were in disloyal hands. They nearly succeeded in tearing Missouri from her moorings, but Price and Frost & Jackson while they took from the state the semblance of ~~military~~ & the prestige of the militia power, could not long stand against the undisciplined uprising of the people. Buckner and Breckinridge stood for a while to Young Kentucky as the embodiment of aristocracy & chivalry in the forum and the field, but better men soon drove them from the state they vainly endeavored to betray.[4] Trimble & Winans and the Maryland Guard for a while seemed all-powerful in their sorely-tempted state;[5] but better counsels prevailed. In all these states the protecting arm of the general government gave an opportunity for reason & free discussion to work out their legitimate results. The dictates of prudence and interest and common sense were heard & heeded: after a short & hesitating spasm of treason disguised under the name of neutrality they all came heartily out on the side of their duty and allegiance, & have ever since, in every position, maintained their loyal relations with their associate States, nobly & well. At the polls they have spoken in a voice not to be misunderstood even by the willfully prejudiced: on every battlefield of the war their dead have mingled their blood with that of their Northern brothers, and their surviving heroes have hailed with the same shout of triumph the same victorious standard of bravery and glory & individual nationality. "By communion &c &c"

There are no states in the Union whose status is more firmly fixed than those whose virtue was so ~~fiercely~~ tempted and tried. You might as well try to drag the Keystone from the completed arch, as these battle swept commonwealths from the embrace of the National Union.

If there could be one lingering relic of hope for rebellion in the attitude of the border states it would be in that contagion of like social systems that first endangered their loyalty. But that has at last vanished. I should wrong your intelligence and my own sense of honor, citizens of Florida, if I should attempt to conceal, in deference to worn-out prejudices what I in common with 9/10 of the people of the United States now think in regard to the national bearing of this dead question of negro slavery. I believe it caused the war and I believe its removal from national politics by its own destruction will under God close the war, and the only argument I care to offer in support of that belief, is the free and ~~untrammelled voice~~ dispassionate utterance of those slave states who have been allowed to give their testimony in regard to this momentous issue.

For many years they have cherished this institution as their palladium. ~~their sacred idol~~ They have forbidden all discussion upon its merits. They have compelled dumb silence or unreasoning praise. They have fiercely persecuted comment from without: they have strongly repressed question or inquiry from within their borders. For a man to express a doubt as to the expediency or morality of this system ~~was to~~ involved the risk of his life, and the more dreadful certainty of social ostracism. The instances of spirits of such eccentric courage were rare. At the beginning of this war, the border slave states could justly claim a united public sentiment in favor of slavery.

The enormous prosperity we had for years enjoyed under the benign and fostering influences of our Republican government, which extended to the slave states as well as to the free, ~~in spite of the drawbacks of their vicious system of labor,~~ gave currency & color of truth to their constant assertion that their prosperity depended on the perpetuation of their system of labor. They stubbornly refused to recognize the fact that the comparative progress of free and slave communities showed incontestably that they were prosperous not by means, but in spite of their vicious social system. An error thus bred of endless fair weather must be dissipated by storm.

The storm came, the awfulest in intensity and terror the ~~world~~ earth has yet seen: Elemental forces contending in the moral ~~world~~ atmosphere: good & evil marshalling on either side the principalities & powers of the air. ~~a grand diapason of groans and showering tears & blood wailing in dismal concord with the tempest.~~ Among the wrecks of that tempest there is one thing we cannot regret, the utter discredit and destruction of the delusion that slavery in any circumstances, is better than freedom. This foundered in the first rough weather. ~~The airy structure of passion and~~ The currents of men's minds were disturbed. They lost their bearings in the stress of new events and were forced to take new observations & points of departure. In the heat of this fiery revolution old party ties parted like cobwebs, and the mists of passion & prejudice vanished & ceased to cloud the minds of men, sobered by the presence of issues greater than any that had ever confronted them before.

To the eternal honor of the men of the border states let it be told that they rose to the level of the occasion. They did not shirk or seek to evade the great issues before them. They examined the whole subject with what calmness and temper they could bring to the consideration of a matter so near to their hearts. ~~They saw themselves in danger of being dragged into the vortex of a revolution which they~~ They saw the government and the institutions with which they were satisfied and of which they were proud attacked by a treacherous & bloody conspiracy: they sought for the cause: they found it was slavery. They saw themselves in danger of being dragged into the vortex of this destructive revolution: they questioned what were the influences which could tend to cause them to link their fate with this causeless and insane revolt. They saw that a sympathy bred of a similar social system alone impelled their heedless and impulsive citizens into that ruinous alliance.

In a danger so great and so near the etiquette of ~~discussion~~ reticence which prevails in all slave communities had not power enough to prevent discussion. Their minds were sobered & their tongues freed. And when free discussion once begins it will never end in an intelligent community but ~~with the abatement of the nuisance which~~ in the settlement of the question which has provoked it. You know better than I, that a system of social servitude is incompatible with free discussion. It lives in an atmosphere of repression. It is walled round by silence and darkness. It crumbles when brought to the light and air, as long buried corpses do.

Among peoples so intelligent as ours, and under a tuition so powerful as war, thought travels like lightning and discussion works out its legitimate results with wonderful rapidity. Two years have worked a revolution in the sentiment of the border states. You will see them now steadily confronting the conviction that slavery cannot survive the war, that the fight inaugurated by slavery has drifted into such a shape that the question is now between the preservation of the Union & the preservation of slavery. And having arrived at that conviction no candid man, approaching the subject without bias or passion, can long hesitate how he will stand.

On the One hand, the perpetuation of a system of government the best that human wisdom has yet devised, so perfect, that the accomplished traitors who seek to destroy it, could invent no better, but copied servilely its constitution and its laws: an asylum for the oppressed of all nations: a [vow?] of promise to the world: a great and powerful nationality loved by the weak and free and feared by the despot and tyrant throughout the earth: A name of which every American is proud. And a flag which blazes through history in glory & power, and streams meteor light, a protection of commerce & a defiance to oppression, to the uttermost isles of the sea.

On the other hand, the stain of treason & rebellion for the protection of a system of labor, proved bad in economy, and of worse than doubtful morality.

The Border states have considered and ~~answered that~~ decided question. You can gather their decision in advance of their final action by looking at their representatives recently elected to Congress.

Delaware sends to the National legislature Col. Smithers an unconditional Anti Slavery man, who caucuses with the Republicans & voted for Mr Colfax for Speaker.[6] They are only discussing the time and way of Emancipation in Delaware; the fact is settled.

Maryland has recently elected by an overwhelming majority an unconditional Emancipation ticket & has sent her whole delegation to Congress right on the great issues with one exception. [four lines are crossed out] The hours of slavery in Maryland are numbered.

West Virginia having sloughed off the corrupting influences of her neighbor to the East has openly declared for Emancipation.

Kentucky, though somewhat behind the front rank of her sisters is steadily advancing in the same path of deliverance. Four of her Congressmen Randall, Anderson, Brutus Clay and the young and gallant soldier general Green Clay Smith, representatives not only of ~~the~~ a large and populous regions but of a powerful and controlling social influence, are avowed emancipationists, favoring all the great radical measures of the Administration, and standing like pioneers in the ~~morning~~ dawn of their states enfranchisement marshalling her the way that she is going.[7]

And Missouri whose true breast has been most savagely torn by the harrying tread of Arms—Missouri, the last to take up the heavy burden is the first to lay it down. Schooled by severe affliction, her people have profited by their experience and in solemn council have resolved to separate themselves forever from the body of death whose contact was destroying them. And hurried on by an excess of noble ardor carried forward by a rush of progress beyond the limits of discretion, her reformers have at last begun to claim that they are ~~become~~ more radical than Abolition, more warlike than our armies, more patriotic than our martyred dead and more loyal than the President. While we may smile at these vagaries we must recognize the courage and the practical wisdom born of this tumult, which has seized the occasion to burn the only bridge which could ever convey them back to the land of peril and disaster from which they are forever delivered.

You cannot but see, that these movements towards the inevitable result of speedy emancipation in the border states, destroys the only substantial hope with which the leaders of the Southern revolt began it. By making the nation homogeneous it vastly increases its strength and its prospect of perpetuity.

All this is outside of the progress of our Armies. These moral and political forces have all worked independently of any thing else but in harmony with the general result. The Army has been especially fortunate during the year that has passed, if you may ~~call~~ designate as good fortune that success, which is due to their own merit and strength and not in any sense to luck or circumstance. The results are too vast and too glorious to need recapitulation here. The control of the great river of the Continent, the possession of Louisiana and the Texas Coast, the great victories of Grant at Vicksburg & Chattanooga and the defeat of Gen. Lee at Gettysburg are successes of that decisive character that foreshadow the end of the war.

There seemed to me to be an omen of good in that crowning battle of Joe Hooker where sweeping with his legions up the precipitous slope of Lookout Mountain, plunging into the clouds and the mists that hung heavy on the mountain-side, fighting his way through with that pluck and energy that he there found for the first time fitly seconded, he came out at last victorious in the higher daylight of those regions where the dew never falls, and his triumphant banners, bathed in the double baptism of battle & storm, shook out their crimson folds to the eternal sunshine.

So I cannot but think that we, having passed through the worst of our trouble and our distress, are now coming out into the faithful promise of assured success. The mists of doubt and danger are under our feet & the rest of the fight we may hope, is to be in the sunshine.

We do not wish to disparage our enemies, or indulge in any thing like unseemly exultation. They have fought gallantly as Americans always do in a cause bad in the beginning and, growing continually more absurd and hopeless. The shadow of foreign recognition which has allured them so long, has vanished. Their credit is gone, their currency is depreciated beyond possibility of restoration. Their armies are wasting: they have already so severely taxed the strength of the country that their depleted ranks can never be filled. They have been driven from point to point, fighting with the energy of desperation, until there are few points left for further retreat. The opening of the coming Spring Campaign will in all probability complete the active work of the war.

It is at this time that the President has thought fit to mingle statesmanship with arms: not to sheath the sword but to wrap it in the olive branch. In his proclamation of the 8th of December he announces to the people of the South that the war is not waged upon them, but upon their wicked and interested leaders for their deliverance. He offers with a generous magnanimity unparalleled in history to restore the entire population of rebellious districts to all their rights of liberty and property, save only those that have been already lost by the inevitable chances of war. And all this upon the sole condition of subscription to an oath of allegiance, in which the accomplished events of the war are recognized. I do not see how more could have been asked by the people. I do not see how less could have been required by the Government. The laws and executive acts made and promulgated by the government in the suppression of the rebellion are facts, to the support of which the whole power of the nation is solemnly pledged. Rights of property & more especially rights of person have accrued under them to disregard which would be an outrageous breach of faith. The government is bound to sustain them.

You may think these laws and acts illegal and unconstitutional. I do not. I believe them sound in law, expedient in fact and righteous in morals, but admitting the contrary you have your remedy in the Supreme Court and the revisory power of the National Legislature What better security could you possibly want? There can be nothing oppressive or arbitrary in the requirement of a support which leaves you so complete a redress if you are wronged.

The indications are that the people of the South will not reject this easy and fair solution of the trouble. I say the people ~~emphatically~~ advisedly. Of course it is not to be expected that the corrupt and ambitious leaders who have so long made the lives and happiness of their fellow citizens the mere playthings and counters of their remorseless game, will approve of a proposition which consigns them to ignominy & exposes them to the just consequences of their crimes. But it seems that the impression is everywhere gaining ground, that enough has already been sacrificed to the bloody experiment of these men and that the time has come for the people to reassert their power in the South, and put a stop to this slaughterous struggle, which has been aptly called the Rich Mans War and the Poor Man's Fight.

Tennessee under the lead of the heroic Governor Andrew Johnson is taking steps to reassume her relations with the ~~Federal~~ National Government. The most loyal population in the land have been for two years & more, ground under the iron heel of oppression in that State, but the fires of liberty have ever been kept [trimmed?] & burning in the fastnesses of the Cumberland Mountains & now the power of the oppressor is broken forever and they may enjoy the freedom for which they have suffered so much.

In Arkansas the movements for reconstruction are most energetic and earnest. A delegation of her leading citizens are now in Washington engaged in making arrangements for extending the benefits of the President's proclamation to that state. The restoration of the loyal state Government of Louisiana which is even now being consummated, will result before very many weeks in the supremacy of law and order west of the Mississippi and will herald the close of that mad revel of anarchy & rapine which has so long ravaged that fertile and opulent region.

Citizens of Florida, one of the most cheering pieces of news that we have recently heard in the North ~~for a great while~~ is the announcement that you are moving in this important matter. It is regarded as especially fitting and especially significant that the most Southern state should be the first to wheel into line. Florida is the child of the Union, bought with the treasure and defended with the blood of the Union. Secession has nowhere seemed more baseless and absurd than here. The state of Florida has nothing to gain by the rebellion. Here dignity & her rights are sage nowhere but in the Union. I suppose she has had enough of anarchy & enough of war to last to the end of time. She can at once deliver herself from anarchy & reestablish the mild reign of law and order: and she will in this way do much to hasten the return of peace, a peace worth having, a peace that will endure.

One word in relation to my own presence among you. I come, under the direction of the President to extend to the citizens of Florida the benefits of the Proclamation of the 8th of December. I will open a book for the registry of those who desire to declare their allegiance to the United States and I will issue to every one signing the oath of allegiance a certificate of such signature, which will be thereafter conclusive evidence of their being entitled to the benefit of that executive act. All are expected to sign this oath: those who are loyal, those who have always been so, as well as, with certain specific exceptions, those who have heretofore favored and participated in the rebellion. The loyal are asked to enroll their names, not only for the sake of example but that the aggregate of the signatures may be used as evidence to show that the minimum proportion of the voters of the state required by the Procn. are really desirous of reorganizing the state in accordance with the executive recommendation. In moral effect such action will be fraught with beneficial results not only to your own state ~~yourselves~~ but to the nation.

Citizens of Florida, the time has come for you to take your ground upon this matter. The moment of supreme decision is here. It is for you to choose whether you will have a continuance of anarchy and lawless waste and all the hideous concomitants of a state of civil war: or a fixed and stable government bringing with it all the blessings of a well-ordered civilization. It is for you to say whether you will embark your hopes and your interests in the shattered and sinking ship of rebellion, "built in eclipse and rigged with curses dark," trembling with the final throes of dissolution in the majestic presence of the national power, like the fated bark of the eastern fable, before the Mountain of Lodestar, losing the bolts and bar & rivet in the stress of that awful attraction, and drifting on helpless, incoherent, and undone to break in disordered fragments on the wavewashed base of the everlasting rocks: or whether, taught by experience and taking counsel of the solemn voices of events, you will wisely adhere to the good ship ~~Union~~ whose timbers are staunch and true, whose mighty frame is still defiant of time and chance, whose keel was laid in justice for the perpetuation of liberty, whose helm has been consecrated by the firm hands of dead worthies whose vigilant eyes watch her protectingly from Heaven—whose wake is a pathway bright with glory and honor—whose prow is turned forever to ~~yet undiscovered regions of~~ the shining shores of limitless wealth and progress hid in the mists of distant centuries.

NOTES

The following abbreviations for frequently cited sources are used in the notes:

AL MSS   Abraham Lincoln Papers.

CWL   *The Collected Works of Abraham Lincoln.* Edited by Roy P. Basler, Marion Dolores Pratt, and Lloyd A. Dunlap. (New Brunswick: Rutgers University Press, 1953–55).

DLC   Library of Congress.

IHi   Illinois State Historical Library, Springfield

O. R.   *The War of the Rebellion: A Compilation of the Official Records of the Union and Confederate Armies.* (Washington, D.C.: Government Printing Office, 1880–1901).

RPB   John Hay Library, Brown University.

EDITORS' INTRODUCTION

1. [William R. Thayer?], "John Hay," Cambridge, Mass., 1918, Hay MSS, RPB; Horace White to Frank J. Garrison, New York, 8 Nov. 1914, William R. Thayer MSS, RPB. White had read the three-volume *Letters of John Hay and Extracts from Diary,* edited by Clara Louise Stone Hay and Henry Adams (Washington: privately printed, 1908).

2. Charles G. Halpine's headnote to Hay's poem, "God's Vengeance," *New York Citizen,* n.d., scrapbook, Hay MSS, RPB; Grow, quoted in James T. DuBois and Gertrude S. Mathews, *Galusha A. Grow: Father of the Homestead Law* (Boston: Houghton Mifflin, 1917), 266–67; Nicolay and Hay, *Abraham Lincoln: A History* (New York: Century, 1890), 1:xii; [Nicolay?], draft of introduction to *Abraham Lincoln: A History,* Nicolay-Hay MSS, IHi.

According to Hay's biographer, Tyler Dennett, "The personal relations of Lincoln and Hay came closely to resemble those of father and son." *John Hay: From Poetry to Politics* (New York: Dodd, 1934), 39. A pair of more recent scholars has maintained that "John Hay's relationship with Abraham Lincoln was a paramount influence over his life. For Hay, Lincoln proved to be a father figure who combined the values and personalities of both John's father and uncle." Howard I. Kushner and Anne Hummel Sherrill, *John Milton Hay: The Union of Poetry and Politics* (Boston: Twayne, 1977), 27. On Lincoln's tendency to act as a surrogate father to young men, see "Surrogate Father Abraham," in Michael Burlingame, *The Inner World of Abraham Lincoln* (Urbana: Univ. of Illinois Press, 1994), 73–91.

3. Hay to Nora Perry, Springfield, Ill., 20 May 1859, Hay MSS, RPB.

4. [Nicolay?], draft of introduction.

5. Milton Hay, quoted in John W. Bunn to Jesse W. Weik, Springfield, Ill., 20 July 1916, in Jesse W. Weik, *The Real Lincoln: A Portrait* (Boston: Houghton Mifflin, 1922), 282–88. During the Civil War, other White House secretaries and clerks, including Gustave Matile and Nathaniel S. Howe, were similarly employed in the Interior De-

partment. Hay was commissioned a major on 12 January 1864 and was promoted on 31 May 1865 to brevet colonel of volunteers for faithful and meritorious service in the war. On 8 April 1867, he was honorably mustered out of the service.

6. Young, "John Hay, Secretary of State," *Munsey's Magazine*, 8 Jan. 1929, 247. On the relationship between Hamilton and Washington, see Fawn Brodie, *Thomas Jefferson: An Intimate History* (New York: Norton, 1974), 257–75.

7. Young, *Philadelphia Evening Star*, 22 Aug. 1891, p. 4. Commenting on this article, Hay told Young: "I read what you say of me, with the tender interest with which we hear a dead friend praised. The boy you describe in such charming language was once very dear to me—and although I cannot rate him so highly as you do, I am pleased and flattered more than I can tell you to know he made any such impression on a mind like yours." Hay to Young, Newbury, N.H., 27 Aug. 1891, John Russell Young MSS, DLC.

8. Young (ca. 1898), quoted in T. C. Evans, "Personal Reminiscences of John Hay," *Chattanooga (Tenn.) Sunday Times*, 30 July 1905.

9. Stone, "John Hay, 1858," in *Memories of Brown: Traditions and Recollections Gathered from Many Sources*, ed. Robert Perkins Brown et al. (Providence, R.I.: Brown Alumni Magazine, 1909), 153–54; Logan Hay, "Notes on the History of the Logan and Hay Families," 30 May 1939, Stuart-Hay MSS, IHi; *St. Louis Dispatch*, 30 May [?], clipping in a scrapbook, Hay MSS, RPB; Mitchel to Hay, East Orange, N.J., 12 Feb. 1905, Hay MSS, RPB.

10. Stone, "John Hay, 1858," 152; Anna Ridgely diary, 22 Jan. 1860, IHi; Anna Ridgely Hudson, "Springfield, Illinois, in 1860, by a Native Springfielder" (typescript dated Dec. 1912), Hay MSS, RPB.

11. Amy Duer to Elizabeth Meads Duer, Washington, 6 May 1862, Hay MSS, RPB; Helen Nicolay, interview by William R. Thayer, Washington, 18 Jan. 1914, Hay MSS, RPB; Hannah Angell, interview by William R. Thayer, Providence, R.I., 6 Dec. 1913, Hay MSS, RPB; Octavia Roberts Corneau, "A Girl in the Sixties: Excerpts from the Journal of Anna Ridgely (Mrs. James L. Hudson)," *Journal of the Illinois State Historical Society* 22 (Oct. 1929): 437 (entry for 26 June 1864).

12. Evans, "Personal Reminiscences of John Hay," *Chattanooga (Tenn.) Sunday Times*, 30 July 1905. Evans befriended Hay on the train trip to Washington in February 1861. Evans represented the *New York World*.

13. *Sedalia (Mo.) Times*, 11 May 1871.

14. Stoddard, "White House Sketches," *New York Citizen*, 25 Aug. 1866, p. 1; *Lincoln's Third Secretary: The Memoirs of William O. Stoddard*, ed. William O. Stoddard Jr. (New York: Exposition, 1955), 166. Stoddard was at first the "Secretary to the President to Sign Land Patents." After the war began, as Nicolay recalled, "business became very slack so that he had scarcely any official work to do. He was therefore assigned to duty as one of my clerks at the White House, being able just as well to sign there the few Land Patents which were issued from time to time. Also on one or two occasions when Hay and I were both absent, he carried a message to Congress. So that you see he ... was not in any proper sense either a real or acting Presidents Private Secretary." Draft of a letter, Nicolay to Paul Selby, Washington, 11 Mar. 1895, Nicolay MSS, DLC.

15. Philbrick to Ozias M. Hatch, 30 Dec. 1864, Hatch MSS, IHi (the "three others" refer to Philbrick, Nicolay, and Edward D. Neill); Higginson to his mother, 25 May 1863, *Letters and Journals of Thomas Wentworth Higginson, 1846–1906*, ed. Mary Thatcher Higginson (Boston: Houghton Mifflin, 1921), 201–2; King (formerly, editor of the *Topeka Record*), quoted in "Col. John Hay—A Sketch of His Life," unidentified clipping, scrapbook, Hay MSS, RPB; Weed to John Bigelow, n.d., quoted in William Roscoe Thayer, *The Life and Letters of John Hay* (Boston: Houghton Mifflin, 1929), 1:222.

16. Smith to Charles Henry Ray and Joseph Medill, [Washington], 4 Nov. 1861, Charles H. Ray MSS, Huntington Library, San Marino, Calif.; "Hay's Florida Expedition," unidentified clipping, John Hay scrapbook, vol. 57, Hay MSS, DLC; Barbee to Stephen I. Gilchrist, Washington, 2 Apr. 1933, quoted in William H. Townsend to Edward C. Stone, Lexington, Ky., 6 Mar. 1945, copy, F. Lauriston Bullard MSS, Boston Univ.; Hay to Nicolay, Warsaw, Ill., 22 Nov. 1870, Hay MSS, RPB.

17. Hay to Nicolay, Washington, 9 Apr. 1862, and Hay to James A. Garfield, Cleveland, 16 Feb. 1881, Hay MSS, RPB. Mary Lincoln disliked Hay in part because he thwarted some of her unethical attempts to tap government funds. See Michael Burlingame, *The Inner World of Abraham Lincoln* (Urbana: Univ. of Illinois Press, 1994), 304. See also Burlingame, *Honest Abe, Dishonest Mary* (Racine: Lincoln Fellowship of Wisconsin, 1994).

18. *Lincoln and the Civil War in the Diaries and Letters of John Hay*, ed. Tyler Dennett (New York: Dodd, 1939).

19. *New York Herald Tribune*, 12 Feb. 1939, Book section, p. 1. After pointing out that Dennett misspelled several names and misidentified some people, Nevins concluded gently, "With all gratitude to Dr. Dennett for what he has presented us, we must hope that when he carries the diary and letters forward . . . he will give closer attention to the niceties of editing." Dennett did not produce another volume of Hay's diaries and letters.

20. Nicolay and Hay, *Lincoln*, 1:212.

21. Dennett, *From Poetry to Politics*, 38.

22. Part of the collective entry presumably written in July and August 1863.

23. Entries for 24 Mar. and 27 Sept. 1864.

24. *Diaries and Letters*, 107.

25. See, for example, Hay's suggestive remark about his pleasure at a wedding party: "Everything was lovely and the goose hung in a more elevated position than usual" (entry for 21 July 1863); and his account of the story told by Gustavus Fox, the assistant secretary of the navy, about an African king who decided to wear some unfamiliar European gifts (entry for 10 Sept. 1863).

1. 1861

1. James H. Lane (1814–66), a U.S. senator from Kansas, raised two regiments and became a general in the fall of 1861. In 1847 Edwin D. and Henry A. Willard took over Fuller's City Hotel, which stood two blocks from the White House at 14th Street and Pennsylvania Avenue, remodeled it, and named it the Willard Hotel. Nathaniel

Hawthorne said that "it may much more justly be called the center of Washington and the Union than . . . the Capitol, the White House, or the State Department." David Hunter (1802–86), a West Point graduate, became a controversial Union general during the Civil War. "Jayhawkers" were Bands of Free State men who participated in the Missouri-Kansas border warfare in the 1850s; later, the term became a sobriquet for Kansans in general. Samuel C. Pomeroy (1816–91), a U.S. senator from Kansas and a spokesman for the Radical Republicans in Congress, achieved wide notice in 1864 when he issued a circular denigrating Lincoln and promoting the candidacy of Salmon P. Chase. Anthony J. Bleecker (1790–1884) was a prominent New York real estate broker and auctioneer as well as an active Republican; in 1862 Lincoln appointed him an assessor of internal revenue.

2. Moses Hicks Grinnell (1803–77) and Robert Browne Minturn (1805–66) were New York merchants in partnership. Grinnell, Minturn, and the other signers of the appeal were given funds and the authorization to forward ships, troops, and supplies.

3. This document is not in the AL MSS, DLC.

4. Edward McManus was a doorkeeper at the White House. Ann Sophia Winterbotham Stephens (1813–86), the author of many sentimental stories and romantic novels, played a leading role in New York literary society. Jean Margaret Davenport Lander (1829–1903), a celebrated English-born actress, took over the direction of Union hospitals in Port Royal, S.C., shortly after the death of her husband, Gen. Frederick West Lander, on 2 March 1862. After the war, she returned to the stage, where she won acclaim. General Lander (1821–62), well known for his work on transcontinental surveys in the 1850s, had assisted McClellan in the West Virginia campaigns in the spring of 1861. In charge of a division, he successfully defended Hancock, Md., from a Confederate assault in January 1862 and the following month led an attack near Bloomery Gap. B. F. Ficklin of Richmond was arrested in April 1865 for allegedly conspiring to assassinate the president. Two months later, he was released at the urging of Orville H. Browning. No formal charges were ever brought against Ficklin.

5. The "Captain" referred to is probably Cassius M. Clay (1810–1903), a leader of antislavery forces in Kentucky who organized the "Clay Battalion," similar to Lane's "Frontier Guards." They were stationed at Willard's hotel, near the White House.

6. Ward Hill Lamon (1828–93) was a close friend and business associate of Lincoln. A native of Virginia, Lamon settled in Danville, Ill., where he practiced law. In 1861 the president appointed him a marshal of the District of Columbia. He frequently served as Lincoln's bodyguard.

7. On 18 April, as Union troops abandoned the U.S. armory at Harper's Ferry, they set it afire. On the previous day, the Virginia state convention had adopted an ordinance of secession.

8. Joseph Jefferson (1829–1905) was a noted actor. Maria Louisa Lander (1826–1923), a native of Salem, Mass., and the sister of Gen. Frederick Lander, studied with Thomas Crawford in Rome, where she executed a bust of Nathaniel Hawthorne. On 19 April, a mob in Baltimore attacked the 6th Massachusetts Regiment as it marched toward the Washington depot en route to the capital. Several soldiers and civilians were killed.

9. James Partridge (1823–84) of Baltimore was appointed by Lincoln as the U.S. minister to Honduras and later as the minister to El Salvador. Edward R. Petherbridge served as a major in the Army of the Potomac, commanding the Maryland Light Artillery and later a cavalry unit of civil forces under Gen. Lew Wallace, whose headquarters were in Baltimore. Thomas H. Hicks (1798–1865) was the governor of Maryland (1858–62). George W. Brown was the mayor of Baltimore.

Hicks and Brown sent the following telegram to Lincoln from Baltimore on 19 April 1861: "A collision between the citizens & the Northern troops has taken place in Baltimore & the excitement is fearful—send no troops here[.] we will endeavor to prevent all bloodshed. A public meeting of citizens has been called and the troops of the State in the city have been called out to preserve the peace. They will be enough." AL MSS, DLC. On the following morning, Lincoln received another letter from the mayor and the governor; the president in reply summoned both to the capital.

On 21 September, after Brown had been arrested for disloyalty, a Maryland delegation appealed for his release. Lincoln replied that the previous spring he had spoken with Brown, who indicated his sympathy with the rebels. He added: "I have not heard of any act of Mayor Brown since, which would lead to the belief that he was in favor of supporting the Government to put down this rebellion." Washington correspondence, *Philadelphia Gazette* n.d., reprinted in the *Chicago Tribune*, 28 Sept. 1861.

10. William S. Wood was later named the commissioner of public buildings. Fort Washington was a dilapidated structure on the Maryland side of the Potomac, facing Mt. Vernon.

11. Dorothea Dix (1802–87) won renown for her efforts to improve treatment of the insane. In May 1861, the secretary of war accepted her offer to set up hospitals and care for sick and wounded troops. On 10 June, she became the "Superintendent to Women Nurses." One of her charges, Louisa May Alcott, called her "a kind old soul, but very queer and arbitrary."

12. Col. Peter G. Washington wished to command the militia of Washington, D.C.

13. Henry Pangborn (1839–66), a journalist who contributed columns to the *New York Times*, among other papers, joined the navy as a paymaster when the war broke out. He died in Pensacola, Fla., immediately after his wedding. A veteran of Baltimore journalism, L. A. Whitely was at this time a reporter for the *New York Herald* and a clerk in the Treasury Department. The 6th Massachusetts, which had arrived the previous evening, was billeted in the Senate chamber. Later, the 7th New York and 8th Massachusetts took up residence in the Capitol. Galusha Grow (1823–1907), a congressman from Pennsylvania, became the Speaker of the House (1861–63).

After the war, Grow wrote: "While visiting Lincoln one evening, I met his young private secretary, John Hay, who afterwards brought me personal communications from the White House. In time we became good friends, and in those early days I used to say to my political colleagues, 'Young Hay, if he lives, will become a very useful public servant, for he has the highest and best views of public life I ever heard expressed by one so young, and he also has a personality which will be of the greatest service to him in his career.'" Quoted in James T. DuBois and Gertrude S. Mathews, *Galusha A. Grow: Father of the Homestead Law* (Boston: Houghton Mifflin, 1917), 266.

14. The son of Lincoln's good friend William Butler of Springfield, Speed Butler was made the commissary of subsistence in Illinois, and in September 1861 he became a major in the 5th Illinois Cavalry. Simon Cameron (1799–1889) was the secretary of war (1861–62). On the night of 22 April, Illinois troops occupied Cairo, at the confluence of the Mississippi and Ohio Rivers. Nathaniel Lyon, the commander of the St. Louis arsenal, assumed direction of loyal forces in St. Louis and helped secure Missouri for the Union.

15. Fort McHenry, in Baltimore, under the command of captains John C. Robinson and George Washington Hazzard, was not attacked. Hazzard, who had been a member of the presidential party on the train trip from Springfield to Washington in February 1861, was a member of the 4th Artillery, a graduate of West Point, class of 1847, and served in the Mexican War. Later, he was posted to Florida and Kansas. In 1861 he was stationed in Utah. He was wounded at White Oak Swamp, Va., on 30 June 1862 and died on 14 August.

16. Upon the outbreak of war, Elmer Ephriam Ellsworth (1837–61), a kind of surrogate son to Lincoln, had abandoned his post as an adjutant and inspector general of militia to recruit a regiment in New York. Hay, who loved Ellsworth, wrote several articles about him. Fort Hamilton was in New York. The telegram is not among those in the AL MSS, DLC.

17. On 18 April, the first Northern soldiers had reached the capital—four companies from the Keystone State: the Washington Light Artillery, the Ringgold Flying Artillery, the Logan Guards, and the Allen Infantry. They had been hastily summoned and had yet to be formed into a regiment or to be issued arms.

18. See Lane to Lincoln, Washington, 20 Apr. 1861, AL MSS, DLC.

19. In the morning and afternoon, Baltimore mayor George W. Brown and three companions met with the president and the cabinet.

20. John B. Magruder (1810–71) had been the commander of the U.S. artillery in Washington. After he deserted to the Confederacy in April, he was entrusted with the defense of the Virginia peninsula. "Capt. Fry" was perhaps James B. Fry (1827–94), the commander of a light artillery battery in the capital who later served as the chief of staff to generals Irvin McDowell and Don Carlos Buell; eventually he became a provost marshal general. Or it may have been John Fry of Kentucky.

Gen. Samuel D. Sturgis recalled Lincoln's telling him:

> Sturgis, I cannot call to mind now any single event of my administration that gave me so much pain or wounded me so deeply as the singular behavior of Colonel Magruder on the very night before he abandoned us. . . . he came to see me the very evening before he left and voluntarily said, while expressing his abhorrence of secession, "Sir, I was brought up and educated under the glorious old flag. I have lived under it and have fought under it, and, sir, with the help of God, I shall fight under it again and, if need be, shall die under it." The very next day, Magruder abandoned us, so that at the very mo-

ment he was making to me these protestations of loyalty and devotion, he must have had his mind fully made up to leave; and it seemed the more wanton and cruel in him because he knew that I had implicit confidence in his integrity. The fact is, when I learned that he had gone over to the enemy and I had been so completely deceived in him, my confidence was shaken in everybody, and I hardly knew who to trust anymore. (Quoted in Sturgis to the editor, *Philadelphia Evening Transcript*, 12 June 1870, autograph draft, in Don E. Fehrenbacher and Virginia Fehrenbacher, eds., *Recollected Words of Abraham Lincoln* [Stanford: Stanford Univ. Press, 1996], 431–32)

21. A slang term meaning "a fruitless effort."

22. See William Meade Addison to Lincoln, Annapolis Junction, [21 Apr. 1861], AL MSS, DLC. Addison, the U.S. district attorney for Maryland, was based in Baltimore.

23. Fanny Campbell Eames (d. 1890) was one of the most prominent hostesses in the capital. Her husband, Charles (1812–67), was the counsel of the Navy Department. When nearly all the officers at the navy yard deserted to the South, that installation lay practically defenseless. Comdr. John A. Dahlgren took charge of it the following day, replacing Capt. Franklin Buchanan.

Society often gathered at the Eames home. John G. Nicolay described a party there:

Both he and his wife are very intelligent, amiable, and hospitable, and by reason of their position and long residence here as well as abroad, know almost everybody, and constantly draw around them the most interesting people who visit Washington. Although they have but a small house, and live in a very moderate style, their parlor is really a sort of focal point in Washington society, where one meets the best people who come here. By the "best" I do not mean mere fashionable "society people," but rather the brains of society—politicians, diplomats, authors and artists, and occasionally too, persons whose social and political positions merely, and not their brains, entitle them to consideration, such as titled foreigners, pretty women &c. Politically it is a sort of neutral ground, where men of all shades of opinion—Republicans, Democrats, Fossil Whigs, with even an occasional spice of Secessionist, come together quietly and socially. Usually we go there on Sunday evenings—say from 8 to 11—without any formality whatever; merely "drop in," coming and going entirely at pleasure, and talking to whom and about whatever one pleases. A variety of people, of course, bring with them a variety of languages; and so, while the key note is almost always English, the conversation runs into variations of French, German, and Spanish. (Nicolay to Therena Bates, Washington, 30 June 1861, Nicolay MSS, DLC)

24. William W. Peck, the son of Lincoln's friend and political ally Ebenezer Peck, became a captain. With his father, he had established a Chicago newspaper, the *De-*

mocratic Argus. John Blair Smith Todd (1814–72) was the brother of Elizabeth Todd Grimsley, Mary Todd Lincoln's cousin and friend. An 1837 graduate of West Point, he received appointment as a brigadier general of volunteers on 19 September 1861 and became the first delegate to Congress from the Dakota Territory later in the year. The post of quartermaster general was eventually won by Montgomery C. Meigs (1816–92). Salmon P. Chase (1808–73) was the secretary of the treasury (1861–64).

25. This committee from the Baltimore Y.M.C.A. proposed that Lincoln recognize the independence of the South. He replied: "You, gentlemen, come here to me and ask for peace on any terms, and yet have no word of condemnation for those who are making war on us. . . . I have no desire to invade the South; but I must have troops to defend this Capital. . . . There is no way but to march across [Maryland], and that they must do.'" *CWL,* 4:341–42.

The president's appeasement of the Baltimore delegation did not suit all members of his cabinet, especially Secretary of the Navy Gideon Welles. According to a close ally of the secretary, who heard it from Welles: "At the Cabinet meeting after the Balt[imore] troubles, the President was for letting the matter slide—taking no steps then or hereafter to straighten things by opening a passage for Northern troops. Mr. Welles jumped up, swung his hat under his arm and hastily walked out, telling them that if that was their policy *he* would have no responsibility in the matter. He was so mad that he don't remember exactly what he did say." William Faxon to Mark Howard, Washington, 12 May [1862], Mark Howard MSS, Connecticut Historical Society, Hartford.

In the summer of 1863, Lincoln was urged to pardon a young man named Compton who had been condemned to death. When the appeals seemed unavailing, one visitor asked, "Will you, Mr. President, receive a delegation of the most influential citizens of Baltimore, with the Hon. Reverdy Johnson at their head, if they will come in person and present a petition of behalf of Mr. Compton?" Lincoln, "with the fire of indignation," replied: "No! I will not receive a delegation from Baltimore for any purpose. I have received many delegations from Baltimore, since I came into office, composed of its most prominent citizens. They have always come to gain some advantage for themselves, or for their city. They have always had some end of their own to reach, without regard to the interests of the government. But no delegation has ever come to me to express sympathy or give me any aid in upholding the government and putting down the rebellion. No! I will receive no delegation from Baltimore." Robert Livingston Stanton, "Reminiscences of President Lincoln," ca. 1883, Robert Brewster Livingston Stanton MSS, New York Public Library.

26. See Pollock's memorandum, Baltimore, 22 Apr. 1861, AL MSS, DLC. Simon de Montfort (1165?–1218) was a French leader of the Crusades; Eleanor of Aquitaine, the wife of Louis VII of France and then of Henry II of England, inspired courtly love poetry in the twelfth century; the "girl of Dom Remy" was Joan of Arc.

27. The *Pocahantas* was a 694-ton screw steamer that had taken part in the expedition to relieve Fort Sumter. The *Anacostia* was a single-engine, 217-ton screw steamer. On 19 April, the *Pocahantas* left New York, where she had been undergoing repairs, and arrived in Washington on 22 April. Her ability to sail to Washington meant that the Potomac was still open.

28. The 7th New York and the 8th Massachusetts Regiments.

29. Henry A. Willard (1822–1909) was the proprietor of Washington's most important hotel.

30. W. Douglas Wallach was the proprietor of the *Washington Evening Star*, which had the largest circulation of any Washington newspaper during the war. Originally a Democrat, Wallach strongly supported the Lincoln administration. He had earlier alerted the administration to Confederate troop movements near his farm in Culpepper, Va. Wallach to Simon Cameron, 19 Apr. 1860 [1861], AL MSS, DLC.

Designed by John W. Griffiths (1809?–82), the *Pawnee* was a controversial twin-screw, 1289-ton steamer built in Philadelphia between 1858 and 1860. Criticized as clumsy, it nevertheless did good service in the South Atlantic Blockading Squadron. Adm. S. F. Du Pont praised her highly: "Her light draft, heavy armament, and comfortable and healthy quarters made her a very superior vessel in the inland waters of my station." *Samuel Francis Du Pont: A Selection from His Civil War Letters*, ed. John D. Hayes (Ithaca: Cornell Univ. Press, 1969), 1:31n. The *Keystone State* was a 1364-ton side-wheel steamer chartered from its owners on 19 April 1861. On 20 April, Comdt. Charles S. McCauley, fearing that the Gosport Navy Yard would be captured, abandoned that facility, ordering it and its ships burned. The "premier" refers to Secretary of State Seward. The *Baltic*, a U.S. transport steamer that Gustavus Fox had rented from its owners for the expedition to relieve Fort Sumter, had left New York the previous day with Elmer E. Ellsworth's Fire Zouaves aboard. *Delenda est* is Latin for "must be destroyed."

31. Francis Elias Spinner (1802–90) was a banker from Mohawk, N.Y., who served in the U.S. House (1855–61) and as treasurer of the United States (1861–75).

32. Col. James Montgomery (1814–71) was a Kansas jayhawker who later commanded the 2nd South Carolina Colored Regiment.

33. The rail line between Annapolis and Annapolis Junction had been torn up.

34. Richard Bickerton Pemell Lyons (1817–87) was Great Britain's minister to the United States.

35. Bennett (1795–1872) owned and edited the *New York Herald*.

36. The 6th Massachusetts Regiment, which had been attacked in Baltimore on 19 April, was thanked by Lincoln in a letter to its colonel: "Allow me to express to you, and through you to the officers under your command, my sincere thanks for the zeal, energy and gallantry, and especially for the great efficiency in opening the communication between the North and this city, displayed by you and them." Army correspondence, 27 Apr. 1861, *Newburyport (Mass.) Herald*, n.d., copied in the *Boston Daily Evening Traveller*, 3 May 1861.

37. Henry Villard recalled the "impatience, gloom, and depression" that had settled over the capital at that time. "No one felt it more than the President. I saw him repeatedly, and he fairly groaned at the inexplicable delay in the advent of help from the loyal States." Villard heard Lincoln utter the words recorded in Hay's diary. *Memoirs of Henry Villard, Journalist and Financier: 1835–1900* (New York: Houghton Mifflin, 1904), 1:169–70. Gen. Benjamin F. Butler (1818–93) was in charge of the District of Annapolis. A Massachusetts Democrat who in 1860 had supported Jefferson Davis for president, Butler abruptly became a Radical Republican when the war began.

38. The *Pocahantas* was ordered to go down the Potomac as far as the White House and to escort any ships bringing Union troops to Washington. The New York companies were the 6th, 12th, and 71st Regiments.

39. The *Mt. Vernon* was a 500-ton side-wheel mail steamer turned over to the War Department on 21 April. Its name was changed in November 1861 to *Mt. Washington*. The boatswain in charge reported that the river was open as far as Cedar Point, which is as far as he went.

40. Marshall C. Lefferts (1821–76) was the colonel of the 7th New York. Hannibal Hamlin (1809–91) of Maine was Lincoln's vice president. See Hamlin to Lincoln, 23 Apr. 1861, AL MSS, DLC; for the president's reply, see *CWL*, 4:343.

The arrival of this elite New York unit cheered all Unionists in the capital. That morning, word arrived that Butler had landed at Annapolis with the New York 7th and 8,000 other men and would march to Washington. According to one journalist, "The President remarked to his cabinet 'that if Gen. Butler was at Annapolis with half that number of men, they would open a road and keep it open. He had every confidence in the pluck of old Massachusetts.'" Washington correspondence, 1 May 1861, *Boston Daily Evening Traveller*, 3 May 1861, p. 1.

41. Lincoln ordered Scott not to disrupt the meeting of the Maryland legislature, scheduled for 26 April.

42. "Ash" was perhaps J. Hubley Ashton of Philadelphia, the assistant U.S. attorney for Eastern Pennsylvania.

43. Arriving from Annapolis were the 1st Rhode Island and the 5th and 8th Massachusetts Regiments. "Helme" was perhaps William H. Helme of Providence, one of Hay's correspondents.

44. William Sprague (1830–1915) was the governor of Rhode Island (1860–63) and later a U.S. senator from that state (1863–75). Henry Villard thought Sprague a man with "very limited mental capacity" who "had reached political distinction at an early age . . . through the influence of real or reputed great wealth." *Memoirs*, 1:175.

45. Carl Schurz (1829–1906) was a German-born Republican leader who lived in Wisconsin. Hay later added the words "That seems scarcely possible but it must be true."

46. Joseph Jackson Grimshaw (1820–75), an Illinois lawyer and Republican politician, had practiced law in Pittsfield from 1843 to 1857, then moved to Quincy, where he ran unsuccessfully for Congress in 1856 and 1858.

47. The only letter from a Channing in the AL MSS, DLC, is one dated 26 April 1863, from William H. Channing (1810–84), a Unitarian minister in Washington, D.C., and a vigorous opponent of slavery.

48. The president, Nicolay, Hay, Cameron, "the ladies of the household," and Willie and Tad Lincoln gathered on the portico to listen to this concert, which included some "soul-stirring national airs." *Washington National Republican*, 29 Apr. 1861, p. 2. White House concerts were given on Wednesday and Saturday evenings.

49. See *CWL*, 4:346–47.

50. See *CWL*, 4:347.

51. The roof was on the Marshall House Hotel, where Elmer Ellsworth was killed on 24 May after removing the offending flag.

52. The plan fell through, and Schurz went off to Spain to serve as the U.S. minister.

53. William W. Hoppin, of the 1st Rhode Island Volunteers, was a graduate of Brown University, class of 1861, and the son of William W. Hoppin, who had been the governor of Rhode Island (1854–57). James A. DeWolf and Frederic M. Sackett (1840–1913) also graduated Brown in 1861 and belonged to the 1st Rhode Island Volunteers. William W. Pearce, another graduate of Brown, class of 1846, belonged to the 1st Light Battery, Rhode Island Volunteers. In February the Confederate Congress had authorized the issuance of 8 percent bonds in the amount of $15,000,000.

54. Born in New Hampshire, Perry (1824–91) won appointment in 1849 as the secretary of the U.S. legation in Spain, where he served until 1855. In 1861 he was reappointed to the post. Schurz, who had lobbied hard for the post of U.S. minister to Spain, decided after war broke out that he would rather serve in the army than in an embassy. He worked to raise German-American troops during his leave and eventually went to Spain, only to return after a few months to join the army. A novelist and poet from Badajos, Carolina Coronado (1823–1911) was the poet laureate of Spain.

55. Friedrich Hassaurek (1832–85) emigrated from Austria to the United States after the failure of the Revolution of 1848 and settled in Cincinnati, where he won renown as a journalist, a lawyer, and a fiery antislavery orator. He was an Ohio delegate at the Chicago convention. Upon being named to represent the United States in Quito, Ecuador, a city 9,500 feet above sea level, he thanked Lincoln for appointing him "to the highest place in his gift." His book *Four Years among Spanish Americans* appeared in 1867.

56. Montgomery Blair (1813–83), a Maryland politician and scion of a powerful political family, was the postmaster general (1861–64). Gustavus Vasa Fox (1821–83), the chief clerk of the Navy Department, became the assistant secretary of the navy on 1 August 1861.

57. Editor-in-chief Henry J. Raymond wrote the editorials that appeared in the *New York Times*, 24 and 25 April 1861. A Boston newspaper charged that a group of Republicans in mid-April had laid plans for removing Lincoln and had chosen Raymond to publish a "feeler." *Boston Courier*, 14 Aug. 1861.

58. Charles H. Van Wyck (1824–95), a congressman from New York, had applied to the president for an active commission. Van Wyck served in the U.S. House (1859–63, 1867–69, 1870–71) and the U.S. Senate (1881–87). He was also a general during the war, leading a unit in the siege of Charleston in 1863. Egbert L. Viele (1825–1902), an engineer in the 7th New York Militia, helped with the defense of the capital.

59. See George W. Caldwell to Lincoln, Wellsburg, Va., 25 Apr. 1861, and Nicolay to George W. Caldwell, Washington, 1 May 1861, AL MSS, DLC. According to one journalist, a committee of delegates from Butler County, Va., had "long and satisfactory interviews with Messrs. Lincoln and Cameron" on the night of 1 May. "Their object," the reporter noted, "was to induce the Administration to pledge itself to support them, if, at the coming election, the loyal citizens of that county showed need of protection. They are determined to assert the rights of citizenship, to resort to

arms in self-defence if attacked, and thus, being backed by a Governmental force, they feel sure of success. No written pledges were given them, but such assurances as made them confident of ultimate triumph and entire impunity." Washington correspondence, 2 May 1861, *New York Tribune*, n.d., copied in the *Chicago Tribune*, 6 May 1861, p. 1.

Several important men, including William E. Dodge, urged the president to honor the Virginians' request for $100,000 and 5,000 rifles. Washington correspondence, 3 May 1861, *New York* Tribune, n.d., copied in the *Chicago* Tribune, 7 May 1861, p. 1. Edwin M. Stanton wrote a legal justification for the secretary of war to transfer federal arms to private parties in Virginia, then pledged all his personal assets as bond to guarantee that the weapons would be used properly. Cameron saw to it that the guns were properly dispatched to the Unionists of western Virginia. George Plummer Smith to Edwin M. Stanton, 14 Oct. 1865, Stanton MSS, DLC; Benjamin P. Thomas and Harold M. Hyman, *Stanton: The Life and Times of Lincoln's Secretary of War* (New York: Knopf, 1962), 127.

60. The Rhode Island Marine Artillery arrived on 3 May.

61. Ellsworth recruited his Zouaves from the fire departments of New York. Col. William Wilson's 6th New York Infantry, known as "Wilson's Zouaves," was sent to Santa Rosa Island, Fla., where Confederates under Gen. Richard Heron Anderson routed them during the night and following morning of 8–9 October 1861.

62. The previous year, Ellsworth's drill team, the "Chicago Zouaves," had won acclaim as it toured the North. Most of the 69th New York Regiment arrived the same day as the Zouaves.

63. Hammacks was a Washington restaurant, which one patron described thus: "It was a fortunate day for those who are forced to put up with the scanty fare of our Washington hotels, as well as for citizens who love an occasional good supper, when Hammack opened his eating-house here. Since then he has been forced by a press of custom to enlarge his establishment, and he now serves up fish, flesh, and fowl in a style worthy of Soyer, Delmonico, or even Francatelli. His game, oysters, and terrapin are noted, and his wines have an undeniable bouquet and flavor." "An Idler," *Washington Sunday Chronicle*, 6 Apr. 1862, p. 2.

64. The governor of New York thrice forbade Ellsworth to leave with the regiment, which was deemed too large. When shown the governor's orders, Gen. John E. Wool overruled the objection, saying, "Go on. It won't make any difference if you've got 11,000." Quoted in Frank E. Brownell, "Lincoln and Ellsworth," interview by Walter B. Stevens, *St. Louis Globe-Democrat*, 3 June 1888.

65. Fernando Wood (1812–81) was the mayor of New York (1855–58, 1861–62) and a member of the U.S. House (1863–65, 1867–81). Isham G. Harris (1818–97) was elected the governor of Tennessee in 1857 and reelected in 1859 and 1861. See Harris to Lincoln, Nashville, 29 Apr. 1861, AL MSS, DLC. In his written reply, Lincoln alleged that the governor had planned to use the arms aboard the *Hillman* against the United States. Lincoln to Harris, Washington, 1[?] May 1861, *CWL*, 4:351–52. Maj. Gen. Edwin R. V. Wright (1812–71) became a congressman from New Jersey (1865–67) and the governor of the state (1869–71).

66. Robert Milligan McLane (1815–98) represented a Maryland district in Congress (1847–51, 1879–83). He was accompanied by Otho Scott and William J. Ross; these three comprised a committee appointed by the legislature of Maryland. During their meeting on the afternoon of 4 May, Lincoln "plainly" told them "that while the Government had no intention to retaliate for Baltimore outrages by force of arms, it had determined upon measures to secure the unobstructed passage of troops through their State, and would carry them out at all hazards." Washington correspondence, 5 May 1861, *Chicago Tribune*, 7 May 1861, p. 1.

67. The Relay House was a station on the Baltimore & Ohio line south of Baltimore.

68. "Maj. Sparks" was perhaps the city's sheriff, Edward R. Sparks. Ben McCulloch (1811–62) was a Texan who had received the surrender of General Twiggs at San Antonio in February. "Howard" was perhaps Joseph Howard Jr. (1833–1908), a Washington correspondent for several New York journals. At this time, McCulloch was stationed west of the Mississippi River. Rumor had it that McCulloch planned to dash from Richmond to Washington with five hundred men and abduct the president, the cabinet, and General Scott. Charles Winslow Elliott, *Winfield Scott: The Soldier and the Man* (New York: Macmillan, 1937), 710.

69. See *CWL*, 4:357–58.

70. Soon after this date, Col. Lovell H. Rousseau called on the president seeking permission to raise troops in Kentucky. Before discussing this project, Lincoln asked, "Rousseau, I want you to tell me where you got that joke about Senator Johnson, of your state." Rousseau, who had heard about Lincoln's letter and had recounted it in a speech in the Kentucky state senate, replied: "The joke was too good to keep, sir, and so Johnson told it himself." Quoted in William F. G. Shanks, *Personal Recollections of Distinguished Generals* (New York: Harper, 1866), 213–14.

71. James W. Singleton (1811–92) was a wealthy Virginia-born Illinois Whig politician who turned Democrat in 1854. In Quincy he practiced both law and medicine. In January 1861, Hay described Singleton as "the genial and gentlemanly President of the Quincy and Toledo Railroad, and one of the most liberal and enlightened patrons of scientific agriculture in the State, the idol of his friends." Springfield correspondence, 8 Jan. 1861, *St. Louis Missouri Democrat*, n.d., clipping pasted in a scrapbook of Hay's writings, vol. 54, Hay MSS, DLC.

During the Civil War, Singleton worked on several proposals to effect a compromise peace. In 1864 he vigorously opposed Lincoln's reelection. The president said to him, "you were pretty hard on me in your New York speech." "No," came the reply; "not on you personally, Mr. President, but on your Administration." Lincoln concluded, "They are appealing to me on all hands to have you arrested, but while I regret your belief and your speeches, I think you have the right to make them, and I have said to outsiders that if I could stand it, they could." Singleton evidently helped to set up the Hampton Roads conference in February 1865. The day after Lincoln's death, Singleton wrote to his wife: "My intercourse with him for the past six months has been so free, frequent and confidential that I was fully advised of all his plans, and thoroughly persuaded of the honesty of his heart and the wisdom of his humane intentions." Quoted in Matthew Page Andrews, "Lincoln's Lost Friend," *New York Times,* 12 Feb. 1928, sec. 9, p. 6. Cf. Andrews's article in the *Baltimore Sun,* 9 Feb. 1930, and Singelton's interview, *Chicago Republican,* 21 June 1865. Singleton's speech was published in the *New York Daily News,* 27 July 1864.

72. Orville H. Browning (1806–81) of Quincy, a longtime friend of Lincoln, was a U.S. senator from Illinois (1861–63). See Browning to Lincoln, Quincy, Ill., 30 Apr. 1861, AL MSS, DLC. See also *The Diary of Orville Hickman Browning,* ed. Theodore Calvin Pease and James G. Randall (Springfield: Illinois State Historical Library, 1925, 1933), 1:467 (entry for 30 Apr. 1861). James Rood Doolittle (1815–97) was a Republican senator from Wisconsin (1857–69). James Alexander Hamilton (1788–1878) was the son of Alexander Hamilton. Cf. *Reminiscences of James A. Hamilton* (New York: Scribner, 1869), 477–79.

Ten years after Lincoln's death, when Browning was asked about Lincoln's religious views, he told an interviewer:

> Perhaps the nearest approach to any religious talk was in the summer or fall of 1861. We were alone together in his room. I said to him substantially:
>
> "Mr. Lincoln we can't hope for the blessing of God on the efforts of our armies, until we strike a decisive blow at the institution of slavery. This is the great curse of our land, and we must make an effort to remove it before we can hope to receive the help of the Almighty."
>
> I remember being much impressed by his reply, because it caused me to reflect that perhaps he had thought more deeply upon this subject than I had. Said he:
>
> "Browning, suppose God is against us in our view on the subject of slavery in this country, and our method of dealing with it?" (Interview with John G. Nicolay, Springfield, Ill., 17 June 1875, Hay MSS, RPB)

73. Nicolay noted the same day, "Going into the P[resident]'s room this morning found Hay with him. The conversation turning on the subject of the existing contest he remarked that the real question involved in it, (as he had about made up his mind, though he would still think further about it, while writing his message) was whether a free and representative government had the right and power to protect and maintain itself. Admit the right of a minority to secede at will, and the occasion for such secession would almost as likely be any other as the slavery question." Memorandum, 7 May 1861, Nicolay MSS, DLC.

74. For Lincoln's message to Congress, delivered on 4 July 1861, see *CWL,* 4:421–41.

75. Ellsworth's men were accused of breaking into taverns, of refusing to pay for restaurant meals, and other "irreverent feats." *Philadelphia Press,* n.d., copied in the *Boston Daily Evening Traveller,* 10 May 1861, p. 1. Cf. *New York Times,* 8 May 1861.

76. The "dandy regiment" was the 7th New York.

77. Davis's manifesto was contained in his message of 29 April to the Confederate Congress.

78. Robert Anderson (1805–71) commanded the Fort Sumter garrison at the outbreak of the war.

79. The *Pensacola* was a 3000-ton steam sloop launched in 1859. Invented by John A. Dahlgren, the Dahlgren gun was a rifled cannon called the "soda-water bottle" because of its peculiar shape. The largest version fired 20-inch shells, and the smallest, 9-inch shells. Comdr. John P. Gillis (1831–1910) took command of the *Pocahantas* on 19 March.

80. When a tailor's shop adjacent to the hotel caught fire, the general commanding Washington ordered the New Yorkers to the scene because the local firemen were notoriously incompetent. The tailor's burned to the ground, but the hotel was saved.

81. When Benjamin F. Butler assumed command of Fort Monroe later in May, he reversed the policy of his predecessor and declined to return fugitive slaves on the grounds that they were "contraband of war."

82. The poet Sarah Helen Power Whitman (1803–78) of Providence, R.I., had been a friend of Hay since his days at Brown University. Thomas Earl was a soldier in the 25th Massachusetts Regiment and a friend of Thomas Wentworth Higginson (1823–1911), an antislavery writer and financial backer of the abolitionist John Brown of Harper's Ferry. Higginson worked behind the scenes to organize a company of soldiers under the leadership of Brown's son, John Brown Jr. "I want to at least get the *name* of John Brown rumored on the border & then the whole party may come back & go to bed—they will frighten Virginia into fits all the same," he wrote on 23 April. The plan came to nothing. Tilden G. Edelstein, *Strange Enthusiasm: A Life of Thomas Wentworth Higginson* (New Haven: Yale Univ. Press, 1968), 244.

83. Hay described Ellsworth's Zouaves in detail; see Washington correspondence signed "Ecarte," 15 May 1861, *Springfield (Ill.) Daily State Journal*, 20 May 1861, p. 2. "Col. Pritchard" was perhaps W. H. Pritchartt, the secretary of the Phoenix Insurance Company of St. Louis, which insured "cargo risks, hull risks, and fire risks." *Campbell and Richardson's St. Louis Business Directory for 1863*, front cover. Gen. Daniel Marsh Frost (1823–1900) commanded approximately 700 pro-Confederate Missouri militia at Camp Jackson in St. Louis. On 10 May, Nathaniel Lyon, with nearly ten times as many men, surrounded the camp and bloodlessly took Frost's men prisoner. Francis P. Blair Jr. (1821–75), leader of the Unionist forces in Missouri and the brother of Lincoln's postmaster general, Montgomery Blair, played a key role in saving Missouri for the Union.

84. As a congressman from Kentucky (1843–47), Thomasson (1797–1882) was the only Southerner to vote for the Wilmot Proviso. Lovell Harrison Rousseau (1818–69) was a soldier and politician from Kentucky who quit his post in the state senate in order to recruit troops there. See Shanks, *Personal Recollections*, 214ff.

85. Beriah Magoffin (1815–85) was the governor of Kentucky (1859–62). On 20 May, Governor Magoffin had proclaimed his state neutral; his constituents, however, favored the Union. On 15 August, pro-Union candidates captured 103 of the 138 seats in the state legislature. Magoffin dispatched the two commissioners, W. A. Dudley and Frank Hunt, both from Lexington, to persuade Lincoln to abide by the May proclamation. See Magoffin to Lincoln, Frankfort, Ky., 19 Aug. 1861, AL MSS, DLC. On 24 August, the president wrote Magoffin that he had neither the power nor the inclination to remove from Kentucky pro-Union forces spontaneously forming in

that state. *CWL*, 4:497. On 3 September, Confederate troops under Gideon Pillow invaded Kentucky and ended its pretense of neutrality. Gen. U. S. Grant responded by seizing Paducah on 6 September.

86. Gen. George B. McClellan (1826–85) replaced Irvin McDowell (1818–85), the hapless commander of Union forces at the Battle of Bull Run the previous month. McClellan, who lived at 15th and H Streets near the White House, had assumed command of the Army of the Potomac in August and quickly restored morale among the discouraged troops. When sixty men of the 2nd Maine refused to obey orders, they were reassigned to fatigue duty on Dry Tortugas, off Key West, Fla., on 15 August. David Hunter had been promoted to a major general of volunteers and assigned to Illinois on 13 August.

87. Hay was sick and returned to the West for a few weeks. John Charles Frémont (1813–90), the commander of the Department of Missouri, had been the Republican presidential candidate in 1856. His wife, Jessie Benton Frémont (1824–1902), daughter of Sen. Thomas Hart Benton of Missouri, was a high-spirited woman who would later clash with Lincoln. See *infra*, entry for 9 Dec. 1863.

88. Hay's dispatch dated 20 September 1861 to the *New York World* is pasted into one of his scrapbooks in the Hay MSS, DLC. Weed (1797–1882), the founder and editor of the *Albany Evening Journal*, was a political operator and Secretary of State Seward's alter ego.

89. The exiled Orléans prince and pretender to the throne, Louis Philippe Albert d'Orléans, Comte de Paris (1838–94), served as an officer on McClellan's staff, as did his brother, Robert Philippe Louis Eugéne Ferdinand d'Orléans, Duc de Chartres (1840–1910). The Union troops called them "Capt. Perry" and "Capt. Chatters."

90. Headed by Gen. Thomas West Sherman and Flag Officer Samuel F. Du Pont, this expedition left Hampton Roads on 29 October with 27 ships and 12,000 troops, which on 7 November attacked and captured Port Royal, S.C. Its departure was delayed because of a dispute between Sherman and McClellan about troops that Sherman wanted to take with him from McClellan's command. See *infra*, entries for 12 and 18 Oct. 1861. For Lincoln's role in planning this operation, see Samuel F. Du Pont to Henry Winter Davis, New York, 8 Oct. 1861, *Du Pont Letters*, 1:162–64.

91. Shortly after this meeting, McClellan expressed his contempt for Seward and Lincoln to his wife: "I can't tell you how disgusted I am becoming with these wretched politicians—they are a most dispicable set of men & I think Seward is the meanest of them all—a meddling, officious, incompetent little puppy—he has done more than any other one man to bring all this misery upon the country & is one of the least competent to get us out of the scrape. The Presdt is nothing more than a well meaning baboon." At the end of the month, he reiterated his opinion of political leaders: "it is terrible to stand by & see the cowardice of the Presdt, the vileness of Seward, & the rascality of Cameron—Welles is an old woman—Bates an old fool." McClellan to his wife, ca. 11 Oct. and 31 Oct. 1861, *The Civil War Papers of George B. McClellan: Selected Correspondence, 1860–1865*, ed. Stephen W. Sears (New York: Ticknor & Fields, 1989), 106–7, 114.

92. Nothing came of this threat of attack.

93. Lander conducted the only active campaigning near Washington during the fall and winter of 1861–62, fighting at Hancock and at Bloomery Gap. In part because of the hardships involved, he died on 2 March 1862.

94. Thomas A. Scott (1824–81) was a leading executive of the Pennsylvania Railroad and the assistant secretary of war (1861–62). Gen. Joseph Hooker (1814–79) was later to command the Army of the Potomac (1863).

95. Gen. Thomas W. Sherman's expedition against Port Royal, S.C., departed on 29 October.

96. John Lothrop Motley (1814–77), the U.S. minister to the Austro-Hungarian empire, had stopped off in Great Britain en route to Vienna and spoke at length with leaders of British society and politics. See Motley to his mother, Wharfside, Yorkshire, 5 Sept. 1861, and East Sheen, 22 Sept. 1861, *The Correspondence of John Lothrop Motley*, ed. George William Curtis (New York: Harper, 1889), 2:33–36. Lord John Russell (1792–1878) was the foreign minister of Great Britain. Sir George Grey (1799–1882) was the home secretary of Great Britain. In Parliament, Richard Cobden (1804–65) was one of the leading defenders of the American Union. Sir Austen Henry Layard (1817–94) was the British undersecretary of state.

Alluding to Motley's dispatch, Hay wrote in mid-October:

> From sources whose trustworthiness cannot be for an instant impugned, our Government has information that only the kindest and heartiest expressions of good will and sympathy are heard in the best circles of the best class of England. Recent conversations, in the unrestrained freedom of friendly intimacy, with men so high in fame, and position, and power as Earl Russell, Mr. Layard, the Under-Secretary of State, Mr. Cobden, Earl Grey, Colonial Secretary, His Royal Highness Albert, and the gracious lady, Victoria herself, evince only the most cordial sympathy with the Federal Government, and show conclusively that the bearings of this great controversy between civilization and barbarism, between law and anarchy, is as fully understood and appreciated in the Court of St. James as in the Cabinet at Washington. (Washington correspondence, 14 Oct. 1861, *St. Louis Missouri Republican*, 19 Oct. 1861, p. 2)

97. "Capt. Schulz" was perhaps Frederick Schultz of the 1st Ohio Light Artillery. Lincoln had defeated Seward at the Republican National Convention in Chicago the previous year.

98. The Connecticut-born Lyman Trumbull (1813–96) had beaten Lincoln for a seat in the U.S. Senate in 1855. He represented Illinois in that body until 1873. "Long John" Wentworth (1815–88), an Illinois politician, was elected the mayor of Chicago in 1857 and 1860; he also served in the U.S. House (1843–51, 1853–55, 1865–67). This story refers to Lincoln's unsuccessful bid for a seat in the U.S. Senate in 1855, when he lost to Trumbull. The "feller" who ran Seward was Thurlow Weed.

99. William Howard Russell recorded that "Sir James Ferguson and Mr. R. Bourke, who have been travelling in the South and have seen something of the Confederate

government and armies, visited us this evening after dinner. They do not seem at all desirous of testing by comparison the relative efficiency of the two armies, which Sir James, at all events, is competent to do. They are impressed by the energy and animosity of the South." *My Diary North and South* (Boston: Burnham, 1863), 555 (entry for 15 Oct. 1861). When Ferguson was informed that it was illegal to post letters he had brought with him from the South, he immediately turned them over to the State Department. Washington correspondence, 29 Nov. 1861, *New York Herald*, 30 Nov. 1861, p. 2.

100. Nathaniel P. Banks (1816–94), a prominent Massachusetts politician whom Lincoln had named a major general of volunteers, had arrived in Washington that day and held long interviews with McClellan in the morning and evening. He was optimistic about defeating the Confederates on the Upper Potomac. Washington correspondence, 17 Oct. 1861, *New York Herald*, 18 Oct. 1861, p. 1.

Lincoln called on McClellan often in the fall. On the day before Hay made this entry in his diary, McClellan told his wife, "I have just been interrupted here by the Presdt & Secty Seward who had nothing very particular to say, except some stories to tell, which were as usual very pertinent & some pretty good. I never in my life met anyone so full of anecdote as our friend Abraham—he is never at a loss for a story apropos of any known subject or incident." Washington, 16 Oct. 1861, *Papers of McClellan*, 107.

101. The actual text of the telegram is slightly different. See *CWL*, 4:577. McClellan had objected strongly to the proposed transfer of troops from his army to Sherman's.

102. In a news dispatch, Hay described this scene more fully:

> Yesterday, at noon, it became generally known that Gen. Stone had crossed the Potomac, and that a spirited skirmish was going on upon the Virginia side of the river. The enemy were taken to be the remnant of the rear guard, who were covering the evacuation of Leesburg. Towards dusk, however, the skirmish began to assume more important proportions, and people began to realize that a battle at Leesburg was imminent. The meagre instalments of intelligence that percolated through admitted channels into the street were far from satisfying the eager interest of the town. McClellan's headquarters were besieged by an anxious throng, whom the bayonets of the sentries only kept outside. In the telegraph office within, sat the President conversing with Gen. Marcy, and evincing the deepest interest in the issue of the engagement, "because," as he said, "Baker is in the fight, and I am afraid his impetuous daring will endanger his life." In a pause of the conversation, the quick clicking of the instrument attracted the attention of the operator—he listened for a moment—then seized a sheet of paper and writing a few lines, handed them to the President. An expression of awe and grief solemnized the massive features of Lincoln as he read the dispatch, and laying down the paper, after a moment's silence, he said, impressively, "Colonel Baker is dead."
>
> When this was heard there was little further interest taken in the affair. . . .

A king might have been proud of the simple and hearty eulogies uttered last night in McClellan's room, where the President, and Seward, and Cameron, and M'Clellan, and another, in deep but not unmanly grief, received the heavy news of the fate of their friend. Each had his word of earnest sorrow and honest praise. The President mourned the sundering of the dearest of those ties that connected him with the memory of a happier and more careless day. The philosopher of Auburn [Seward] deplored the stainless statesman, and Cameron the dauntless patriot. And McClellan pronounced his bluff and soldierly epitaph: "I would rather have lost a battle than Baker; yet no loss is so great but it can be repaired, and though many a good fellow with shoulder straps go under the sod before this row is over, the cause must triumph." (Washington correspondence, 22 Oct. 1861, *St. Louis Missouri Republican*, 27 Oct. 1861, p. 2)

103. Charles P. Stone (1824–87) had commanded a division at the Battle of Ball's Bluff. He was later confined for 189 days without charges for his role in that debacle. The last sentence of the paragraph was evidently added later.

104. George W. Summers (1804–68), a judge from Virginia, was a former congressman and a delegate to the Washington Peace Convention in early 1861. Shortly after his arrival in Washington on 23 February, Lincoln spent an evening talking with Peace Convention delegates, including Summers. When William C. Rives warned of the danger of civil war, the president-elect said, according to Charles S. Morehead of Kentucky, "Mr. Rives, Mr. Rives! If Virginia will stay in I will withdraw the troops from Fort Sumter." *Liverpool (Ohio) Mercury*, 13 Oct. 1862, reprinted in David R. Barbee and Milledge L. Bonham Jr., eds., "Fort Sumter Again," *Mississippi Valley Historical Review* 28 (1941): 63–73.

In early April, the president had dispatched Allan B. Magruder to Richmond to set up a meeting with a prominent Virginia Unionist like Summers. Magruder returned on 4 April with John B. Baldwin of Virginia, who spoke with Lincoln. It is unclear exactly what was said, but at least one source other than Hay claims that Lincoln repeated the offer made earlier to Rives. John B. Baldwin, "Interview Between President Lincoln and John B. Baldwin" (Stanton, Va.: "Spectator" Job Office, 1866). George Plummer Smith gave a similar version of this interview. See Smith to Hay, Washington, 9 Jan. 1863, AL MSS, DLC. Cf. John B. Baldwin's testimony, 10 Feb. 1866, *Report of the Joint Congressional Committee on the Conduct of the War*, 39th Cong., 1st sess., 1866, pt. 2, 102–6.

105. "Kennedy" was perhaps Anthony Kennedy (1810–92), a U.S. senator from Maryland, or Joseph Camp Griffith Kennedy (1813–87), the superintendent of the census. Charles P. McIlvaine (1799–1873), the Episcopal bishop of Ohio, had served as the president of Kenyon College (1833–40).

106. On 19 October, William M. Merrick of Maryland, a justice of the U.S. Circuit Court in Washington, D.C., issued a writ of habeas corpus demanding that Provost Marshal Andrew Porter surrender a prisoner. After Porter refused, the judge cited him for contempt and instructed the deputy marshal to deliver the citation to

the accused. Lincoln had ordered that no such writs be served. The judge was then put under virtual house arrest and his salary was cut off. Washington correspondence, 22 Oct. 1861, *Chicago Tribune*, 23 Oct. 1861, p. 2. See also Mark E. Neely Jr., *The Fate of Liberty: Abraham Lincoln and Civil Liberties* (New York: Oxford Univ. Press, 1991), 27.

107. New Hampshire-born Zachariah Chandler (1813–79) at the age of twenty settled in Detroit, where he grew rich in business. Elected to the U.S. Senate in 1857, he became a truculent critic of the Confederates and their Northern sympathizers. Benjamin Franklin Wade (1800–1878), a leading Radical Republican senator from Ohio, was born in Massachusetts and settled in the Western Reserve section of Ohio. A militant opponent of slavery, his frank manner and hot temper won him the sobriquet "Bluff Ben." During the war, he was a fierce opponent of the Confederacy and conservative Union generals. Thomas M. Key, who before the war served as a jurist and legislator in Cincinnati, was a member of McClellan's staff. Tension between Scott and McClellan had been mounting throughout the summer and fall.

The day after this entry was made, Senator Chandler wrote:

> Trumbull, Wade and myself have been busy night and day since my arrival, but whether our labor has been in vain or not, time alone must disclose. . . . If Wade and I fail in our mission, the end is at hand. If we fail I *may* take my seat in the Senate this winter, but doubt it—in fact I told Mr. Lincoln last night that I was in favor of sending for Jeff Davis *at once* if their views were carried out. I was with McLellan until one oclock A.M. night before last and with the President until 12 P.M. last night. The prospects are gloomy indeed to this date 4 P.M. Sunday. Wade and Trumbull are with me constantly at all interviews. . . . If we fail in getting a battle here now all is lost, and up to this time a fight is scarcely contemplated. Washington is safe and that seems to be all they care for. Washington is safe therefore let the country go to the devil. (Chandler to his wife, Washington, 27 Oct. 1861, Chandler MSS, DLC, copy, Allan Nevins MSS, Columbia Univ.)

The Radicals had clamored for an advance against Richmond in the summer. That fall they criticized McClellan for not sending his 152,000 men to attack the 41,000 Confederates at Manassas. Senator Wade said in October that "I begin to despair of ever putting down this rebellion through the instrumentality of this administration. They are blundering, cowardly and inefficient. . . . You could not inspire Old Abe, Seward, Chase, or Bates with courage, decision, and enterprise, with a galvanic battery." Wade to Zachariah Chandler, Jefferson, Ohio, 8 Oct. 1861, Chandler MSS, DLC, copy, Allan Nevins MSS, Columbia Univ. "Several Western Senators, who had been urging an advance of the army on the President, were told that all was left to Gen. McClellan's direction, uninfluenced." Washington correspondence, 31 Oct. 1861, *Chicago Tribune*, 1 Nov. 1861, p. 1. Wade later reported that when he complained to the president about McClellan's timidity, "Mr. Lincoln replied that McClellan was a good General, whom it would not do to disturb." Wade's speech in Pittsburgh, 24 Oct. 1864, *Chicago Tribune*, 1 Nov. 1864, p. 3.

108. See Lincoln to McClellan, Washington, 26 Oct. 1861, *CWL*, 5:4–5. Lincoln dubbed this precursor of the machine gun "the coffee-mill gun." It had been invented by either Edward Nugent or William Palmer and was promoted by J. D. Mills. Reverdy Johnson (1796–1876) was a U.S. senator from Maryland (1863–68). He had played a key role in keeping his state in the Union.

109. McClellan described this meeting with Wade and the others thus: "For the last 3 hours I have been at Montgomery Blair's talking with Senators Wade, Trumbull & Chandler about war matters—They will make a desperate effort tomorrow to have Genl Scott retired at once. Until that is accomplished I can effect but little good—he is ever in my way & I am sure does not desire effective action." McClellan to his wife, Washington, 26 Oct. 1861, *Papers of McClellan*, 112.

Wade had a different recollection of this meeting. In 1864 he said that he and Senator Chandler, after arriving in Washington on 25 October, called on McClellan: "Mr. Chandler and myself, feeling that the army was laboring under some serious defect somewhere, by reason of which no progress was made, went off to the army to satisfy ourselves, and if possible discover where the difficulty lay." They found McClellan at Blair's, where for three hours they spoke. "We exhorted him for God's sake, to at least push back the defiant traitors." McClellan protested that he wanted to undertake an offensive, but was thwarted by his superior, General Scott. *Facts for the People* (Cincinnati, 1864), 1–2, quoted in T. Harry Williams, *Lincoln and the Radicals* (Madison: Univ. of Wisconsin Press, 1941), 44.

110. In November, Senator Chandler described the pressure he and his Radical colleagues applied to the chief executive: "Lincoln means well but he has no force of character. He is surrounded by Old Fogy Army officers more than half of whom are downright traitors and the other one half sympathize with the South. One month ago I began to doubt whether this accursed rebellion could be put down without a Revolution in the present Administration. Wade, Trumbull, [Morton S.] Wilkinson, Pomeroy and myself made a descent upon them and spent two weeks with the President, Cabinet, McClellan &c. We raised an awful commotion and I think accomplished our object." Chandler to Henry W. Lord, 16 Nov. 1861, quoted in Hans L. Trefousse, *The Radical Republicans: Lincoln's Vanguard for Racial Justice* (New York: Knopf, 1969), 180–81.

111. See Lincoln to Hunter, Washington, 24 Oct. 1861, *CWL*, 5:1–2. Gen. Sterling Price (1809–67) commanded Confederate forces in Missouri.

112. Oliver P. Morton (1823–77), the governor of Indiana (1861–67), feared that disloyal elements in neighboring Kentucky posed a serious threat to his state and begged Lincoln to send him arms and men. Kentuckian Joshua Fry Speed (1814–82), Lincoln's closest friend in his early adulthood and his bunkmate in Springfield, 1837–41, was in Washington trying to procure weapons for Unionists in his state. On 21 September, Lincoln took him to Gen. Lorenzo Thomas to make sure that arms were promptly supplied to Gen. Robert Anderson in Kentucky. Henry Wilson (1812–75) of Massachusetts chaired the Senate Committee on Military Affairs. The "Leesburg business" was the Battle of Ball's Bluff.

113. "Just returned from Warsaw. Saw Gen Fremont. Doubt the policy of his removal. Will be Home in a few days." Telegram, Lamon to Lincoln, St. Louis, 26 Oct.

1861, AL MSS, DLC. "Things look more & more alarming here entirely outside of contracts. In my judgment events are drifting towards resisting Government authority. This opinion concurred in by best men here. 'Forewarned fore-armed.'" Telegram, E. B. Washburne to Lincoln, St. Louis, 26 Oct. 1861, AL MSS, DLC. Elihu B. Washburne (1816–87), a congressman from Galena, Ill., championed the interests of his fellow townsman, Ulysses S. Grant.

114. Brig. Gen. Benjamin F. Kelley (1807–91) captured Romney in northwest Virginia on 26 October. Maj. Charles Zangonyi led Frémont's cavalry into Springfield, Mo., where they defeated a small Confederate force. See Fremont to Lincoln, in the field near Hammansville, Mo., 26 Oct. 1861, AL MSS, DLC.

115. On 1 November, McClellan took over the command of the Union army from Scott.

116. "A dinner, celebrating General McClellan's assumption of the chief command of the U.S. Army, was given him last night by the Secretary of State, at which all the members of the Cabinet were present. During the evening Gen. McClellan was engaged in his new duties, the President being with him for several hours." Washington correspondence, 2 Nov. 1861, *New York Commercial Advertiser*, n.d., copied in the *Chicago Tribune*, 4 Nov. 1861, p. 1.

117. François Ferdinand-Philippe-Louis-Marie d'Orléans (1818–1900), the Prince de Joinville, drew on his experiences with McClellan's staff to write *The Army of the Potomac: Its Organization, Its Commander, and Its Campaign* (New York: Randolph, 1862).

118. The administration was considering whether to allow cotton trading in Beaufort, S.C., which Union forces had recently captured.

119. Neither this letter nor any response to it has survived. John E. Wool (1784–1869) commanded the Department of Virginia.

120. Louis Blenker (1812–63), the German-born leader of a brigade in the Army of the Potomac, achieved notoriety in 1862 when his division, while en route to assist Frémont in West Virginia, engaged in looting and thievery after the War Department had failed to supply it adequately. For a description of the parade, see the Washington correspondence, 11 Nov. 1861, *New York Herald*, 12 Nov. 1861, p. 5. The president was cheered by the success of the expedition under Sherman and Du Pont, which captured Port Royal on 7 November.

121. See Washington correspondence, 10 Nov. 1861, *New York Herald*, 11 Nov. 1861, p. 1. Lt. Col. Frank Wheaton (1833–1903) served in the 2nd Rhode Island Infantry. Don Carlos Buell (1818–98) commanded a division in the Army of the Potomac.

122. This snub was not unprecedented. On 9 October 1861, William Howard Russell wrote in his dairy: "Calling on the General [McClellan] the other night at his usual time of return, I was told by the orderly, who was closing the door, 'The General's gone to bed tired, and can see no one. He sent the same message to the President, who came inquiring after him ten minutes ago.'" Russell commented: "This poor President! He is to be pitied; surrounded by such scenes, and trying with all his might to understand strategy, naval warfare, big guns, the movements of troops, military maps, reconnaissances, occupations, interior and exterior lines, and all the tech-

nical details of the art of slaying. He runs from one house to another, armed with plans, mss, reports, recommendations, sometimes good humored, never angry, occasionally dejected, and always a little fussy." Russell, *My Diary North and South,* ed. Eugene H. Berwanger (New York: Knopf, 1988), 317.

The following year, Lincoln again found the general unwilling to get out of bed to meet with him. According to a member of McClellan's staff, the president called at McClellan's house one Sunday morning in September 1862 and asked to see him. A short while later, McClellan's chief of staff, Gen. Randolph Marcy, "came down and with flushed face and confused manner said he was very sorry but McClellan was not yet up. A strange expression came over Lincoln's face, as he rose and said, 'Of course he's very busy now, and no doubt was laboring far into the night.' He departed hastily." Memorandum by C. C. Buel, New York, 23 Nov. 1885 (recalling the words uttered the previous evening by Horace Porter), Richard Watson Gilder MSS, New York Public Library.

On another occasion, McClellan had not deigned to interrupt his breakfast when the president called; Lincoln was kept waiting till the general finished eating, much to the surprise of one observer. Reminiscences of John M. Wilson, then a lieutenant on McClellan's staff, *Brooklyn Eagle,* 12 Feb. 1913.

McClellan's poor opinion of Lincoln was also manifested in the general's letters to his wife, in which he called Lincoln "an idiot," "the *original gorilla*," and "'an old stick'—& of pretty poor timber at that." He spoke of "the cowardice of the Presdt" and said that "I can never regard him with feelings other than those of thorough contempt—for his mind, heart, & morality." McClellan to his wife, Washington, 16 Aug., 31 Oct., and 17 Nov. 1861, and McClellan to his wife, Berkeley, Va., 17 July and 27 July 1862, *Papers of McClellan,* 85, 114, 135, 362, 374.

123. Lincoln's patience with McClellan was demonstrated one day when the general failed to keep an appointment with the president, Gen. Ormsby M. Mitchel, and Ohio governor William Dennison. After a long wait, Lincoln said: "Never mind; I will hold McClellan's horse if he will only bring us success." F. A. Mitchel to John Hay, E. Orange, N.J., 3 Jan. 1889, Nicolay-Hay MSS, IHi.

124. Hay went to New York to help smooth the way for the "New York Executive Committee," which planned to visit Washington to facilitate the exchange of prisoners of war.

125. Samuel Sullivan Cox (1824–89) was a militantly Democratic representative from Ohio (1857–65, 1869–85) and an alumnus of Brown University, class of 1846. On 4 December, he introduced into the U.S. House a resolution on the exchange of war prisoners. *Congressional Globe,* 38th Cong., 2nd sess., 1861, 33. Richard O'Gorman (1821–95) was a New York lawyer who, along with Judge Charles P. Daly and John Savage, constituted "the New York Executive Committee," which urged the administration to exchange prisoners with the Confederacy. They were aided by Hiram Barney, collector of the Port of New York. They met frequently in December with the president, the cabinet, the military committees of Congress, and McClellan and eventually achieved their goal. They were especially concerned about Col. Michael Corcoran (1827–63) of the New York State Militia, a captive in Confederate hands

who faced a death sentence. In August 1862, he was exchanged and was then offered a generalship by Lincoln. Washington correspondence, 29 Aug. 1862, *New York Express*, 1 Sept. 1862, p. 4.

126. Lt. Col. James Allen Hardie (1823–76) was an aide-de-camp to General McClellan. Charles Patrick Daly (1816–99), the first judge of the New York City Court of Common Pleas, was a Unionist Democrat who consulted with Lincoln about a number of matters, including the seizure of Confederate commissioners Mason and Slidell. Hiram Barney (1811–95) was a New York attorney, an antislavery leader, and the collector of the Port of New York. John J. Crittenden (1786–1863) of Kentucky was a Unionist member of the U.S. House (1861–63) and a former U.S. senator (1817–19, 1835–41, 1842–48, 1855–61). James Alexander McDougall (1817–67) was a Democratic senator from California (1861–67). Milton S. Latham (1827–82) also was a Democratic senator from California (1860–63).

127. John Savage (1828–88) at the age of twenty left his native Ireland for New York, where he became a prolific journalist and playwright. When the war broke out, he helped organize the Irish brigade. He was a militant supporter of Stephen A. Douglas. For the House resolution, see the *Congressional Globe*, 38th Cong., 2nd sess., 1861, 15. Frederick William Seward (1830–1915) was the assistant secretary of state and the son of Secretary of State Seward.

O'Gorman, Daly, and Savage wrote to Cameron on 7 December:

> The condition of the officers and privates of the United States army, taken prisoners at Manassas and since then, in captivity in Southern prisons has excited the grave attention of the Citizens of New York.
>
> The sufferings of Colonel Michael Corcoran of the 69th Regiment N. Y. S. M. especially have enlisted their sympathies.
>
> He is, as we learn from letters received from him and his fellow-prisoners, closely confined in a felon's cell at Charleston, and treated in all respects as a felon, convicted, and about to suffer death for an infamous crime.
>
> The unflinching loyalty, patriotism and capacity for command exhibited by that officer have particularly endeared him to our fellow-citizens of Irish birth and extraction.
>
> We express the urgent desire of millions of our fellow-citizens when we most anxiously and respectfully recommend his case to the earnest consideration of the Government, with the confident hope that immediate steps will be taken to effect his restoration to active duty.
>
> The continued imprisonment of Colonel Corcoran is, in many ways, detrimental to the Public Service; and we have the best reasons for believing that his release will confer prompt and efficient aid to the National cause. (Hay MSS, DLC)

128. James Fowler Simmons (1795–1864) was a Republican senator from Rhode Island (1841–47, 1857–62). Jabez C. Knight was a cotton merchant in addition to being the mayor. Daniel Butterfield (1831–1901), a New York merchant, was a brigadier general of volunteers. He served as General Meade's chief of staff at Gettysburg, and in

the autumn of 1863 he went with Hooker to join the Union army in the West. Gen. James S. Wadsworth (1807–64), a well-to-do New Yorker, helped organize the Free Soil party in that state. Early in the war he served as an aide to Gen. Irvin McDowell at First Bull Run, then became the military governor of Washington, D.C. He ran unsuccessfully for governor of New York in 1862. Two years later, at the battle of the Wilderness, he was killed. Gen. Rufus King (1814–76), who organized the famous "Iron Brigade" of Wisconsin, played an active role in the defense of Washington in the first year of the war. At Second Bull Run in August 1862, his division was ignominiously defeated, and he resigned from the army in 1863.

Salmon Chase noted in his diary on 10 December 1861: "At 12, went to President's to Cabinet Meeting. A deputation from New York, consisting of *Judge* [Henry Ebenezer] *Davies* [of the New York Court of Appeals], *Mr.* [Richard] *O'Gorman* and *Mr.* [John] *Savage*, represented the importance of an exchange of prisoners, with special reference to the case of Col. [Michael] Corcoran." *The Salmon P. Chase Papers*, vol. 1, *Journals, 1829–1872*, ed. John Niven (Kent, Ohio: Kent State Univ. Press, 1993), 313.

A journalist reported the following from Washington on 11 December:

> The question of the exchange of prisoners seems to be fairly settled. The New York Executive Committee had several lengthy and interesting interviews with the President, Gen. McClellan, and Senators and members of the House, all of whom favor it. The Committee's interview with Gen. McClellan was especially gratifying. He spoke of the subject briefly but warmly, and from his conversation had evidently given the subject much study. The Military Committee in both Houses have reported favorably on the subject, and a joint resolution, which passed the House, requesting the President to make an exchange, will pass the Senate. An exchange has been practically going on. Thirty prisoners were sent from here yesterday to Fort Monroe, and large numbers have been likewise released from Fort Warren. (*Chicago Tribune*, 12 Dec. 1861, p. 1)

129. "Mulligan" was probably James Adelbert Mulligan (1830–64), the colonel of the 23rd Illinois Regiment (known as the Irish Brigade). He had been captured at the battle of Lexington, Mo., in September and was exchanged two months later. Gen. Julius Stahel (1825–1912) was the Hungarian-born commander of a brigade in Blenker's division. Gen. Adolph Wilhelm August Friedrich von Steinwehr (1822–77) was the German-born commander of the second brigade of Blenker's division. Prince Felix Salm-Salm (1828–70) was the German-born aide-de-camp to General Blenker.

2. 1862

1. War Order 1 stated "That the 22nd day of February, 1862, be the day for a general movement of the Land and Naval forces of the United States against the insurgent forces." *CWL*, 5:111–12. Two years later the president told General Grant that "the

pressure from the people at the North and Congress . . . forced him into issuing his series of 'Military orders.'" *Personal Memoirs of U. S. Grant* (New York: Webster, 1894), 407. Forts Henry and Donelson in Tennessee were captured by Grant on 6 and 16 February. "The President's General War Order No. 2," issued on 8 March, provided that sufficient forces must be left to protect Washington if McClellan took his army by water to the Virginia peninsula. It also established five army corps. See *CWL*, 5:149–50. Samuel P. Heintzelman (1805–80) was a West Point graduate who had been wounded while leading a division at First Bull Run. Erasmus D. Keyes (1810–95) had led a brigade at First Bull Run. Nathaniel P. Banks was awaiting his assignment to command the Military District of Washington, which was made on 12 September.

2. On 8 March, Lincoln ordered that those batteries be taken. See *CWL*, 5:151.

3. After the Confederates withdrew from Manassas, it was discovered that it had been protected by logs painted to resemble artillery ("Quaker guns"). The news hurt McClellan's reputation.

4. War Order 3 relieved McClellan of responsibility for other military departments while he was in the field with the Army of the Potomac. See *CWL*, 5:151.

5. A movement from Harper's Ferry was frustrated by canal locks that were too narrow for the barges employed. When he learned the bad news, Lincoln "swore like a Philistine." Horace White to Joseph Medill, Washington, 3 March 1862, Charles H. Ray MSS, Huntington Library, San Marino, Calif. White House secretary William O. Stoddard "never knew Mr. Lincoln so really angry, so out of all patience, as when it was reported impossible to obey his celebrated order for a general advance of the army on the 22d of February, 1862." "White House Sketches, No. VI," *New York Citizen*, 22 Sept. 1866. Stoddard recalled that Lincoln

> was alone in his room when an officer of General McClellan's staff was announced by the doorkeeper and admitted. The President turned in his chair to hear, and was informed, in respectful terms, that the advance movement [against Winchester] could not be made.
> "Why?" he curtly demanded.
> "The pontoon trains are not ready—"
> "Why in ——— ain't they ready?"

Unable to think of a reply, the officer abruptly left the room. "Lincoln also turned to the table and resumed the work before him, but wrote at about double his ordinary speed."

When Secretary of War Stanton confirmed the bad news, Lincoln asked, "What does this mean?"

"It means that it is a d——d fizzle. It means that he doesn't intend to do anything," replied Stanton. Dirk P. de Young, "Lincoln's Secretary Talks of His Chief," *Dearborn Independent*, 7 Feb. 1925, p. 4

John G. Nicolay observed that Lincoln "was much cast down and dejected at the news of the failure of the enterprise. Why could he not have known whether his arrangements were practicable?" The President summoned McClellan's chief of staff, Gen. Randolph B. Marcy, and said:

> Why in the Nation, General Marcy, couldn't the General have known whether a boat would go through that lock before spending a million dollars getting them there? I am no engineer, but it seems to me that if I wished to know whether a boat would go through a hole or a lock, common sense would teach me to go and measure it. I am almost despairing at these results. Everything seems to fail. The general impression is daily gaining ground that the General does not intend to do anything. By a failure like this we lose all the prestige we gained by the capture of Fort Donelson. I am grievously disappointed—almost in despair.

When Marcy defended McClellan, Lincoln abruptly dismissed him. Memorandum, 27 Feb. 1862, Nicolay MSS, DLC. On 1 March Lincoln "angrily" described to Charles Sumner the canal boat fiasco, which "excited him very much." Sumner to John A. Andrew, Washington, 2 Mar. 1862, *Selected Letters of Charles Sumner*, ed. Beverly Wilson Palmer (Boston: Northeastern Univ. Press, 1990), 2:115.

6. Lincoln had placed Frémont in command of the newly created Mountain Department. The feud in Missouri between Frémont and his former champions, the Blairs, had culminated in the arrest of Frank Blair.

7. Schuyler Colfax (1823–85), a congressman from Indiana, served as the Speaker of the House (1863–69). Justus McKinstry (1814–97), the quartermaster for Frémont's army, was the only Union general dismissed from the service "for neglect and violation of duty, to the prejudice and good order and military discipline." He engaged in extortion and other corrupt practices in Missouri. Frémont, McKinstry, and Blair all played parts in the mismanagement and corruption in St. Louis.

8. The "Soldiers' Home" was Lincoln's summer retreat, three miles outside the District of Columbia. Located on a hilltop, this facility for disabled troops was far cooler than the White House. In 1862, 1863, and 1864, the president and his family spent the summers in a stone cottage on this site.

9. Pope's Army of Virginia had been attacked in the rear by Jackson on 29 August. Lee's plan at the Second Battle of Bull Run was to smash Pope before the Army of the Potomac, returning from McClellan's peninsula campaign, could fully reinforce it. No reliable news of the battle had reached Washington until Sunday afternoon, 31 August. A journalist who observed the president on the thirtieth wrote that he had never seen him "so wrathful as last night against George." Adams Hill to Sidney Howard Gay, Washington, 31 Aug. 1862, Gay MSS, Columbia Univ. McClellan's dispatch about Pope was sent on 29 August. Gen. William B. Franklin (1823–1903) was the commander of the 6th Corps of the Army of the Potomac.

At 6 A.M. on 29 August, the first day of the battle, McClellan, pressed by Halleck, sent Franklin off toward Pope, but after the troops had gone only seven miles, McClellan ordered a halt. The soldiers spent the rest of the day listening to the cannons boom in the distance. Halleck was furious. The next day at dusk they reached the battlefield, only to encounter thousands of retreating troops. McClellan could have dispatched, if he had felt so inclined, 25,000 troops under Franklin and Sumner to reinforce Pope on the second day of the battle. Halleck had ordered him to send Franklin's troops; McClellan in effect ignored the command. McClellan mistakenly believed that Lee was approaching Chain Bridge with over 100,000 troops. McClellan had returned to Alexandria on 27 August. On that day and in his dispatch of 29 August he requested orders defining the scope of his authority. No clear definition was given him either before or after his resumption of the chief command.

One of McClellan's biographers concluded that the general was not "deliberately conspiring to have the Army of Virginia beaten" but added that "his bruised sensibilities and his unreasoning contempt for Pope convinced him that general would be—and deserved to be—defeated. Nor can it be doubted that he would have acted far more vigorously at Alexandria had one of his favorites, such as Fitz John Porter, commanded the Army of Virginia. Instead, the captive of his delusions, he put his own interests and messianic vision ahead of doing everything possible to rush reinforcements to the battlefield." Stephen W. Sears, *George B. McClellan: The Young Napoleon* (New York: Ticknor & Fields, 1988), 254.

10. Hay was not the only one to characterize Ellen Stanton unfavorably; during the war, an Iowa woman noted that "she is very handsome, but much complaint is made of her freezing manner and repellent address." She was also known to have a "waspish and uncertain" temper. Benjamin P. Thomas and Harold Hyman, *Stanton: The Life and Times of Lincoln's Secretary of War* (New York: Knopf, 1962), 393. Possibly Stanton intended to pump Hay about Lincoln's intentions concerning McClellan (220).

11. An officer in the field telegraphed the next day: "Near a thousand came last night, half of them drunk. We do not want any more of them." Clerks from the Treasury Department, including the assistant secretary, also went as nurses. Herman Haupt, *Reminiscences of General Herman Haupt* (Milwaukee: Weight & Joys, 1901), 127.

12. Herman Haupt (1817–1905) was the chief of construction and transportation on the U.S. military railroads. Lincoln telegraphed Haupt seven times during the battle. The "whilom General-in-chief" was George B. McClellan.

13. Jackson's move heralded the beginning of Lee's invasion of Maryland, which culminated in the Battle of Antietam on 17 September. McClellan had been reappointed to command the forces guarding Washington on 2 September. As Nicolay and Hay noted, "There is no other official act of his life for which he has been more severely criticized." *Lincoln*, 6:21. The president assumed the full responsibility; Stanton was not officially informed until the cabinet met later that day. Feelings there were strong because Stanton and Chase had been circulating a protest to the president demanding McClellan's dismissal. Hay's "yesterday" may have been a slip of the pen, for there is no other evidence of a second cabinet discussion.

According to Ward Hill Lamon, Lincoln explained to his incredulous cabinet that "something had to be done, but there did not appear to be any one to do it, and he therefore took the responsibility on himself. . . . [and] that McClellan had the confidence of the troops beyond any other officer and could, under the circumstances, more speedily and effectually reorganize them and put them into fighting trim than any other general." *New York Tribune*, 26 July 1885, p. 3.

Lincoln told Welles, "I must have McClellan to reorganize the army and bring it out of chaos. But there has been a design, a purpose in breaking down Pope, without regard of consequences to the country. It is shocking to see and know this; but there is no remedy at present. McClellan has the army with him." *The Diary of Gideon Welles, Secretary of the Navy under Lincoln and Johnson, 1861–1869*, ed. Howard K. Beale (New York: Norton, 1960) 1:112 (entry for 7 Sept. 1862).

14. On 3 September, the National War Committee, meeting in New York, passed a resolution calling for this measure. The "Mitchell" referred to was probably Gen. Robert Byington Mitchell (1823–82), who had served in Missouri when Frémont was in charge of that department.

15. Joseph M. Wightman was the mayor of Boston.

16. Seward had been visiting his home in Auburn, N.Y.

17. Hay refers to the final draft of the preliminary Emancipation Proclamation. Lincoln had submitted a previous draft to his cabinet on 22 July. No attached document marked "a" can be found.

18. See *CWL*, 5:438–39.

19. The "old fogies" included Gen. Cassius M. Clay; William F. Clark, the collector of internal revenue in Pennsylvania's 20th district; Gen. Jesse H. Robinson of Pittsburgh, a member of the U.S. military telegraph service; and William David Lewis (1792–1881), the president of the Philadelphia Academy of Fine Arts. See *The Salmon P. Chase Papers*, vol. 1, *Journals, 1829–1872*, ed. John Niven (Kent, Ohio: Kent State Univ. Press, 1993), 400 (entry for 24 Sept. 1862).

20. Maj. John J. Key, the brother of Col. Thomas M. Key, a judge advocate on McClellan's staff, was the suspect. The following day Lincoln interrogated Key and Judge Advocate Levi C. Turner and then wrote a copy of the record: "Major Turner says . . . 'I asked the question why we did not bag them after Sharpsburg [Antietam]?' Major Key's reply was that was not the game, that we should tire the rebels out, and ourselves, that that was the only way the Union could be preserved, we come together fraternally, and slavery be saved." Lincoln promptly dismissed Key. He later refused to remit the sentence. *CWL*, 5:442–43. See also Washington correspondence, 30 Sept. 1862, *Chicago Tribune*, 1 Oct. 1862, p. 1. According to Welles, Turner had passed the information to Secretary of the Interior Caleb B. Smith, who evidently told the president. *Diary of Welles*, 1:146, 156 (entries for 24 and 30 Sept. 1862).

21. Two years later the president told Hay that he had been unable to make McClellan move against Lee after Antietam. McClellan was fired on 7 November. See *infra*, entry for 25 Sept. 1864.

3. 1863

1. Hay's official mission was to deliver dispatches from the Navy Department to Adm. Samuel Francis Du Pont. The carefully prepared attack on Charleston by the navy's armored monitors was then imminent. The extension of Hay's visit was probably in part designed to allow Hay to report on the situation in the Department of

the South, but it was also a form of vacation and a chance to visit his brother Charles. On 5 April, Nicolay told his fiancee that "I am literally alone in the house here today. John Hay left last Thursday morning [2 April] for New York, and sailed in the 'Arago' yesterday morning for Hilton Head. He expects to help Gen. Hunter capture Charleston. I hope he may—but am afraid that Charleston problem is a harder one than we imagine." Nicolay to Therena Bates, Washington, 5 Apr. 1863, Nicolay MSS, DLC.

2. Gen. Israel Vogdes (1816–89) helped plan the artillery locations and strategy in the Charleston campaign.

3. Built in Scotland, the Confederate commerce raider *Alabama* was devastating the Union merchant marine around the world.

4. Located sixty miles southwest of Charleston, Hilton Head was headquarters of the Army Department of the South. "Smith" was perhaps Maj. Edward W. Smith, the assistant adjutant general to Gen. David Hunter. "Skinner" was perhaps Capt. Benjamin H. Skinner of the 7th Connecticut Infantry. Col. Joseph R. Hawley (1826–1905), a Connecticut journalist and politician, was at this time in command of Hilton Head Island.

5. The *Wabash* was a U.S. steam frigate.

6. The *Nahant* was an ironclad steamer of the monitor class. The attack on Sumter had begun soon after 1 P.M. on 7 April; it was called off after forty minutes, during which time the monitors suffered heavy damage, as did Union prestige at home and abroad. Charles G. Halpine (1829–68) was an Irish-born New York journalist who served as an assistant adjutant to General Hunter, as well as a liaison with the press. Written under the pen name of Miles O'Reilly, his contributions to the *New York Herald* were extremely popular. Joseph R. Hawley described him as "a beautiful hater of . . . [the] swindlers" who infested Florida. Joseph R. Hawley to Charles Dudley Warner, St. Augustine, Fla., 14 July 1863, "Letters of Joseph R. Hawley" (typescript dated 1929), ed. Arthur L. Shipman, Connecticut Historical Society, Hartford, p. 154.

7. The *Canonicus* was a light-draft single-turreted monitor.

8. Alfred Howe Terry (1827–90), head of the 7th Connecticut Regiment, had helped to seize Port Royal in November 1861 and to besiege Fort Pulaski, Ga., in April 1862. "Fess" was James Deering Fessenden (1833–82), an aide-de-camp to General Hunter and the son of Sen. William P. Fessenden of Maine. In 1862 he had organized one of the first regiments of black troops for service in the U.S. Army. The *Ben De Ford* was a U.S. transport steamer. The ironclad *Keokuk* had been sunk the day after the battle. The USS *New Ironsides*, an ironclad steamer, served as flagship during the Union assault on Charleston. John Rodgers (1812–82) was the commander of the *Weehawken*. The dispatches were from Welles and Fox transmitting the president's orders to send most of the ironclads to the Mississippi.

9. The interview with Captain Rodgers and Admiral Du Pont drastically changed Hay's optimism about the future prospects of the operations, which he had derived from the army officers.

10. Thomas Turner (1808–83) was the commander of the *New Ironsides*.

11. Robert Smalls (1839–1915), a slave pilot who had escaped from Charleston har-

bor with the steamer *Planter*, became a pilot in the U.S. Navy during the war and a prominent politician after it. In 1876 he was convicted of taking bribes.

12. See Hay to Lincoln, Stono River, S.C., 10 Apr. 1863, Hay MSS, RPB.

13. Gen. Orris S. Ferry (1823–75) was the commander of the 5th Connecticut.

14. In the Connecticut elections on 6 April, the Republicans managed to retain a reduced majority in the legislature.

15. Rufus Saxton (1824–1908) administered abandoned plantations on the Sea Islands and helped recruit blacks into the Union army. The *Wyoming* was a 997-ton steam sloop of the second class. The Rev. Dr. Richard Fuller (1804–76) was the minister of the Seventh Baptist Church in Baltimore (1847–71) and a landowner on St. Helena Island. William Elliott owned the Oak Lawn plantation on the Pon-Pon River and much land elsewhere in South Carolina.

Joseph R. Hawley called Saxton a "muddle headed . . . *darned fool*" who "gets continually imposed upon. . . . His eye-teeth, yea and his eyes, can be humbugged out of him any day." Conceding that Saxton "is honest and honorable," Hawley declared that "he knew *nothing* of the Liberty and Slavery question before the war and don't read and can't *think* it out now. He has adopted some good ideas but it will be years before his slow intellectual digestion gets them into his blood and some of them will be found whole in his stomach when he dies." Hawley to Charles Dudley Warner, St. Augustine, Fla., 14 June 1863, "Letters of Hawley," 135–36.

16. Col. Milton Smith Littlefield (1830–99) of the 21st U.S. Colored Troops was in charge of recruiting at Hilton Head. During Reconstruction, he achieved notoriety as a corrupt railroad lobbyist in North Carolina and Florida. Capt. Edward W. Hooper, formerly a superintendent of freedmen, was an aide-de-camp on Saxton's staff. After the war, he served as the treasurer of Harvard University. Nathaniel Heyward was one of the richest planters in South Carolina. Robert Barnwell Rhett (1800–1876) was a leading South Carolina secessionist.

17. The 1st South Carolina Infantry was the first black unit mustered into the U.S. Army.

18. Maj. Edward Wright and Capt. Samuel W. Stockton (1834–99) were aides-de-camp to General Hunter.

19. Lt. Charles E. Hay, John's younger brother, was the acting aide-de-camp to General Hunter. Hunter told Hay in February that Charlie "is quite well and his conduct is such as to give me perfect satisfaction." Hunter to Hay, Hilton Head, S.C., 11 Feb. 1863, AL MSS, DLC. Halpine also reported in February that "your brother is well & in good spirits." Halpine to Hay, ca. 24 Feb. 1863, AL MSS, DLC. Charles was later ordered north from South Carolina and worked as a recruiter in Springfield, Ill. He wed Mary Ridgeley in May 1865 and became a prosperous grocer and the mayor of Springfield.

20. Surgeon John Joseph Craven (1822–93) was the chief medical officer of the Department of the South. Whitemarsh Benjamin Seabrook (1793–1855) had been the governor of South Carolina (1848–50).

21. Lincoln ordered Hunter and Du Pont to keep up their campaign against Charleston. See Hay to Nicolay, Hilton Head, S.C., 16 Apr. 1863, Hay MSS, RPB.

22. Capt. Arthur M. Kinzie was an aide-de-camp to General Hunter and the nephew of Mrs. Hunter. Commanding the Savannah River, Fort Pulaski had been captured by Gillmore on 2 April 1862. Before surrendering the fort, the Confederates vandalized it. "They filled one at least of the cisterns with rubbish; they defaced the walls of their quarters by throwing ink-stands and other objects at them; they did, in fact, all the damage they dared, for it is held a crime in military law for a garrison surrendering to destroy its material." "Two Weeks on Hilton Head," *Washington Sunday Chronicle*, 31 May 1863.

23. The Olympic Theater at Fort Pulaski was established in a wooden building outside the fort. One playgoer noted that the "scenery, in fact all the outfit, is astonishingly perfect; there are even two private boxes; there are resplendent chandeliers, curled strips of tin can taking the place of cut glass." "Two Weeks at Port Royal," *Washington Sunday Chronicle*, 31 May 1863. *John Bull, or, An Englishman's Fire-Side*, by George Colman (1762–1836), was published in 1803. *The Rough Diamond* was written by Benjamin Franklin Craig (b. 1814).

24. The Rev. Mr. Mansfield French (1810–76) of the Methodist Episcopal Church was an army chaplain and a general agent of the New York Freedmen's Relief Association. Maj. J. D. Strong was part of Company B, 1st South Carolina Infantry (Colored). In March, Hiram Barney, collector of the Port of New York, had sworn in the members of the "Port Royal experiment," including Hooper, before they sailed from New York. See Elizabeth Ware Pearson, ed., *Letters from Port Royal, Written at the Time of the Civil War* (Boston: Clarke, 1906), 2.

25. Dr. Joseph Means had a plantation on Parris Island. John Hamilton (1823–1900) commanded Battery E of the 3rd U.S. Artillery.

26. "In a prayer-meeting at Hilton Head one night a young negro said he would like to see Linkum. A gray-headed patriarch rebuked the rash wish, saying 'No man see Linkum. Linkum walk as Jesus walk. No man see Linkum.'" John Hay, "Heroic Times in Washington" (lecture dated 1871), Hay MSS, RPB.

27. "Pope" was probably Daniel Pope, whose plantation was described in a letter by Laura Towne, 21 Apr. 1862, *Letters and Diary of Laura M. Towne, Written from the Sea Islands of South Carolina, 1862–1884*, ed. Rupert Sargent Holland (Cambridge: Riverside, 1912), 11. Edward L. Pierce (1829–97) of Massachusetts, appointed by Treasury Secretary Chase as a special agent to help the freedmen on the Sea Islands produce a cotton crop, used this plantation on St. Helena Island as his headquarters.

28. See Hay to Nicolay, Hilton Head, S.C., 23 Apr. 1863, Hay MSS, RPB. "Marston" could be Congressman Gilman Marston (1811–90) or William H. Marston, a friend and correspondent of Nicolay. Cf. Nicolay to Marston, Washington, 4 June 1864, Nicolay MSS, DLC.

29. Perhaps the first-named play was an adaptation of Washington Irving's story, "The Spectre Bridegroom." *The Jacobite*, by James Robinson Planche (1796–1880), was published in 1847. *The New Footman: A Burletta in One Act* (1842) was by Charles Selby (1802?–63).

30. Fernandina had been in Federal hands since March 1862. Dungeness was an estate on Cumberland Island given by the state of Georgia to Gen. Nathanael Greene

as a token of gratitude for his services in the Revolutionary War. James M. Latta, an assistant district tax commissioner for Florida and civil provost marshal at Fernandina, was an associate of Judge Lyman D. Stickney. Joseph R. Hawley described him unflatteringly: "An Indiana judge named James M. Latta, a man of about 30 who calls himself the friend of Colfax, etc., knows Washington, thinks he can *manage* everybody, sets up for something of a literary chap and a good deal of a politician, came down here last fall and got Saxton to appoint him Civil Provost Marshal General of Florida. . . . Latta really came down here to speculate and steal; thinks himself a Talleyrand." Hawley to "My dear Boy," St. Augustine, Fla., 14 July 1863, "Letters of Hawley," 153.

31. Confederate general Joseph Finegan (1814–85), who commanded the Department of Middle and East Florida, had been active in the secession of the state. The Direct Tax Law of 7 June 1862 authorized the sale of land owned by absentee Confederate landowners. The Treasury Department appointed tax commissioners to conduct the sales. Hay's involvement with them through the agency of Judge Stickney would cause him much embarrassment the following year. Charles G. Halpine reported that Hay "has gone junketeering with some feminine female women." Halpine to John G. Nicolay, Hilton Head, S.C., 25 Apr. 1863, Nicolay MSS, DLC.

32. Located at the northern end of Amelia Island, Fort Clinch guarded the approaches to Fernandina. Alfred F. Sears (1826?–95) was the captain of Company E, New York Volunteer Engineers.

33. George F. Gardiner was described thus by Joseph R. Hawley:

a troublesome, seditious, insubordinate, half treasonable, quite disloyal intriguer and mischief maker, formerly a Breckinridge man, a hater of temperance and virtue, a believer in universal female frailty, a *goat* in his practices so far as opportunity offers, though much afraid of public opinion, sensual and enormously selfish. He struts in command and puts on severe discipline but turns around and spoils discipline by demagogue efforts for *popularity*. Five sixths of the officers bitterly hate him, only one or two associate with him at all and no one's fancy for or association with him lasts a month. He is sure to crowd or defraud them. (Hawley to Charles Dudley Warner, 15 Mar. 1863, "Letters of Hawley," 135–36)

Alfred G. Gray (1818–76) commanded the transport *McClellan*.

34. Samuel L. Burritt of Jacksonville was described as "a Union man with strong Southern proclivities." Samuel F. Du Pont to his wife, Port Royal, S.C., 19 June 1862, *Samuel Francis Du Pont: A Selection from His Civil War Letters*, ed. John D. Hayes (Ithaca: Cornell Univ. Press, 1969), 2:120–21.

35. Harrison Reed (1813–99) was the U.S. tax commissioner for Florida. During Reconstruction, he served as the state's governor. Harriet L. Harris came from Portland, Maine. Carrie L. Smith came from Manchester, N.H. Chloe Merrick (d. 1897) of Syracuse, N.Y., the daughter of Susbanus Merrick, taught liberated slaves in Fernandina and St. Augustine as an agent of the Freedman's Aid Society of Syracuse.

The black orphanage and school were located in St. Augustine. To accommodate the students and orphans, Merrick, the principal, bought General Finnegan's house at a tax sale in June 1862. See *New York Tribune*, 17 Aug. 1864. She later married Reed.

36. The *Jeff Davis* was a Confederate blockade-runner that wrecked 8 April 1862. The "Fort of St Mark" was the Castillo de San Marcos, a Spanish colonial citadel.

37. Orloff M. Dorman was then a paymaster in the Department of the South. A long-time resident of Florida, he had sought appointment as the provisional governor in 1862, and Orville Browning had introduced him to Lincoln on 30 June 1862.

38. Sarah Mather (1818–94) and Rebecca L. Perit (or Peret) (1823–93) were teachers from Massachusetts.

39. Joseph R. Hawley described the conduct of Col. Haldimand S. Putnam of the 7th New Hampshire Infantry thus: he "staid here too long and got too fond of secesh, let the people run in and out of the lines, socially went with secesh., didn't attend to business generally . . . but let all the good loyal people *feel almost ostracized as old abolitionists* used to." Hawley to Charles Dudley Warner, 14 June 1863, "Letters of Hawley," 162.

40. "Merriam" was perhaps Lt. Eli C. Merriam of the 1st South Carolina Volunteers.

41. Hay had written a poem entitled "The Army Gambolier" on 10 April 1863 at Folly Island. See Hay scrapbook, Hay MSS, RPB.

42. Nathaniel Prentiss Banks (1816–94), a Democrat who had been the Speaker of the House (1856–58) and the governor of Massachusetts (1858–61), was in charge of Union forces in the New Orleans area from late 1862 to 1865.

43. Horatio G. Wright (1820–99) was an engineer.

44. "Genl. Com." refers to David Hunter.

45. The *Arago* was a U.S. transport steamer. The accounts were early reports of the Battle of Chancellorsville.

46. Union general William S. Rosecrans (1819–98) commanded the Army of the Cumberland. Dahlonegah was a small town in northern Georgia.

47. *No Name* (1862) was a novel by Wilkie Collins (1824–89). Five monitors moved from Charleston harbor for refitting after the attack. Thomas Greeley Stevenson (1836–64) commanded Union forces on Seabrook Island. Daniel Ammen (1819–98) commanded the monitor *Petapsco* and later wrote *The Atlantic Coast* (1883) and *The Old Navy and the New* (1891). Du Pont called him "a kindly and hospitable person as well as a good officer." Du Pont to his wife, Port Royal, S.C., 13 Nov. 1861, *Du Pont Letters*, 1:236. "Beaumont" was Capt. John C. Beaumont (1821–82). The *Delaware* was a 357-ton U.S. transport side-wheel steamer.

48. During such conversations, Halpine gave Hay "insight into those 'mysteries of iniquity.'—N. Y. City politics." Halpine to Hay, New York, 12 Nov. 1863, Hay MSS, RPB.

49. Henry R. Guss of the 97th Pennsylvania Infantry commanded Union forces on St. Helena Island.

50. The *Nantucket* was an ironclad steamer of the monitor class.

51. John A. Downes (1822–65) commanded the *Nahant*. The USS *Catskill* was an ironclad monitor commanded by George W. Rodgers (1822–63). Donald McNeill

Fairfax (1821–94) commanded both the *Montauk* and the *Nantucket* in the Charleston campaign.

52. "Col Seabrook" was perhaps Paul H. Seabrook of the 23rd South Carolina Infantry.

53. Some Confederate artillery units fired Whitworth solid shot from the English-made Whitworth rifled cannons. Robert F. Stockton (1795–1866) designed the *Princeton*, one of the earliest steam-powered vessels in the U.S. Navy. On 28 February 1844, an explosion aboard that sloop of war killed several people, including the secretary of state and the secretary of the navy.

54. "Ives" was probably Lt. Thomas Poynton Ives (1834–65), USN, who graduated from Brown University in 1854.

55. *Barren Honour* was a novel by Guy Livingston published in 1862. See Hay's letter to Nicolay, 12 May 1863, Hay MSS, RPB. The *James Adger* was a 1152-ton side-wheel steamer that had been towing the damaged monitor *Passaic* to New York.

56. *The Silver Cord: A Story* (London: Bradbury, 1862) was written by Shirley Brooks (1815–74).

57. Early in the war, Franz Sigel (1824–1902), a leading German American general, and Francis P. Blair Jr. (1821–75) had taken part in the attack on the Confederate Camp Jackson in St. Louis.

58. General Lander's widow was doing hospital work in the department.

59. Abram D. Smith, U.S. direct tax commissioner in South Carolina, was from Wisconsin.

60. Laura Matilda Towne (1825–1901) of Philadelphia, a teacher and doctor, was among the first Northerners to travel to South Carolina to assist the freedmen; she was joined by her friend Ellen Murray of Milton, Mass. In the summer of 1862, they established the Penn School for freed slaves on St. Helena Island. Charlotte Forten (1837–1914) was teaching in the Sea Islands under the auspices of the Port Royal Relief Association. Among her pupils were members of the 1st South Carolina Volunteers, black troops under the command of Col. Thomas W. Higginson.

61. On 25 May, Thomas W. Higginson described this event to his mother: "Only think of the picnic here the other day! Mrs. Lander got one up at the Barnwell place, the most beautiful on the island, and I helped her a good deal. It was got up for a young Mr. Hay, President Lincoln's private secretary, a nice young fellow, who unfortunately looks about seventeen and is oppressed with the necessity of behaving like seventy. . . . About four came the band, the officers, the young ladies, Gen. Saxton without his livelier half, Mr. Hay laboring not to appear newmown." *Letters and Journals of Thomas Wentworth Higginson, 1846–1906*, ed. Mary Thatcher Higginson (Boston: Houghton Mifflin, 1921), 201–2. For an extensive account of this event, see Beaufort correspondence by N. P., 26 May 1863, *New York Tribune*, n.d., clipping in Hay's scrapbook, vol. 54, Hay MSS, DLC.

62. Frances Dana Barker Gage (1808–84), an abolitionist author and lecturer, was working with the National Freedmen's Relief Association. She had charge of five hundred blacks on Parris Island. Maj. Dwight Bannister of Ohio was the chief paymaster on General Gillmore's staff.

63. One observer of this scene wrote the following a few days later:

Mr. Hay, in eloquent yet to the blacks comprehensible language, as one who in official position stood near the person of their good friend, told them that the President took the greatest interest in their welfare; that he considered this military department one of the most important in the country, not simply on account of its military character, but that here great social and educational projects were being worked out, upon the success of which would probably depend the future welfare of the race. It gratified the President, he said, to hear that they were learning to read and write, to work for themselves, to accumulate property, and manifest a disposition to fight, if necessary, for its defense....

The speeches being over, the blacks all came forward to shake hands with their distinguished visitors. A warmer, a more cordial and honest greeting was never given to any party, distinguished or obscure....

After all who desired had come up and shaken hands, three cheers were called for Gen. Saxton, three for the President, and one old negro, carried away with excitement, mounting an old broken plow, called out for three cheers for the "President's General," meaning Secretary Hay. This last round, together with the one for Mrs. Saxton and Mrs. Lander, were given with a will which fairly made the old oak overhead thrill with joy. (Beaufort correspondence by N. P., 29 May 1863, *New York Tribune*, n.d., clipping, Hay scrapbook, vol. 54, Hay MSS, DLC)

64. The Reverend J. C. Zachos was the superintendent of Parris Island.

65. Henry A. Gadsden was commander of the *Arago*. Hay's argument about McClellan probably resembled the one he made in 1881: "that McClellan was really never interfered with [by Lincoln], that he was treated by Lincoln with a long-suffering forbearance without parallel in history, that he had at all times more troops than he knew how to use, and that he failed from sheer moral incapacity ever to assume the initiative when an enemy stood in the way." Hay lamented that "The country has not even yet come to comprehend the depths of McClellan's incapacity." Unsigned review of *The Peninsula: McClellan's Campaign of 1862*, by Alexander Webb, *New York Tribune*, 23 Dec. 1881, p. 6, reprinted in George Monteiro, ed., "John Hay and the Union Generals," *Journal of the Illinois State Historical Society* 69 (1976): 49. Cf. John G. Nicolay and John Hay, *Abraham Lincoln: A History* (New York: Century, 1890), 6:189–95 (a passage written by Hay, not by Nicolay); see also [John Hay], "Lincoln and the Army of the Potomac," 283–89, Evelyn W. Symington Collection, DLC.)

66. "Gus" was Augustus Leonard Hay. The Tombs was a prison.

67. George Gordon Meade (1815–72) commanded the Army of the Potomac at Gettysburg. Lee's invasion of the North in the spring 1863 had aroused Lincoln's hope that the Army of Northern Virginia could be trapped, especially after its defeat at Gettysburg. Between 3 July, when the fighting ended, and 14 July, when Lee safely returned to Virginia, Lincoln's "anxiety seemed as great as it had been during the battle itself," according to an officer in the Washington telegraph office. The president, he recalled, "walked up and down the floor, his face grave and anxious, wringing his

hands and showing every sign of deep solicitude. As the telegrams came in, he traced the positions of the two armies on the map, and several times called me up to point out their location, seeming to feel the need of talking to some one. Finally, a telegram came from Meade saying that under such and such circumstances he would engage the enemy at such and such a time. 'Yes,' said the President bitterly, 'he will be ready to fight a magnificent battle when there is no enemy there to fight!'" "Notes of an Interview with A. B. Chandler, September 16, 1898," Ida M. Tarbell MSS, Allegheny College.

On 15 July, Lincoln told Simon Cameron, "I would give much to be relieved of the impression that Meade, Couch, Smith and all, since the battle of Gettysburg, have striven only to get Lee over the river without another fight." *CWL*, 6:329–30. Two months later, Gideon Welles asked what Meade was doing; Lincoln replied: "It is the same old story of this Army of the Potomac. Imbecility, inefficiency—don't want to *do*—is defending the Capital." The president then "groaned," saying "Oh, it is terrible, terrible, this weakness, this indifference of our Potomac generals, with such armies of good and brave men." *The Diary of Gideon Welles, Secretary of the Navy under Lincoln and Johnson, 1861–1869*, ed. Howard K. Beale (New York: Norton, 1960), 1:439 (entry for 21 Sept. 1863). See also Gabor S. Boritt, "'Unfinished Work'; Lincoln, Meade, and Gettysburg," in Gabor S. Boritt, ed., *Lincoln's Generals* (New York: Oxford Univ. Press, 1994), 81–120.

68. Thomas T. Eckert (1825–1910) was the chief of the War Department Telegraph Office. Gen. Benjamin F. Kelley (1807–91) commanded the Department of West Virginia.

69. When word arrived that the Army of Northern Virginia had crossed the Potomac, Lincoln's "grief and anger were something sorrowful to behold," according to Noah Brooks, the journalist who brought him the bad news on 14 July. *Washington, D.C., in Lincoln's Time*, ed. Herbert Mitgang (New York: Rinehart, 1958), 94.

70. It is hard to determine which dispatch by Lincoln Hay refers to. Several days after the battle, Lincoln, according to his son Robert, "summoned Gen. [Herman] Haupt, in whom he had great confidence as a bridge builder, and asked him how long in view of the materials which might be . . . available under Lee, would it take him to devise the means and get his army across the river." Haupt guessed that it would require no more than twenty-four hours. Lincoln "at once sent an order to Gen. Meade," either by telegraph or by special messenger, "directing him to attack Lee's army with all his force immediately, and that if he was successful in the attack he might destroy the order but if he was unsuccessful he might preserve it for his vindication." Memorandum by Robert Todd Lincoln of a conversation with his father on 14 July 1863, dated 5 Jan. 1885, enclosed in R. T. Lincoln to John G. Nicolay, Washington, 5 Jan. 1885, Hay MSS, DLC.

Gabor S. Boritt speculates that the messenger bearing the dispatch was Vice President Hannibal Hamlin. Boritt, "'Unfinished Work,'" 99–100. Cf. Joseph Medill's statement to Newton Macmillan, *Portland Oregonian*, 28 Apr. 1895; and a memorandum by Rush C. Hawkins, Hombourg-les-Bains, Prussia, 17 Aug. 1872, Hawkins MSS, RPB. In the latter document, Hawkins reports, evidently based on what he had just heard, that on the day before Lincoln received Meade's dispatch saying he would not attack Lee, "the President had telegraphed to Genl. Mead to follow up and attack, and that he (the President) would hold himself responsible for the result. The telegram, as I now understand it was, read as follows: 'To Major General Mead Commanding the Army of the Potomac. You will follow up and attack Genl. Lee as soon as possible before he can cross the river. If you fail this dispatch will clear you from all responsibility and if you succeed you may destroy it.'"

A Lincoln collector in Seattle allegedly bought a copy of Lincoln's order to Meade, which read something like this: "This is your order to pursue the retreating army and annihilate them. If you succeed you may keep this order and take the credit. If you fail destroy this order I will take the blame." Roger L. Scaife to Albert J. Beveridge, Boston, 27 Apr. 1925, enclosing an undated letter from "H. L." in Seattle to Scaife, Beveridge MSS, DLC.

Robert Todd Lincoln told others about this order. See R. T. Lincoln to Isaac N. Arnold, Washington, 11 Nov. 1883 and 27 Mar. 1884, Abraham Lincoln Collection, and R. T. Lincoln to Isaac Markens, Washington, 6 Apr. 1918, R. T. Lincoln MSS, Chicago Historical Society; R. T. Lincoln to Helen Nicolay, Manchester, Vt., 29 May 1912, R. T. Lincoln to John G. Nicolay, Chicago, 14 June 1878, John G. Nicolay to R. T. Lincoln (draft), Burlingame, Kans., 25 June 1878, and John G. Nicolay to R. T. Lincoln, Colorado Springs, 5 Sept. 1881, Nicolay MSS, DLC; Isaac N. Phillips, *Abraham Lincoln: A Short Study of a Great Man and His Work* (Bloomington, Ill.: privately printed, 1901), 45–46; George H. Thacher, "Lincoln and Meade After Gettysburg," *American Historical Review* 32 (1926–27): 282–83. See also F. Lauriston Bullard, "President Lincoln and General Meade after Gettysburg," *Lincoln Herald* 47 (Feb. 1945): 30–34, and 47 (Oct.–Dec. 1945): 3–4, 13–16; and the remarks of Andrew S. Draper in "A Story of Lincoln," unidentified clipping, 18 Apr. 1887, Lincoln Museum, Fort Wayne, Ind.

In October 1863, Lincoln sent to Meade through Halleck a telegram stating, among other things, "If Gen. Meade can now attack him [Lee] on a field no worse than equal for us, and will do so with all the skill and courage, which he, his officers and men possess, the honor will be his if he succeeds, and the blame may be mine if he fails." *CWL,* 6:518. On 8 July, Halleck told Meade: "The President is urgent and anxious that your Army should move against him [Lee] by forced marches." Halleck to Meade, 8 July 1863, 12:30 P.M., *The Life and Letters of George Gordon Meade,* ed. George Gordon Meade (New York: Scribner, 1913), 2:308.

71. See General Orders, No. 68, 4 July 1863, *Life and Letters of Meade,* 2:122–23. On 14 July Lincoln wrote Meade a harsh letter: "I do not believe you appreciate the magnitude of the misfortune involved in Lee's escape. He was within your easy grasp, and to have closed upon him would, in connection with our other late successes, have ended the war. As it is, the war will be prolonged indefinitely. . . . Your golden opportunity is gone, and I am distressed immeasurably because of it." Lincoln to Meade, Washington, 14 July 1863, *CWL,* 6:328. Lincoln filed this document away with the endorsement "never sent, or signed," though earlier that day General Halleck had telegraphed Meade that "the escape of Lee's army without another battle has created great dissatisfaction in the mind of the President, and it will require an active and

energetic pursuit on your part to remove the impression that it has not been suffi-ciently active heretofore." Halleck to Meade, 14 July 1863, *CWL*, 6:328. Lincoln later told Meade, "The fruit seemed so ripe, so ready for plucking, that it was very hard to lose it." Quoted in William Swinton, *Campaigns of the Army of the Potomac* (New York: Richardson, 1866).

To Gideon Welles, Lincoln expressed the fear that the Army of the Potomac was determined to allow Lee to escape: "There is bad faith somewhere," he said. "Meade has been pressed and urged, but only one of his generals was for an immediate at-tack . . . on Lee. . . . What does it mean, Mr. Welles? Great God! what does it mean?" *Diary of Welles*, 1:370–71 (entry for 14 July 1863).

72. Where people drink and smoke.

73. Robert Todd Lincoln said that his father wept when he learned that Lee had escaped across the Potomac. Memorandum dated 5 Jan. 1885, enclosed in R. T. Lin-coln to John G. Nicolay, Washington, 5 Jan. 1885, Hay MSS, DLC.

74. Gen. Robert H. Milroy (1816–90) of Indiana had been trapped at Winchester on 13 June and saw 3,400 of his 6,000 men taken prisoner by Confederate forces under Richard Ewell. Robert C. Schenck (1809–90) of Ohio commanded the Mid-dle Department, with headquarters in Baltimore, and was Milroy's superior officer. Lincoln wrote a frank letter to Milroy and an opinion of the subsequent inquiry. See *CWL*, 6:308.

75. "Lt. Col Alexander" may have been Barton Stone Alexander (1819–78), an en-gineer with the Army of the Potomac, who was instrumental in designing and build-ing the defenses of Washington, or T. L. Alexander, about whom Lincoln wrote: "The relations between Col. T. L. Alexander and myself, at the Soldier's Home, have been very agreeable, and I feel great kindness for him and his family." Lincoln to Halleck, Washington, 3 Mar. 1864, *CWL: Supplement 1*, 228. William Whiting (1813–73) was the solicitor of the War Department (1862–65). Braxton Bragg (1817–76), the com-mander of the Confederate Army of Tennessee, left northern Mississippi on 21 July and headed for Chattanogga. Disaffected North Carolinians, calling themselves the "Heroes of America," banded together to resist the Confederacy. Concentrated in the western part of the state and in the Piedmont, they numbered as many as ten thousand.

76. Some authorities support Hay's view, while others dissent. Cf. A. Wilson Greene, "Meade's Pursuit of Lee: From Gettysburg to Falling Waters," in Gary W. Gallagher, ed., *The Third Day at Gettysburg and Beyond* (Chapel Hill: Univ. of North Carolina, 1994), 161–201.

77. On 12 June, Gillmore had replaced Hunter in command of the Army of the South.

78. According to the judge advocate general, the president when reviewing court-martial decisions "shrank with evident pain from even the idea of shedding human blood. . . . In every case he always leaned to the side of mercy. His constant desire was to save life. There was only one class of crimes I always found him prompt to punish—a crime which occurs more or less frequently about all armies—namely, outrages upon women. He never hesitated to approve the sentence in these cases."

Joseph Holt, interview by John G. Nicolay, 29 Oct. 1879, Nicolay MSS, DLC. See also Michael Burlingame, ed., *An Oral History of Abraham Lincoln* (Carbondale: Southern Illinois Univ. Press 1996), 69–70. Of the 276 Union soldiers executed during the Civil War, twenty-two were found guilty of rape. Robert I. Alotta, *Civil War Justice: Union Army Executions under Lincoln* (Shippensburg, Penn.: White Mane, 1989), 30. Alotta notes that Lincoln "provided clemency for all types of military offenders, except rapists" (31). Gen. George Stoneman recalled that late one night at the telegraph office at McClellan's headquarters, Lincoln "arose from his chair to leave, straightened himself up and remarked: 'Tomorrow night I shall have a terrible headache.' When asked the cause, he replied: 'Tomorrow is hangman's day and I shall have to act upon death sentences;' and I shall never forget the sad and sorrowful expression that came over his face." Quoted in Osborn H. Oldroyd, ed., *The Lincoln Memorial: Album Immortelles* (New York: Carleton, 1882), 221.

79. Usher F. Linder (1809–76) was an Illinois lawyer and politician who had frequent contact with Lincoln in the 1840s and 1850s. In 1857 Lincoln allegedly counseled Melissa Grovings, a 70-year-old woman he was defending in a murder trial, that she could find good drinking water in Tennessee; she then disappeared and forfeited her bail bond.

80. Gen. Lee's invasion of the North, written by himself.
  "In Eighteen sixty three, with pomp, and mighty swell
  Me and Jeff's Confederacy, went forth to sack Phil-del,
  The Yankees they got arter us and giv us particular hell,
  And we skedadeled back again, and didn't sack Phil-del."
Written Sunday morning July 19, 1863. Attest John Hay. (*CWL: Supplement 1*, 194)

81. John A. McClernand (1812–1900) commanded the 13th Corps in the Vicksburg campaign until Grant relieved him on 18 June. McClernand claimed credit for the success of that campaign. William Butler (1797–1876) was a good friend of Lincoln in Springfield with whom Lincoln boarded, 1837–42.

82. On 17 June, Montgomery Blair had advocated compulsory colonization of the freed slaves.

83. Phillips had said: "President Lincoln told a Massachusetts Committee—I being one of them—the last week of January 'Gentlemen, I know that I am to lose 200,000 men before the first day of July; I know that when they go out of the ranks the Confederate will time his deadliest effort at that moment, and I mean before that time comes to put the 200,000 muskets which they drop, into the hands of the negroes of the Southern states' . . . pledging himself to have the work finished in sixty days." *The Liberator*, 10 July 1863, in Don E. Fehrenbacher and Virginia Fehrenbacher, eds., *Recollected Words of Abraham Lincoln* (Stanford: Stanford Univ. Press, 1996), 356.

84. The Rev. Dr. Smith Pyne was the minister at St. John's Episcopal Church in Washington. Lee told a friend, "If Virginia stands by the old Union, so will I. But if she secedes (though I do not believe in secession as a constitutional right, nor that there is a sufficient cause for revolution), then I will follow my native State with my

sword, and, if need be, with my life." Quoted in Emory Thomas, *Robert E. Lee: A Biography* (New York: Norton, 1995), 187.

85. See O. O. Howard to Lincoln, 18 July 1863, AL MSS, DLC.

86. See Lincoln to Howard, Washington, 21 July 1863, *CWL*, 6:341.

87. Hamilton R. Gamble (1798–1864) became provisional governor of Missouri in 1861 when the incumbent, Claiborn F. Jackson, sided with the Confederacy. See Gamble to Lincoln, 13 July 1863, AL MSS, DLC. John M. Schofield (1831–1906) was the commander of the Department of Missouri. See Lincoln to Schofield, 27 May, 13 July, and 20 July 1863, and Lincoln to Gamble, Washington, 23 July 1863, *CWL*, 6:234, 326, 338, 344.

88. Horatio Seymour (1810–86) was the governor of New York (1853–55, 1863–65). Draft riots swept through New York, 13–16 July.

89. Southerners had bestowed upon Gen. Benjamin F. Butler, who sought the 1864 presidential nomination, the sobriquet "Beast." Gen. John W. Turner (1833–99) was Gillmore's chief of staff. Gen. George C. Strong (1832–63) had served on Butler's staff in New Orleans.

90. Andrew Jackson Butler (d. 1864), the general's elder brother, had reputedly made a great deal of money through suspect trading practices in New Orleans in 1862.

91. Editor of the influential *New York Tribune*, Horace Greeley (1811–72) had pressed the Lincoln administration in his editorials to launch an offensive against Richmond early in the war. Some blamed him for the fiasco at First Bull Run in July 1861.

92. See Lincoln to Halleck, Washington, 29 July 1863, *CWL*, 6:354.

93. Schurz was in town to discuss the future of the 11th Corps. Evidently, he saw Lincoln this day.

94. See Meade to Lincoln, Warrenton, Va., 30 July 1863, AL MSS, DLC.

95. See Lincoln to Hurlbut, Washington, 31 July 1863, *CWL*, 6:358.

96. William King Sebastian (1812–65) of Arkansas had been expelled from the U.S. Senate in 1861 for disloyalty. The "dilatory and half-hearted" Missouri emancipation ordinance had been passed on 31 July; it offered freedom to slaves under the age of forty at future dates varying from 1870 to 1876.

97. See "Order of Retaliation," 30 July 1863, *CWL*, 6:357.

98. Pennsylvanian John W. Forney (1817–81) was the editor of the *Philadelphia Press* and the *Washington Chronicle*. Lorenzo Thomas (1804–75) was an adjutant general of the army. Forney's new building was the first in Washington devoted exclusively to a newspaper office. Other dignitaries attending the event included generals S. P. Heintzelman and John Henry Martindale as well as secretaries Seward and Welles. Washington correspondence, 1 Aug. 1863, *Chicago Tribune*, 2 Aug. 1863, p. 1. The event is described in detail in the *Washington Chronicle*, 4 Aug. 1863, p. 2.

99. The USS *Baltimore* was a 500-ton steamer used primarily as an ordnance vessel at the Washington Navy Yard. William Faxon (b. 1822), the chief clerk of the Navy Department, had been a Connecticut newspaper publisher before the war. Phineas Jonathan Horwitz (1822–77) was the assistant chief of the Bureau of Medicine and

Surgery in the Navy Department. The party traveled approximately fifty miles down-river and returned around 8 P.M. G. V. Fox to his wife, Washington, 4 Aug. 1863, Fox MSS, New-York Historical Society.

100. Henry A. Wise was the chief of the navy's Bureau of Ordnance and Hydrography. Richmond Aulick was the assistant chief. Five years after the war, Hay recalled: "Wise and Fox and Aulick & I have dined together hundreds of pleasant evenings. I can see them and hear them all tonight. Wise's fantastic fun Fox's lambent humor Leutze's crabbed wit and Aulick's gentle culture. I knew so many clever people in Washington that there will be a sort of insipidity about society the rest of my life, I suppose." Hay to Harriet Loring, Madrid, 30 June 1870, Hay MSS, RPB. In 1857, George Alfred Lawrence (1827–76) published the controversial novel *Guy Livingston, or Thorough*, which scandalized polite society. He tried to join the Confederate army but was arrested by Union forces. Eventually, he was released on the condition that he return immediately to England. His other books included *Sword and Gown* (1859), *Barren Honour* (1862), and *Border and Bastille* (1863). In May Hay had written Nicolay about him: "I see by the papers that Lawrence, the Englishman who wrote Guy Livingston has been caught near Washington going over to the enemy & jugged. I hope you will use all your influence to prevent his getting loose, until I get home & then I will relieve you. It was bad enough for him to write the most immoral novels of the age, but to fall in love with that 'flamboyant deminess' Secessia, is worse. Dont let up on him. Go to Judge Turner & tell him to keep him a while longer. When I get home your mind may be easy." Hay to Nicolay, Hilton Head, S.C., 12 May 1863, Hay MSS, RPB.

101. Byron Sunderland (1819–1901) was the chaplain of the U.S. Senate and the pastor of the First Presbyterian Church in Washington. Phineas D. Gurley (1816–68) was the pastor of the New York Avenue Presbyterian Church.

102. Sen. John P. Hale (1806–73) of New Hampshire chaired the Senate Naval Affairs Committee. Navy Secretary Welles loathed him.

103. See Seymour to Lincoln, Albany, 3 Aug. 1863, AL MSS, DLC.

104. George S. Boutwell (1818–1905) was a prominent lawyer and antislavery Democrat in Massachusetts. In 1850 and 1851, he was chosen governor; in 1855, he was instrumental in organizing the Republican party. From 1863 to 1869, he served in Congress, where he championed the Radical cause. See Lincoln to Banks, Washington, 5 Aug. 1863, *CWL*, 6:364–65.

105. Bullitt was a New Orleans loyalist who served as acting collector of customs in November 1862. He was demoted in the fall of 1863 to naval officer as a rebuke to the Conservative Loyalists. He headed the "Lincoln Club" in 1864, incurring Chase's wrath; the president later that year named him U.S. marshal for Louisiana. He was the brother-in-law of Hugh Kennedy, editor of the *New Orleans True Delta*. Bullitt wrote to Lincoln on 12 August: "On my arrival here I found every piece of official machinery in motion for one object exclusively, namely the advancement president-wise of Mr. Chase." AL MSS, DLC.

106. Photographer Alexander Gardner had been an associate of Matthew Brady; in 1863 he established his own studio at 7th and D Streets.

107. The French had established Maximilian of Austria as emperor of Mexico. Lincoln took a dim view of French meddling in North America. In response to the threat of French intervention in the Civil War, he allegedly said he would "be d——d if he wouldn't get 1,000,000 men if France dares to interfere." Josephine Shaw Lowell diary, 20 May 1862, copy, Allan Nevins MSS, Columbia Univ. See Lincoln to Grant, Washington, 9 Aug. 1863, *CWL*, 6:374.

108. See Rosecrans to Lincoln, Winchester, Tenn., 1 Aug. 1863, AL MSS, DLC.

109. See Lincoln to Rosecrans, Washington, 10 Aug. 1863, *CWL*, 6:377–78.

110. See Lincoln to Seymour, Washington, 7 Aug. 1863, *CWL*, 6:369–70. "Sockdolager" was a slang term for something that settles a matter.

111. See Lincoln to John M. Fleming and Robert Morrow, Washington, 9 Aug. 1863, *CWL*, 6:373. The petition is enclosed in John M. Fleming and Robert Morrow to Lincoln, Washington, 8 Aug. 1863, AL MSS, DLC. Horace Maynard (1814–82), a devout Tennessee Unionist, was the state attorney general (1863–65) and had served in Congress (1857–63). Andrew Johnson (1808–75), a leading Tennessee Unionist, was the military governor of the state. Andrew J. Clements (1832–1913) was a Unionist Congressman from Kentucky.

112. See Seymour to Lincoln, Albany, 8 Aug. 1863, AL MSS, DLC.

113. Seymour's letter of 8 August was read by Lincoln to the cabinet on this date. He answered Seymour on the same day, reducing quotas in more districts but maintaining "the principle to which I purpose adhering—which is to proceed with the draft." Lincoln to Seymour, Washington, 11 Aug. 1863, *CWL*, 6:381–82.

114. See Charles D. Drake to Lincoln, St. Louis, 13 July 1863, Al MSS, DLC. Drake (1811–92), a leading Missouri Radical, represented that state in the U.S. Senate (1867–70).

115. Douglass described this interview at length in *The Life and Times of Frederick Douglass* (1892; reprint, New York: Collier Books, 1962), 346–349. Douglass's plan to join the staff of Gen. Lorenzo Thomas, who was in Mississippi recruiting black troops, fell through when he failed to receive a commission (350).

116. Sculptor Hiram Powers (1805–73) created several statues for the building.

117. The Anti-Masonic movement in New York began in 1826 and lasted into the 1830s.

118. "Brady" was perhaps James T. Brady (1815–1869), a leading New York lawyer who had been the gubernatorial nominee of the New York Democrats favoring states rights in 1860.

119. In 1857–58, President Buchanan sent federal troops to Utah to compel the Mormons to obey federal laws. William Pitt Fessenden (1806–69), a U.S. senator from Maine, served as Lincoln's secretary of the treasury (1864–65).

120. A native of New Hampshire and a Williams College alumnus, Justin Butterfield (1790–1855) practiced law in New York before moving to Chicago, where he became a prominent lawyer. From 1841 to 1844, he was the U.S. district attorney in Chicago. In 1849 Butterfield won the commissionership of the general land office, a post for which Lincoln had fought hard.

121. The secretary of state invited prominent diplomats to join him on a tour of

New York state, evidently to demonstrate the continued prosperity and war potential of the North. Apparently, Hay was unable to accept.

122. Andrew G. Curtin (1815–94), the governor of Pennsylvania, was reelected in October. The feud between Cameron and Curtin dominated Pennsylvania Republican politics.

123. John Conness (1821–1909) was a U.S. senator from California (1863–69). Charles James is listed as the collector and disbursing agent at San Francisco in the 1863 *U.S. Official Register*. Frederick Ferdinand Low (1828–94) served as a representative in Congress from California (1862–63) and as the collector of the Port of San Francisco (1863) until his election later that year as governor of California. The collectors of the major ports were particularly important for dispensing the political patronage controlled by the Treasury Department because of the number of customshouse positions. See *supra*, entry for 6 Aug. 1863.

124. See Lincoln to Meade, Washington, 27 July 1863, *CWL*, 6:350; and Meade to Lincoln, Warrenton, Va., 30 July 1863, AL MSS, DLC.

125. The draft was resumed on 19 August. Gen. John A. Dix (1798–1879) was in command of Union forces in New York. Charles W. Sandford (1796?–1878), mustered out in July 1861, nevertheless helped the Union cause in many informal ways, including efforts to control the draft rioters in New York.

126. See Hurlbut to Lincoln, Memphis, 10 and 11 Aug. 1863, AL MSS, DLC.

127. In 1860 Christopher Miner Spencer (1833–1922) invented a self-loading (repeating) rifle that the U.S. Army adopted; by the end of the war, over 200,000 had been manufactured. The president was presented with Spencer's "seven-shooter magazine rifle" on 17 August and practiced with it on the two succeeding days. Many years later, Spencer described his experiences with the president. See W. A. Bartlett, "Lincoln's Seven Hits with a Rifle," *Boston Transcipt*, n.d., reprinted in *The Magazine of History* 19, no. 73 (1921): 68–72.

William O. Stoddard also accompanied the president on similar occasions. He later recalled:

> On the grounds near the Potomac, south of the White House, was a huge pile of old lumber, not to be damaged by balls, and a good many mornings I have been out there with the President, by previous appointment, to try such rifles as were sent in. There was no danger of hitting any one, and the President, who was a very good shot, enjoyed the relaxation very much. One morning early we were having a good time—he with his favorite "Spencer," and I with a villainous kicking nondescript, with a sort of patent backaction breech, that left my shoulder black and blue—when a squad from some regiment which had just been put on guard in that locality pounced on us for what seemed to them a manifest disobedience of all "regulations." I heard the shout of the officer in command and saw them coming, but as the President was busy drawing a very particular bead—for I had been beating him a little—I said nothing until down they came. In response to a decidedly unceremonious hail, the President, in some astonishment, drew back from his stooping posture, and turned upon them the full length six feet four of their beloved "Commander-in-Chief." They stood and looked one moment, and then fairly

ran away, leaving his Excellency laughing heartily at their needless discomfiture. He only remarked: "Well, they might have stayed and seen the shooting." (Stoddard, "White House Sketches, No. V," *New York Citizen,* 22 Sept. 1866, p. 1)

128. "Lincoln had a quick comprehension of mechanical principles, and often detected a flaw in an invention which the contriver had overlooked. He would sometimes go out into the waste fields that then lay south of the Executive Mansion to test an experimental gun or torpedo. He used to quote with much merriment the solemn dictum of one rural inventor that 'a gun ought not to rekyle; if it rekyled at all, it ought to rekyle a little forrid.'" Hay, "Life in the White House in the Time of Lincoln," Hay MSS, DLC. The essay was published, with slight variations, in *Century Magazine,* Nov. 1890.

129. The former Democratic representative from Carbondale, Ill., John A. Logan (1826–86), was making speeches in Illinois favoring the Lincoln administration.

130. William Clarke Quantrill (1837–65) commanded Confederate guerilla forces in Kansas.

131. The observatory was at 23rd and E Streets. James C. Conkling (1816–99) was an Illinois Republican leader who invited Lincoln to address a Union rally in Springfield in August 1863. See Lincoln to Conkling, Washington, 20 Aug. 1863, *CWL,* 6:399. The long political statement was to be read at "a mass meeting of unconditional pro-Union men" at Springfield on 3 September. Conkling had requested the president's presence, and Lincoln's reply held out a possibility that he could attend. It finally went out on 26 August.

Hay left for a vacation at Long Branch the next day. Before departing, he told Fry: "I am going to the sea-shore; burst not with envy." Hay to Col. James B. Fry, Washington, 24 Aug. 1863, *O. R.,* 3d ser., vol. 3, 712. A Washington dispatch of late August noted: "Col. John Hay, Private Secretary to the President, has gone to Long Branch for a short visit. W. O. Stoddard, Esq., will fill his position until his return." *Illinois Daily State Journal* (Springfield), 28 Aug. 1863, p. 3.

132. The dating of the entries that follow is only an estimate. The handwriting indicates they were made at different times.

133. Richard C. McCormick recalled Lincoln using this image:

[H]e talked at length of the battles of Antietam and South Mountain, and of the difficulty in accounting for the number of men upon the army rolls, yet not in action. He said he had a list of the men in the several corps, provided him by Gen. McClellan, and that he also had a list of those who took part in the battle, and that there was a wonderful discrepancy, for which he could not account except upon the ground that the men were let off by the company officers. He concluded by pronouncing it a most difficult matter to retain men, to put your finger upon them when needed. "They are like fleas," said he, "the more you shovel them up in the corner the more they get away from you." (R. C. McCormick's reminiscences, New York, 29 Apr. 1865, *New York Evening Post,* 5 May 1865, semi-weekly edition, p. 4)

Lincoln used the same image in a conversation with members of the Sanitary Commission on 24 November 1862. One of them recorded that the president "said that the great difficulty was that our army couldn't be got together. . . . He said he couldn't figure out where the leakage was but there stood the fact, & he then made use of the elegant illustration that 'it was just like trying to shovel fleas,—before the shovel load fell the fleas were all gone.'" Horace Howard Furness to his wife, 24 Nov. 1863, *The Letters of Horace Howard Furness*, ed. Henry Howard Furness Jr. (Boston: Houghton Mifflin, 1922), 1:126–27. Another member of the Sanitary Commission, Mary A. Livermore, recalled Lincoln's using this image at that meeting. See Fehrenbacher and Fehrenbacher, *Recollected Words of Lincoln*, 301.

134. Capt. James Madison Cutts Jr., brother of Stephen A. Douglas's second wife, was found guilty of using unbecoming language to Capt. Charles G. Hutton, writing a derogatory complaint about Hutton, and being a Peeping Tom at a Cincinnati hotel. He was convicted on all three counts and sentenced to be cashiered. Lincoln remitted the sentence. A contentious, belligerent soul, Cutts won the Medal of Honor for bravery in combat. See *CWL*, 6:538n. Lincoln's pun on "peeper" alludes to Count Edward Piper, the minister resident of Sweden and Norway.

135. The raid of Confederate cavalryman John Hunt Morgan (1825–64) into Ohio in July 1863 ended with the capture of the Confederate force.

136. Roger B. Taney (b. 1777) of Maryland, the chief justice of the U.S. Supreme Court, did not die until 12 October 1864.

137. The C.S.S. *Arkansas* was destroyed in August 1862.

138. Hay recounted Lincoln's use of this story in November 1863: "The Honest Abraham . . . [told] a story of his friend Jesse Dubois, who, being State Auditor, had control of the State House at Springfield, Ill. An itinerant quack preacher wanted the use of the Representatives Hall to deliver a religious lecture. 'What's it about' said Jesse. 'The Second Coming of Christ' said the parson. 'Nonsense' roared Uncle Jesse, 'If Christ had been to Springfield once, and got away, he'd be damned clear of coming again.'" Hay to Charles G. Halpine, Washington, 22 Nov. 1863, Halpine MSS, Huntington Library, San Marino, Calif.

139. At the Second Battle of Winchester on 14–15 June, over 4,000 Union troops were reported captured or missing. Gen. Robert H. Milroy (1816–90) was widely blamed for the defeat.

140. The Canterbury was a music hall with a dubious reputation. A journalist called it "a sink of corruption . . . whose matinees are attended by the shameless sort of Treasury girls." *New York Citizen*, 27 Oct. 1866. Another correspondent, describing both the Canterbury and the Oxford music halls, labeled them "very low theaters—something between a 'model artist' establishment and a Bowery—where the principal attraction is the 'development' of the female performers, and where *double entendre* always brings down the house." *Cincinnati Commercial*, 4 Dec. 1865. David Kellogg Cartter (1812–87), who had represented an Ohio district in the U.S. House (1849–53), served as the U.S. minister to Bolivia (1861–62) and as the chief justice of the Supreme Court of the District of Columbia (1863–87).

141. "Capt LeRoy" was perhaps Robert Le Roy, an assistant adjutant general of volunteers. Wayne McVeagh (1815–1917) of West Chester served as a major and an aide-de-camp to the general commanding the Pennsylvania home guards.

142. Joseph King Fenno Mansfield (1803–62) was killed at Antietam.

143. Henry J. Raymond remembered Lincoln's saying:

My brother and I were once plowing corn on a Kentucky farm, I driving the horse and he holding the plow. The horse was lazy, but on one occasion rushed across the field so that I, with my long legs, could scarcely keep pace with him. On reaching the end of the furrow, I found an enormous chin-fly fastened upon him, and knocked him off. My brother asked me what I did that for. I told him I didn't want the old horse bitten in that way. "Why," said my brother, "that's all that made him go." Now, if Mr. [Chase] has a presidential chin-fly biting him, I'm not going to knock him off, if it will only make his department *go*. (Quoted in Fehrenbacher and Fehrenbacher, *Recollected Words of Lincoln*, 375–76)

144. Thomas Corwin (1794–1865), formerly a congressman from Ohio, was the U.S. minister to Mexico. "Bob Blackwell" was perhaps Robert S. Blackwell of Rushville, Ill., whom Lincoln had known in the 1840s.

145. Horace Porter recalled Lincoln's telling a different version of this story:

[H]e spoke of the improvement in arms and ammunition, and of the new powder prepared for the fifteen-inch guns. He said he had never seen the latter article, but he understood it differed very much from any other powder that had ever been used. I told him that I happened to have in my tent a specimen which had been sent to headquarters as a curiosity, and that I would bring it to him. When I returned with a grain of the powder about the size of a walnut, he took it, turned it over in his hand, and after examining it carefully, said: "Well, it's rather larger than the powder we used to buy in my shooting days. It reminds me of what occurred once in a country meeting-house in Sangamon County. You see, there were very few newspapers then, and the country storekeepers had to resort to some other means of advertising their wares. If, for instance, the preacher happened to be late in coming to a prayer-meeting of an evening, the shopkeepers would often put in the time while the people were waiting by notifying them of any new arrival of an attractive line of goods. One evening a man rose up and said: 'Brethren, let me take occasion to say, while we're a-waitin', that I have jest received a new inv'ice of sportin' powder. The grains are so small you kin sca'cely see 'em with the naked eye, and polished up so fine you kin stand up and comb yer ha'r in front of one o' them grains jest like it was a lookin'-glass. Hope you'll come down to my store at the cross-roads and examine that powder for yourselves.' When he had got about this far a rival powder-merchant in the meeting, who had been boiling over with indignation at the amount of advertising the opposition powder was getting, jumped up and cried out: 'Brethren, I hope you'll not believe a single word Brother Jones has been sayin' about that powder. I've been down thar and seen it for myself, and I pledge you my word that the grains is bigger than the lumps in a coal-pile; and any one of you, brethren, ef you was in your future state, could put a ar'l o' that powder on your shoulder and march squar' through the sulphurious flames surroundin' you without the least danger of an explosion.'" (*Campaigning with Grant* [New York: Century, 1897], 221–22)

146. Rufus F. Andrews was the assistant to the collector of the Port of New York, Hiram Barney. Henry J. Raymond (1820–69) had established the *New York* Times in 1851 and was its editor. He served in Congress from 1865 to 1867. Editorials in the *New York* Times on 17, 18, 22, and 24 August and 3 September 1863 supported the draft policy of the administration.

147. Count Adam Gurowski (1805–66), who had been a Polish revolutionary, worked in the State Department as a translator.

148. The 95th Annual Commencement at Brown took place on 2 September 1863. The *Providence* Journal of the following day reported that at the close of the dinner, "Professor Lincoln in a few felicitous words, called out the Class Poet of 1858, Mr. John Hay, Private Secretary of President Lincoln. Mr. Hay responded with verses of great beauty and grace, which showed that the lyre, which in former days charmed the hearers, had not lost its charms even in the prosaic atmosphere of Washington."

149. Gen. Daniel Butterfield (1831–1901) was Hooker's chief of staff. On 26 June 1863, Hooker asked permission to evacuate Maryland Heights at Harper's Ferry. The Union reoccupied the position on 7 July. Hooker was relieved of the command of the Army of the Potomac on 27 June. The immediate cause of Hooker's resignation was Halleck's refusal to permit the withdrawal of Union forces from Harper's Ferry.

150. Gen. George Stoneman (1822–94) had commanded the cavalry of the Army of the Potomac under Hooker.

151. The battles of Malvern Hill (1 July 1862) and Fair Oaks (1 June 1862), or Seven Pines, were fought on the Virginia peninsula.

152. Maj. Albert J. Meyer (d. 1880) was McClellan's chief signal officer. On 27 June 1862, the battle of Gaines' Mill was fought on the Virginia peninsula.

153. "Tucker" was probably the assistant secretary of war, John Tucker (1812–83).

154. William B. Franklin (1823–1903) commanded the 6th Corps during the Peninsular campaign. Lincoln shared the belief that McClellan could have seized Richmond after the Battle of Malvern Hill. Henry C. Deming, *Eulogy of Abraham Lincoln* (Hartford: Clark, 1865), 40.

155. Hooker had resigned from the service in 1853 and lived on the West Coast until the outbreak of the war.

156. Eugene de Beauharnais (1781–1824) was the adopted son of Napoleon.

157. See Rosecrans to Halleck, Trenton, Ga., telegram, 8 Sept. 1863, AL MSS, DLC.

158. In a speech the previous month, Blair had advocated readmission of the seceded states and reenfranchisment of former rebels.

159. The merchant George Opdyke (1805–80) was at this time the mayor of New York and a member of the Radical faction in the state's politics. See *infra*, entry for 30 Oct. 1863, and *supra*, entry for 23 Aug. 1863.

160. Wormley's hotel and restaurant on I Street was run by a free black man, James Wormley (1819–84). "Col. Rush" was perhaps Benjamin Rush (1811–77).

161. Edward, the prince of Wales, visited Canada and the United States in 1860. Thomas D'Arcy McGee (1825–68), formerly an Anglophobic Irish expatriate in Boston, was then a Canadian minister and a supporter of the Crown.

162. The Canadian rebellions of 1837–38 were known as the "Patriot War."

163. Gen. John Buford (1826–63) commanded the cavalry of the Army of the Potomac during the Antietam and Fredericksburg campaigns in 1862 and the reserve brigade of cavalry under Hooker in 1863. He had played a distinguished role in the first day's fighting at Gettysburg.

164. Edward Davis Townsend (1817–93) was Scott's chief of staff. George Washington Cullum (1809–92) served on Scott's staff during the early stages of the war. Schuyler Hamilton (1822–1903) was a military secretary to Scott. Horatio G. Wright (1820–99) served as General Heintzelman's chief engineer in 1861.

165. James Longstreet (1821–1904) commanded the 1st Corps of Lee's army.

166. Dr. Elisha K. Kane (1820–57) was an arctic explorer.

167. Fox, Wise, and Halleck had all served in the Mexican War.

168. See *CWL*, 6:440.

169. George Henry Boker (1823–90), a playwright and poet, was the secretary of the Union League of Philadelphia from 1862 to 1871 and a friend of Pennsylvania politicians and journalists like Simon Cameron and John W. Forney. Lincoln had been his father's lawyer in Springfield. "Mrs LeRoy" was perhaps the wife of Capt. Robert Le Roy.

170. Curtin won the governorship in the state elections.

171. When Lincoln received word that Burnside was moving away from Chattanooga and towards Jonesboro, he exclaimed: "Jonesboro? Jonesboro?? D—— Jonesboro!" Quoted in Albert B. Chandler, "As Lincoln Appeared in the War Department," in William Hayes Ward, ed., *Abraham Lincoln: Tributes from His Associates, Reminiscences of Soldiers, Statesmen and Citizens* (New York: Crowell, 1895), 222.

172. George H. Thomas (1816–70) of Virginia earned the sobriquet "The Rock of Chickamauga" for his heroic stand at that battle. When he obliterated John B. Hood's army in November 1864 outside the capital of Tennessee, he added another, "The Sledge of Nashville."

173. Confederate general Benjamin Hardin Helm (1831–63) was the husband of Emilie Todd, Mary Todd Lincoln's half sister. At the outset of the war, Lincoln had unsuccessfully offered Helm, a West Point graduate, the post of paymaster with the rank of major in the Union army. Helm later said, "The most painful moment of my life was when I declined the generous offer of my brother-in-law." Quoted in Katherine Helm, *The True Story of Mary, Wife of Lincoln* (New York: Harper, 1928), 188. David Davis was quoted in 1877 as saying that when Helm was killed at the battle of Chickamauga in September 1863, Lincoln lamented, "I feel as David of old did when he heard of the death of Absalom. 'Would God I had died for thee, O Absalom, my son, my son!'" *Washington City Herald*, n.d., quoted in Emanuel Hertz, ed., *Lincoln Talks: A Biography in Anecdote* (New York: Viking, 1939), 660.

174. The message was not from Rosecrans, but from Charles A. Dana at the general's headquarters. See *O. R.*, 1st ser., vol. 30, pt. 1, 198–199. Dana (1819–97), a journalist who acted as a troubleshooter for the War Department, kept in direct contact

with Stanton and had great influence in molding the president's and the War Department's opinions of Rosecrans's conduct during and after the battle. In January 1864, he became the assistant secretary of war. Alexander M. McCook (1831–1903), the brother of Stanton's former law partner, was blamed by Rosecrans for the debacle at Chickamauga. Though cleared, McCook saw his reputation so badly injured that he was denied any further field commands. At Chickamauga, Thomas L. Crittenden (1819–93) commanded the 21st Corps, which was sent reeling by the Confederate attack. McCook and Crittenden were relieved on 28 September.

175. Peter H. Watson, the shrewd and energetic assistant secretary of war, was the nation's foremost patent lawyer. Maj. James Allen Hardie (1823–76) was the assistant adjutant general of the Army of the Potomac. Col. Daniel C. McCallum (1815–78) was the director of military railroads. The movement of the 11th and 12th Corps was one of the war's major feats of railroad transportation.

176. Gen. Henry Warner Slocum (1827–94) commanded the 12th Corps of the Army of the Potomac (1862–63). Slocum, refusing to serve under Hooker, had submitted his resignation.

177. At Lincoln's suggestion, Stanton consulted with Halleck about Burnside's request for instructions. Burnside feared that his movement to aid Rosecrans would mean the abandonment of East Tennessee. *O. R.*, 1st ser., vol. 30, pt. 3, 883, 904. Lincoln himself replied to Burnside twice that evening. See *CWL*, 6:483–84. Halleck also telegraphed. See *O. R.*, 1st ser., vol. 30, pt. 3, 906.

178. Hay had hoped to join Hooker's staff. Gen. Ambrose Powell Hill (1825–65) was one of Lee's corps commanders.

179. The Radical delegations from Missouri and Kansas came to Washington in the wake of the Lawrence massacre, 21–22 August, perpetrated by William C. Quantrill and his bushwackers. A Republican leader from Keokuk, Iowa, Taylor had been appointed a mail agent in Kansas at the behest of Jim Lane. He lined up support for Lincoln and Lane. See Taylor to David Davis, Lawrence, Kans., 12 Sept. 1864, David Davis MSS, IHi.

180. Cartter saw Lincoln about Missouri matters on 1 October.

181. In their biography of Lincoln, Nicolay and Hay enclose part of this sentence, from "if they can show" to the end, in quotation marks, indicating that these were Lincoln's exact words. *Lincoln*, 8:214.

182. See Lincoln to Schofield, Washington, 22 June 1863, and Schofield to Lincoln, 20 June 1863, *CWL*, 6:291, 289n.

183. See *CWL*, 6:486–87.

184. For Hay's verbatim minutes of this meeting, see Nicolay-Hay MSS, IHi.

185. Simon P. Hanscom, one of Lincoln's favorite journalists, edited the *Washington National Republican*. Hay and his brother Gus were to return home the next day for a vacation.

186. John Brough (1811–65) was the governor of Ohio. Samuel Galloway (1811–72) was a Republican congressman from Ohio.

187. "A. L." was Hay's brother, Augustus Leonard.

188. David Tod (1805–68) was the governor of Ohio (1861–63).

189. Hay's elder sister married Austin Coleman Woolfolk, a captain and quarter-master in the Union army. After the war, he became a circuit court judge. Because of failing health, he moved to Denver.

190. Congressman Shelby M. Cullom (1829–1914) of Springfield had been the Speaker of the Illinois House of Representatives (1861). Milton Hay (1817–93), the uncle of John Hay, was a Springfield lawyer and friend of Lincoln. The appointment of former newspaper editor Mark William Delahay (1817–79), whose wife was dis-tantly related to Lincoln, provoked serious criticism. Stephen Trigg Logan (1800–80) had been Lincoln's second law partner (1841–44).

Two historians deemed the president's choice of Delahay "the most disastrous of Lincoln's personal appointments." Harry J. Carman and Reinhard H. Luthin, *Lincoln and the Patronage* (New York: Columbia Univ. Press, 1943), 118. A contemporary called Delahay "an empty-headed, self-puffing vain-glorious strut." *New York Herald*, 9 Dec. 1860, in Carman and Luthin, *Lincoln and the Patronage*, 77. Grimshaw protested to Lyman Trumbull: "Will the Senate confirm that miserable man Dela-hay for Judge in Kansas. The appointment is disgraceful to the President who knew Delahay and all his faults, but the disgrace will be greater if the Senate confirms him. He is no lawyer, could not try a case properly even in a Justice's Court, and has no character." Grimshaw to Trumbull, 16 Nov. 1863, quoted in Carman and Luthin, *Lincoln and the Patronage*, 118. He resigned from the bench in the midst of impeach-ment proceedings against him.

191. The Republicans carried these two critically important "October states." This day Lincoln told Welles that "he had more anxiety in regard to the election results of yesterday than he had in 1860 when he was chosen." *Diary of Welles*, 1:470 (entry for 14 Oct. 1863).

192. "Marston" was William H. Marston of 26 Wall Street.

193. At the urging of his Springfield friend Robert Irwin, Lincoln had overruled Treasury Secretary Chase and appointed George Denison (or Dennison) the naval officer for the Port of New York in 1861.

194. A radical antislavery leader, Henry B. Stanton (1805–87) had been appointed by Lincoln to an important post in the New York Custom House in 1861. His wife, the well-known abolitionist and feminist Elizabeth Cady Stanton (1815–1902), had helped launch the women's rights movement at Seneca Falls, N.Y., in 1848. Patron-age problems in the New York Custom House had long plagued Lincoln.

195. William Maxwell Evarts (1818–1901) was a prominent New York lawyer, politi-cian, and diplomat.

196. Chase's plan to woo the Radicals and capture the presidential nomination in 1864 was well advanced. Attorney General Bates noted on 17 October: "Chase's head is turned by his eagerness in pursuit of the presidency. For a long time back he has been filling all the offices in his own vast patronage, with extreme partizans, and con-trives also to fill many vacancies, properly belonging to other departments." *The Diary of Edward Bates, 1859–1866*, ed. Howard K. Beale (Washington, D.C.: Govern-ment Printing Office, 1933), 310.

197. Hamilton R. Gamble (1798–1864) became the provisional governor of Mis-

souri in June 1861 when the elected governor, Claiborne Jackson, joined the Confederacy. For Lincoln's reply, see *CWL*, 6:499–504, 526–27.

198. Attorney and politician Joseph Gillespie (1809–85) was a good friend of Lincoln and a judge of the Illinois state circuit court (1861–73).

199. On 14 October, near Bristoe Station, Va., Lee unsuccessfully attacked Union forces.

200. See *O. R.*, 1st ser., vol. 29, pt. 2, 345.

201. William H. Kent wrote for the *New York Tribune*. Adams S. Hill, a Harvard graduate, was a principal Washington correspondent for the *Tribune*. Henry Villard called him "a sharp-witted and indefatigable collector of news." *Memoirs*, 1:339.

202. Lincoln removed Rosecrans at Grant's request.

203. Titian J. Coffey (1824–67) of Pennsylvania had studied law in St. Louis with Edward Bates, who had him appointed the assistant attorney general. John Covode (1808–71) represented a Pennsylvania district in the U.S. House (1855–63) and served on the Joint Committee on the Conduct of the War. William B. Mann (b. 1816), the U.S. district attorney in Philadelphia, was a well-known political manager who allegedly helped Simon Cameron bribe Pennsylvania legislators in 1857. See *CWL*, 4:165.

204. Gen. Daniel E. Sickles (1825–1914) commanded the 3rd Corps of the Army of the Potomac. He became notorious in 1859 when he murdered his wife's paramour. At the battle of Gettysburg, he lost a leg.

205. "Andrews" was perhaps Timothy Patrick Andrews (1794–1868), the paymaster general of the army. Gen. William Henry French (1815–81), the commander of the 3rd Corps in the Army of the Potomac, saw his career ruined when Hooker charged him with tardiness in bringing up his troops in the Mine Run campaign the following month.

206. Charles G. Halpine used the pen name "Miles O'Reilly".

207. Stephen C. Rowan (1808–90), the commander of the *New Ironsides*, took charge of Union naval forces in North Carolina in 1864. In July, Dahlgren had assumed command of the South Atlantic Fleet from Du Pont and remained in charge till war's end. Upon Dahlgren's appointment, Welles noted: "As a bureau officer he is capable and intelligent, but he shuns and evades responsibility." Four months later Welles noted: "Dahlgren has been feeble from illness. He is proud and very sensitive and the strictures of the press he would feel keenly. . . . His cold, selfish and ambitious nature has been wounded." *Diary of Welles*, 1:341, 475 (entries for 23 June and 24 Oct. 1863).

208. This letter is no longer extant. Hay added a note to this entry: "March, 1878. I was not old enough to know that a good idea is worthless in the hands of a 'humbug.'"

209. Indiana politician John Palmer Usher (1816–89) became the secretary of the interior on 3 January 1863. Lucius H. Chandler and Sen. Lemuel Jackson Bowden (1815–64), both of Norfolk, were in Washington to appeal for the life of their client, Dr. David Minton Wright (1809–63) of Norfolk, who had been condemned to death for the July 1863 murder of a white Union officer drilling black troops. The two attorneys pleaded an insanity defense to Lincoln, who carefully reviewed the case and

consulted with mental health experts. He upheld the death sentence, which was carried out on 23 October. Allen D. Spiegel, "Abraham Lincoln and the Insanity Plea," *Lincoln Herald* 97 (summer 1995): 60–70. Joel Parker (1816–88) was elected the governor as a Democrat in 1862.

210. "Bibb" was perhaps William C. Bibb, a Unionist from Montgomery, Ala. See W. C. Bibb to Lincoln, Washington, 12 Apr. 1865, AL MSS, DLC; and *The Diary of Orville Hickman Browning*, ed. Theodore Calvin Pease and James G. Randall (Springfield: Illinois State Historical Library, 1925, 1933) 2:16, 17 (entries for 1 and 12 Apr. 1865).

211. Hay added a manuscript note to this entry, evidently in 1878: "He selected for this work Amasa Stone of Cleveland [Hay's father-in-law] & appointed him a Brigadier General for the purpose."

212. "Rogers" was perhaps Henry Munroe Rogers (1839–1937), an assistant paymaster in the navy who had been a classmate of Robert Todd Lincoln at Harvard. See Rogers, *Memories of Ninety Years* (Boston: Houghton Mifflin, 1928), 70–75. "Taylor" was perhaps William Rogers Taylor (1811–89), USN, Admiral Dahlgren's chief of staff.

213. In an address delivered on 3 October at Rockville, Md., Blair denounced Sumner's reconstruction plan: "The Abolition party, whilst pronouncing philippics against slavery, seek to make a caste of another color by amalgamating the black element with the free white labor of our land and so to expand far beyond the present confines of slavery the evil which makes it obnoxious to republican statesmen. And now . . . they would make the manumission of the slaves the means of infusing their blood into our whole system by blending with it 'amalgamation, equality and fraternity.'" Quoted in William Ernest Smith, *The Francis Preston Blair Family in Politics* (New York: Macmillan, 1933), 2:238. Thomas Swann (1809–83) was a conservative Unionist elected the governor of Maryland in 1864. Henry Winter Davis (1817–65), Montgomery Blair's chief rival in Maryland politics, was a bitter opponent of the Lincoln administration. He represented a Maryland district in the U.S. House (1855–61, 1863–65).

214. Francis Thomas (1799–1876) of Maryland had been the governor of that state (1841–44) and served in the U.S. House (1831–41, 1861–69). John A. J. Creswell (1828–91) of Baltimore won his bid for a seat in the U.S. House in the fall. He later served as a U.S. senator from Maryland (1865–67). The previous day Lincoln purportedly told a delegation of Marylanders who protested against the recruitment of blacks in their state "that if the recruiting squads did not conduct themselves properly, their places should be supplied by others, but that the orders under which the enlistments were being made could not be revoked, since the country needed ablebodied soldiers, and was not squeamish as to their complexion." Washington correspondence, 21 Oct. 1863, *New York Tribune*, 22 Oct. 1863, p. 1. William Birney (1819–1907), the son of the abolitionist James G. Birney, commanded the 22nd U.S. Colored Troops. He recruited seven black regiments, liberated the prisoners in the Baltimore slave jails, and worked hard to get Maryland to emancipate her slaves. On 21 October, Lt. Eben White of the 7th U.S. Colored Troops was killed by the slaveholder John H. Sothoron and his son at Benedict, Md. A former member of the

Maryland legislature, Sothoron was about to be arrested for recruiting Maryland citizens into the Confederate army. Baltimore correspondence, 22 Oct. 1863, *New York
Tribune*, 23 Oct. 1863, p. 1. He and his son escaped to Richmond and avoided all prosecution. The president summoned Schenck and his chief of staff, Donn Piatt, to
Washington, where they received a dressing down. Piatt later wrote, "I do not care
to recall the words of Mr. Lincoln. . . . They were exceedingly severe, for the President was in a rage." *Memories of the Men Who Saved the Union* (New York: Belford,
Clarke, 1887), 44–45.

215. A social reformer from Indiana, Owen (1801–77) chaired a commission to inquire into the condition of the freed slaves. A vehicle for the celebrated actress Maggie Mitchell, "The Pearl of Savoy" was an adaptation of Gaetano Rossi's *Linda di
Chamounix*.

216. Dr. Robert King Stone, a professor of medicine and ophthalmology at Columbia Medical College, was the White House physician.

217. Schenk's chief aide Donn Piatt (1819–91) was a lawyer and a journalist from
Ohio.

218. Charles G. Halpine's story in the *New York Herald*, 23 October, described
"Miles O'Reilly's" dinner. Hay later noted, perhaps in 1878, that "I cannot make out
this word," referring to what is rendered here as "Mr K's." Perhaps "K" is William D.
("Pig Iron") Kelley (1814–90), a leading Radical from Philadelphia, who served in
the U.S. House (1861–90).

219. "Dana" was the journalist Charles A. Dana.

220. Acting Master Charles B. Dahlgren (1839–1912) had just returned with dispatches from his father's squadron.

221. On the previous day, Terry and Hawley had called on Gideon Welles and had
denounced Admiral Dahlgren "as incompetent, imbecile, and insane . . . [and] totally unfit for his position." *Diary of Welles*, 1:474–75 (entry for 24 Oct. 1863).

222. The lull in the shelling of Charleston ended on 26 October.

223. Oliver Spencer Halstead Jr. (1819–71), a notable lawyer and lobbyist from
Newark, N.J., moved to Washington in 1861 and returned to Newark in 1865. Horatio Ames, an ironmaster from Falls Village, Conn., manufactured wrought-iron rifled cannon that, in his view, had been unfairly rejected by the Navy Department.
Ames felt that Adm. John Dahlgren, who had invented a cannon himself, had not
tested Ames's weapon adequately. Augustus Brandegee (1828–1904) was a congressman from southeast Connecticut (1863–67).

A *New York Tribune* account depicted Halstead as more than "a mere uncon-
scionable braggart; his was a swagger which was more than magnificent. He went
everywhere, knew everybody, and cut a large figure in social as well as political life.
There was nothing he did not know—nothing he could not do. There were no
bounds to his ambition and no limit to his glowing imagination. He was lavish in
his expenditure and as generous as a prince, when he had money; and when money
failed him, his credit was liberally bestowed." Quoted in Robert V. Bruce, *Lincoln and
the Tools of War* (Indianapolis: Bobbs-Merrill, 1956), 231.

In late September, Brandegee and Ames had called at the White House to ask that

Ames's cannon be given new and fair tests. Years later Brandegee described the interviews with Lincoln thus:

> As he rose—and seemed to keep on rising—before me, his hair was black, coarse and of an unkempt appearance, his nose prominent, his cheek bones high, his cheeks very hollow, his complexion swarthy, his manner gracious but subdued, while his eyes had an expression that I find myself incapable of describing, as though they lay in ambush in their deep caverns, ready to spring forth or retreat further within, as occasion required. He was awkward, but it was the awkwardness of nature, which is akin to grace. The expression of his face was earnest, with a shade of sadness, and his voice was soft, and at times as tender as a woman's.
>
> I had prepared what I thought a neat little speech of introduction, but he at once put my rhetoric and embarrassment to flight by taking me by the hand and saying, "Well, what does little Connecticut want?"
>
> The tone, the familiar address, the friendly manner, the gracious smile at once put me at my ease, and I stated my case as to a friend and almost an equal. As I proceeded with gathering warmth, commenting upon the unfairness of submitting the Connecticut invention to a rival gun-maker, the unfriendly tests adopted and the supreme importance of a gun which would do more execution at the muzzle than at the breech, Mr. Lincoln listened with evident interest. Ames had stated that a record existed of the various charges, the number of firings, and the respective results to each gun, and that it would vindicate all he claimed, but he had been denied access to it. Mr. Lincoln closed the interview by requesting me to procure it, and bring it to him at 8 o'clock that evening. And to my suggestion that I was unknown at the [Navy] department, he took an Executive envelope from a bundle which lay always on his table and wrote the following: "Let Mr. ———, of Connecticut, have a copy of such record as he indicates. A. Lincoln."

That evening Brandegee called again at the White House. He later wrote of the meeting:

> Mr. Lincoln sat at an office desk, under which his long legs protruded to an extent which made them conspicuous. At first he had on a pair of carpet slippers, but as the conversation progressed he unconsciously withdrew his feet, disclosing what seemed to be a pair of dark yarn stockings, through which had worked his great toe, and this he kept in almost perpetual motion.
>
> The record [of tests at the Navy Department] verified the claim of Mr. Ames, and after much discussion and searching questions Mr. Lincoln took an Executive envelope and wrote the following: "If Horatio Ames will make ten wrought iron guns after his method, which will answer satisfactorily such tests as I shall order, I will see that he gets paid $1 per pound for each gun. A. Lincoln." (*New York Tribune*, 23 Jan. 1887, p. 1)

224. Col. J. Henry Puleston, a native of England, was a military agent of Pennsylvania and a longtime resident of the state, where he became deeply involved in politics. After the Civil War, he returned to England and entered Parliament as the representative of Davenport. *Forney's Progress*, 2 Aug. 1879. George B. McClellan wrote to the chairman of the Pennsylvania Democratic party endorsing Judge George W. Woodward, the Democratic gubernatorial candidate running against Curtin. The last sentence of this paragraph was uttered by Curtin. See Nicolay and Hay, *Lincoln*, 7:376n.

225. Homer G. Plantz, a Treasury clerk who served as Chase's secretary, was appointed to this post on 3 November. Washington correspondence, 3 Nov. 1863, *New York Times*, 4 Nov. 1863, p. 4. Elisha Peyre Ferry (1825–95), a lawyer and politician of Waukegan, Ill., was appointed the tax commissioner for Tennessee. After the war, Ferry served as the governor of the Territory of Washington and retained the governorship when Washington became a state.

226. Capt. Charles G. Hutton, an aide-de-camp to General Burnside, had challenged Capt. J. Madison Cutts to a duel. For this offense, he was dismissed from the service on 28 September; he was reappointed on 30 October.

227. This document was not discovered in its entirety until 1947, when the Lincoln papers at the Library of Congress were opened to the public. Tyler Dennett did not include it in his edition of the Hay diary, which appeared in 1939. In their compilation of Lincoln's works, Nicolay and Hay published an excerpt as a footnote to Lincoln to W. G. Anderson, 31 Oct. 1840.

228. See *CWL*, 6:533–34.

229. George W. Beardslee invented a portable military telegraph and an electric detonating system. Hay ate at Harvey's Oyster Saloon.

230. Hay originally wrote "Butler" but later changed it to "Boteler."

231. "Ritchie" was perhaps Capt. Montgomery Ritchie, who had been on the staff of generals Reno and Burnside. On 11 November, one "M. Ritchie" thanked Hay for his kindness in introducing him to Kate Chase. Hay MSS, RPB.

232. See *CWL*, 6:543–44.

233. Lincoln's problems with the Radicals had more to do with their style than with their ideology. He and they shared much in common. See *infra*, entry for 4 July 1864. Lincoln, however, objected to "the self-righteousness of the Abolitionists," as he told William D. Kelley. Kelley to the editor of the *New York Tribune*, Philadelphia, 23 Sept. 1885, in William D. Kelley, *Lincoln and Stanton* (New York: Putnam's, 1885), 86. According to Eli Thayer, Lincoln spoke of abolitionists "in terms of contempt and derision." Quoted in an undated memorandum by F. P. Rice, Eli Thayer MSS, RPB. That was true of at least one "well-known abolitionist and orator" whom he called "a thistle" and about whom he exclaimed, "I don't see why God lets him live!" Quoted in John Eaton, *Grant, Lincoln and the Freedmen* (New York: Longmans, Green, 1907), 184.

234. Union forces on 26 October had resumed the bombardment of Charleston, which lasted forty-one days. But the city held out and was not captured until 18 February 1865.

235. Gen. Henry W. Benham (1813–84) was the chief engineer of the Army of the Potomac.

236. Albert Marshman Palmer (1838–1905), confidential secretary to the collector of the Port of New York, Hiram Barney, was thought to be "the Collector *de facto.*" Whitman knew Hay well enough to call on him at the White House. It is possible that such political services were responsible for the poet's appointment to a clerkship in the Interior Department in 1865.

237. Gen. James A. Garfield (1831–81), Rosecrans's chief of staff, resigned his commission in December to represent Ohio in the U.S. House. In 1880 he was elected president. Nicolay was in Colorado helping to arrange a treaty with the Ute Indians.

238. Conservative Unionist Emerson Etheridge (1819–1902), a slaveholder from west Tennessee, was the clerk of the U.S. House. He hoped to disqualify many Republican representatives on a technicality. Lincoln sent his letter to three senators, James W. Grimes, Zachariah Chandler, and Jacob Collamer, as well as to Vice President Hannibal Hamlin. See *CWL*, 6:546–50.

239. John R. Briggs Jr., the assistant clerk to the U.S. House, visited Lincoln on 23 October. For his letter about heading off Etheridge's plot, see Briggs to Lincoln, Washington, 24 Oct. 1863, AL MSS, DLC.

240. Gen. James Blair Steedmen (1817–83) led his division so ably that he virtually saved the day for the Union army.

241. A year later, on the night before it was announced that he had appointed Chase as the chief justice of the Supreme Court, Lincoln told an unidentifed Massachusetts politician that Chase's "head was so full of Presidential *maggots* he would never be able to get them out" and that his overweening ambition might interfere with the execution of his judicial duties. Quoted in [John B. Alley?] to Josiah G. Holland, Washington, 8 Aug. 1865, J. G. Holland MSS, New York Public Library. The president named Chase to the high court despite his own personal feelings, for he would, to use his own language, "rather have swallowed his buckhorn chair" or "have eat[en] flat irons" than to have made that appointment. William E. Chandler, quoting Lincoln, in *Diary of Welles*, 2:196 (entry for 15 Dec. 1864); Lincoln, quoted in Virginia Fox diary, 10 Dec. 1864, in *Lincoln Day by Day: A Chronology, 1809–1865*, ed. Earl Schenck Miers (Washington, D.C.: Lincoln Sesquicentennial Commission, 1960), 3:301.

242. An accomplice in the crime.

243. William H. Aspinwall (1807–75) was a New York merchant and a philanthropist. Charles Henry Marshall (1792–1865) was a New York merchant, a member of the Union Defense Committee, and the president of the Union League of New York.

244. "Webster" was perhaps Erastus D. Webster, a frequent correspondent of Seward. "Murphy" was perhaps Thomas Murphy, a New York ward heeler who became the collector of the Port of New York in 1870. "Smalley" was perhaps journalist George W. Smalley (1833–1916) of the *New York Tribune*. In 1862 Joseph K. Barnes (1817–83) replaced William Alexander Hammond (1828–1900) as the surgeon general. He was at Lincoln's bedside when the president died.

245. Rosecrans, who had been removed from the command of the Department of the Cumberland on 17 October, was given command of the Department of Missouri on 22 January 1864.

246. Theodore Tilton (1835–1907), an abolitionist who championed women's rights, edited the *New York Independent*. He objected to the president's letter to the Missouri Radicals.

247. "Captain de Lacy" was perhaps William de Lacy of the 37th New York Infantry.

248. Augustus Waldauer's *Fanchon, the Cricket: A Domestic Drama in Five Acts, from a Tale of Georges Sand*, starring Maggie Mitchell, was given at Ford's Theater, which had opened in August 1863. This was Lincoln's first visit to the new theater.

249. The visit took place on 16 January 1861. John T. Hogeboom, the general appraiser in the New York Custom House, was a friend of Salmon Chase and belonged to the Old Democrat faction in New York politics.

250. See *supra*, entry for 17 Oct. 1863.

251. David Dudley Field (1805–94) was a prominent New York lawyer and a member of the Old Democrat faction of the New York Republican Party. This interview had taken place on 17 January 1863. According to one source, it was "unpleasant," with Lincoln "distinctly avowing his belief that the Government was better informed as to the necessities of the country than outsiders could be, no matter how able or intelligent." Washington correspondence, 18 Jan. 1863, *New York Times*, 19 Jan. 1863, p. 4.

252. Cf. *Lincoln's Third Secretary: The Memoirs of William O. Stoddard*, ed. William O. Stoddard Jr. (New York: Exposition, 1955), 192–93. In 1878 Stoddard was accused of having availed himself of inside information to gamble in stocks and bonds. See Stoddard to Hay, Brooklyn, 13 Mar. 1878, Hay MSS, RPB.

253. "Chad" was perhaps Adm. Charles Henry Davis (1807–77), the chief of the Bureau of Navigation in the Navy Department.

254. "Kelley" was Congressman William D. Kelley of Pennsylvania.

255. See *supra*, entry for 22 Oct. 1863.

256. A prominent Virginia Unionist, Botts (1802–69) was arrested by the Confederate government during the war.

257. John Woodland Crisfield (1806–97) represented a Maryland district in the U.S. House (1847–49, 1861–63).

258. The engagement at Wauhatchie took place on 28 October.

259. George Hunt Pendleton (1825–89), a Democratic representative from Ohio (1857–65), was to be George B. McClellan's vice presidential running mate in 1864. See *infra*, entry for 21 Nov. 1863.

260. Reid (1837–1912), a correspondent for the *Cincinnati Gazette* (1861–65), became an intimate friend of Hay's after the war.

261. Augustus Williamson Bradford (1806–81) was the governor of Maryland (1862–66).

262. Samuel Wilkeson, a native of Buffalo and a graduate of Union College, headed the Washington bureau of the *New York Tribune*. Before the war, he had been

an editor and part owner of Thurlow Weed's *Albany Evening Journal,* but after a falling out with Weed, Wilkeson joined forces with Horace Greeley, Weed's nemesis in New York politics.

263. Gen. John G. Foster (1823–74) at this time headed the Department of Virginia and North Carolina. Burnside resigned his post with the Department of the Ohio on 22 October but did not turn over the command to Foster till 11 December. Butler took command of the Department of Virginia and North Carolina on 11 November.

264. See *CWL,* 6:555–58.

265. Col. Edward Sewall Sanford (1827?–82), a former president of the American Telegraph Company, was the military supervisor of the telegraph. His dispatch is not among the AL MSS, DLC. The Republicans made significant gains in the New York state elections.

266. Judge Lyman D. Stickney was a Northern-born Florida Unionist who served as the superintendent of freedmen in his adopted state. A friend of Salmon Chase, the judge speculated financially and politically. He was accused of corruption and misfeasance in office. See Herbert Reed to Salmon P. Chase, New York, 3 Nov. 1863, Chase MSS, DLC; U.S. House, 38th Cong., 2nd sess., 1864, Executive Doc. 18; and *infra,* entries for 28 Dec. 1863, 3 and 7 Mar. 1864.

267. For three months, Nicolay had been in the West, helping to negotiate a treaty with the Ute Indians.

268. Meade crossed the Rappahannock on 7 November, forcing Lee to retreat to the line of the Rapidan. Grant's move, to be led by Gen. George H. Thomas, was countermanded.

269. Seward refers here to Robert Augustus Toombs (1810–85) of Georgia, Jefferson Davis, and John C. Breckinridge (1821–75) of Kentucky.

270. Eduoard Henri Mercier (1816–86) was France's minister to the United States (1860–63).

271. Charles Selby (1802?–63) based his play *The Marble Heart, or The Sculptor's Dream* (first performed in 1854) on the 1853 play by Theodore Barriere and Lambert Thiboust, *Les Filles de Marbre.* Earlier in 1863, the *Washington Chronicle* announced that Booth, a "popular young tragedian, who appears to have taken our citizens by storm," would play the roles of Phidias and Raphael in "the beautiful emotional play," *The Marble Heart.* "The performance of these characters by Mr. Booth has won the highest encomiums from the press and the public wherever he has appeared." *Washington Chronicle,* 29 Apr. 1863, p. 3.

According to George Alfred Townsend, Lincoln "applauded the actor [Booth] rapturously, and with all the genial heartiness for which he was distinguished. Booth, when told of the President's delight, said to his informant that he would rather have the applause of a Nigger. The President sent word back stage that he would like to make the actor's acquaintance, but Booth evaded the interview." *New York World,* 19 Apr. 1865, quoted in David Rankin Barbee, "Mr. Lincoln Goes to the Theater," Barbee MSS, Georgetown Univ., 46. The actor Frank Mordaunt, a member of the National Theater Stock Company, corroborated Townsend's account: "President

Lincoln was an admirer of the man who assassinated him. I know that, for he said to me one day that there was a young actor over in Ford's Theater whom he desired to meet, but that the actor had on one pretext or another avoided any invitations to visit the White House. That actor was John Wilkes Booth." *Chicago Inter-Ocean,* 10 June 1905. Lincoln had seen Booth in *Richard III, Hamlet,* and other plays. See Barbee, "Mr. Lincoln," 44–48.

272. Janet (Nettie) Ralston Chase (1847–1925) was Kate Chase's younger sister. "Miss Nichols" was perhaps Ida Nichols, the niece of William Sprague. "Miss Skinner" was perhaps Helen Skinner, the niece of Salmon P. Chase. "Albrecht" was perhaps Claire Albrecht, who is mentioned in Chase's diary entries for 3 and 8 Sept. 1864. *The Salmon P. Chase Papers,* vol. 1, *Journals, 1829–1872,* ed. John Niven (Kent, Ohio: Kent State Univ. Press, 1993), 499, 501. "Capt. Ives" was perhaps Thomas P. Ives. One "M. (Montgomery?) Ritchie" apologized the next day. Ritchie to Hay, Washington, 11 Nov. 1863, Hay MSS, RPB.

273. The son of Adm. John Dahlgren, Ulric Dahlgren (1842–64) had lost a leg at Gettysburg and was later killed while participating in Judson Kilpatrick's raid on Richmond. Gen. Julius Stahel (1825–1912) was a cavalry commander. "Kirkland" was perhaps the "Maj. Kirkland" listed in the 1863 Washington city directory, or perhaps E. L. Kirkland, listed in the 1864 directory as a clerk in the Pension Office. William Wheatley (1816–76), an actor and theater manager, was at the time managing Niblo's Garden in New York.

274. French S. Evans, editor of the *Baltimore Patriot,* had been persecuted for his Unionism; Lincoln insisted that he be given a government post, and he became deputy naval officer at Baltimore in 1861. Lincoln to Francis S. Corkran, Washington, 6 May 1861, *CWL,* 4:485. Henry W. Hoffman was the collector of the Port of Baltimore.

275. Mary Lincoln refused to attend Kate Chase's wedding and wanted her husband to boycott that occasion, the social event of the season.

276. Joseph Bertinatti was Italy's minister to the United States. Isola and Martinez were members of the Italian navy. Cora was the secretary of the Italian legation. Charlotte Brooks Everett Wise, the daughter of Edward Everett, was married to Henry A. Wise. McDougal was a member of the Canadian ministry.

277. Radical William W. Edwards of St. Charles, the U.S. district attorney for the Eastern District of Missouri, had been removed by Bates for "active participation in political enterprises hostile to the known views and wishes of the Executive Government of both the nation and State." Bates to Edwards, Washington, 2 Nov. 1863, Washington correspondence, 16 Nov. 1863, *New York Times,* 17 Nov. 1863, p. 1; *Diary of Bates,* 460 (entry for 10 Mar. 1865). See *infra,* entry for 9 Dec. 1863.

278. Judge David Wills had originated the idea to establish the military cemetery and was in charge of arrangements. He invited the president not only to speak at the ceremony but also to stay at his house, which Lincoln did. Edwin Lamson Stanton (1842–77) assisted his father, Edwin M. Stanton, at the War Department. Harris Charles Fahnestock (1835–1914) was a banker whose family came from Harrisburg and Ephrata, Penn. With Henry D. Cooke, Fahnestock ran the Washington branch

of Jay Cooke's banking house. The dignitaries accompanying Lincoln spent the night at his house. Cornelius Cole, "Lincoln's Gettysburg Address," *The Wesleyan Alumnus* 6, no. 6 (July 1922): 5.

279. See *supra*, entry for 13 Aug. 1863.

280. See *CWL*, 7:16–17.

281. "Shannon" was probably the Hon. P. C. Shannon of Pittsburgh.

282. John Russell Young (1840–99) was the managing editor of Forney's newspapers, the *Philadelphia Press* and the *Washington Chronicle*.

283. Thomas H. Stockton (1808–68) was the chaplain of the U.S. Senate.

284. Edwin D. Morgan (1811–83) served as the governor of New York (1859–63) and as a U.S. senator (1863–69). Zachariah Chandler had told the president that Weed, Seward, and Blair "are a millstone about your neck." Chandler to Lincoln, Detroit, 15 Nov. 1863, AL MSS, DLC.

285. Everett wrote on 20 November: "Permit me . . . to express my great admiration of the thoughts expressed by you, with such eloquent simplicity & appropriateness, at the consecration of the Cemetery. I should be glad, if I could flatter myself that I came as near to the central idea of the occasion, in two hours, as you did in two minutes." AL MSS, DLC. For Lincoln's reply, see *CWL*, 7:24–25.

286. See *supra*, entry for 2 Nov. 1863, and *infra*, entry for 9 Dec. 1863.

287. Galusha Grow had defeated Blair for the speakership of the 37th Congress.

288. Lincoln had appointed his friend and political ally Norman B. Judd (1815–78) of Chicago as the U.S. minister to Prussia in 1861.

289. Clay had returned to Russia to serve as the U.S. minister.

290. Matamoras was the Mexican entrepôt for Confederate trade.

291. Thomas E. Bramlette (1817–75), the governor of Kentucky (1863–67), wrote this letter to Capt. Edward Cahill.

292. Gen. Jeremiah Tilford Boyle (1818–71), the military governor of Kentucky (1862–64), had opposed black recruitment as recently as June.

293. Burnside was beleaguered in Knoxville.

294. The clipping is not in Hay's diary.

295. Samuel Lewis Casey (1821–1902) represented Kentucky in the U.S. House (1862–63). Edwin Hanson Webster (1829–93) represented Maryland in the U.S. House (1859–65).

296. A longer version on this story is given by Hay in his 1871 lecture "The Heroic Age in Washington," Hay MSS, RPB. See also Paul M. Zall, ed., *Abe Lincoln Laughing: Humorous Anecdotes from Original Sources by and about Abraham Lincoln* (Knoxville: Univ. of Tennessee Press, 1995), 30.

297. In accordance with the president's proclamation of 3 October, Thanksgiving was established as a national holiday. This was its first observance as such.

298. "Hall" was perhaps Rev. Dr. Charles Hall of the Church of the Epiphany (Episcopal).

299. He had contracted varioloid fever, which lasted till 4 December. To his physician, he quipped, "There is one consolation about the matter, . . . it cannot in the least disfigure me!" Washington correspondence by "Zeta," 3 Dec. 1863, *Chicago Tri-*

bune, 8 Dec. 1863, p. 2. While recuperating from the disease, he said "that since he has been President he had always had a crowd of people asking him to give them something, but that *now he has something he can give them all.*" Washington correspondence, 14 Dec. 1863, *Chicago Tribune*, 15 Dec. 1863, p. 1.

300. See *infra*, entry for 10 Dec. 1863. The consul general at London was Freeman H. Morse. The U.S. minister to Great Britain was Charles Francis Adams (1807–86).

301. Cornelius A. Walborn was named the postmaster of Philadelphia in 1861 on Simon Cameron's recommendation. Mary A. E. Halborn was the postmaster of Middletown, Penn., in 1865, according to the *Official Register of the U.S.* for 1865. The 1863 edition lists Walter H. Kendig as postmaster of Middletown. The sentence in parentheses was added later by Hay, perhaps in 1878.

302. Henry C. Bowen (1813–96) was the cofounder of the *New York Independent*. The article referred to was perhaps "Signs of the Times," *Independent*, 12 Nov. 1863, p. 4.

303. Lincoln had appointed John D. Defrees, a leading Republican of Indiana, as the superintendent of public printing.

304. This action was taken during a Republican caucus. Etheridge's scheme (see *supra*, entry for 29 Oct. 1863) was exposed on Saturday, 5 December. That evening a delegation of House Republicans was created to investigate the matter. They called on Etheridge on Sunday but received no satisfactory answer to their inquiries. Washington correspondence, 6 Dec. 1863, *New York Times*, 7 Dec. 1863, p. 4. That same day an observer reported that "There is great anxiety to learn what tomorrow may bring forth, and many anticipate a very stormy time in the House." Washington correspondence, 6 Dec. 1863, *Chicago Tribune*, 11 Dec. 1863, p. 2.

305. Evidently, Lincoln wanted to confer with Colfax about the Etheridge plot. He may also have discussed with him the coming battle for the speakership of the House, which Colfax desired. Gideon Welles thought Lincoln opposed Colfax, whom the president allegedly considered "a little intriguer,—plausible, aspiring beyond his capacity, and not trustworthy." One journalist claimed that Lincoln "openly electioneered" for Colfax's principal opponent, E. B. Washburne of Illinois. But others thought Lincoln had been neutral in the contest. Willard H. Smith, *Schuyler Colfax: The Changing Fortunes of a Political Idol* (Indianapolis: Indiana Historical Bureau, 1952), 187. Frank Blair and Elihu B. Washburne contended that Colfax was Chase's candidate for the speakership. When Colfax learned that he was labeled the Chase candidate, he "at once sought an audience with the President, and positively repudiated any such connection." Nicolay and Hay, *Lincoln*, 8:315. But in January 1864, he publicly announced that he favored no particular candidate for the Republican presidential nomination. Smith, *Colfax*, 196.

306. Congressman Owen Lovejoy (1811–64) of Illinois was a leading Radical and a friend of Lincoln. *Mauvaise plaisanterie* is French for "an untimely joke." Anna E. Dickinson (1842–1932) of Philadelphia was a mesmerizing antislavery lecturer and an outspoken Radical. See Edward Magdol, *Owen Lovejoy: Abolitionist in Congress* (New Brunswick: Rutgers Univ. Press, 1967), 395–96.

307. Etheridge lost his nerve when it came time to call the roll. According to one

observer, "The happy and speedy organization of the House . . . is due to the timidity of Emerson Etheridge rather than to any lack of dishonest efforts. He went just far enough to demonstrate his capacity for high handed outrages, but got frightened and stopped short before going far enough to realize any benefit from it." Washington correspondence, 7 Dec. 1863, *Chicago Tribune*, 8 Dec. 1863, p. 1. James Cameron Allen (1822–1912) was a representative from Illinois (1853–57, 1863–65) and the clerk of the U.S. House (1857–59). A journalist said of him: "The Democrats confess that the faction now controlling the party lacks brains. It looks very much that way, when such men as Jim Allen . . . are put forward as leaders. Allen has a good, loud voice, a fair personal appearance, but possesses but medium talent." Washington correspondence by "Zeta," 7 Dec. 1863, *Chicago Tribune*, 12 Dec. 1863, p. 1. Congressman Moses F. Odell (1818–66) of New York served on the Joint Committee on the Conduct of the War. Lincoln's former law partner, John Todd Stuart (1807–85) served as a representative from Illinois (1839–43, 1863–65). William Ralls Morrison (1824–1909) was a Democratic representative from Illinois (1863–65, 1873–87).

308. In his message, Lincoln established criteria for the readmission of the seceded states and included a Proclamation of Amnesty and Reconstruction.

309. James Dixon (1814–73) was a conservative Republican senator from Connecticut (1857–69).

310. Francis William Kellogg (1810–79) represented a Michigan district in the U.S. House (1859–65).

311. The reference is to Lincoln's speech of 16 June 1858.

312. Blow (1817–1907) represented Missouri in the U.S. House (1863–67). Peter Osterhaus (1823–1917), a veteran of the German Revolution of 1848 and a prominent member of the St. Louis German community, was promoted to brevet major general on 24 July 1864.

313. See the *New York Tribune*, 10 Dec. 1863.

314. One journalist noted that while the message was favorably received at first, the Radicals "became more cautious in their praise" as they "began to look at it more closely." Washington correspondence, 9 Dec. 1863, *Chicago Tribune*, 10 Dec. 1863, p. 1. "Gurley" was perhaps William H. F. Gurley of Davenport.

315. Lincoln despised the retainers who flocked to Frémont in Missouri. When a friend of the general called to smooth over the troubled relations between the two men, Lincoln told him: "Sir, I believe General Fremont to be a thoroughly honest man, but he has unfortunately surrounded himself with some of the greatest scoundrels on this continent; you are one of them and the worst of them." E. P. Whipple, quoting Lincoln, quoted in Thomas Wentworth Higginson to his mother, 1 Nov. 1861, *Letters and Journals of Thomas Wentworth Higginson, 1846–1906*, ed. Mary Thatcher Higginson (Boston: Houghton Mifflin, 1921), 160. Jessie Frémont offered a different version of her interview with Lincoln. See her memoirs, "Great Events" (1891), *The Letters of Jessie Benton Frémont*, ed. Pamela Herr and Mary Lee Spence (Urbana: Univ. of Illinois Press, 1993), 266. In 1888 and 1890, Mrs. Frémont wrote two other versions of this interview that are not reproduced in the published memoirs. See the Frémont MSS, Bancroft Library, Univ, of California, Berkeley.

316. Blair resigned on 23 September 1864, and Bates followed suit two months later.

317. It was anticipated that the Loyal Leagues would become hotbeds of support for Chase, but they did not.

318. The visit of the Russian fleet commanded by Admiral Lesovesky (or Lisovskii) was a significant diplomatic event.

319. Isaac N. Arnold (1815–84) of Chicago represented an Illinois district in the U.S. House (1861–65). This day he gave a well-received and rousing speech endorsing Lincoln before the Union League conclave. A leading authority on Lincoln's humor, Paul M. Zall, speculates that a story recounted by David Paul Brown (*The Forum* 2 [1856]: 375–76) is the one Lincoln related. It pits a defense attorney against a quack (i.e., a "steam doctor") who was suing for unpaid fees:

> *Counsel*—"Did you treat the patient according to the most approved principles of surgery?"
> *Witness*—"By all means—certainly I did."
> *Counsel*—"Did you decapitate him?"
> *Witness*—"Undoubtedly I did—that was a matter of course."
> *Counsel*—"Did you perform the Cesarean operation upon him?"
> *Witness*—"Why, of course, his condition required it, and it was attended with great success."
> *Counsel*—"Did you, now Doctor, subject his person to an autopsy?"
> *Witness*—"Certainly, that was the last remedy adopted."
> *Counsel*—"Well, then, Doctor, as you performed a *post mortem* operation upon the defendant, and he survived it, I have not more to ask, and if your claim will survive it, quackery deserves to be immortal." (Quoted in Zall, *Abe Lincoln Laughing*, 30–31)

320. Joseph K. C. Forrest (1820–96) was the Springfield correspondent for the *Chicago Tribune* and an aide-de-camp to Illinois governor Richard Yates. Paul Selby called him "a lively sensationalist and very vain and egotistical." Selby to Nicolay, Chicago, 2 Mar. 1895, Nicolay MSS, DLC. Theophilus Lyle Dickie (1811–85) was a prominent attorney in Ottawa, Ill. In 1858 he switched his allegiance from the Republican to the Democratic party. During the Civil War, he served as a colonel in the 4th Illinois Cavalry. Thomas B. Florence (1812–75) was the editor of the *Washington Constitutional Union* (1863–68) and formerly a member of the U.S. House from Pennsylvania (1851–61).

321. Sumner told a journalist that "he is fully and perfectly satisfied" with the message and "endorses it to the fullest extent," even though some details about readmitting states into the Union needed to be worked out. Washington correspondence by "Zeta," 13 Dec. 1863, *Chicago Tribune*, 14 Dec. 1863, p. 1. To Orestes Brownson, he declared that Lincoln's stand on reconstruction was "identical with ours." Sumner to Brownson, Washington, 27 Dec. 1863, *The Selected Letters of Charles Sumner*, ed. Beverly Wilson Palmer (Boston: Northeastern Univ. Press, 1990), 2:216–17. Sumner's

ally, Sen. Zachariah Chandler of Michigan, was "delighted" with the message. Wilmer C. Harris, quoting Chandler, in *The Public Life of Zachariah Chandler*, quoted in William Frank Zornow, *Lincoln and the Party Divided* (Norman: Univ. of Oklahoma Press, 1954), 18.

322. Hay does not indicate where this quote begins. See *supra*, entry for 1 Nov. 1863.

323. For Hay's verbatim minutes of this important meeting, see Nicolay-Hay MSS, IHi. John B. Henderson (1826–1913) was a U.S. senator from Missouri (1862–69). Benjamin Gratz Brown (1826–85) was also a U.S. senator from Missouri (1863–67).

324. James Sidney Rollins (1812–88) represented a Missouri district in the U.S. House (1861–65). "Ci-devant rebels" are former rebels.

325. Lincoln, "greatly outraged" at Kentuckians who were "running off slaves from Missouri and other states into Kentucky and selling them," ordered the arrest of such persons. Washington correspondence, 4 Feb. 1864, *Chicago Tribune*, 5 Feb. 1864, p. 2.

326. See Harlan Hoyt Horner, *Lincoln and Greeley* (Urbana: Univ. of Illinois Press, 1953), 284.

327. Ada and Emma Webb were known as the "Fairy Star Sisters." The Russian officers apparently "made lascivious signs to the ladies on the stage" at Ford's. Washington correspondence by "Zeta," 14 Dec. 1863, *Chicago Tribune*, 18 Dec. 1863, p. 2.

328. Christopher Columbus Augur (1821–98) commanded the 22nd Corps and the Department of Washington.

329. On 11 December, Brown reported to a friend: "Have just returned from a long and satisfactory interview with the President, and if he will adhere to the purpose expressed all will be well in Mo. very briefly. He said he would put his hand in and see if he could not push the Comr. Bill through, and expressed an inclination to order Schofield elsewhere and substitute in his place Rozencrans. He ordered Schofield to Washington for an interview. The only matter is whether he may not come under some other influence in the next two days and all the good be destroyed." Brown to N. B. Judd, Washington, 11 Dec. 1863, Lincoln Collection, RPB.

On 12 December, a delegation from the Grand Council of the Loyal Leagues, consisting of John Covode, George S. Boutwell, and James M. Ashley, called on Lincoln to demand that General Schofield be removed as head of the Department of Missouri. Shortly thereafter, the president summoned Schofield to Washington. Washington correspondence, 14 Dec. 1863, *Chicago Tribune*, 15 Dec. 1863, p. 1. Schofield came to Washington and explained his side of the story. On 18 December, Lincoln told Stanton: "I believe Gen. Schofield must be relieved from command of the Department of Missouri, otherwise a question of veracity, in relation to his declarations as to his interfering, or not, with the Missouri Legislature, will be made." *CWL*, 7:78.

330. Curtis heard that false and malicious rumors about him were circulating in Washington, so he dispatched his principal aide to Washington, where he discovered that malcontents had been spreading untruths about Curtis for over a year. Curtis requested a court of inquiry, but Lincoln did not think it necessary. The president asked Curtis to give a statement, which he did immediately, to the evident satisfaction of Lincoln. Samuel R. Curtis, autobiographical sketch, Samuel R. Curtis MSS,

Western Americana MSS, Beinecke Library, Yale Univ. Curtis had been accused of illegal cotton speculation. Washington correspondence, 21 Dec. 1863, *Chicago Tribune*, 22 Dec. 1863, p. 1. In January the president appointed Curtis to head the Department of Kansas and Rosecrans to command the Department of Missouri.

331. Pomeroy helped lead the boom for Chase. In February 1864, his circular calling for Chase's nomination was made public. "Vaughn" was perhaps Brig. Gen. Richard C. Vaughn of Lexington, Mo.

332. Charles Henry Ray (1821–70) was the editor of the *Chicago Tribune*. In addition to writing dispatches for the *Cincinnati Gazette* under the byline "Agate," Whitelaw Reid produced telegraphic reports for several newspapers. Chase was Reid's "chief sponsor." Royal Cortissoz, *The Life of Whitelaw Reid* (New York: Scribner, 1921), 1:105.

333. James Henry Hackett (1800–71) was a noted Shakespearean actor. David Homer Bates said that Lincoln "was very fond of Hackett personally and of the character of *Falstaff*, and frequently repeated some of the latter's quaint sallies. I recall in his recitation for my benefit he criticized some of Hackett's readings." *Lincoln in the Telegraph Office: Recollections of the United States Military Telegraph Corps During the Civil War* (New York: Century, 1907), 223. Lincoln corresponded with the actor until finally Hackett asked for an appointment as U.S. consul to London. Cf. Barbee, "Mr. Lincoln," 24–40. The play was *Henry IV*, part 1.

334. Samuel Houston (1793–1863) was the president of the Republic of Texas, a U.S. senator from Texas (1846–59), and the governor of the state (1859–61). David "Davy" Crockett (1786–1836), a congressman from Tennessee (1827–31, 1833–35), was killed at the Battle of the Alamo. "McCarty" was perhaps William Monroe McCarty (b. 1816), an Indiana lawyer who served in the Mexican War. "Prentiss" was perhaps Sergeant Smith Prentiss (1808–50), a congressman from Mississippi, or Union general Benjamin Maybury Prentiss (1819–1901).

335. Emily Todd Helm (1836–1930), Mary Lincoln's half sister, was the widow of Confederate general Ben Hardin Helm. Lincoln had provided her a pass on 15 October. She spent approximately a week visiting at the White House.

336. The *Washington Chronicle* reported on 15 December that the president saw Hackett's Falstaff on the night of the fourteenth. Either Lincoln visited Ford's theater on two successive nights or Hay mistook the date.

337. Bayard Taylor (1825–78), who had recently returned from a diplomatic post in Russia, lectured on that country. Lincoln recommended that he also talk on "Serfs, Serfdom and Emancipation in Russia." Lincoln to Taylor, Washington, 25 Dec. 1863, *CWL*, 7:93.

338. On 11 December, it was reported that "The President has signed the pardon, exempting E. W. Gantt of Arkansas, from the penalty of treason of which he is accused by accepting and exercising the office of Brigadier General in the service of the rebels. The pardon also reinstates Gen. Gantt in all his rights of property excepting those relating to slaves." Washington correspondence, 11 Dec. 1863, *Chicago Tribune*, 12 Dec. 1863, p. 1. Edward Walton Gantt (1812–83) repented and told Lincoln he wanted "to induce the withdrawal of my State from its allies in rebellion and its

reentry into the Federal Union." Quoted in Nicolay and Hay, *Lincoln*, 8:410. He did so with a pamphlet, *Address of E. W. Gantt, of Arkansas (Brigadier General in the Confederate Army) in Favor of Re-union in 1863*, which urged Arkansans to quit the war, reorganize the state, and bring it back into the Union. *New York Times*, 6 Feb. 1864. Samuel Allen Rice (1828–64) distinguished himself at the battle of Helena, Ark., and later helped capture Little Rock. The U.S. merchant steamer *Chesapeake*, seized by Confederate sympathizers, had been recaptured by a U.S. gunboat in British territorial waters off Nova Scotia.

339. "Miss Ramsay" was perhaps the daughter of Gen. George Douglas Ramsay (1802–82), the chief of ordnance and the commander of the Washington arsenal. "Miss Loring" was perhaps Harriet Loring, the daughter of Dr. Francis Bott Loring of Washington. Hay received a dinner invitation from F. B. Loring of Washington. Loring to Hay, Washington, 2 Jan. [?], Hay MSS, RPB. See also Hay to Harriet Loring, Madrid, 30 June 1870, Hay MSS, RPB. "Miss Hetzel" was perhaps the daughter of Maj. Sheldon Hetzel, who lived with Margaret Hetzel at 139 F Street North in Washington. Joseph Camp Griffith Kennedy (1813–87), the superintendent of the census, was among the participants in the play that was being rehearsed. Edward B. Malet to Hay, Washington, 8 Jan. 1864, Hay MSS, RPB. Edward Baldwin Malet (1837–1908) worked in Washington for the British minister Lord Lyons. See his memoirs, *Shifting Scenes, or Memories of Many Men in Many Lands* (London: John Murray, 1901). Charles Hueage was an attaché at the British legation.

340. John Sherman (1823–1900), a U.S. senator from Ohio, was the brother of Gen. William T. Sherman. Ira Harris (1802–75) was a U.S. senator from New York. James Rood Doolittle (1815–97) was a U.S. senator from Wisconsin. Solomon Foot (1802–66) was a U.S. senator from Vermont. Jacob M. Howard (1805–71) was a U.S. senator from Michigan. John M. Schofield later wrote, "Mr. Lincoln declared decidedly to me, and to my friends in the Senate, that he would make no change [in the command of the Department of Missouri] until the Senate united with him in vindicating me by confirming my nomination . . . and he would then give me a more important command." *Forty-Six Years in the Army* (New York: Century, 1897), 109.

341. George F. Shepley (1819–78) was the military governor of Louisiana. Thomas J. Durant (1817–82) was a New Orleans Unionist. See *CWL*, 7:89–91.

342. Edward H. Durell (1810–87) was a federal judge (1863–74).

343. Alexander K. McClure recalled Lincoln's saying, "I have always felt that God must love common people, or he wouldn't have made so many of them." McClure, "His Career Was a Climax of Ceaseless Self-Culture," *Success*, Feb. 1904, 91, quoted in Fehrenbacher and Fehrenbacher, *Recollected Words of Lincoln*, 319. Similarly, James Grant Wilson reported that Lincoln said, "I think the Lord must love the plain people, he has made so many of them." Wilson, "Recollections of Lincoln," *Putnam's Monthly*, Feb. 1909, 516, quoted in Fehrenbacher and Fehrenbacher, *Recollected Words of Lincoln*, 502.

344. Congressman Kelley's aversion to Blair grew even more intense the following year when the postmaster of Philadelphia worked to block his renomination.

345. Charles O'Neill (1821–93) of Philadelphia served in the U.S. House (1863–71).

346. The Republicans in the Ohio state legislature endorsed Lincoln's candidacy in March 1864.

347. McClellan wrote that he favored the Democratic candidate for governor of Pennsylvania, Judge George W. Woodward of the state supreme court. See McClellan to Charles J. Biddle, Orange, N.J., 12 Oct. 1863, *The Civil War Papers of George B. McClellan: Selected Correspondence, 1860–1865*, ed. Stephen W. Sears (New York: Ticknor & Fields, 1989), 558–59.

348. The *New York Herald* had been promoting Grant's candidacy throughout December.

349. Grant expressed strong antislavery views in that document. See Grant to Washburne, Vicksburg, 30 Aug. 1863, *The Papers of Ulysses S. Grant*, ed. John Y. Simon (Carbondale: Southern Illinois Univ. Press, 1967–), 9:217–18.

350. Lincoln's draft of the placard has not been located.

351. Francis H. Peirpont (1814–99) was the governor of the loyal portion of Virginia under the control of Union troops. His name was also spelled Pierpoint or Pierpont.

352. See "Wendell Phillips–Gov. Chase," editorial, *New York Tribune*, 24 Dec. 1863, p. 4. In his 22 December lecture, Phillips had criticized Chase's financial plan as a "magnificent project of pouring the whole bank capital of the Union into a tub without a bottom." *New York Tribune*, 23 Dec. 1863, p. 1.

353. Benjamin H. Hutton (1809?–84) was a New York merchant. John Jay Cisco (1806–84), a Wall Street banker, had been appointed the assistant U.S. treasurer in charge of the subtreasury in New York by President Pierce in 1853. Lincoln not only retained him in that place but insisted that he serve as treasurer of the Union Pacific Railroad. *New York Times*, 24 Mar. 1884, p. 1. Chase's proposal to establish a national banking system was the heart of his plan for financing the war.

354. The cabinet discussed Lincoln's "Opinion on the Draft" on 14 and 15 September. Atty. Gen. Edward Bates confided to his diary on 14 September that Lincoln "was greatly moved—more angry than I ever saw him" because state judges had freed civilians arrested by the military. Lincoln "declared that it was a formed plan of the democratic copperheads, deliberately acted out to defeat the Govt., and aid the enemy" and that "no honest man did or could believe that the State Judges have any such power." *Diary of Bates*, 306. The president, Welles noted, threatened to expel refractory state judges to the Confederacy. *Diary of Welles*, 1:432. Later that day, Lincoln wrote an opinion on the draft criticizing its opponents for "effrontery" and for their use of "false arguments," calling into question their patriotism, and asking, "Are we degenerate? Has the manhood of our race run out?" The next day, he suspended the privilege of the writ of habeas corpus and ordered provost marshals to reject any attempts by judges to counter the proclamation. *CWL*, 6:444–49. See also Mark E. Neely Jr., *The Fate of Liberty: Abraham Lincoln and Civil Liberties* (New York: Oxford Univ. Press, 1991), 69–74; and a statement by the son of Robert B. Carnahan (U.S. district attorney for the western district of Pennsylvania), Pittsburgh, May 1896, Ida M. Tarbell MSS, Allegheny College. The Pennsylvania Supreme Court eventually reversed its earlier finding that the draft was unconstitutional.

355. Indiana governor O. P. Morton's presidential hopes were dashed when the Indiana Republican Convention in February 1864 endorsed Lincoln for reelection. Stickney and Plantz were busy organizing Florida in accordance with Lincoln's reconstruction plan, announced earlier that month in the president's message to Congress. See Stickney to Chase, St. Augustine, Fla., 21 Dec. 1863, and Plantz to Chase, Key West, Fla., 12 Jan. 1864, Chase MSS, DLC.

356. Hay's visit to the prisoner-of-war camp is described *infra*, entry for 4 Jan. 1864. The Florida mission lasted from mid-January till mid-March. Lincoln planned to help form a loyal state government based on his 8 December proclamation of amnesty and pardon. Hay's efforts coincided with a military expedition into Florida, suggested by Gen. Quincy A. Gillmore, who told Halleck on 15 December that he aimed to cut Confederate supply lines, to recruit black troops, and to capture the most important region in Florida. Six weeks later he added two more objectives to the mission: to open a Florida port and to "inaugurate measures for the speedy restoration of Florida to her allegiance." Quoted in William H. Nulty, *Confederate Florida: The Road to Olustee* (Tuscaloosa: Univ. of Alabama Press, 1990), 73–74. The St Augustine meeting took place on 19 December. A petition was sent to the president.

357. Poor health forced Gen. John Henry Martindale (1815–81) to resign his commission in September 1864.

358. Leonard Grover was the proprietor of Grover's Theater. Franklin Philp, with his partner Adolpheus S. Solomon (1826–1910), ran the Metropolitan Book Store at 332 Pennsylvania Avenue. "Eastman" was perhaps Norman Eastman, listed in the 1864 Washington city directory as a clerk in the Interior Department.

4. 1864

1. Hay probably refers to the Metropolitan Club. Hay, Nicolay, and their friends, as one of them later recalled, made the Metropolitan "our headquarters." William E. Doster, *Lincoln and Episodes of the Civil War* (New York: Putnam's, 1915), 31.

2. See Lincoln to Butler, Washington, 2 Jan. 1864, *CWL*, 7:103.

3. The prisoner population of Point Lookout was 8,385, of which approximately 1,000 (mostly from North Carolina, Kentucky, and Tennessee) wanted to take the oath and join the U.S. Army. They were intimidated, however, by their patriotic Confederate fellow-prisoners. Washington correspondence, 4 Jan. 1864, *Chicago Tribune*, 5 Jan. 1864, p. 1. In his memoirs, Butler claimed that two regiments of Union troops were recruited from the prisoners at Point Lookout. *Autobiography and Personal Reminiscences of Major-General Benjamin F. Butler: Butler's Book* (Boston: Thayer, 1892), 587.

4. Hay refers to the oath prescribed in Lincoln's proclamation of 8 December 1863.

5. On 5 January, Butler pressed these views upon Lincoln, Halleck, and Stanton, proposing "that the President issue a Proclamation for 100,000 volunteers, for a limited number of days, for the special purpose of a crusade on Richmond, and liberating our starving prisoners there. He says he can with that number take the whole

concern and thus clean out that rebel nest." Washington correspondence, 5 Jan. 1864, *Chicago Tribune*, 7 Jan. 1864, weekly edition, p. 2.

When a New England visitor soon thereafter recommended this plan to the president, saying that Butler's forces would be aided by the Unionists in Richmond, Lincoln replied:

> I have great confidence in General Butler, but I am not so sure about Richmond. Your plans remind me of a story told of a lot of Methodist ministers, who were the trustees of a Western college. It so happened that the college was connected with a neighboring town by a bridge, and that this bridge was subject to be carried away by freshets. At last they held a special session to receive the plans of a noted bridge builder, a good mechanic, but rather a profane man. "Can you build this bridge?" asked a reverend gentleman. "Build it," bluntly replied the mechanic, "I could build a bridge to ———." This horrified the trustees, and after the bridge builder had retired, the minister who had recommended him thought proper to apologize. "I feel confident," said he, "that our energetic friend could build a safe bridge to Hades, although I am not so sure of the abutment on the other side." And so with your plan . . . I have great confidence in Gen. Butler, but doubt the strength of Unionists in Richmond. (Ben Perley Poore in the *Boston Journal*, copied in the *Chicago Tribune*, 9 Jan. 1864, p. 1)

6. Butler had commanded the troops in the joint army and navy expedition that occupied New Orleans in April 1862.

7. See *supra*, entry for 22 Oct. 1861.

8. Robert Ould (1820–81) was the chief of the Confederate Bureau of Exchange of Prisoners; Butler was his Union counterpart.

9. Caleb B. Smith, who died on 7 January, had been appointed to a Federal judgeship in October 1862 and was succeeded as secretary of the interior by John Palmer Usher, formerly the assistant secretary. William Tod Otto (1816–1905), an attorney from Indiana, who had been appointed the assistant secretary of the interior by Usher after Smith retired, remained in the post until 1871.

10. This message from Cameron is not among the AL MSS, DLC.

11. On 7 January, the New Hampshire Republican Convention endorsed Lincoln for a second term. The Union League Club of Philadelphia followed suit on 11 January.

12. In 1857, Cameron defeated Forney, at the time a Buchanan Democrat.

13. In addition to being named an assistant adjutant general, Hay was also given the rank of major.

14. Hay's mission to Florida generated controversy after the Union repulse at Olustee on 20 February. Some criticized the military movement that culminated in that battle as a brainchild of the president who, it was said, merely wanted to capture more votes at the Republican National Convention and recklessly endangered troops for short-term political gain. In the *Washington National Republican*, that charge was rebutted thus: "It was not until after the President gave his consent that

Gen. Gillmore, in cooperation with a naval force, should undertake the expedition, that the idea of sending Mr. Hay to report to Gen. Gillmore was thought of. Mr. Hay, desiring more active life, made a personal application to the President to go with the expedition, and the latter consented, commissioned Mr. Hay, and ordered him to report to Gen. Gillmore, who subsequently informed the President, officially, that he (Gillmore) had ordered Maj. Hay to proceed to Florida to superintend certain civil and military duties under the Amnesty Proclamation." *New York Times*, 7 Mar. 1864, p. 4.

15. A reference perhaps to Mrs. John Wood, the proprietress of the Olimpic Theater in New York.

16. The *Fulton* was a U.S. transport steamer. The 54th Massachusetts Regiment was the black unit that had so gallantly assaulted Fort Wagner near Charleston, S.C., the previous July.

17. Lt. Col. Edward W. Smith was the assistant adjutant general to General Gillmore.

18. John Wesley Turner (1833–99) was the chief of staff of the Department of the South.

19. See *supra*, entry for 29 Apr. 1863. On 21 January, Dorman asked the president through Jesse O. Norton for permission to accompany the expedition to Florida.

20. A. G. Browne was a treasury agent. Cf. Hay to Nicolay, 21 Jan. 1864, Hay MSS, RPB.

21. In civilian garb.

22. The *Cosmopolitan* was a U.S. transport steamer.

23. In October 1862, Union forces broke up the inauguration of a Confederate governor at Frankfort, Ky. "Meriwether" was perhaps W. A. Merriweather, a U.S. marshal in Kentucky.

24. "Barton" was perhaps William B. Barton, the commander of a brigade in the 54th Massachusetts Regiment.

25. Alfred Howe Terry had made his reconnaisance in Charleston harbor, before the bombardment of Fort Sumter in October 1863.

26. Banks issued orders accordingly on 10 February. Hay arrived in Key West on 7 March.

27. "Ellwell" was perhaps John J. Elwell, the assistant quartermaster on Gillmore's staff.

28. "Jackson" was perhaps Lt. Col. Richard Jackson. Thomas B. Brooks was an aide-de-camp to General Gillmore. Chauncey B. Reese was a member of the corps of engineers. "Frothingham" was perhaps Benjamin Thompson Frothingham (1843–1902).

29. Union troops had taken Fort Wagner on 7 September, after two failed attempts in July. Gen. George C. Strong (1832–63) had crossed the inlet to occupy Morris Island before the first attack; he was killed in the second.

30. Battery Gregg had been taken by Union forces on 7 September 1863.

31. "Ames" was perhaps William Ames of the 3rd Rhode Island Artillery, the chief of artillery in the area. Peter S. Michie belonged to the corps of engineers.

32. Stickney reported on this day that "John Hay arrived . . . He says the President

was highly pleased with the result of our meeting at St. Augustine [on 19 December 1863]. . . . He says he was directed to cooperate with me & will do so." Stickney to Salmon P. Chase, Beaufort, S.C., 26 Jan. 1864, Chase MSS, DLC.

33. In late January, Gillmore acknowledged receipt of the blank books and stated that Hay had been ordered to proceed to Florida. Gillmore to Lincoln, Hilton Head, [31 Jan. 1864], *O. R.*, 1st ser., vol. 35, pt. 1, 294–95; Gillmore's General Order 16, 31 Jan. 1864, U.S. Senate, *Report of the Joint Committee on the Conduct and Expenditures of the War*, 38th Cong., 1st sess., 1864, S. Rept. 47, 23.

34. In the 62nd regiment, 287 men reenlisted.

35. The 8th U.S. Colored participated in the Florida campaign and suffered heavy casualties, losing over 300 of the 550 men in the unit.

36. Apparently, duplicates of this letter were prepared for Col. Henry R. Guss, 97th Pennsylvania, commanding at Fernandina, and Col. Thomas O. Osborne of the 24th Massachusetts Infantry, commanding at St. Augustine.

37. William W. H. Davis belonged to the 104th Pennsylvania Volunteers.

38. The stranded blockade-runner was the *Presto* from Nassau.

39. "Drayton" was perhaps James Spencer Drayton, who had commanded a black unit under Gen. E. A. Wild.

40. Bayard Taylor, *Hannah Thurston: A Story of American Life* (London: S. Low, 1863).

41. "Abot" was perhaps Joseph C. Abbott of the 7th New Hampshire Volunteers.

42. Embarkation orders listed the units as the 7th Connecticut; the 7th New Hampshire; the 8th U.S. Colored; the 3rd U.S. Colored; the 40th Massachusetts; a battalion of Massachusetts cavalry; and ten guns.

43. Only one locomotive operated on the road.

44. John McGowan of New Jersey was a captain in the U.S. Revenue Cutter Service. He was described by Stickney as "a careful President man," that is, a supporter of Lincoln's renomination. Stickney to Chase, 5 Feb. 1864, quoted in John E. Johns, *Florida During the Civil War* (Gainsville: Univ. of Florida Press, 1963), 194.

45. William Alsop, a Florida resident for many years, succeeded John S. Sammis as a direct tax commissioner in November and was prominent at the St. Augustine meeting.

46. The firm of Calvin L. Robinson, William C. Morrill, and L. D. Stickney was the object of an investigation by Austin Smith, a special agent of the Treasury Department. Robinson, who ceased to be a partner in the following month, gave testimony critical of Stickney's merchandising of government property that had been intended for use by the Tax Commission. U.S. House, 38th Cong., 2nd sess., 1864, Executive Doc. 18.

47. Jacksonville had been captured the same day.

48. "Sears" was perhaps Captain Sears, who had been in charge of Fort Clinch. "Freeman" was perhaps Acting Master Simeon N. Freeman, USN.

49. Maj. James E. Place commanded the 1st New York Engineers under Colonel Hawley.

50. *Mauvaise honte* is French for "self-consciousness" or "bashfulness."

51. A written order.

52. Admiral Dahlgren described Jacksonville the same day in his dairy: "The people have all gone. Quiet as death. It has every evidence that trade and industry were about to build up a flourishing city. All over for the present." *Memoir of John A. Dahlgren*, ed. Madeleine Vinton Dahlgren (Boston: Osgood, 1882), 439.

53. Union forces had occupied Jacksonville 12 March–9 April 1862.

54. "Walker" was perhaps Samuel G. Walker, who had attended the Union meeting at St. Augustine held on 19 December 1863.

55. Col. Guy V. Henry was in charge of a mounted brigade, comprising the 40th Massachusetts Mounted Infantry and an independent battalion of Massachusetts cavalry. On 8 February, Henry's men captured five artillery pieces.

56. The trapped blockade-runner *St. Mary's*, loaded with cotton, had been scuttled on 9 February.

57. The pilgrims were the returning Florida Unionists.

58. Col. John S. Sammis of Jacksonville had vigorously opposed secession; when he declined to purchase Confederate bonds, authorities seized his property. He then fled the state. He returned as a leader of Unionism in east Florida and became a district tax commissioner and a bitter opponent of Stickney, who was investigated by the Treasury Department in response to Sammis's complaints. In 1864 he served as a pro-Lincoln delegate to the Republican Convention in Baltimore.

59. G. N. Papy had been secretary at the Union meeting held at St. Augustine on 19 December 1863. Hay had William C. Morrill purchase several lots for him at the St. Augustine tax sale of 21–28 December 1863. On 29 February 1864, he evidently bought three lots from Morrill; on 12 March 1864, he bought a lot in St. Augustine for $270.75 from Calvin L. Robinson. In 1864 the land apparently produced a crop worth $2,500, though Hay told Whitelaw Reid that "incidental expenses" had consumed the profits and that "he had never seen an orange or received a penny from it!" He also bought property in Fernandina in a joint venture with Morrill, Lyman Stickney, William Alsop, and gentlemen named Ayer and Hoyt. Hay sank all his capital ($4,000) into Florida real estate, thinking he would reap profits of "several hundred percent." Hay's notations are on the final pages of the notebook he used as a diary from 1866 to 1870. See Hay to William Alsop, Paris, 9 Oct. and 12 Dec. 1865, to an unknown correspondent, Paris, 26 Sept. 1866, to Lyman Stickney, Paris, 4 June 1866; and Alsop to Hay, New York, 29 Aug. 1866, in a letterpress copybook, Hay MSS, RPB. Also see Whitelaw Reid, *After the War: A Tour of the Southern States, 1865–1866* (1866; reprint, New York: Harper Torchbooks, 1965), 171–72.

Hay found Reid's mention of his orange groves painful: "it would have been more merciful for him to have passed that orange grove in St. Augustine without the *infandum renovare dolorem* ["to renew my unspeakable grief," an allusion to Vergil's *Aeneid*] of my enterprise." Hay to Salmon P. Chase, Paris, 19 Oct. 1866, letterpress copybook, Hay MSS, RPB.

60. Col. Thomas O. Osborn served in the 24th Massachusetts Volunteers.

61. Capt. John Jackson Dickinson, a wealthy landowner from Orange Springs, commanded a militia unit known as the Leo Dragoons, which defended the west bank of the St. John's River and conducted raids against Union forces in the area.

62. Stickney reported to Chase that on this day he had talked with Hay. "The Pres-

ident's plan for the restoration of Florida will be a failure, and that is now the opinion of his secretary Mr Hay. We discussed the subject yesterday & the conclusion arrived at was, that Mr Hay would make an effort to enroll one tenth of the voters in 1860. In case of failure, which he thought certain, he would go back to the President and ask a change of program like that with which I started." Stickney to Chase, St. Augustine, Fla., 16 Feb. 1864, Chase MSS, DLC.

63. Col. John L. Otis served in the 10th Regiment, Connecticut Volunteers.

64. Bartolo Oliveros had attended the Union meeting at St. Augustine, 19 December 1863.

65. Stickney claimed to have had Alley appointed as the commander of the *John Adams* and also as an assessor of the direct tax.

66. Col. Alfred S. Hartwell commanded the 55th Massachusetts Volunteers.

67. "Bingham" was perhaps Lt. J. M. Bingham, the quartermaster of the 1st South Carolina Volunteers. On 20 February, at the Battle of Olustee, the Union forces suffered a bloody defeat. Colonel Henry, however, was not killed and five guns, not seven, were lost.

68. Gillmore's orders of 18 February had not arrived before the battle.

69. Gen. Truman Seymour (1824–91), a veteran artillery officer, at various times between 1862 and 1864 had commanded Port Royal Island, Morris Island, and Hilton Head. He led the Florida expedition to disastrous defeat and was subsequently transferred to the Army of the Potomac, where he served in the 6th Corps. Beauregard had substantially reinforced Finegan before the battle.

70. Capt. James A. Hamilton commanded a battery of the 3rd U.S. Artillery. Lt. John R. Myrick served with Battery E, 3rd U.S. Artillery. Lt. Tully McRae served with the 1st U.S. Artillery. Charles W. Fribley served with the 8th U.S. Colored Troops.

71. For three days, Vogdes took command of one of the divisions from Seymour, who was relieved on 24 March.

72. Gen. Adelbert Ames (1835–1933) was ordered to dispatch 1,300 troops to Jacksonville. Gen. Robert S. Foster was ordered to send his troops from South Carolina to Jacksonville promptly.

73. Lieutenant Colonel Reed served with the 1st North Carolina Colored Troops. Lieutenant Eddy served with the 3rd Rhode Island Battery.

74. On this date, Stickney reported that:

Maj. Hay now agrees heartily with me about the readiest way of restoring Florida to the Union—to call a convention which shall change the Constitution in what relates to suffrage & slavery—by making all residents of the State at the time of election, of lawful age, voters, and all the inhabitants thereof *free*. That accomplished, by opening the ports of Fernandina, St. Augustine and Jacksonville, removing hindrances to northern emigrants, and giving me the use of a revenue cutter or any seagoing vessel for three or four weeks, I pledge to you that Florida shall be as bright a star as shine in freedom's constellation. . . . This is the only way to make the State what the friends of freedom desire. Maj Hay is sanguine the President will adopt the plan here given. (Stickney to Chase, Jacksonville, Fla., 24 Feb. 1864, Chase MSS, DLC)

75. Dr. Sylvanus S. Mulford was the chief medical officer on the staff of the post commander on the south end of Folly Island (Gen. George H. Gordon's division).

76. Dahlgren described this conversation at length in his diary. See *Memoir of Dahlgren*, 441–42 (entry for 26 Feb. 1864).

77. The *New York Herald*, 23 Feb. 1864, p. 4, reported the following:

It is stated that a curious development of Executive intermeddling with military movements has been developed by inquiries about the recent Florida expedition. It is said that upon hearing of it General Halleck was quite taken by surprise, and wrote to General Gillmore to know what he was doing at Jacksonville, a place that had been two or three times in our possession and was not considered worth holding, and asking how he came to go there, not only without orders but without the knowledge and contrary to the positive instructions of the Secretary of War and General Halleck. In reply General Gillmore is said to have enclosed a letter of instructions from the President, transmitted to him by Mr. Hay, late private secretary of Mr. Lincoln, directing the movement to be made. Since this statement has been in circulation it is rumored that the expedition was intended simply for the occupation of Florida for the purpose of securing the election of three Lincoln delegates to the National Nominating Convention, and that of John Hay to Congress. The cost of the operation to the government is estimated at about one million of dollars.

Stickney observed that "Maj Hay was greatly excited at the notice taken of his Florida mission by the Herald. I have not opposed him, but rather moulded his views in harmony with my own. He now works with them, and for the measures I wish to prevail." Stickney to Chase, 2 Mar. 1864, Chase MSS, DLC.

78. The *Dictator* was an ironclad steamer of the monitor class.

79. Sargent, *Peculiar: A Tale of the Great Transition* (New York: Carleton, 1864).

80. Philip Frasure, a Jacksonville Unionist, served as a U.S. district judge for the Northern District of Florida.

81. William C. Morrill had been a musician in the 9th Maine until October 1862 and remained in St. Augustine.

82. Latin for "You will go most safely in the bunk," a play on Ovid's expression "In medio tutissimus ibis."

83. "Gen. W." was Daniel P. Woodbury (1812–64), the commander of the District of Key West and the Tortugas. Capt. Henry W. Bowers was the assistant adjutant general to General Woodbury. Banks issued orders on 10 February calling on all officers in Key West, Dry Tortugas, and elsewhere in Florida to assist Hay in his work of enrolling voters. *O. R.*, 1st ser., vol. 35, pt. 1, 473.

84. William J. Boynton was a district judge on Key West. "Admiral Bailey" was Theodorus Bailey (1805–77).

85. "Mr. Howe" was perhaps Charles Howe, who had attended the Union meeting at St. Augustine, 19 December 1863.

86. The British sloop *Hannah* from Nassau, New Providence, was captured that same day by the U.S. schooner *Beauregard*.

87. A controversy emerged in the press about responsibility for the Olustee dis-

aster. The *New York Herald* protested that "brigades of our brave armies are sent into rebellious states to water with their precious blood the soil that may produce Presidential votes." In late February, one journalist reported that "the very highest authority" claimed "that the President never issued any order or made any suggestion to Gen. Gillmore relative to military operations in Florida. . . . that the contrary statement . . . is untrue," and "that the expedition was made by Gen. Gillmore on his own responsibility." Washington correspondence, 28 Feb. 1864, *Chicago Tribune*, 29 Feb. 1864, p. 1. Press criticism continued into March. On the first of that month, the *New York Herald* condemned "the President and his private secretary, who are the recognized originators and managers of this whole movement" and endorsed "the popular conviction that the President and his secretary are the only ones to blame in the business" (p. 4).

88. On 2 March, Admiral Dahlgren's son was killed while participating in Judson Kilpatrick's unsuccessful cavalry raid against Richmond.

89. George Meredith Clymer (b. 1817) was the medical director of the Department of the South.

90. On the previous day, Lyman Stickney reported that "Maj Hay will return to Washington by the next steamer. I think I could do much good with the President to pass a week in Washington myself. Maj Hay thinks so too." Stickney to Chase, Fernandina, Fla., 15 Mar. 1864, Chase MSS, DLC.

91. A play on the word *varioloid*, a mild form of smallpox.

92. *The Idiot Witness, or A Tale of Blood* was a melodrama by John Thomas Haines (1799?–1843). *Boots at the Swan: A Farce in One Act* by Charles Selby was published in London in 1842.

93. After making several such requests in February and March, Gillmore was ordered north on 4 April.

94. Capt. William L. M. Burger was an assistant adjutant general under Gen. John G. Foster.

95. Sand's novel was first published in 1846.

96. Charles Dickens, *American Notes for General Circulation* (New York: Winchester, 1842).

97. Mary Elizabeth Braddon (Mrs. John Maxwell) (1837–1915) was an English novelist. *Eleanor's Victory* was published in London in 1863.

98. The *Arago* arrived at New York with about 500 passengers. *New York Tribune*, 24 Mar. 1864.

99. French for "Is the game worth the candle?"

100. On 5 April, Stanton supplied copies of this correspondence to the Joint Committee on the Conduct of the War. That committee had evidently interrogated Hay, who, according to a press account, "exculpates the President from any interference in that [Olustee] affair." Washington correspondence, 25 Mar. 1864, *New York Times*, 25 Mar. 1864, p. 1. Grant was nominated lieutenant general on 29 February; Halleck resigned the command of the army on 9 March. For further comments by Lincoln about Halleck, see *infra*, entry for 28 Apr. 1864.

101. The Missouri Radicals chose anti-Lincoln delegates to the Republican National Convention.

102. Hay conferred with Grant on 27 March. Two days earlier Nicolay had left for New York to consult about appointments in the customhouse.

103. Thomas Carney (1824–88), the second governor of Kansas, was elected to the U.S. Senate by the anti-Lane forces in 1864, but the election was ruled illegal. The "Pomeroy Circular," touting Chase for the presidency, had been made public in February.

104. Col. Edwin H. Webster (1829–93), of the 7th Maryland Volunteers, represented a Maryland district in the U.S. House (1859–65). In 1865 Lincoln appointed him collector of the Port of Baltimore. On 6 April, Marylanders voted on the question of holding a state convention to abolish slavery.

105. See Grant to Halleck, Culpepper, Va., 25 Mar. 1864, *The Papers of Ulysses S. Grant*, ed. John Y. Simon (Carbondale: Southern Illinois Univ. Press, 1982), 10:223–24.

106. Henry Wikoff had worked for the *New York Herald* as a kind of sub-rosa correspondent and had befriended Mary Lincoln, which scandalized polite society. See David Davis to his wife, St. Louis, 15 Dec. 1861, Davis MSS, Chicago Historical Society; Henry Smith to Charles Henry Ray and Joseph Medill, [Washington], 4 Nov. 1861, Charles H. Ray MSS, Huntington Library, San Marino, Calif.; Adam Gurowski to Horace Greeley, Washington, 1 Oct. 1861, Greeley MSS, New York Public Library; Joseph Hawley to Charles Dudley Warner, n.d., "Letters of Joseph R. Hawley" (typescript dated 1929), ed. Arthur L. Shipman, Connecticut Historical Society, Hartford, p. 387; Washington correspondence, 21 Oct. 1861, *St. Louis Missouri Republican*, 25 Oct. 1861, p. 3; *Memoirs of Henry Villard, Journalist and Financier: 1835–1900* (New York: Houghton Mifflin, 1904), 1:157; and *infra*, entry for 23 Sept. 1864.

107. Samuel Hooper (1808–75) was a Boston merchant and ironmaster who served in the U.S. House (1861–74). Édouard Drouyn de Lhuys (1805–81) was France's minister of foreign affairs (1848, 1851, 1852–55, 1862–66). William L. Dayton (1807–64) was the U.S. minister to France (1861–64). Emperor Maximilian's acceptance of the crown of Mexico had strained U.S. relations with France.

108. In May, Hunter replaced Franz Sigel in the Department of West Virginia.

109. This letter, in Hay's hand and on White House stationery, is pasted into the diary.

110. Commo. Charles Wilkes (1798–1877) was court-martialed for publishing a critical letter sent to him by Welles. On 8 April, Edwin Forrest performed *King Lear* before an audience that included Lincoln. Daniel Dougherty (1826–92), an attorney and orator, helped found the Union League Club in Philadelphia and worked hard for Lincoln's reelection. Dougherty was celebrated as a brilliant public speaker.

111. "Kinney" was perhaps John Fitch Kinney (1816–1902), a Democrat who represented a Nebraska district in the U.S. House (1863–65).

112. The presence of the Kentuckians may have been connected with discussions among the president and Governor Bramlette of Kentucky, former senator Archibald Dixon, and journalist Albert G. Hodges. The governor urged that his state's draft quota be reduced and protested against the way that black troops were recruited in Kentucky. Bramlette to A. G. Hodges, Frankfort, 22 Apr. 1864, *Chicago Tribune*, 27 Apr. 1864, p. 1.

113. The Lincolns attended this performance of Carl Maria von Weber's opera. For the letter, see Lincoln to Albert G. Hodges, Washington, 4 Apr. 1864, *CWL*, 7:281–82. "Drabs" was a slang term for slatternly women.

114. Field (1822–75) was the deputy assistant treasurer in New York and a close associate of Chase. See *infra*, entry for 30 June 1864.

115. See *supra*, entries for 28 Feb. and 12 Mar. 1864. Among the nastier comments were these: "In this Florida expedition may be seen, compactly gathered together, all the elements which characterize the course of the Administration in its general policy. The object, the manner of attempting it, the abandonment of one purpose to attempt another, the reckless expenditure of national money and life to achieve the object, the headlong course, the disaster." *New York Journal of Commerce*, n.d., copied in an unidentified newspaper, clipping in Hay's scrapbook, vol. 57, 101, Hay MSS, DLC. In another unidentified clipping included in the scrapbook, its author asked querulously: "Why was Hay made a major and then an assistant adjutant-general over the heads of brave officers who were periling their lives upon the battle-field for honorable promotion?" Francis B. Carpenter recalled that on 2 March, Lincoln seemed "deeply disturbed" by the press charges that he had ordered the expedition to Florida in order to win more votes at the Republican Convention in Baltimore that June. *Six Months at the White House with Abraham Lincoln* (New York: Hurd and Houghton, 1866), 48–49.

116. The original of this letter is in the Halpine MSS, Huntington Library, San Marino, Calif.

117. The *New York World* was the leading Democratic newspaper in the North.

118. Edward Lyulph Stanley (1840–1925) was Baron Sheffield of Roscommon. Edward John Stanley (1802–69) was the postmaster general of Great Britain.

119. The Confederates had captured Plymouth, N.C., on 20 April.

120. The siege took place in November and December 1863.

121. "Foster" was probably Gen. John Gray Foster (1823–74).

122. Burnside's 9th Corps was moving from Annapolis to join the Army of the Potomac. It had just been reviewed by the president. Welles wrote: "General Butler has telegraphed to Fox, who is an old boyhood associate and acquaintance, to come down to Hampton Roads. Wants help. Asks F. to induce the President to go down, but he declines." *The Diary of Gideon Welles, Secretary of the Navy under Lincoln and Johnson, 1861–1869*, ed. Howard K. Beale (New York: Norton, 1960), 2:16 (entry for 23 Apr. 1864).

123. The *Iriquois* was a steam sloop. Christopher Raymond Perry Rodgers (1819–92) later served as superintendent of the Naval Academy (1874–78). John Wilson Shaffer of Freeport, Ill., was serving as General Butler's chief of staff.

124. Butler told the American Freedman's Inquiry Commission that the discipline instilled by slavery was "an advantage in favor of the negro as soldiers," for they had grown accustomed "to do as they are told." Quoted in Joseph T. Glatthaar, *Forged in Battle: The Civil War Alliance of Black Soldiers and White Officers* (New York: Free Press, 1990), 84. Many Union officers in command of black troops reached similar conclusions (87–88).

125. "Rip-Raps" was a knickname for Fort Wool, which was built on an artificial island in Hampton Roads. Gen. August Valentine Kautz (1828–95) commanded a cavalry division in Butler's Army of the James.

126. John S. Barnes (1836–1911) was a flag captain of the North Atlantic Blockad-

ing Squadron. "Davis" was perhaps Maj. Nelson Henry Davis. Possibly Hay sought a positon on the staff of Gillmore, who arrived on 3 May.

127. Godfrey Weitzel (1835–84) was the chief engineer of the Army of the James. The "coming movement" was the planned attack on Richmond by that army.

128. Gen. William Farrar Smith (1824–1903) served under Butler.

129. The Army of the Potomac moved shortly after midnight, 4 May.

130. The episode occurred at the end of the Peninsular Campaign in July 1862.

131. See *supra*, entry for 24 Mar. 1864.

132. Moody was a Methodist clergyman from Ohio.

133. The delegates were instructed not only to vote for Lincoln but also to vote "against all attempts the postpone the day of nomination." Telegram, Cameron to Lincoln, Harrisburg, 28 Apr. 1864, AL MSS, DLC.

134. "Wilder" was presumably Abel C. Wilder (1828–75), a congressman from Kansas (1863–65). Pasted into the diary at this point is a letter from John W. Turner to Hay, Fort Monroe, Va., 27 Apr. 1864:

> Yours of yesterday is received—I was much disappointed not to have seen you. I had much to say to you.
>
> I am trying to fix up the 10th Corps, [illegible word] and try to come with it. G[illmore] is not arrived. I am afraid he will be too late. Your friend F——
> is to be notified when the time arrives. Come with him. My advices will reach you too late.
>
> Dont let them throw G out.
>
> I am in hopes to have a division but [illegible words].
>
> I left Smith jubilant.

135. See Lincoln to Grant, Washington, 30 Apr. 1864, *CWL*, 7:324.

136. Fry was promoted to brigadier general on 21 April.

137. See Lincoln to Albert G. Hodges, Washington, 4 Apr. 1864, *CWL*, 7:281–82. Immediately after the first battle of Bull Run, Greeley had urged the president to surrender, if he thought the rebels too strong to conquer. See Greeley to Lincoln, New York, 29 July 1861, in Harlan Hoyt Horner, *Lincoln and Greeley* (Urbana: Univ. of Illinois Press, 1953), 233–35.

138. See Lincoln to Buell, Washington, 13 Jan. 1862, *CWL*, 5:98–99.

139. Gen. George H. Thomas (1816–70) commanded the Army of the Cumberland. Gen. James B. McPherson (1828–64) commanded the Army of the Tennessee.

140. "Hood" was the poet Thomas Hood (1799–1845). Orville H. Browning noted in his diary on 1 May: "In conversation with the President last night he expressed great solicitude about the coming struggle with the Army of the Potomac." *The Diary of Orville Hickman Browning*, ed. Theodore Calvin Pease and James G. Randall (Springfield: Illinois State Historical Library, 1925), 1:668.

Hay reportedly told Elihu Root that at times during the war:

> I would be awakened by some one seating himself on the side of my bed, and Lincoln's voice would say, "Lie still; don't get up. Would you mind if I read

to you a little while?" Then he would begin a poem of Hood's, a passage from Shakespeare, or a portion of the Bible. After perhaps twenty minutes or half an hour, his mind having become calm, the tall gaunt figure would rise from the edge of my bed and start for the door and on down the dark corridor. The candle carried high in his hand would light the disheveled hair as the President in flapping night-shirt, his feet padding along in carpet slippers, would disappear into the darkness.

Root related this story to the sculptor James R. Fraser. William L. Slade, quoting Fraser, in "Abraham Lincoln's Shakespeare" (typescript), James G. Randall MSS, DLC.

141. See Grant to Halleck, Germania Ford, Va., 4 May 1864, *Papers of Grant*, 10:397.

142. Gen. Green Clay Smith (1826–95) was a congressman from Kentucky (1863–66). James M. Ashley (1824–96) was a congressman from Ohio (1859–69). The call was for a convention to meet in Cleveland on 31 May to nominate a more radical Republican than Lincoln for president.

143. See Grant to Halleck, "Wilderness," 9 May 1864, *Papers of Grant*, 10:414–15.

144. James W. Nesmith (1820–85) was a U.S. senator from Oregon (1861–67). Rufus Ingalls (1820–93) was the quartermaster of Grant's army. The despatch appeared on the front page of the *New York Tribune*, 14 May. Meade reprimanded Ingalls for sending it.

145. See Thomas L. Carney to Lincoln, 13 May 1864, and Lincoln to Carney, [Washington,] 14 May 1864, *CWL*, 7:340–341.

146. Anna Elizabeth Dickinson (1842–1932) was a young antislavery orator. James Miller McKim (1810–74) was a leading Pennsylvania abolitionist who was traveling throughout the South to promote education among the freedmen.

In 1864 Dickinson called Lincoln "the wisest scoundrel in the country" and told a friend that "I would rather lose all the reputation I possess & sell apples & peanuts on the street, than say aught, that would gain a vote for him." Dickinson to [Elizabeth Cady Stanton?], Philadelphia, 12 July 1864, Harper Collection, Huntington Library, San Marino, Calif. That year Dickinson urged Lincoln to enforce more vigorously the Emancipation Proclamation. The president tried to tell her a story, but she interrupted: "I didn't come to hear stories. I can read better ones in the papers any day than you can tell me." The President asked her opinion of his reconstruction policy, which she called "all wrong; as radically bad as can be." The president closed the interview by saying, "if the radicals want me to lead, let them get out of the way and let me lead." The gravely offended Ms. Dickinson told a friend, "I have spoken my last word to President Lincoln." As she recounted this story, she ridiculed Lincoln's appearance, especially "his old coat, out at the elbows which look as if he had worn it three years and used it as a pen wiper" and his stocking "limp and soiled." *Boston Daily Courier*, 28 Apr. 1864, in James Harvey Young, "Anna Elizabeth Dickinson and the Civil War: For and Against Lincoln," *Mississippi Valley Historical Review* 31 (June 1944): 72.

McKim heard the interview described in much different terms: "A. E. D. said but very few words. She was more a witness than a party. What she did say was 'foolish' according to her own acknowledgment at the time. She burst into tears—struck an attitude and begged Mr. L. to excuse her for coming there to make a fool of herself. The President was paternally kind and considerate in what he said to her." McKim to William Lloyd Garrison, 5 May 1864, quoted in Young, "For and Against Lincoln," 73. Dickinson eventually endorsed Lincoln's candidacy as a necessary evil. Dickinson to "My dear friend," Philadelphia, 3 Sept. 1864, *Chicago Tribune*, 12 Sept. 1864, p. 2.

On 10 May, at a meeting of the American Antislavery Society in New York, Wendell Phillips attacked Lincoln. Garrison dissented, saying of the president:

> when I remember the trials through which he has passed, and the perils which have surrounded him . . . when I remember how fearfully pro-slavery was the public sentiment of the North . . . when I remember how nearly a majority, even at this hour, is the seditious element of the North, and then remember that Abraham Lincoln struck the chains from the limbs of more than three millions of slaves . . . when I remember that we have now nearly reached the culmination of our great struggle for the suppression of the rebellion and its cause, I do not feel disposed, for one, to take this occasion . . . to say anything very harshly against Abraham Lincoln. (*The Letters of William Lloyd Garrison*, ed. Walter M. Merrill [Cambridge: Harvard Univ. Press, 1971–81], 5:181–82)

147. John Sedgwick (1813–64), the commander of the 6th Corps of the Army of the Potomac, was killed on 9 May.

148. The wife of Samuel Gridley Howe, Julia Ward Howe (1819–1910) won fame as the author of the text for the "Battle Hymn of the Republic." She championed the causes of peace, abolition, and woman suffrage. Her parlor lectures included "Moral Triangulation, or the Third Party."

149. The foremost female pianist of her time, the Venezuelan-born Teresa Carreno (1853–1917) debuted in Philadelphia at the age of nine. She was known as "the Valkyrie of the piano."

150. William M. Fishback (1831–1903), an attorney who had worked with Lincoln in the late 1850s, was a leading Unionist in Arkansas. In January 1864, he wrote much of the state's new constitution, which limited voting to whites. Partly as a result of that clause, the U.S. Senate refused to seat him. He later served as governor of Arkansas (1893–95). In part because Fishback recommended him, Stoddard was commissioned a U.S. marshal for the Eastern District of Arkansas on 24 September 1864.

151. *Jessie Brown, or the Relief of Lucknow*, by Dionysius L. Boucicault (1820?–90).

152. Butler's Army of the James bungled its assignment so badly that the Confederates were able to concentrate almost all their reinforcements against the Army of the Potomac.

153. Sigel was removed after humiliating defeats in the Shenandoah Valley, most notably at the Battle of New Market in May.

154. Alexander W. Randall (1819–72), the assistant postmaster general, was a Wisconsin politician who became Andrew Johnson's postmaster general after the war. A. D. Smith, a direct tax commissioner for South Carolina, was a brother-in-law of Harrison Reed. See *supra*, entries for 27 Apr. and 4 Nov. 1863. An investigation by Special Treasury Agent Austin Smith in 1864 cleared Harrison Reed's reputation from the charges made by his colleague, Judge Lyman D. Stickney, who had accused him of defrauding the government by selling land to blacks below its fair market value.

155. The person saved was perhaps Henry Slack, whose sister had appealed on 21 May to Lincoln. Three days later the president commuted the sentence.

156. On 4 April, Davis had introduced the following resolution, which passed unanimously: "the Congress of the United States are unwilling by silence to leave the nations of the world under the impression that they are indifferent spectators of the deplorable events now transpiring in the republic of Mexico, and that they therefore think fit to declare that it does not accord with the policy of the United States to acknowledge any monarchical Government erected on the ruins of any republican Government in America under the auspices of any European Power." *Congressiional Globe*, 38th Cong., 1st sess., 1864, pt. 2, p. 1408. Whitelaw Reid agreed with Hay: "A foolish effort has been made by some people . . . to distort Mr. Winter Davis' resolution about French interference in Mexico, into an attack upon the Administration. Some one said something of the sort to Mr. Davis himself yesterday. Perhaps his reply was about the most satisfactory that could be made: 'If the friends of the Administration want to commit suicide that's what they had better do. If they don't, they had better not create the impression that that resolution differed in the slightest degree from their own desires!'" Washington correspondence by "Agate," 21 Apr. 1864, *Cincinnati Gazette*, 25 Apr. 1864, p. 1.

Davis, according to a Washington journalist, had a large "organ of combativeness," was "always spoiling for a fight," and seemed "to be ever wandering about dragging an imaginary coat upon the floor of the House and daring any one to tread upon it." Early in 1864 "his favorite object of attack" became Lincoln, who said: "Well, well, it appears to do him good, and as it does me no injury, (that is I don't feel that it does) what's the harm in letting him have his fling? If he did not pitch into me he would into some poor fellow whom he might hurt." Washington correspondence, 28 Feb. 1864, *Chicago Tribune*, 3 Mar. 1864, p. 2.

157. Gouverneur K. Warren (1830–82) was the commander of the 5th Corps of the Army of the Potomac. John Gross Barnard (1815–82) had been the superintendent of West Point (1855–56) and was Grant's chief engineer. Meigs and Barnard composed the investigating board sent by Halleck at Grant's suggestion to the Army of the James. Their report of 25 May recommended that Butler be given an administrative post and removed from field command.

158. Anson Stager (1825–85) of Cleveland was the general superintendent of the Western Union Company. The Cleveland convention was a meeting of Radicals unwilling to support Lincoln for reelection.

159. Ebon Clark Ingersoll (1831–79) of Peoria, Ill., occupied the congressional seat of the recently deceased Owen Lovejoy.

160. The Republican National Convention met in Baltimore 7–8 June. The Louisiana delegation was seated.

161. The South Carolina delegation was not seated.

162. The pro-Lincoln Florida delegation won admission but was denied a vote.

163. Gen. Winfield Scott Hancock (1824–86) was from Pennsylvania.

164. William Francis Bartlett (1840–76), a colonel of the 49th Massachusetts, lost a leg at the Battle of Yorktown in 1862 and suffered wounds at the Battle of Port Hudson in 1863 and at the Battle of the Wilderness in 1864. Franklin Philp, according to William E. Doster, "received his gentleman friends every Sunday evening." At Philp's home, "affairs of State were discussed" and Nicolay and Hay "were much courted for their supposed influence." At these gatherings, Hay was, after July 1864, jocularly dubbed the "Niagara Commissioner." Doster, *Episodes of the Civil War*, 31–32.

165. Both before and after the convention, the president was besieged by delegates attending the conventions of the Republican Party and the Union League. To one group, he declared "that the position which he fills is not to be envied, or one to be desired." Washington correspondence, 9 June 1864, *Chicago Tribune*, 11 June 1864, p. 1.

166. See Nicolay to Hay, Baltimore, 5 June 1864, Nicolay MSS, DLC; and Hay to Nicolay, Washington, 6 June 1864, Hay MSS, RPB.

167. Hay's description of his journey to Missouri as the president's special representative to General Rosecrans exists in two versions; they are presented here consecutively. The evidence of the manuscript, a pocket diary, suggests that the first draft was written on or shortly after 15 June, during the final stages of his return trip. The revised, fuller version in Hay's regular diary volume was completed on 17 June, after his arrival in Washington.

168. "Mrs. Pendelton" was perhaps the wife of Elliott Hunt Pendelton (1828–92), a merchant and banker in Cincinnati who was active in the affairs of the Sanitary Commission.

169. Larz Anderson (1803–78) was Robert Anderson's brother and the son-in-law of Nicholas Longworth, who became the Speaker of the House. Nicholas Longworth Anderson was brevetted a major general at the age of twenty-seven.

170. The Lindell was a noted hotel in St. Louis.

171. Maj. Frank S. Bond was one of Rosecrans's favorite staff officers.

172. "S" was Col. John P. Sanderson (1818–64), the provost marshal general of the Department of Missouri, who had been the chief clerk of the War Department early in the war. He exercised great influence over Rosecrans. His exposé of the "Conspiracy to Establish a Northwest Confederacy" appeared in the *St. Louis Missouri Democrat* on 28 July 1864. William P. Hall (1820–82) became the governor of Missouri upon the death of Hamilton R. Gamble on 31 January 1864.

173. William S. Hillyer (1831–74) had been a friend of Grant before the war and served on his staff from 1861 until 15 May 1863, when he resigned. In 1864 he asked the cotton trader James W. Singleton to help arrange for him an interview with the president. See Hillyer to Singleton, Washington, 22 Sept. 1864, AL MSS, DLC. John A. Rawlins (1831–69) was Grant's most trusted staff member.

174. Rosecrans had unsuccessfully sent Bond to Washington in order to secure Senate confirmation of Sanderson's appointment as the provost marshal general of the department.

175. French for "As it should be."

176. John Wynn Davidson (1823–81) was the commander of the Army of Arkansas. Thomas Ewing Jr. (1829–96) commanded the District of St. Louis.

177. Clement L. Vallandigham (1820–71) of Ohio, the leader of the northern Peace Democrats, had been a member of the U.S. House (1858–63) and an unsuccessful candidate for governor of Ohio (1863). General Burnside had him arrested in May 1863 for uttering sedition; Burnside's act embarrassed the president, who banished Vallandigham to the Confederacy. He returned to Ohio in mid-June 1864. The "military commander" of the O.A.K., Gen. Sterling Price (1809–67), invaded Missouri in the fall of 1864 with 12,000 men, hoping that O.A.K. members would rise up and help him defeat the Union forces. Too few cooperated with him, however, and he was defeated at Pilot Knob and elsewhere.

178. Charles L. Hunt was a St. Louis attorney. Joseph E. Johnston (1807–91) was a leading general in the Confederate army.

179. Confederate general Edmund Kirby Smith (1824–93) commanded the Trans-Mississippi Department.

180. Sanderson made a full record of his examination of Mary Ann Pitman, alias "Lieutenant Rawley," alias "Mary Hays." Gen. Nathan Bedford Forrest (1821–77) was in charge of Confederate forces in West Tennessee. In April 1864, Forrest's men overran Fort Pillow and murdered in cold blood many captured Union soldiers.

181. James A. McMaster (1820–86) edited the *New York Freeman's Journal.*

182. See Rosecrans to Lincoln, St. Louis, 14 June 1864, AL MSS, DLC.

183. The Battle of Perryville, Ky., took place on 8 October 1862. The Battle of Chickamauga, Ga., took place 19–21 September 1863.

184. The largest of the Copperhead secret societies, the Knights were organized in the 1850s, when they championed U.S. annexation of various Caribbean nations.

185. In a memorandum dated 14 December 1863, John G. Nicolay recorded the following:

> This morning early Edward came into the President's office and announced that Mr Wood was here to see him. "I am sorry he is here," said the President. "I would rather he should not come about here so much. Tell Mr Wood that I have nothing as yet to tell him on the subject we conversed about when he was here last." Edward went out to deliver the message. "I can tell you what Wood wants," said the President to me. "He came here one day last week to urge me to publish some sort of amnesty for the northern sympathizers and abettors of the rebellion, which would include Vallandigham, and permit him to return; and promised that if I would do so, they would have two Democratic candidates in the field at the next Presidential election." (Nicolay MSS, DLC)

186. The Democratic National Convention, originally scheduled for 4 July, had been postponed till late August.

187. On 20 June, Lincoln drafted, but did not send, a letter to Brough and Heintzelman. See *CWL*, 7:402.

188. Democrat William R. Morrison (1824–1909) was a congressman from Illinois (1863–65, 1873–87).

189. In the margin next to this paragraph, Hay wrote: "'If I didn't know I'd tell you,' Seward once said to a man who asked him a question of State importance."

190. At the end of the week, Gustavus Fox described this visit:

Monday afternoon the Prest Master Tad and Chadwick as caterer, all on board the Balt[imore] ord[nance] boat started down the Potomac and after a delightful run of 20 hours we landed at City Point 57 miles up the James River. At this point Gen Grant has his headquarters. We found him in his tent under the shade trees smoking a cigar, and after a pleasant chat and dining with him we started on horseback for the front near Petersburg. The weather was not hot but the roads were horribly dusty. The army however occupies a healthy country and are in the midst of fields of clover wheat and oats. A nine mile ride brought us within sight of Petersburg and close to the lines of the enemy and here we saw most of the Generals of the Army of the Potomac. The troops cheered the Prest, especially the colored ones, with much fervor. We retd about dusk and after a cup of tea with the Genl and his officers we went on board our boat to sleep. In the morning we went up to Bermuda Hundred and took Genl Butler and Ad[miral] Lee on board and ascended the James River to Howletts House where the enemy have a battery and just below which point lie the iron-clads All the vessels cheered the Prest as he passed and as we were within reach of the enemies guns I wondered they did not open fire. The Prest went on board the Onondaga and thence we landed and took horses and rode across Butlers lines to his headquarters and dined with him, at a place on the Appo-mattox called point of Rocks. After dinner we took a boat in that river and run down to City Point where our own boat was waiting to receive us. Here we had an hours visit from Genl Grant. Everything is very satisfactory and the Prest came back in fine spirits. Grant says he will never be farther from Richmond and that, though he will have some rebuffs he will surely win and I think he will. . . . Our trip back was smooth and pleasant and the Prest expressed him-self delighted. (Fox to his wife, Washington, 25 June 1864, Fox MSS, New-York Historical Society)

191. "Brooks" was perhaps Gen. William T. H. Brooks (1821–70), who had served in the 10th Corps in operations at Cold Harbor and Petersburg.

192. Orville H. Browning recorded that "During the past week, the President vis-ited Grants army. . . . He told me last night that Grant said, when he left him, that 'you Mr President, need be under no apprehension. You will never hear of me far-ther from Richmond than now, till I have taken it. I am just as sure of going into Richmond as I am of any future event. It may take all summer day, but I will go in." *Diary of Browning*, 1:673 (entry for 26 June 1864).

193. Hunter's offensive in the Shenandoah Valley began auspiciously but

foundered when Jubal Early reinforced the Confederates. Gen. Philip H. Sheridan (1831–88) commanded the Army of the Shenandoah. Gen. James Harrison Wilson (1837–1925) led a cavalry raid on 22 and 23 June against the South Side Railroad. In the margin next to this passage appears the following: "Commenced reading French today with Harrison"

194. In 1861 Britain, France, and Spain intervened in Mexico to collect debts. The following year, the British and Spanish withdrew their forces, but French troops remained and overthrew the government of Benito Juárez in 1863, paving the way for the Austrian archduke Ferdinand Maximilian to become emperor of Mexico.

195. Francis B. Carpenter (1830–1900), a portrait painter, spent six months in the White House painting the monumental canvas of Lincoln reading the Emancipation Proclamation to the cabinet. The cabinet meeting that Seward referred to took place on 29 March 1861.

196. Edward Wellman Serrell (1826–1906) was the chief engineer of the Army of the James. Lt. Col. Cyrus B. Comstock (1831–1910) of Massachusetts was the chief engineer of the Army of the Potomac and later the senior aide-de-camp to General Grant. On 29 May, Butler told Gillmore: "Gen. Weitzel will do anything in the way of engineering to which Gen. Gillmore does not feel himself competent on our line. Col. Henry L. Abbot is also a very accomplished engineer officer in your command. In my judgment Col. Serrell is now of more use in his present position than he can be elsewhere." *Private and Official Correspondence of Gen. Benjamin F. Butler During the Period of the Civil War* (Norwood, Mass.: privately printed, 1917), 4:283.

Gillmore endorsed Butler's message thus: "The operator will have this repeated and will request the other station to have it examined by Gen. Butler, before he sends it again." In fact, Butler wired back at 2:15 P.M. on 29 May: "Gen. Gillmore has returned my despatch of 12.30 for examination. I see no word to alter save that Genl. Gillmore may object to the word 'competent.' The sense in which it may be used might be objectionable, but there are many kinds of incompetency and knowledge, and the other's want of time, pressure of other duties for superintendence of details and supervision works, because of which Gen. Gillmore asked for Col. Serrell, and to which I have suggested the services of Genl. Weitzel & Col. Abbot." *Correspondence of Butler*, 4:283.

197. The operations on Morris Island took place in Charleston Harbor during the summer of 1863.

198. Secretary Chase wanted Maunsell B. Field (1822–75), the assistant secretary of the treasury, named the assistant treasurer of the United States at New York, but Lincoln refused because of intense opposition from the New York congressional delegation.

199. Lincoln also admired Tod as a raconteur. See John Sherman, *John Sherman's Recollections of Forty Years in the House, Senate and Cabinet: An Autobiography* (New York: Werner, 1895), 1:337–38.

200. See Chase to Lincoln, Washington, 29 June 1864, *CWL*, 7:414n. Lucius E. Chittenden (1824–1902), the register of the treasury (1861–65), had vainly tried the previous day to arrange for Chase's return. In his recollections of this episode,

Chittenden did not mention this threat of a "general resignation." *Recollections of President Lincoln and His Administration* (New York: Harper, 1891), 370–84.

201. Edwin D. Morgan (1811–83), the former governor of New York (1859–63) and a senator from New York (1863–69), was the chairman of the Republican National Committee. Morgan told a friend, "I never will consent to the appointment of Mr. M. B. Field as Cisco's successor." Morgan to Thomas Hillhouse, 30 June 1864, quoted in James A. Rawley, *Edwin D. Morgan, 1811–1883: Merchant in Politics* (New York: Columbia Univ. Press, 1955), 196. Dudley S. Gregory (1800–74) of New Jersey, a banker, had served with Lincoln as a Whig in Congress (1847–49). Richard M. Blatchford (1798–1875), a New York lawyer, had served as the U.S. minister to the States of the Church in Rome in 1862. Thomas Hillhouse (1816–97) was a New York financier and politician who had served as the assistant adjutant general of volunteers on the staff of Governor Morgan (1861–62). See Morgan to Lincoln, Washington, 27 June 1864, AL MSS, DLC. Cisco did withdraw his resignation on 28 June. See Chase to Lincoln, 29 June 1864, *CWL*, 7:414n.

On 12 July, Brough told William Henry Smith of his conversation with the president, who told him, "this is the third time he [Chase] has thrown this [his resignation] at me, and I do not think I am called on to continue to beg him to take it back, especially when the country would not go to destruction in consequence." When Brough offered to mediate the dispute, Lincoln declined: "I know you doctored the matter up once, but on the whole, Brough, I reckon you had better let it alone this time." Brough's recollections in William Henry Smith, "Private Memoranda of War Times," Smith MSS, Ohio State Archaeological and Historical Society, Columbus.

Chase explained to Jay Cooke:

> When I found that upon the question of Mr. Cisco's successor I was not to be left free from all other considerations, except simple fidelity to the general cause and fitness for the place, but was expected to take into consideration questions of local politics, I felt myself constrained to make it a turning point. I had been so much embarrassed and injured by the standing of one of the members of the cabinet that I could not feel at all safe unless that office was in hands on which I could personally depend. The President differed with me and I tendered my resignation, and he thought it best to accept it. I could not remain and feel that my Department was really under my own control or that I had any real ability to serve the country in it. The President did not see the matter as I did.
>
> It was very painful for me to resign especially at a moment of peril, but at moments of peril the pilot must have command of the ship, whether the best pilot that can be found or not. If the captain won't let him have charge the pilot cannot be expected to be willing to do the piloting. I don't know that I could do the piloting and have nothing to complain of, if, when I tendered my resignation, it was accepted.
>
> After all I did not know but it would be later if not then. It was very doubtful whether Congress would give the additional taxes necessary to a firm basis

of credit, and I am tired of expedients. I want something solid. Congress you know did refuse the tax on state banks necessary to compel them to assume the burden of contracting circulation, and so put that burden wholly on the Treasury. Congress refused also to give the Treasury the benefit of the whole tax on national banks as a basis for loans. I felt therefore that if Congress should refuse also taxes sufficient to produce at least half the expenditure of the next fiscal year, that I could hardly remain anyhow.

These considerations made me more than willing to resign. After all I should have held on as long as I could hope to be useful had not I feared that my insisting on what I thought the true and only safe principle relating to the appointment of Assistant Treasurers made my position disagreeable to the President, and that I must hold my office, if I retained it, either by surrendering a point which I thought vital or against his inclinations. I therefore tendered my resignation and feel its acceptance as a real relief. (Chase to Cooke, 1 July 1864, in Ellis Paxson Oberholtzer, *Jay Cooke: Financier of the Civil War* [Philadelphia: George W. Jacobs, 1907], 1:421–22)

202. John Sherman (1823–1900) was a Republican senator from Ohio (1861–77, 1881–97) and the secretary of the treasury (1877–81). Peter Godwin Van Winkle (1808–72) was a senator from West Virginia (1863–69). A journalist reported that Lincoln "was very low spirited on Thursday—the day on which he sent in the nomination of Dave Tod. He seems to have been deserted of his usual good sense when he sent in this name to the Senate. The feeling was unanimous in Congress that for such a man to succeed Mr. Chase would be ruinous to the finances." Washington correspondence, n.d., *Springfield (Mass.) Republican*, n.d., copied in the *St. Paul (Minn.) Press*, 22 July 1864, p. 3.

Lincoln told Gov. John Brough of Ohio "emphatically that he would not withdraw" Tod's nomination. According to a journalist who spoke with Brough on 12 July:

> The governor advised him to request the Senate Committee to delay their report until the next morning, as he was satisfied Tod would decline the appointment, and in that way the President, the Senate, Tod and the country would be relieved from embarrassment. The President asked for his reasons for supposing Tod would decline. He gave them: The state of his health, and the fact that in the nomination he got all the honor without the hard work; and that Tod was a man of good common sense and would not willingly place himself in a position which he was not capable of filling. The President accepted the advice, and apparently with great pleasure. (William Henry Smith, "Private Memoranda")

203. Chase waited until Congress was about to adjourn to submit his supplemental tax bill. On 29 June, a journalist reported that "Both Senate and House Finance Committees express doubt whether such a measure as he desires could pass

at this late day of the session." Washington correspondence, 29 June 1864, *New York Times*, 30 June 1864, p. 1.

204. Benjamin Rush Plumley (1816–87), a Quaker abolitionist from Pennsylvania, served as General Banks's main civilian assistant in New Orleans and was a leading Radical in Louisiana. Morgan exulted on 1 July, "It is not a dark day, but among the brightest we have seen for many days *lately*." Quoted in Rawley, *Morgan*, 196.

205. George Harrington (1815–92) had long been a clerk in the Treasury Department and in 1861 became the assistant secretary. From 1865 to 1869, he served as the U.S. minister to Switzerland.

206. A journalist gave the following account of Fessenden's appointment:

> On Thursday night Governor Tod sent his declination and Mr. Lincoln went to bed upon it, and as he says, before morning he was satisfied that Pitt Fessenden was the man. Early on Friday he ordered nomination to be made out and Major Hay took it down to the Senate. Five minutes after he had left, Senator Fessenden entered the Presidential apartment and was soon discussing the "situation." Mr. Lincoln did not tell him what he had done, but discussed Mr. Chase's resignation for a short time and then said, "Mr. Fessenden, I have made a new nomination this morning which I trust you will approve; I have sent your name in!" Mr. Fessenden was greatly surprised and amazed. He replied, "You must recall it; you can overtake Hay with a messenger now if you will. Please send for him at once for I cannot possible taken it. My health will not permit me to think of it for a moment." But the President was firm. "You must take it," he said, and later in the day sent word as follows: "Tell Fessenden to stick." Meantime telegrams from all parts of the country came pouring in upon him, congratulating him upon his admirable selection. At night Mr. Lincoln was in high spirits, and he exclaimed to Mr. Seward who was present: "The Lord has never yet deserted me, and I did not believe he would this time!" It was Mr. Lincoln's intention to send in the name of ex-Governor Boutwell, if Mr. Fessenden had positively declined. (Washington correspondence, n.d., *Springfield [Mass.] Republican*, n.d., copied in the *St. Paul [Minn.] Press*, 22 July 1864, p. 3)

207. Abram Wakeman (1824–89) was the postmaster of New York.

208. "Coe" was probably George Simmons Coe (1817–96), president of the American Exchange Bank in New York (1860–94). The Gold Act of 17 June, forbidding speculation in gold futures, failed to check the rise in the price of gold. Timothy O. Howe (1816–83) was a senator from Wisconsin (1861–79). Gen. Alexander Samuel Diven (1809–96) had been a congressman from New York (1861–63).

209. Hugh McCulloch (1808–95), the comptroller of the currency, became the secretary of the treasury when Fessenden stepped down in 1865. Cf. Chittenden, *Recollections of Lincoln*, 381–83.

210. A similar scheme had been suggested to Chase in September 1862.

211. In 1852 Lincoln became a manager of the Illinois State Colonization Society,

and he addressed their annual meetings in 1853 and 1855. During the Civil War, he continued to promote colonization, a pet scheme of his "beau ideal of a statesman," Henry Clay, despite criticism from some Radical Republicans. Bernard Kock was the promoter of the unsuccessful attempt to form a black settlement on Vache Island, off Haiti. Attorney General Bates called him "an arrant humbug" and a "Charleston adventurer," and others thought of him "as a swindler and full-fledged rascal." Frederic Bancroft, *The Colonization of American Negroes*, ed. Jacob E. Cook (Norman: Univ. of Oklahoma Press, 1957), 235–40. On 2 July 1864, Congress revoked the funds it had appropriated for the project. James Mitchell was a clergyman who headed the Emigration Office of the Interior Department. The Chiriqui plan included colonization of American blacks on the Isthmus of Panama. A contract between the U.S. government and the Chiriqui Improvement Company had been signed on 12 September 1862, but the project was dropped later that year. The $25,000 advanced to Senator Pomeroy to implement the scheme was not accounted for. Pomeroy and Caleb B. Smith were involved in the scheme. On 29 June, Lincoln had written a message to the Senate communicating a report by Usher on the subject of colonization, but it was not forwarded.

It should be noted that many other vigorous opponents of slavery favored colonization, including Benjamin F. Wade, Salmon P. Chase, Horace Greeley, Thaddeus Stevens, Samuel C. Pomeroy, Harriet Beecher Stowe, Henry Ward Beecher, James G. Birney, Martin R. Delany, Lyman Trumbull, Henry Wilson, and Gerrit Smith.

212. See Chase to Lincoln, 29 June 1864, *CWL*, 7:414n.

213. The *Tribune* account included the following:

> It is undoubtedly true that Mr. Chase has frequently felt discouraged about his ability to carry the financial load taken upon his shoulders. He has within a week expressed this discouragement. The feeling perhaps is inseparable from his organization.
>
> This, coupled with the irritation caused by the quasi Executive sanction of the warfare of the Blairs upon the purity of his departmental administration and his personal integrity, probably precipitated the resignation which so suddenly startled Congress and Washington this forenoon. (*New York Tribune*, 1 July 1864, p. 1)

"Let 'em wriggle" is an allusion to a story that Lincoln liked to tell about a man whose son, "of a scientific turn," compulsively examined things with his microscope. One day, as the father was about to eat a piece of cheese, the boy exclaimed: "Don't eat that, it is full of wrigglers." The reply came: "My son, let 'em wriggle; I can stand it if they can." Francis B. Carpenter, *Six Months at the White House with Lincoln*, 2nd ed. (New York: Hurd and Houghton, 1867), 145.

214. The Wade-Davis bill, passed on 2 July and then vetoed by Lincoln, challenged the reconstruction plan announced by the president on 8 December 1863. "Pocketed" means pocket vetoed by the president.

215. The previous day, Fessenden had agreed to serve as the secretary of the trea-

sury. On this day, he and Lincoln consulted about patronage matters in the department.

216. In his last public address, Lincoln called the question of whether the Confederate states had been in or out of the Union "a merely pernicious abstraction." *CWL*, 8:403.

217. In the vicinity of Harper's Ferry, Confederates under Jubal Early were driving Sigel's forces back. On 8 July, Sigel was replaced by Gen. Albion P. Howe.

218. Hunter had retreated from the Shenandoah Valley, leaving it open to Jubal Early.

219. "G. C. S." was Green Clay Smith. His nephew was William Cassius Goodloe (1841–89) of Kentucky.

220. A loose newspaper clipping in the diary summarizes the eight scenes that comprise this work. Robert L. Hickman (d. 1873) of Virginia was a celebrated ne'er-do-well, gambler, vagabond, and fancy dresser. He was described by a Washington newspaper as a man "too proud to work" and "too honest to steal," who "levying a tax on all who came in contact with him, made it pay." *New York Times*, 3 Sept. 1873, p. 5.

221. "Fraser" was probably Judge Philip Frasure of the U.S. district court for the northern district of Florida. "Chamberlin" was probably Culver P. Chamberlin, who had served as the U.S. attorney for the northern district of Florida. See *The Diary of Edward Bates, 1859–1866*, ed. Howard K. Beale (Washington, D.C.: Government Printing Office, 1933), 374 (entry for 9 June 1864).

222. The article Hay alludes to appeared in the 7 July issue of the *Tribune*. Chase had requested an interview on 28 June. The president refused, saying that "the difficulty does not, in the main part, lie within the range of a conversation between you and me." Chase did not allude to this rebuff in his letter of resignation. See *CWL*, 7:413.

223. Gen. Lewis Wallace (1827–1905), though defeated by Jubal Early at Monocacy, had slowed him up and thus may well have saved Washington. Lincoln in response urged Grant to send troops to destroy Early. Early's raid brought him close to the capital, but reinforcements from Grant enabled the Union forces to drive him off on 12–13 July. On the fourteenth, he retreated across the Potomac.

224. Horatio G. Wright's 6th Corps helped fend off Early's threat to Washington. "Whiton" was probably William H. Whiton of the Office of Military Railroads. The proximity of the enemy annoyed Lincoln. Gustavus Fox kept the ordnance ship *Baltimore* ready to carry the president off, in case Early did seize the capital.

225. Stanton had urged the presidential family to leave the Soldiers Home and come back to the White House for the sake of their safety. This move irritated the president.

226. Fort Stevens, north of Washington, became the scene of skirmishing between Union forces and Early's advance units shortly after noon. According to some accounts, the soldier who ordered Lincoln to get down was Capt. Oliver Wendell Holmes Jr. (1841–1935), who was to become a celebrated justice of the U.S. Supreme Court. Early's forces burned Montgomery Blair's home in Silver Spring. The home of Francis P. Blair Sr. was unharmed.

227. Gen. E. R. S. Canby (1817–73) had been named the commander of the Department of West Mississippi on 7 May 1864. Gillmore took command of part of the 19th Corps, which had recently arrived from the West. McCook assumed charge of the miscellaneous military and civilian forces hastily assembled in Washington, including members of the quartermaster general's department.

228. While standing near the president, Dr. C. C. V. A. Crawford, a surgeon attached to a unit of Pennsylvania Volunteers, was shot in the leg.

229. Joseph Jackson Lewis (1801–83), a Republican politician from Pennsylvania, served as the commissioner of internal revenue (1863–65).

230. Company K of the 150th Pennsylvania was ordered out to Fort Reno on 11 July. Two days later it returned.

231. Britton A. Hill was a St. Louis lawyer who from 1863 to 1865 had a Supreme Court practice in Washington with Thomas Ewing, Edgar Cowan, and Orville H. Browning.

232. Daniel Henry Rucker (1812–1910) was an assistant quartermaster general. Lt. Thomas G. Welles was an aide-de-camp to General McCook. His father, Gideon Welles, said "I regret his passion for the service and his recklessness and youth." *Welles Diary*, 2:71 (entry for 11 July 1864).

233. Gen. Edward Otho Cresap Ord (1818–83) commanded the 8th corps of the Army of the Potomac. Reinforcements from his command at Baltimore arrived during the night.

234. The attachments are not in the Hay MSS, RPB. The letter referred to as "A" is doubtless Greeley to Lincoln, 7 July 1864; letter C is Greeley to Lincoln, 13 July 1864. For letters A–F, see *CWL*, 7:435–36n, 435, 440–441n, 442, 443n, 443.

235. For letters H and I, see *CWL*, 451n, 451.

236. George N. Sanders was a political figure from Kentucky who, before the Civil War, had spent time in Europe championing the cause of revolutionary Republicans like Garibaldi. In Canada he served as a Confederate agent and became intimate with John Wilkes Booth. James P. Holcombe (1820–73) was a law professor at the University of Virginia (1851–61), a representative in the Confederate Congress (1862–64), and a member of the Confederate Secret Service (1864–65). Clement C. Clay (1816–82) was a former senator from Alabama (1853–61). "St. Kate's" is the town of St. Catherines, Ont., twelve miles from Niagara Falls. See Clay's report to Judah P. Benjamin, St. Catherines, Canada West, 11 Aug. 1864, Clay MSS, Chicago Historical Society.

237. James Gordon Bennett was the editor of the *New York Herald*. The story of Greeley's attempts to effect a compromise peace is told in Horner, *Lincoln and Greeley*, 296–323.

238. William Edward Dorsheimer (1832–88) was a New York lawyer and politician who offered his services to the president the following month to act as a go-between with the Confederate emissaries. His offer was declined.

239. Samuel Nelson (1792–1873) of New York, an associate justice of the U.S. Supreme Court (1845–72), was a Democrat.

240. Hay's second version of his report on the Niagara Falls Conference is writ-

ten on leaves folded and inserted into a notebook that contains the first version. Possibly it was intended as the basis of a newspaper article to counter the effects of the *Tribune* article of 22 July, which omitted the text of the communications written before 17 July. This created the impression that Lincoln had withdrawn from a previous commitment to negotiate unconditionally. The *New York Times* of 4 August called for the publication of the entire correspondence and accused Greeley of having failed to reveal to the Confederate "commissioners" the conditions laid down in the president's letter of 9 July.

Lincoln had specified that he would negotiate with "any person anywhere professing to have any proposition of Jefferson Davis in writing, for peace, embracing the restoration of the Union and the abandonment of slavery." Greeley's own "plan of adjustment" in his letter of 7 July to Lincoln had recommended similar terms: "(1) The Union is restored and declared perpetual. (2) Slavery is utterly and forever abolished throughout the same." The *Times* article showed a knowledge of the earlier letters, which probably came from within the White House. In an editorial published in the *Tribune* of the following day, Greeley replied: "I deny that the overture submitted through Major Hay was the 'same offer' that I had been authorized to make; I deny that I was ever required to impose such 'conditions' as those embodied in Major Hay's rescript." But he reluctantly agreed to publication provided it should be in full.

Correspondence between Greeley, Hay, and Lincoln 4–11 August resulted in an impasse, as Lincoln objected to, and Greeley insisted on, the publication of certain phrases of Greeley's original letter of 7 July, including his words, "our bleeding, bankrupt, almost dying country also longs for peace; shudders at the prospect of further wholesale devastations, and of new rivers of human blood." Lincoln wrote to Raymond on 15 August: "I have concluded that it is better for *me* to submit, for the time, to the consequences of the false position in which he has placed me, than to subject the country to the consequences of publishing these discouraging and injurious parts." *CWL*, 7:494.

241. William Cornell Jewett of Colorado was deemed by Attorney General Bates "a crack-brained simpleton, who aspires to be a knave." *Diary of Bates*, 388 (entry for 22 July 1864). His personal and unauthorized peace negotiations included sending several letters to the president. These were intercepted by Hay, who informed Jewett on 6 December 1863 that "your letters are never . . . submitted." Hay to Jewett, Washington, 6 Dec. 1863, Hay MSS, RPB.

242. James Harlan (1820–99) was a U.S. senator from Iowa (1855–65). Lincoln did woo Bennett, who in the last days of the 1864 campaign told his readers that it made little difference for whom they voted. While this was hardly a ringing endorsement, the *Herald* stopped its assaults on the administration and may have thus helped pave the way for Lincoln's narrow victory in New York state. A week before the election, Lincoln told Bennett's emissary, William O. Bartlett, that he expected to appoint Bennett minister to France. On 20 February 1865, the offer was formally tendered; two weeks later, the editor turned it down. See Bartlett to Lincoln, New York, 20 Oct. 1864, AL MSS, DLC.

243. On 23 September, Lincoln had requested Blair's resignation. This was done in part to placate the Radicals, whose presidential candidate, John C. Frémont, had withdrawn from the contest on 22 September.

244. William Dennison (1815–82), the former governor of Ohio (1859–61), replaced Blair as the postmaster general.

245. Dennison did accept the offer.

246. On 12 October, the people of Maryland voted to make the "Free State" a free state.

247. John Gregory Smith (1818–91) served as the governor of Vermont (1863–65). After the president issued the preliminary Emancipation Proclamation on 22 September, Baldy Smith persuaded McClellan to destroy a letter he had written denouncing that fateful document. Three other generals—John Cochrane, Jacob D. Cox, and Ambrose E. Burnside—also counseled against any public criticism of emancipation. McClellan agreed to give their advice careful thought. The story given by Lincoln to Hay differs from the version written by Governor Smith later in the year:

> I find from a recent interview with Maj. Genl. Wm. F. Smith [the governor's brother], that in the communication which I made to you in Sept last, I was in error as regards some portions of my statement, and hence embrace the first moment at my command to make the correction.
>
> The facts as now related by Genl Smith are, that soon after your emacipation Proclamation was issued, Genl. McLellan called Genl Smith into his tent, and showed him a letter which he (Genl McL.) had written addressed to you condemning the policy of the Proclamation and saying that the Army would never sustain you in it etc. and asking Genl Smiths judgment upon the letter.—Gen Smith advised that he should destroy the letter, that he would neither sustain himself with the army nor the country and that it would only array him in opposition to yourself and result in disaster to him (Gen. McL.). On the strength of Genl Smiths earnest expostulation, Genl McLellan was finally persuaded to destroy the letter.
>
> The statement which I made to you with regard to the letter accepting the proposition for the Presidency, was communicated to me by another person who told me that Genl Smith was knowing to the fact.
>
> Not long after this communication was made to me, in a conversation with Genl Smith, I referred to the letter of Genl McLellan, as a most disgraceful affair, meaning the letter accepting the proposition. Genl Smith supposing that I referred to the letter relating to the proclamation, heartily assented to all I said, and we commented severely upon the course pursued by McLellan and the Copperhead party. This led me to believe that he fully understood the facts and incidents connected with the letter of acceptance, and I have never supposed it otherwise, till he corrected my mistake in his recent conversation with me, and satisfied me that he had no personal knowledge of that letter nor of the proposition which called for it.
>
> I have felt it due to myself, and but an act of justice to Genl Smith that I

should make this explanation and regret that I should have been led into the error (J. G. Smith to Lincoln, St. Albans, 30 Dec. 1864, Univ. of Vermont Library, Burlington)

A copy of this document was enclosed in a letter from Governor Smith to Solomon Foot, a U.S. senator from Vermont, also dated St. Albans, 30 Dec. 1864, and housed in the same collection:

I have been so overwhelmed with pressing duties since my return from Washington that I have not till now, found a moments leisure to correct myself with the President in the matter of my communication with him of Sept last.

I called there several times before leaving Washington, hoping to find him disengaged that I might make the explanation in person, but he was either thronged, or absent on his usual ride, & I failed to see him.

I enclose a copy of my letter to him sent by this mail, that you may understand more fully the extent of the explanation in order that should the matter ever again be referred to between yourself & him you may know what he does.

I trust it will be regarded by him as satisfactory. Should be pleased to hear your views.

248. Smith had graduated in 1845, a year ahead of McClellan.

249. Lincoln visited McClellan at Antietam, 1–4 October 1862. On 6 October, he ordered the general to advance. On 5 November, Lincoln finally removed McClellan. Lincoln told the journalist Albert D. Richardson a similar story:

I do not, as some do, regard McClellan either as a traitor or an officer without capacity. He sometimes has bad counselors, but he is loyal, and he has some fine military qualities. I adhered to him after nearly all my Constitutional advisers lost faith in him. But do you want to know when I gave him up? It was after the battle of Antietam. The Blue Ridge was then between our army and Lee's. We enjoyed the great advantage over them which they usually had over us: we had the short line, and they had the long one, to the Rebel Capital. I directed McClellan peremptorily to move on Richmond. It was eleven days before he crossed his first man over the Potomac; it was eleven days after that before he crossed the last man. Thus, he was twenty-two days in passing the river at a much easier and more practicable ford than that where Lee crossed his entire army between dark one night and daylight the next morning. That was the last grain of sand which broke the camel's back. I relieved McClellan at once. (Quoted in Richardson, *The Secret Service, the Field, the Dungeon and the Escape* [Hartford: American, 1865], 323–24)

Lincoln told Noah Brooks, long after McClellan's dismissal, "I kept McClellan in command long after I had ceased to expect that he would win any victories, simply because I knew that his dismissal would provoke popular indignation and shake the faith of the people in the final success of the war." Brooks, *Statesmen* (New York: Scribner, 1893), 210.

250. See *supra*, entry for 26 Sept. 1862.

251. Lincoln probably alludes to Don Carlos Buell's letter to Halleck, dated 22 October 1862: "The spirit of the rebellion enforces a subordination and patient submission to privation and want, which public sentiment renders absolutely impossible among our troops." *O. R.*, 1st ser., vol. 16, pt. 2, 637. The day after this arrived, Lincoln removed Buell from command. Edward D. Neill (1823–93) was an assistant to Nicolay and Hay in the White House (1864–65).

252. Hay's visit to the Navy Department was described by William Faxon, the chief clerk of the department: "I may as well tell you what I heard not ten minutes ago. . . . Mr. Hay was in the Department, and the subject of Blair's removal was up. Hay said he had just left about a dozen gentlemen with the president and they were talking about Blair's not agreeing with the president's policy, when Lincoln put in that Blair had always agreed with him and that Chase was the only man in the Cabinet who opposed the Emancipation proclamation—which struck me as a very queer thing." Faxon to Mark Howard, Washington, 25 Sept. 1864, Mark Howard MSS, Connecticut Historical Society, Hartford.

An expedition to capture Fort Fisher, commanding the last major Confederate seaport unmolested by an effective Union blockade, was being urged by the Navy Department. The first attack, a fiasco led by Benjamin Butler, took place in December. The following month it was captured. Porter was transferred from the Mississippi Squadron to the North Atlantic Blockading Squadron on 12 October. Godfrey Weitzel did lead the land forces in the first attack.

253. Lincoln wrote Blair on 23 September asking him to resign from the cabinet. *CWL*, 8:18.

254. Blair's memo of 15 March 1861 urged supplying Sumter, while all other cabinet members recommended against it.

255. *Teterrima fons malorum* is Latin for "the most vile source of evils." According to Reuben E. Fenton, Weed was upset at Simeon Draper, the collector of the Port of New York, and Rufus F. Andrews, surveyor of the port, and wanted them replaced. Nicolay and Fenton went to New York to consult with Weed, and Nicolay returned to Washington with Andrews's resignation. Abram Wakeman was appointed surveyor in his place. Allen Thorndike Rice, ed., *Reminiscences of Abraham Lincoln by Distinguished Men of His Time* (New York: North American Review, 1886), 68–70.

256. Forney predicted a victory by at least 50,000 votes. Forney to Lincoln, Philadelphia, 24 Sept. 1864, AL MSS, DLC.

257. William Curtis Noyes (1805–64), a champion of judicial reform, was a U.S. district attorney in New York. Blair told the audience in New York, "Some of my friends . . . have questioned the kindness of the President to me, indicating my resignation under the circumstances of the country. Let me tell you, my friends, the president has at least the support of those who are nearer to me than all the other people on this earth. I retired by the recommendation of my own father to the President." *Chicago Tribune*, 6 Oct. 1864, p. 2.

258. Dean Richmond (1804–66), the vice president of the New York Central Railroad, chaired the New York Democratic State Committee (1850–66).

259. A New York journalist, George Wilkes (1817–85) edited *The Spirit of the Times*. On 18 August, New York mayor George Opdyke hosted a meeting of two dozen leading Republicans who agreed to call for a new nominating convention to meet on 28 September in Cincinnati to replace Lincoln, presumably with either Chase or Grant. Sherman marched into Atlanta on 2 September. The public disliked the Democratic platform, adopted at the convention in Chicago in late August, which declared the war a failure.

260. See *CWL*, 8:29; and *Papers of Grant*, 12:228–29. Gen. David Bell Birney (1825–64) commanded a corps in the Army of the James.

261. William Grover was the U.S. attorney for the Eastern District of Missouri. Robert W. Welles, whose court met in Jefferson City, was a native of Virginia; he was replaced by Arnold Krekel. The three original cabinet members still heading departments were Seward, Welles, and Bates.

262. When Holt declined, Lincoln appointed James Speed of Kentucky as the attorney general.

263. Samuel Treat (1815–1902) was a St. Louis attorney who served on the U.S. District Court (1857–87).

264. William McKee was the editor and proprietor of the *St. Louis Missouri Democrat*. "A change in the St. Louis Post Office would probably be quite feasible in as much as it would coincide with the change in the Postmaster Generals office." Schurz to Lincoln, Bethlehem, Penn., 1 Oct. 1864, AL MSS, DLC.

265. As the head of the western division of the National Union Executive Committee, Lane, among other things, raised money for the campaign in the trans-Mississippi states.

266. "Swinton" was probably John Swinton of the editorial staff rather than his brother, the war correspondent William Swinton.

267. Halpine eventually decided to postpone his bid for office until 1866, when he was elected register.

268. Banks had seen the president. See the *Washington* Star, 7 Oct. 1864.

269. The editor of the *New York Evening Post*, William Cullen Bryant, was angry at Lincoln for dismissing Hiram Barney and Isaac Henderson from the New York Custom House.

270. See Cameron to Lincoln, telegram, Philadelphia, 8 Oct. 1864, and Weed to Lincoln, New York, 7 Oct. 1864, AL MSS, DLC.

271. A "Grand Mass Meeting" was to be held on 10 October to rally support for the proposed abolition of slavery in Maryland.

272. See Lincoln to Henry W. Hoffman, Washington, 10 Oct. 1864, *CWL*, 8:41. The amended passage reads thus: "I attempt no argument. Argument on the question [of slavery] is already exhausted by the abler, better informed, and more immediately interested sons of Maryland itself."

273. "Childs" was perhaps George W. Childs, a Philadelphia publisher. See Childs to Lincoln, Philadelphia, 16 Feb. 1863, AL MSS, DLC.

274. William A. Newell (1817–1901), the former governor of New Jersey (1857–60),

had served in Congress with Lincoln (1847–51). "Cummings" is probably Alexander Cummings (1810–79), the founder of the *Philadelphia Evening Bulletin*, who was notorious for his work as a purchasing agent for the War Department in 1861 and a controversial governor of the Colorado Territory (1865–67).

275. See Weed to Lincoln, New York, 10 Oct. 1864, AL MSS, DLC. See *infra*, entry for 12 Oct. 1864.

276. A gold medal was voted by Congress on 28 January in recognition of Vanderbilt's gift of a steamship, the *Vanderbilt*.

277. William E. Dodge Sr. (1805–83) was running for Congress on the Union ticket in New York. See Dodge to Davis, Newport, R.I., 30 Sept. 1864, AL MSS, DLC. On 18 July, Lincoln wrote the following document, which Hay presented to Greeley on 20 July: "To whom it may concern: Any proposition which embraces the restoration of peace, the integrity of the whole Union, and the abandonment of slavery, and which comes by and with an authority that can control the armies now at war against the United States, and will be met by liberal terms on other substantial and collateral points, and the bearer or bearers thereof shall have safe conduct both ways." *CWL*, 7:451. This statement made Lincoln seem intransigent. George Templeton Strong called it a "blunder" that "may cost him the election. By declaring that abandonment of slavery is a fundamental article in any negotiation for peace and settlement, he has given the disaffected and discontented a weapon that doubles their power of mischief." *The Diary of George Templeton Strong*, ed. Allan Nevins and Milton Halsey Thomas (New York: Macmillan, 1962), 3:474 (entry for 19 Aug. 1864). See also Horner, *Lincoln and Greeley*, 318–24.

278. The Union mayoral candidate won by a large majority. Thomas Swann (1806–83) was elected governor of Maryland in 1866. A letter by Francis P. Blair Sr. to the *National Intelligencer* (Washington), reprinted in the *New York Times*, 10 Oct. 1864, p. 5, described his appeal to McClellan before the Chicago convention to reject the overtures of the Peace Democrats.

279. See Puleston to Nicolay, Philadelphia, 11 Oct. 1864, telegram, Nicolay MSS, DLC. Puleston had been keeping the White House apprised of political developments during the campaign. See Puleston to Nicolay, New York, [?] August and [6 Sept. 1864], Nicolay MSS, DLC.

280. The encouraging dispatches were from the "October States"—Pennsylvania, Indiana, and Ohio, where the Republicans did well.

281. Benjamin Eggleston (1816–88) represented an Ohio district in the U.S. House (1865–69). Rutherford B. Hayes (1822–93) represented an Ohio district in Congress (1865–67) and was elected the U.S. president in 1877. Samuel Shellabarger (1817–96) was a Republican congressman from Ohio (1861–63, 1865–69, 1871–73).

282. "Petroleum V. Nasby" was the pen name of humorist David Ross Locke. John S. Clark was a member of Banks's staff. "Wilson" was perhaps Col. William Wilson of the 6th New York Volunteers. F. S. Aston Buruaga was the Chilean minister to the United States.

283. See *CWL*, 8:43. David Homer Bates recalled that this was Lincoln's last message of the night and that he "stayed in the telegraph office until after midnight."

Lincoln in the Telegraph Office: Recollections of the United States Military Telegraph Corps During the Civil War (New York: Century, 1907), 276–77.

284. Gen. Robert Allen (1812–86), the chief quartermaster of the Department of the West (1861–65), made his headquarters at first in St. Louis and later in Louisville. Col. William Myers was the assistant quartermaster, stationed in St. Louis.

285. Col. George B. Dandy (1830–1911) of the 100th New York, who had served on McClellan's staff, was given the rank of brevet brigadier general on 13 March 1865.

286. McClernand's formal protest against Grant was dated 25 September 1863. *O. R.*, 1st ser., vol. 24, pt. 1, 169–86.

287. Lt. Col. Walter Bennet Scates (1808–87), whom Lincoln described as "an old personal friend & most worthy gentleman," had served as the chief justice of the Illinois Supreme Court (1853–57) and during the war was the assistant adjutant general of the 13th Corps. See Lincoln to Edwin M. Stanton, Washington, 31 Mar. 1864, *CWL*, 7:277.

288. Governor Morton and the rest of the Republican slate received a large majorities. Gen. Henry B. Carrington (1824–1912), who helped recruit many troops in Indiana, issued three reports about sedition in that state. The third, submitted to Governor Morton on 28 June and published in the press on 30 July, maintained that the Sons of Liberty were engaged in a conspiracy to establish a Northwest Republic.

289. Welles recorded the following in his diary on 13 October 1864:

> The President is greatly importuned and pressed by cunning intrigues just at this time. Thurlow Weed and Raymond are abusing his confidence and good nature badly. Hay says they are annoying the President sadly. This he tells Mr. Fox, who informs me. They want, Hay says, to control the Navy Yard but dislike to come to me, for I give them no favorable response. They claim that every mechanic or laborer who does not support the Administration should be turned out of employment. Hay's representations alarmed Fox, who made it a point to call on the President. F. reports that the President was feeling very well over the election returns, and on the subject of the Navy Yard votes, expressed his intention of not further interfering but will turn the whole matter over to me whenever the politicians call upon him. (*Diary of Welles*, 2:175–176)

See also Welles's entries for 8 August (2:97–98), 17 August (2:108–9), 27 August (2:122–23), 5 September (2:136–37), and 13 September (2:142–45).

290. On 6 December, Lincoln reluctantly nominated Chase for chief justice.

291. Justin S. Morrill (1810–98), a Republican congressman from Vermont, had protested to Chase against tax increases. *The Salmon P. Chase Papers*, vol. 1, *Journals, 1829–1872*, ed. John Niven (Kent, Ohio: Kent State Univ. Press, 1993), 470 (entry for 30 June 1864).

292. Robert Murray was the federal marshal of the Southern District of New York. "Brady" was perhaps James Topham Brady (1815–69), a lawyer from New York.

293. See William O. Bartlett to Lincoln, New York, 20 Oct. 1864, AL MSS, DLC.

Bartlett had a long conversation with Lincoln on 1 November about the appointment of James Gordon Bennett to serve as U.S. minister to France. See Bartlett to Bennett, 4 Nov. 1864, *CWL*, 8:239–40n.

294. See Weed to Lincoln, New York, 6 Nov. 1864, AL MSS, DLC.

295. See Henry W. Hoffman to Lincoln, Baltimore, 8 Nov. 1864, AL MSS, DLC.

296. See Forney to Lincoln, telegram, Philadelphia, 8 Nov. 1864, AL MSS, DLC. Samuel M. Felton (1809–89) headed the Philadelphia, Wilmington, and Baltimore Railroad Company. Alexander Hamilton Rice (1818–95) was a congressman from Massachusetts (1859–67). A few weeks later, Fox told Rice that Lincoln was at first incredulous when he read about the size of Rice's lead: "Rice has one of the closest districts in the country, and those figures are more likely to be 40 or perhaps 400." When news from the Associated Press confirmed the earlier reports, the president said, "If the doubtful districts come in in this shape, what may we expect from the certain ones?" Shortly after Fox related this story, Rice encountered the president, who remarked: "Well, your district proved to be a good deal like a jug after all, with the handle all on one side." *Washington Post*, 24 Sept. 1889.

297. Mary Lincoln told a friend, "I could have gone down on my knees to ask votes for him and again and again he said: 'Mary, I am afraid you will be punished for this overweening anxiety. If I am to be re-elected it will be all right; if not, you must bear the disappointment.'" Quoted in *Some Incidents in the Life of Mrs. Benjamin S. Edwards*, ed. M[ary] E[dwards] R[aymond] (n.p., 1909), 16. According to one account, she feared that if Lincoln lost, creditors would demand payment for the huge debts she had incurred buying her clothes. See Elizabeth Keckley, *Behind the Scenes, or, Thirty Years a Slave, and Four Years in the White House* (New York: Carleton, 1868), 147–51.

298. John Hickman (1810–75) was a Republican representative from Pennsylvania (1855–63). James W. Grimes (1816–72) was a Republican senator from Iowa (1859–69). Richard C. McCormick (1832–1901) recalled Lincoln's saying, "I must do something for Grimes. I have tried hard to please him from the start, but he complains, and I must satisfy him." *New York Post*, 3 May 1865, in Don E. Fehrenbacher and Virginia Fehrenbacher, eds., *Recollected Words of Abraham Lincoln* (Stanford: Stanford Univ. Press, 1996), 320.

299. Amos Bebee Eaton (1806–77) was the commissary general of the Subsistence Bureau.

300. Peter L. Foy was the postmaster of St. Louis. Samuel Knox (1815–1905) of St. Louis represented a district in the U.S. House (1864–65). William E. Dodge (1805–83) challenged James Brooks, who seemingly won, but in the spring of 1865, the House determined that election fraud had unfairly deprived Dodge of the victory and seated him. William Augustus Darling (1817–95) represented a New York district in the U.S. House (1865–67).

301. See *CWL*, 8:96.

302. "W. H. L." was Ward Hill Lamon.

303. Hugh J. Hastings (1820–83) founded the *Albany Knickerbocker* in 1844.

304. See Swett to Lincoln, New York, 1 P.M., 9 Nov. 1864, telegram, AL MSS, DLC.

305. See Nicolay to Lincoln, telegram, Springfield, 10 Nov. 1864, AL MSS, DLC.

Among those mentioned as congressmen from Illinois and the years they served were: John Wentworth (1815–88), in 1843–51, 1853–55, and 1865–67; John Franklin Farnsworth (1820–97) in 1863–73; Burton C. Cook (1819–94) in 1865–71; Ebon Clark Ingersoll (1831–79) in 1864–71; Abner Clark Harding (1807–74) in 1865–69; Henry Pelham Holmes Bromwell (1823–1903) in 1865–69; Andrew Jackson Kuykendall (1815–91) in 1865–67; Samuel Wheeler Moulton (1821–1905) in 1865–67 and 1881–85; Anthony Thornton (1814–1904) in 1865–67; Lewis Winans Ross (1812–95) in 1863–69; Samuel Scott Marshall (1821–90) in 1855–59 and 1865–75.

306. The speeches were given on 8 and 10 November 1864. See *CWL*, 8:96, 100–101.

307. On 12 November, Charles H. Philbrick reported that he had

just shipped him [Hay] with Fox on Steamer City of Baltimore for a few days recuperation and a visit to the "Front"—I hope he will be in better plight when he returns—For a while he did well and read French assiduously but the literature which he chose I fear was not of the right kind and corrupted him, being the productions of Paul de Kock, Xavier de [Montepere?] etc You will agree with me that such volumes as "Les [Diseaux?] de nuit" "Confessions d'un Boheme" "La demoiselle du cinquieme" & the like are not pious books suited for the young—I dont know what his bill at Fred Cozzens is, but it must be enormous—His French got so into his head that he frequently signed official papers "Jean Foin A. A. G." & he addresses the Madame's respectable old female tidewaiter with the ribald song "Par bleu Madame, qu faitez vous ici?" (Philbrick to John G. Nicolay, Washington, 12 Nov. 1864, Nicolay MSS, DLC)

The purpose of the visit was evidently "to confer with Admiral Porter in reference to naval activities present and to come." Washington correspondence, 13 Nov. 1864, *New York Tribune*, 14 Nov. 1864, p. 1. "Dyer" was perhaps William W. S. Dyer, a clerk in the office of the navy's Bureau of Equipment and Recruiting. John Murray Forbes (1813–98) was a businessman who assisted Massachusetts governor John A. Andrew in his efforts to organize black regiments.

308. "Captain Steadman" was Charles Steedman (1811–90) of South Carolina.

309. Gen. Fitzhugh Lee (1835–1905) was a Confederate cavalry commander. "F. F. V.s" refers to First Families of Virginia.

310. Grant telegraphed Stanton on 10 November, saying: "Congratulate the President for me for the double victory. The election having passed off quietly, no bloodshed or riot throughout the land, is a victory worth more to the country than a battle won. Rebeldom and Europe will so construe it." *Papers of Grant*, 12:398.

311. The *Martin* was a 25-ton screw steamer. Lt. Col. Orville E. Babcock (1835–84) of Vermont was Grant's aide-de-camp. William M. Dunn Jr. (1814–87) was an assistant judge advocate general of the army.

312. "Mrs. Stackpole" was probably the wife of Maj. Joseph Lewis Stackpole, the judge advocate at Fort Monroe.

313. The Confederate commerce raider *Florida*, obtained from the British in 1862, destroyed thirty-seven Union vessels before being captured by the USS *Wachusett* in

October 1864. Lester Anthony Beardslee (1836–1901) helped capture the *Florida* at Bahia, Brazil, and sailed her back to the United States.

314. Gen. William Hemsley Emory (1811–87) commanded the 19th Corps of the Army of the Shenandoah. Dr. Thomas Emory was an assistant surgeon on the *Florida*. Later, Hay added this sentence at the end of this paragraph: "He afterwards took it before me in Paris."

315. This was evidently a rehearsal of the impending attack on Fort Fisher, N.C.

316. Capt. James Gilchrist Benton (1820–81), the principal assistant to the chief of ordnance, had written a West Point textbook, *A Course of Instruction in Ordnance and Gunnery* (1861). "Jeffers" was perhaps William N. Jeffers (1824–83), USN, commander of the *Underwriter*. Erith, an urban district on the Thames fourteen miles southeast of London, had been the site of a huge gunpowder explosion. Col. Benjamin Chew Tilghman (1821–1901) of the 3rd U.S. Colored Troops was an inventor who took part in the Olustee campaign in February 1864.

317. Thomas H. Hicks (1798–1865), the former governor of Maryland, at this time represented the state in the U.S. Senate. Henry W. Hoffman, collector of the Port of Baltimore, was to be appointed the U.S. minister to Spain; Hicks was to replace him as the collector. Blair suspected Hoffman's loyalty to the administration, for he had been a supporter of the Radical faction in Maryland, led by Henry Winter Davis. Unwilling to alienate the Maryland Radicals, Lincoln offered Blair the Spanish mission, which he declined. When Hicks died in February 1865, Blair tried to win the vacated Senate seat, but the Maryland legislature chose John A. J. Creswell instead.

318. During the secession winter of 1860–61, Sen. John J. Crittenden (1786–1863) of Kentucky introduced a series of compromise measures to settle the differences between North and South. At the heart of his resolutions was a proposal to allow slavery to expand into western territories below 36°30' north latitude and to prohibit it in the western territories above that line. Samuel Latham Mitchell Barlow (1826–89), a New York corporation lawyer and prominent leader of the national Democratic party, was a confidant of McClellan. Blair made his proposal on 1 May 1864. Barlow replied on 3 May rejecting the proposal.

319. On 15 December, Congressman James Ashley of Ohio introduced a compromise between Lincoln's plan of reconstruction and the Radicals' Wade-Davis bill. It adopted the president's 10 percent scheme, allowing Louisiana to be restored under that plan and requiring black political equality in the states to be reconstructed. Lincoln wrote comments on a printed copy of the bill. AL MSS, DLC. Ashley's bill stipulated that "the loyal male citizens" were eligible to vote. On 20 December, Ashley reported an amended version of his bill that incorporated this change.

320. The Emancipation Proclamation had exempted slaves in some districts; the Wade-Davis bill, which Lincoln had vetoed, did not include that distinction, nor did Ashley's measure of 15 December. Ashley's amended bill of 20 December required that the freedom of bondsmen liberated by the Emancipation Proclamation must be "recognized and guaranteed" in the new constitutions adopted by the former Confederate states.

321. On 13 June 1905, Hay made the following entry in his diary: "I dreamt last night that I was in Washington and that I went to the White House to report to the President, who turned out to be Mr. Lincoln. He was very kind and considerate, and sympathetic about my illness. He said there was little work of importance on hand. He gave me two unimportant letters to answer. I was pleased that this slight order was within my power to obey. I was not in the least surprised by Lincoln's presence in the White House. But the whole impression of the dream was one of overpowering melancholy." Hay diary, Hay MSS, DLC. The severe bronchial cold from which Hay was suffering claimed his life on 1 July.

Appendix

1. This undated document is found at the end of the notebook Hay used as a diary in Florida in 1864. It is not clear if this is a draft of a speech or if Hay wrote down later what he had said, if in fact it was ever delivered.

2. After the bombardment of Sumter, Pierce told a New Hampshire audience that "I do not believe aggression by arms is a suitable or possible remedy for existing evils." Privately he condemned the Lincoln administration's attempts to crush the rebellion and was especially indignant when his friend James Berrett, former mayor of Washington, was arrested. He predicted that such actions would precipitate war in the North against the national government. On 4 July 1863, he made an especially bitter speech attacking Lincoln's war measures, a speech that ruined his reputation.

3. On 13 October 1863, Unionist Daniel Agnew defeated Justice Walter Lowrie of the Pennsylvania Supreme Court, who sought reelection to the bench. Lowrie had maintained that the draft was unconstitutional.

4. As an officer in the U.S. Army, Simon Buckner (1823–1914) had attempted to keep his native state of Kentucky neutral in the opening months of the war, but he eventually joined the Confederate army. He surrendered Fort Donelson to Grant in February 1862.

5. Isaac R. Trimble (1802–88) was the general superintendent of the Baltimore and Ohio Railroad (1859–61) who helped burn the bridges north of Baltimore in April 1861, thus impeding the progress of Union troops to Washington. He later served as a general in the Confederate army. Ross Winans (1796–1877) was a wealthy inventor and Democrat who had been elected to the state legislature in 1861. On 14 May 1861, Benjamin Butler arrested him at the Relay House and held him at Fort McHenry.

6. Nathaniel Barratt Smithers (1818–96) won election to the U.S. House as an Unconditional Unionist and served from December 1863 to March 1865.

7. William Harrison Randall (1812–81) served in the U.S. House from 1863 to 1867, Lucian Anderson (1824–98) from 1863 to 1865, and Brutus Junius Clay (1808–78) from 1863 to 1865. All three were elected as Unconditional Unionists.

INDEX

The following abbreviations are used throughout the index:
AL   Abraham Lincoln
JH   John Hay

Michael Burlingame is a professor of history at Connecticut College in New London. His previous books include *The Inner World of Abraham Lincoln* and *An Oral History of Abraham Lincoln*, which won the 1995 Abraham Lincoln Association Prize.

John R. Turner Ettlinger is a professor emeritus at the School of Library and Information Studies, Dalhousie University, in Halifax, Nova Scotia. He has published a number of books and articles in the field of bibliographical studies.